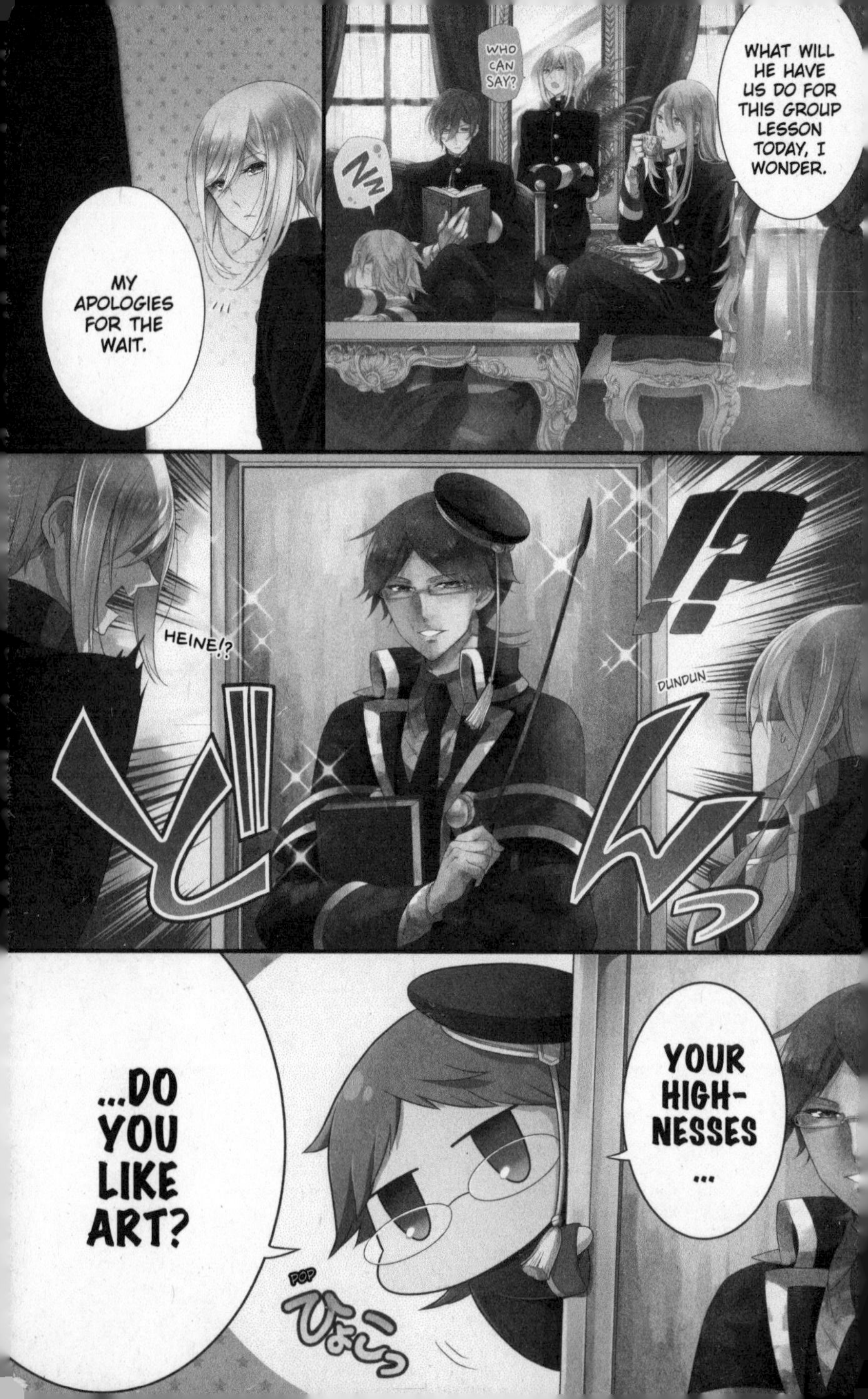
WHAT WILL HE HAVE US DO FOR THIS GROUP LESSON TODAY, I WONDER.
WHO CAN SAY?
ZZ
MY APOLOGIES FOR THE WAIT.
!?
DUNDUN
どんっ
HEINE!?
YOUR HIGH-NESSES ...
...DO YOU LIKE ART?
POP
ひょこっ

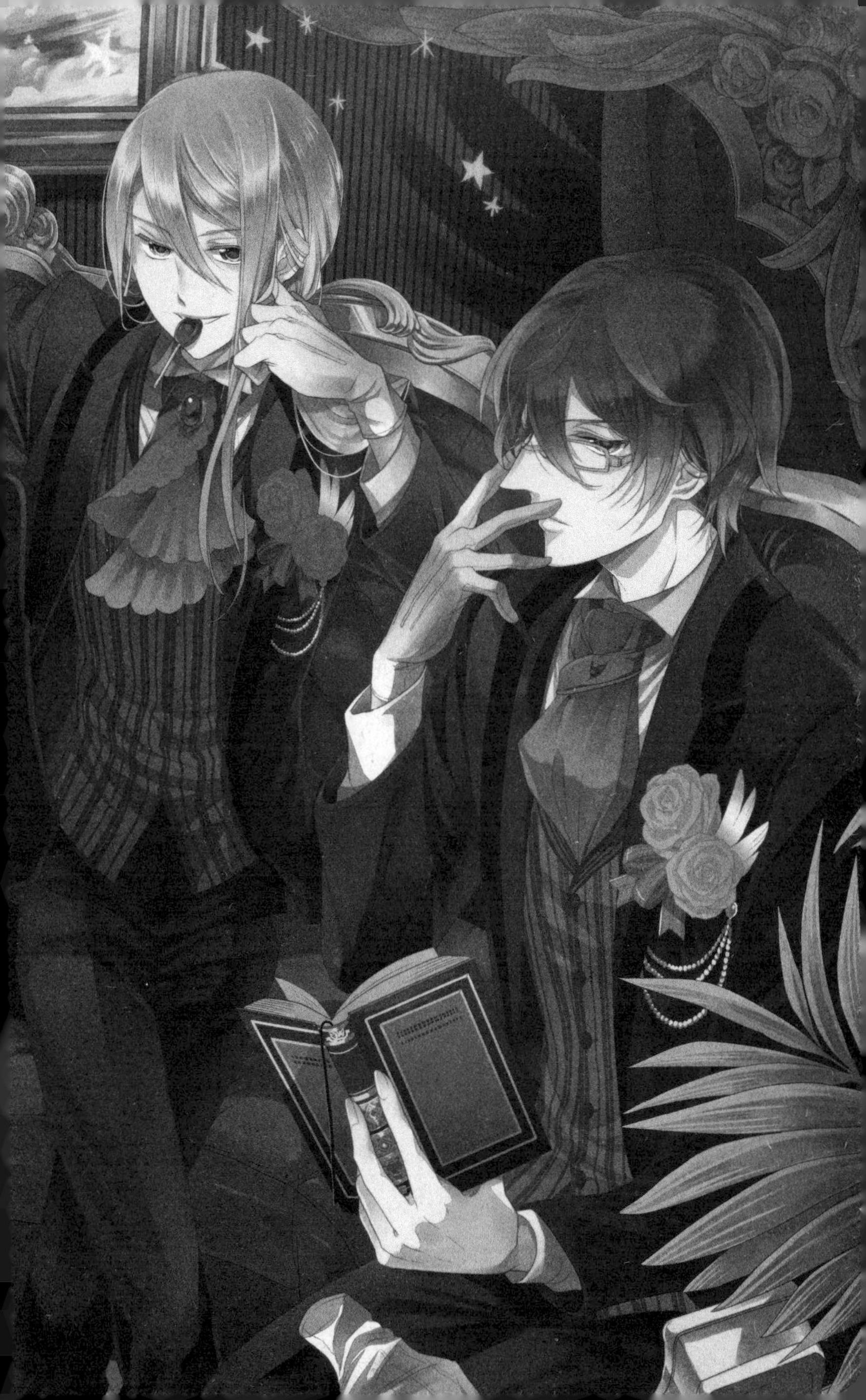

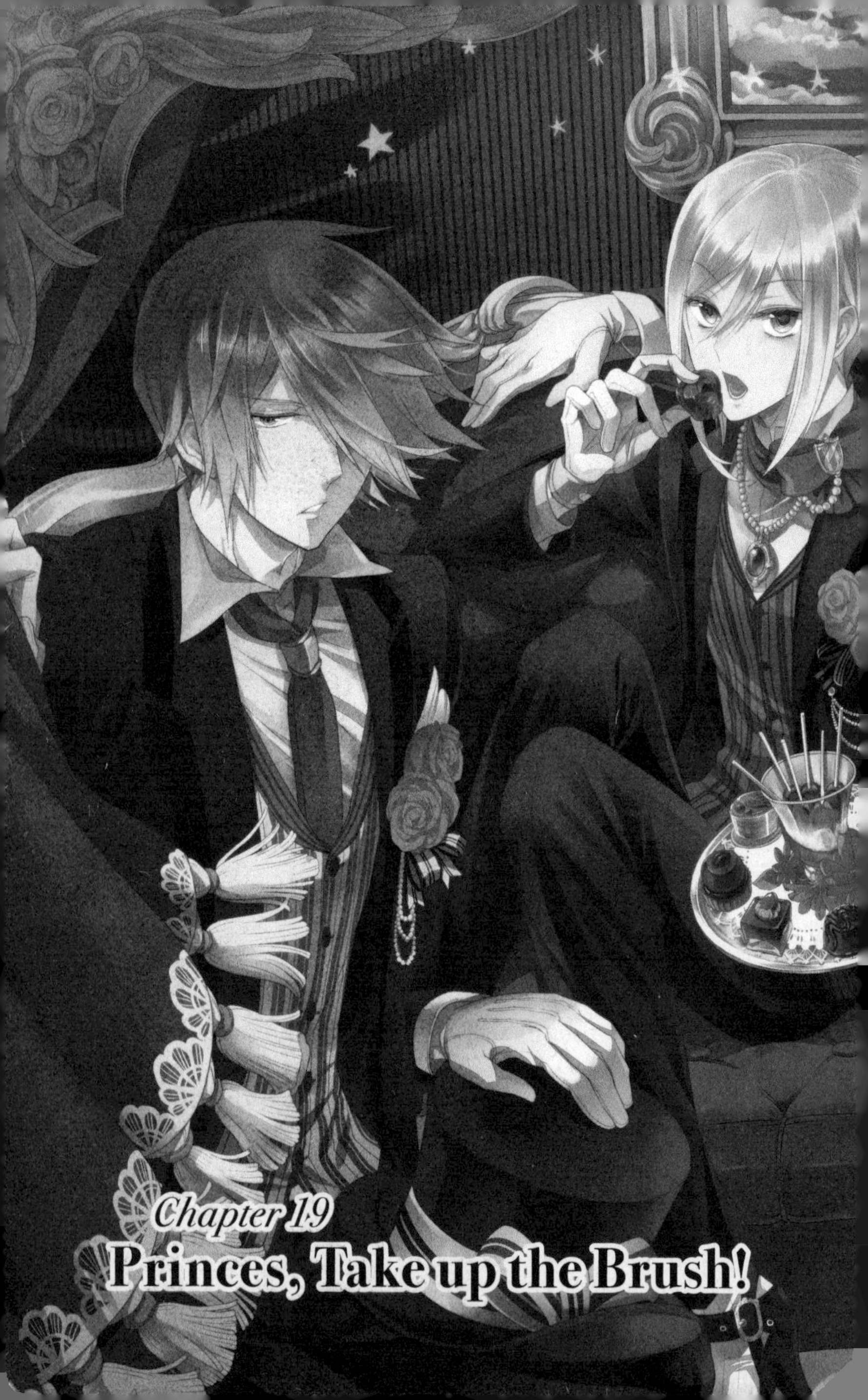
Chapter 19
Princes, Take up the Brush!

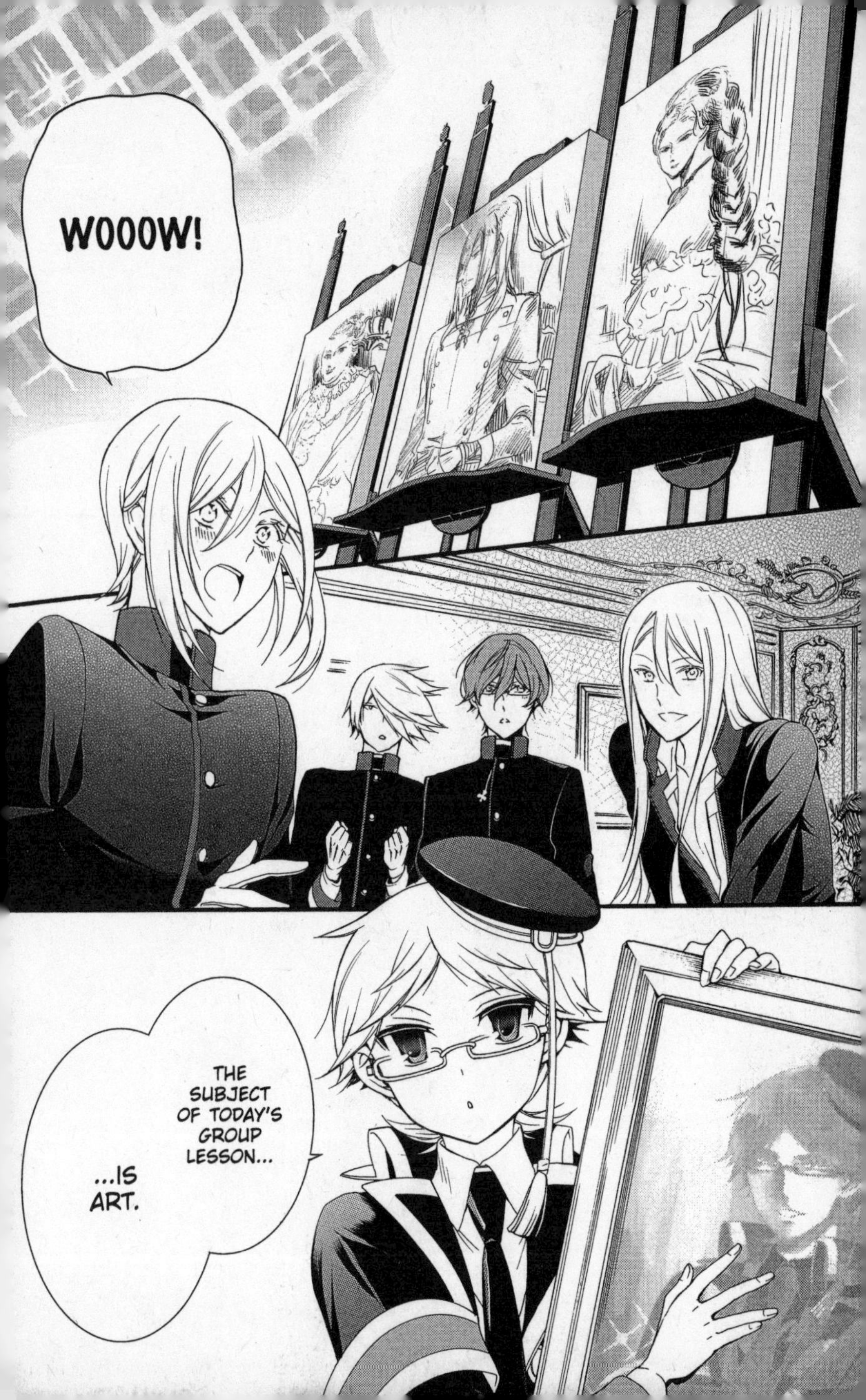
WOOOW!
THE SUBJECT OF TODAY'S GROUP LESSON...
...IS ART.

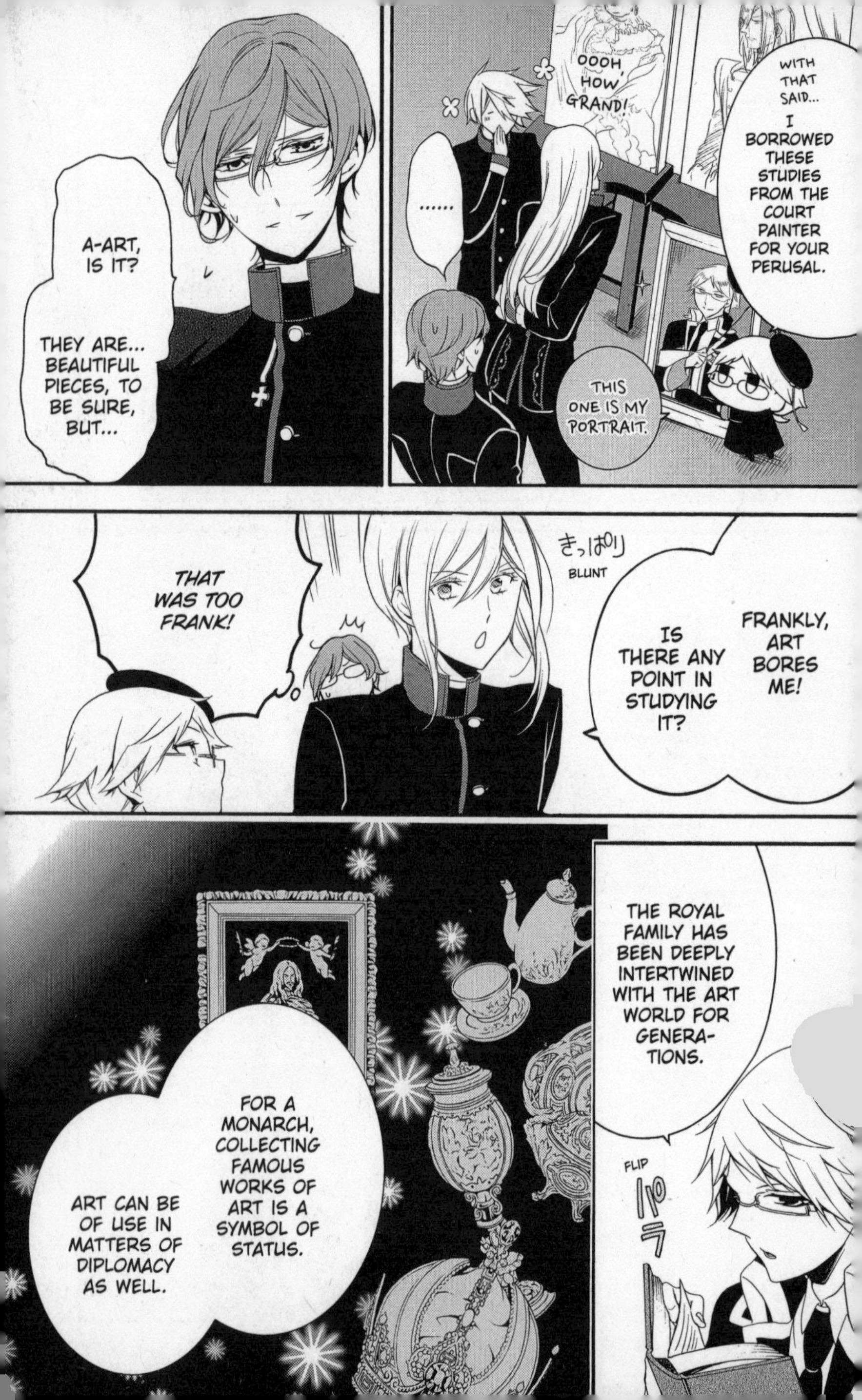
WITH THAT SAID... I BORROWED THESE STUDIES FROM THE COURT PAINTER FOR YOUR PERUSAL.
OOOH, HOW GRAND!
......
THIS ONE IS MY PORTRAIT.
A-ART, IS IT?
THEY ARE... BEAUTIFUL PIECES, TO BE SURE, BUT...
きっぱり
BLUNT
FRANKLY, ART BORES ME!
IS THERE ANY POINT IN STUDYING IT?
THAT WAS TOO FRANK!
THE ROYAL FAMILY HAS BEEN DEEPLY INTERTWINED WITH THE ART WORLD FOR GENERATIONS.
パラ
FLIP
FOR A MONARCH, COLLECTING FAMOUS WORKS OF ART IS A SYMBOL OF STATUS.
ART CAN BE OF USE IN MATTERS OF DIPLOMACY AS WELL.

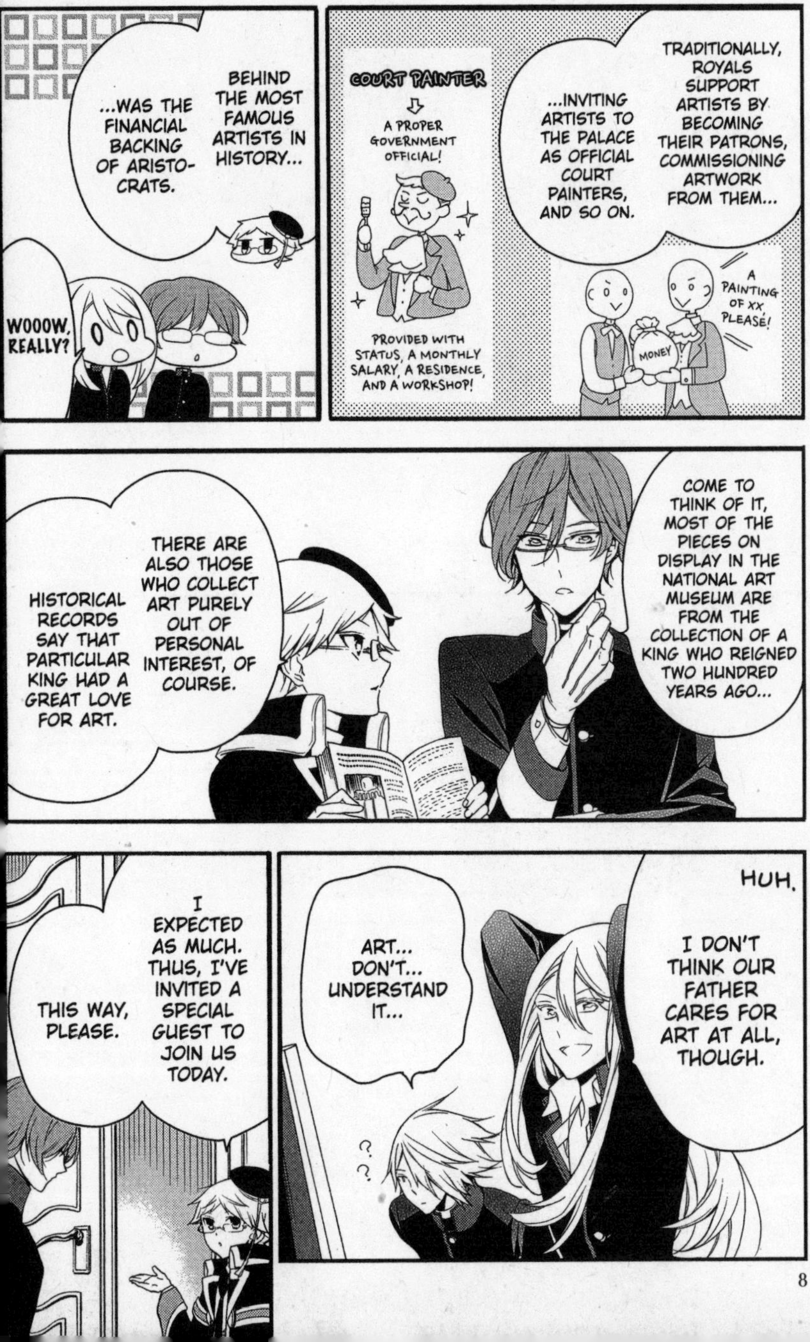
TRADITIONALLY, ROYALS SUPPORT ARTISTS BY BECOMING THEIR PATRONS, COMMISSIONING ARTWORK FROM THEM...
...INVITING ARTISTS TO THE PALACE AS OFFICIAL COURT PAINTERS, AND SO ON.
COURT PAINTER
A PROPER GOVERNMENT OFFICIAL!
PROVIDED WITH STATUS, A MONTHLY SALARY, A RESIDENCE, AND A WORKSHOP!
A PAINTING OF XX, PLEASE!
MONEY
BEHIND THE MOST FAMOUS ARTISTS IN HISTORY...
...WAS THE FINANCIAL BACKING OF ARISTO-CRATS.
WOOOW, REALLY?
COME TO THINK OF IT, MOST OF THE PIECES ON DISPLAY IN THE NATIONAL ART MUSEUM ARE FROM THE COLLECTION OF A KING WHO REIGNED TWO HUNDRED YEARS AGO...
THERE ARE ALSO THOSE WHO COLLECT ART PURELY OUT OF PERSONAL INTEREST, OF COURSE.
HISTORICAL RECORDS SAY THAT PARTICULAR KING HAD A GREAT LOVE FOR ART.
HUH.
I DON'T THINK OUR FATHER CARES FOR ART AT ALL, THOUGH.
ART... DON'T... UNDERSTAND IT...
I EXPECTED AS MUCH. THUS, I'VE INVITED A SPECIAL GUEST TO JOIN US TODAY.
THIS WAY, PLEASE.

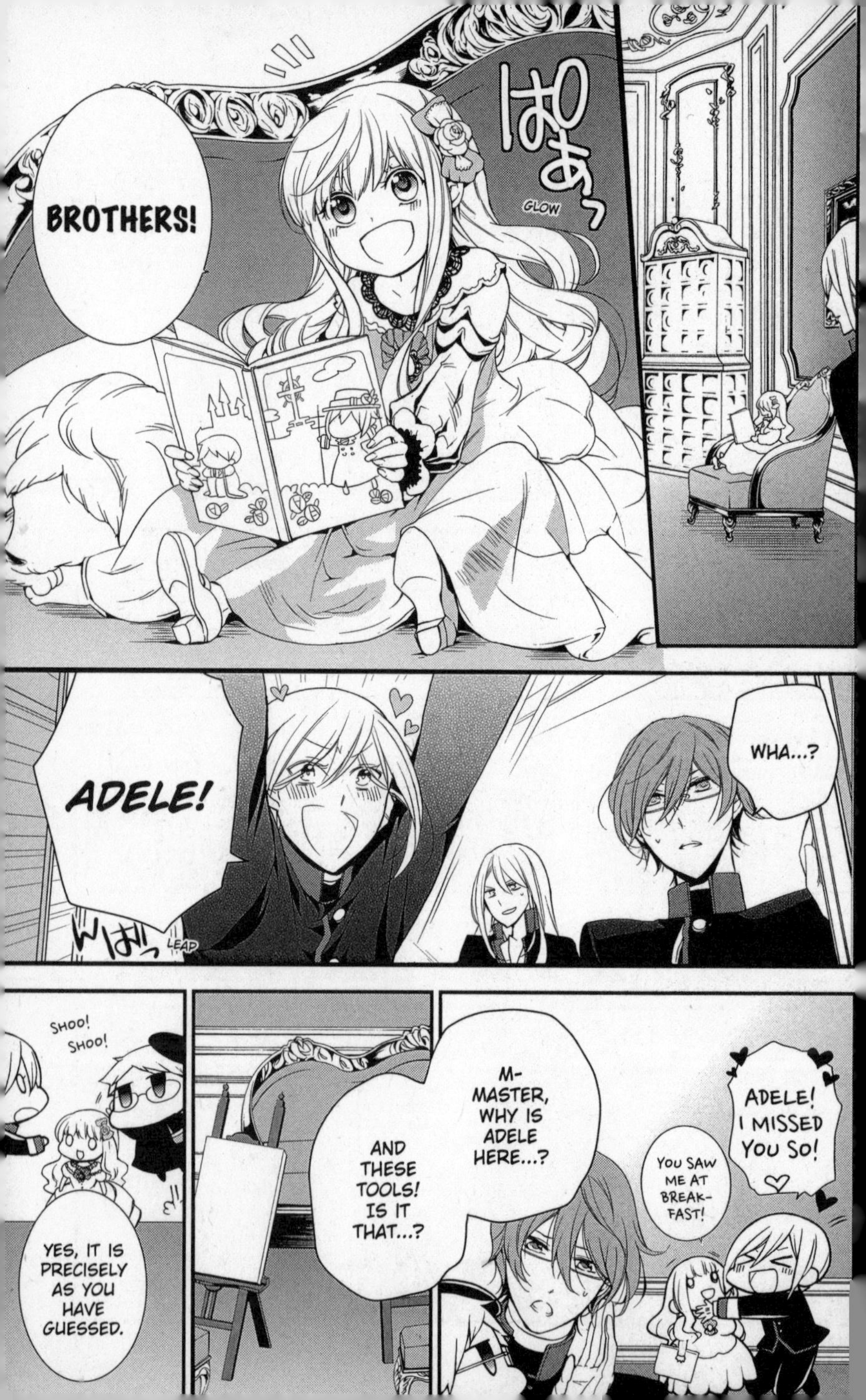
ぱあっ
GLOW
BROTHERS!
WHA...?
ADELE!
LEAP
ADELE! I MISSED YOU SO!
YOU SAW ME AT BREAK-FAST!
M-MASTER, WHY IS ADELE HERE...?
AND THESE TOOLS! IS IT THAT...?
SHOO! SHOO!
YES, IT IS PRECISELY AS YOU HAVE GUESSED.

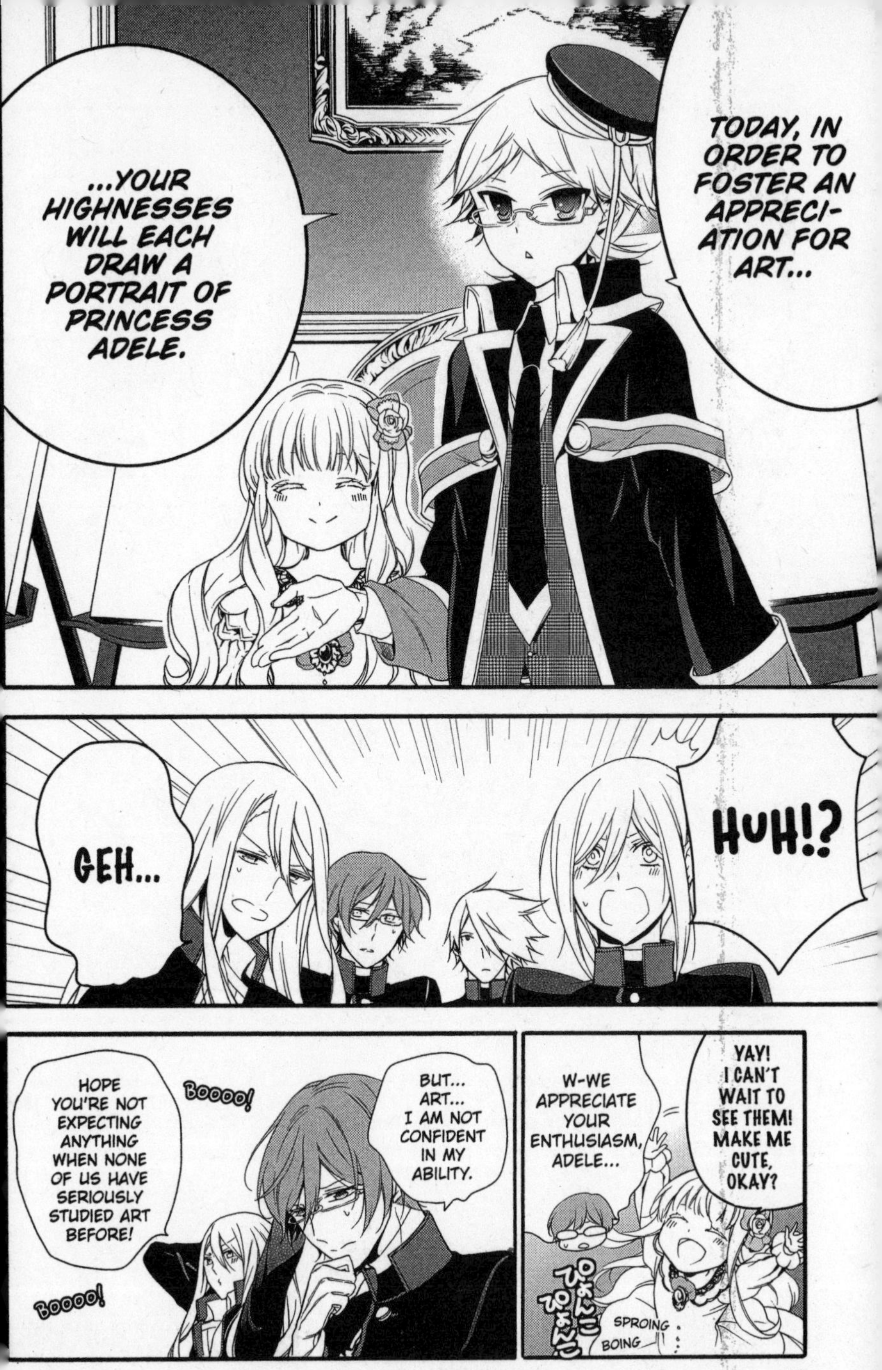
TODAY, IN ORDER TO FOSTER AN APPRECI-ATION FOR ART...
...YOUR HIGHNESSES WILL EACH DRAW A PORTRAIT OF PRINCESS ADELE.
HUH!?
GEH...
YAY! I CAN'T WAIT TO SEE THEM! MAKE ME CUTE, OKAY?
W-WE APPRECIATE YOUR ENTHUSIASM, ADELE...
SPROING
BOING
BUT... ART... I AM NOT CONFIDENT IN MY ABILITY.
BOOOO!
HOPE YOU'RE NOT EXPECTING ANYTHING WHEN NONE OF US HAVE SERIOUSLY STUDIED ART BEFORE!
BOOOO!

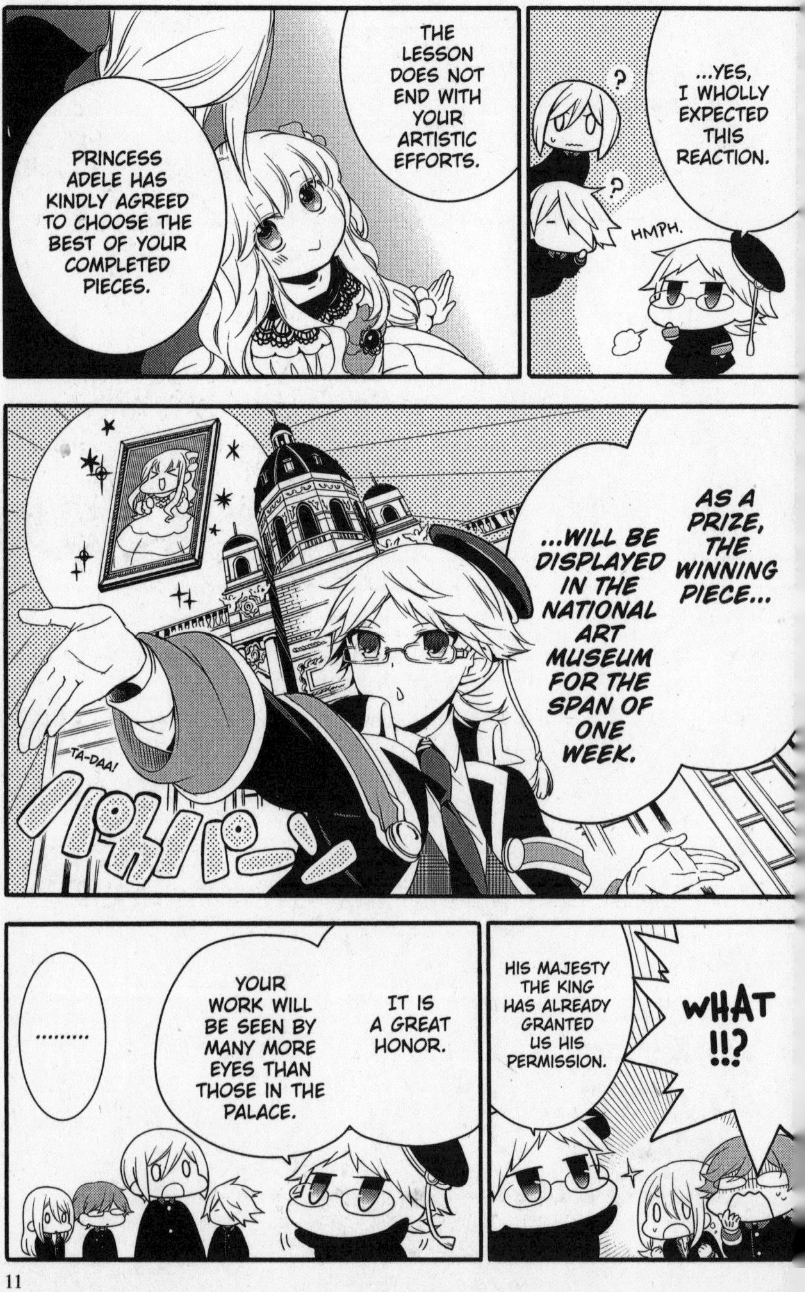
...YES, I WHOLLY EXPECTED THIS REACTION.
?
?
HMPH.
THE LESSON DOES NOT END WITH YOUR ARTISTIC EFFORTS.
PRINCESS ADELE HAS KINDLY AGREED TO CHOOSE THE BEST OF YOUR COMPLETED PIECES.
AS A PRIZE, THE WINNING PIECE...
...WILL BE DISPLAYED IN THE NATIONAL ART MUSEUM FOR THE SPAN OF ONE WEEK.
TA-DAA!
WHAT!!?
HIS MAJESTY THE KING HAS ALREADY GRANTED US HIS PERMISSION.
IT IS A GREAT HONOR.
YOUR WORK WILL BE SEEN BY MANY MORE EYES THAN THOSE IN THE PALACE.
....

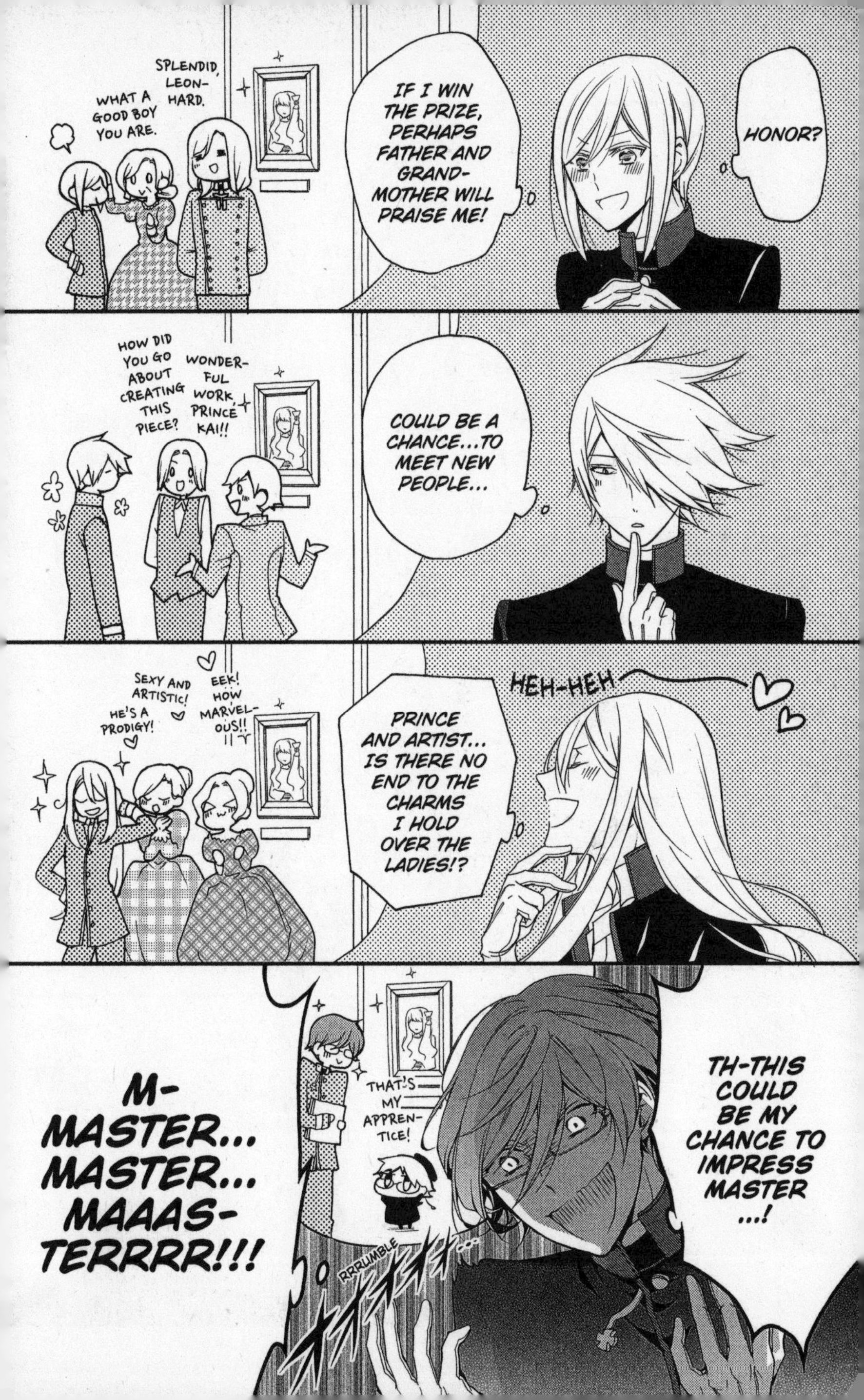
HONOR?
IF I WIN THE PRIZE, PERHAPS FATHER AND GRAND-MOTHER WILL PRAISE ME!
SPLENDID, LEON-HARD.
WHAT A GOOD BOY YOU ARE.
COULD BE A CHANCE...TO MEET NEW PEOPLE...
WONDER-FUL WORK, PRINCE KAI!!
HOW DID YOU GO ABOUT CREATING THIS PIECE?
HEH-HEH
PRINCE AND ARTIST... IS THERE NO END TO THE CHARMS I HOLD OVER THE LADIES!?
EEK! HOW MARVEL-OUS!!
SEXY AND ARTISTIC!
HE'S A PRODIGY!
TH-THIS COULD BE MY CHANCE TO IMPRESS MASTER ...!
THAT'S MY APPREN-TICE!
RRRUMBLE
M-MASTER... MASTER... MAAAS-TERRRRR!!!

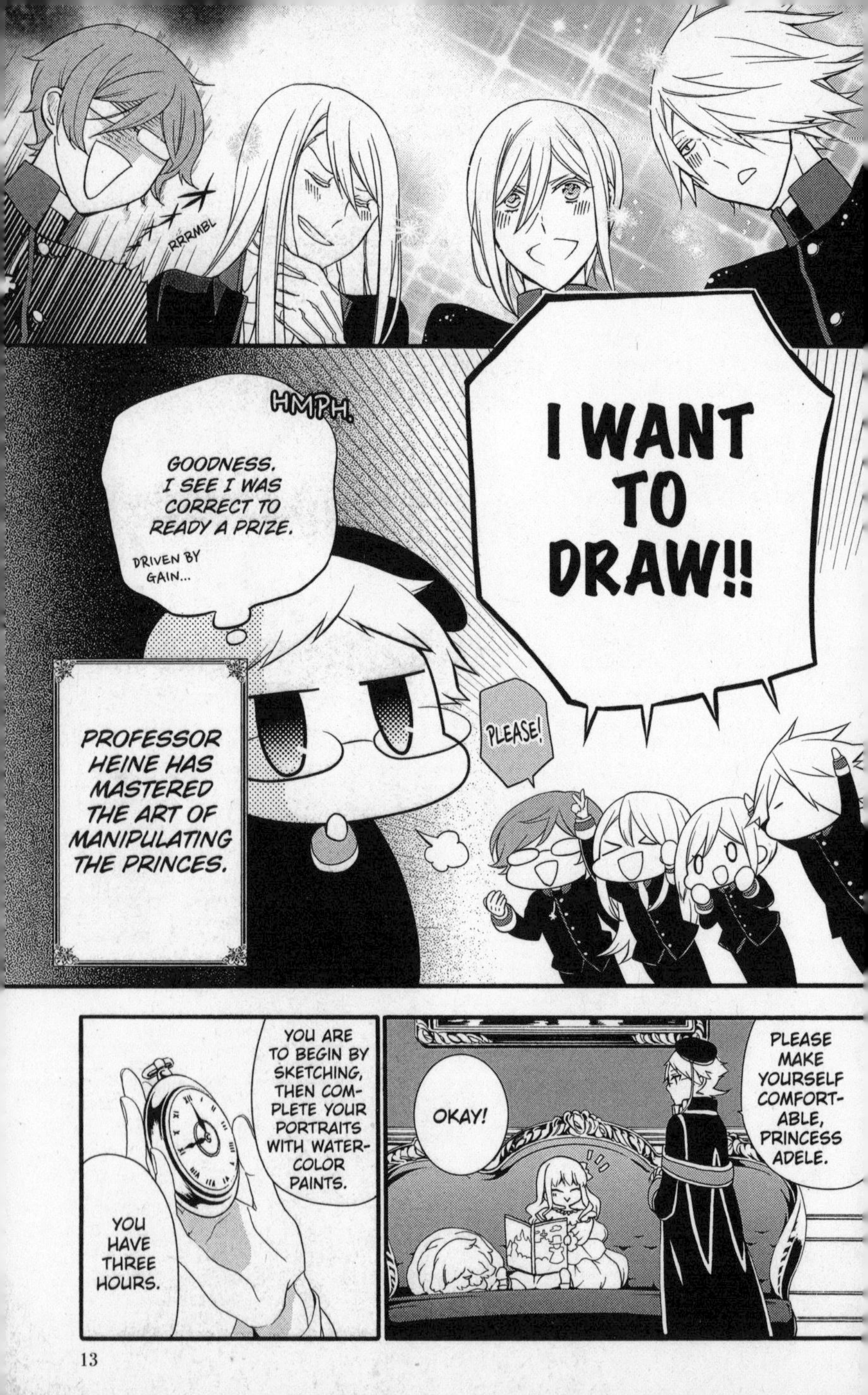
RRRMBL
I WANT TO DRAW!!
PLEASE!
HMPH.
GOODNESS. I SEE I WAS CORRECT TO READY A PRIZE.
DRIVEN BY GAIN...
PROFESSOR HEINE HAS MASTERED THE ART OF MANIPULATING THE PRINCES.
PLEASE MAKE YOURSELF COMFORT-ABLE, PRINCESS ADELE.
OKAY!
YOU ARE TO BEGIN BY SKETCHING, THEN COM-PLETE YOUR PORTRAITS WITH WATER-COLOR PAINTS.
YOU HAVE THREE HOURS.

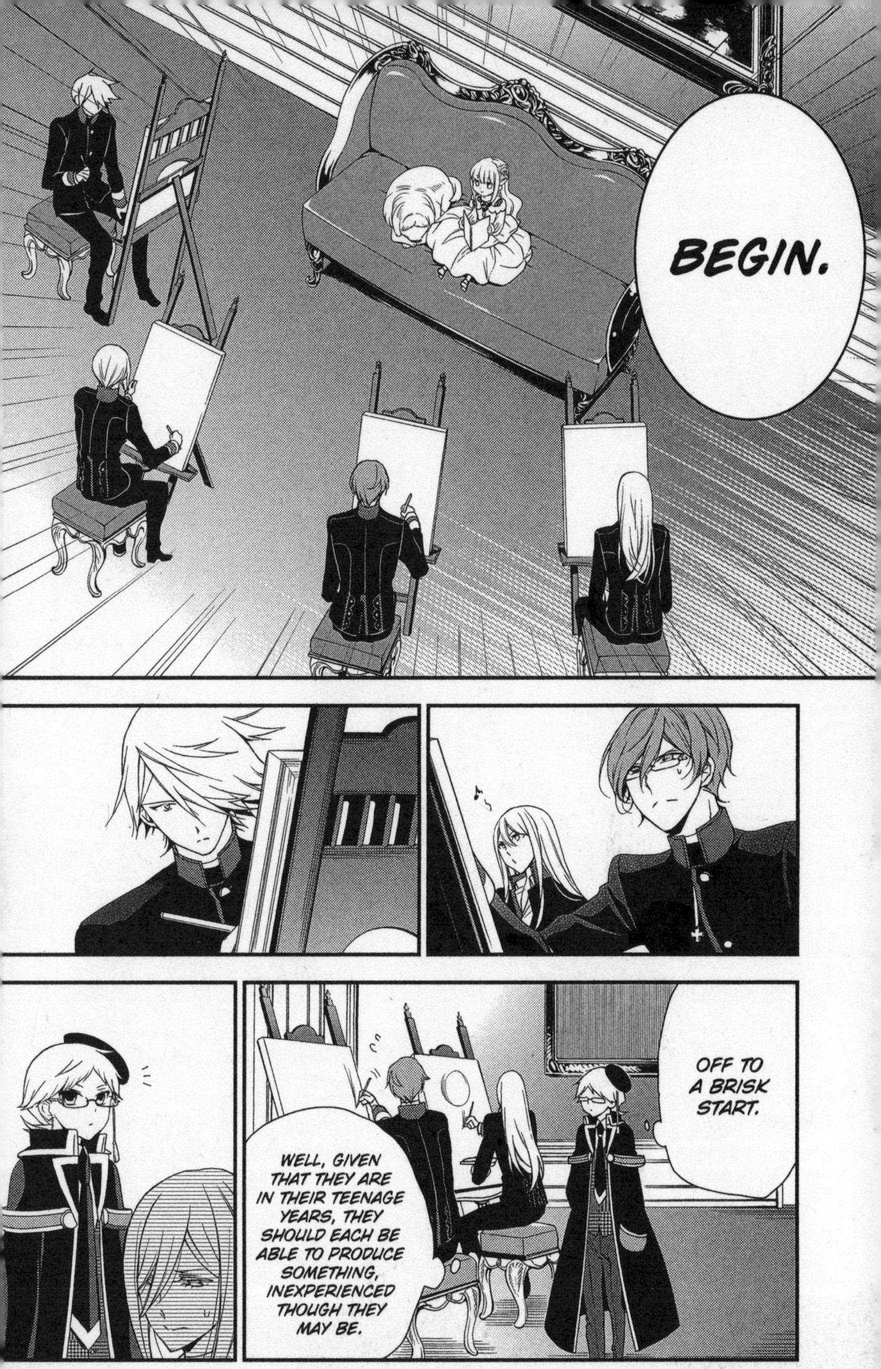
BEGIN.
OFF TO A BRISK START.
WELL, GIVEN THAT THEY ARE IN THEIR TEENAGE YEARS, THEY SHOULD EACH BE ABLE TO PRODUCE SOMETHING, INEXPERIENCED THOUGH THEY MAY BE.

STARE

....

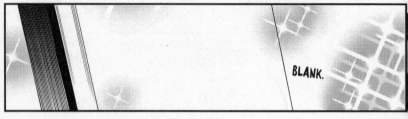

BLANK.

AHEM.

PRINCE
LEON-
HARD...?

......

....

HEINE!

HOW ON
EARTH
DOES ONE
GO ABOUT
DRAWING
ANYWAY!?

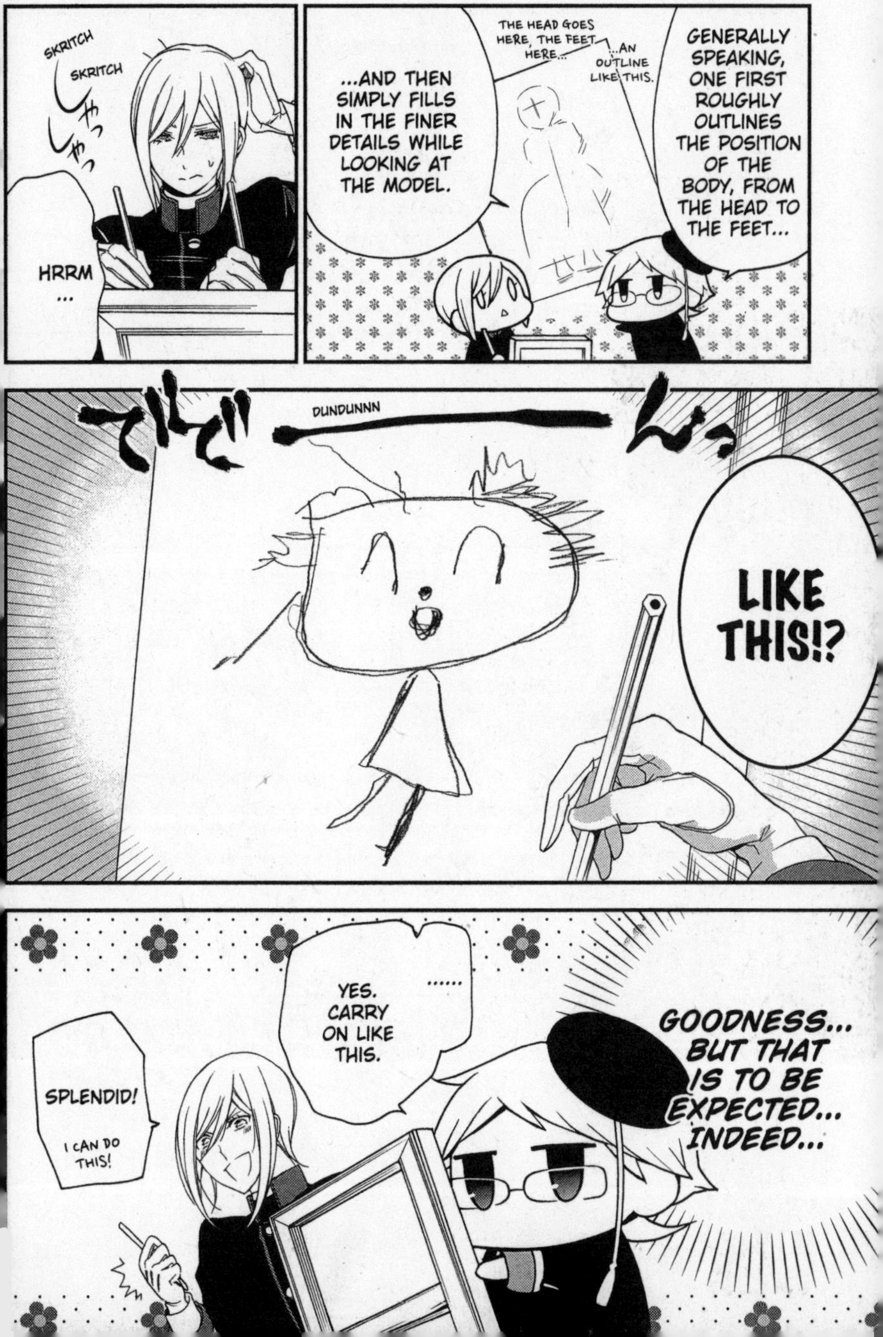
GENERALLY SPEAKING, ONE FIRST ROUGHLY OUTLINES THE POSITION OF THE BODY, FROM THE HEAD TO THE FEET...
THE HEAD GOES HERE, THE FEET HERE...
...AN OUTLINE LIKE THIS.
...AND THEN SIMPLY FILLS IN THE FINER DETAILS WHILE LOOKING AT THE MODEL.
SKRITCH
SKRITCH
しゃっ しゃっ
HRRM...
DUNDUNNN
LIKE THIS!?
GOODNESS... BUT THAT IS TO BE EXPECTED... INDEED...
......
YES. CARRY ON LIKE THIS.
SPLENDID!
I CAN DO THIS!

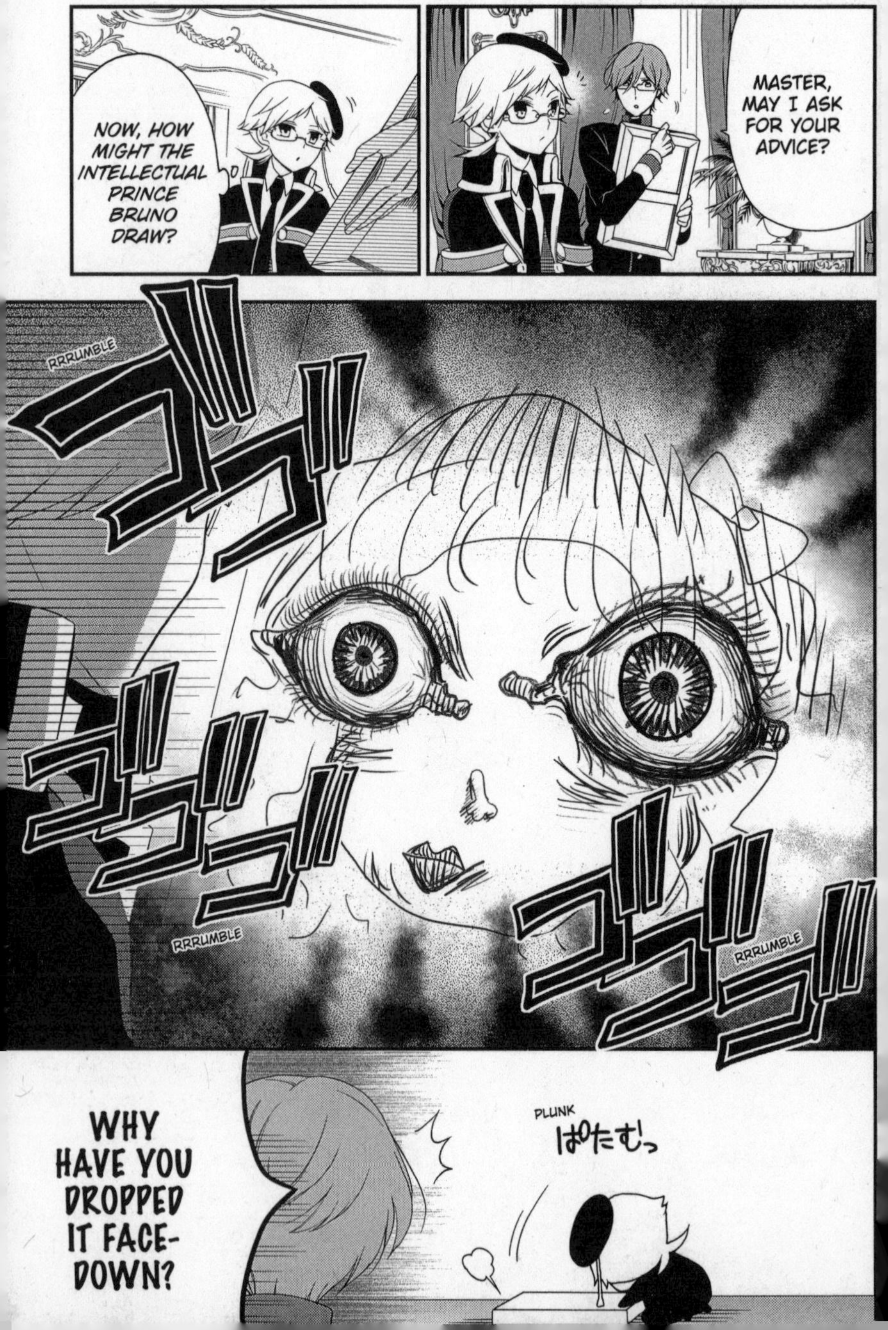
MASTER, MAY I ASK FOR YOUR ADVICE?
NOW, HOW MIGHT THE INTELLECTUAL PRINCE BRUNO DRAW?
RRRUMBLE
ゴゴゴ
RRRUMBLE
ゴゴゴ
RRRUMBLE
ゴゴ
PLUNK
ぱたむっ
WHY HAVE YOU DROPPED IT FACE-DOWN?

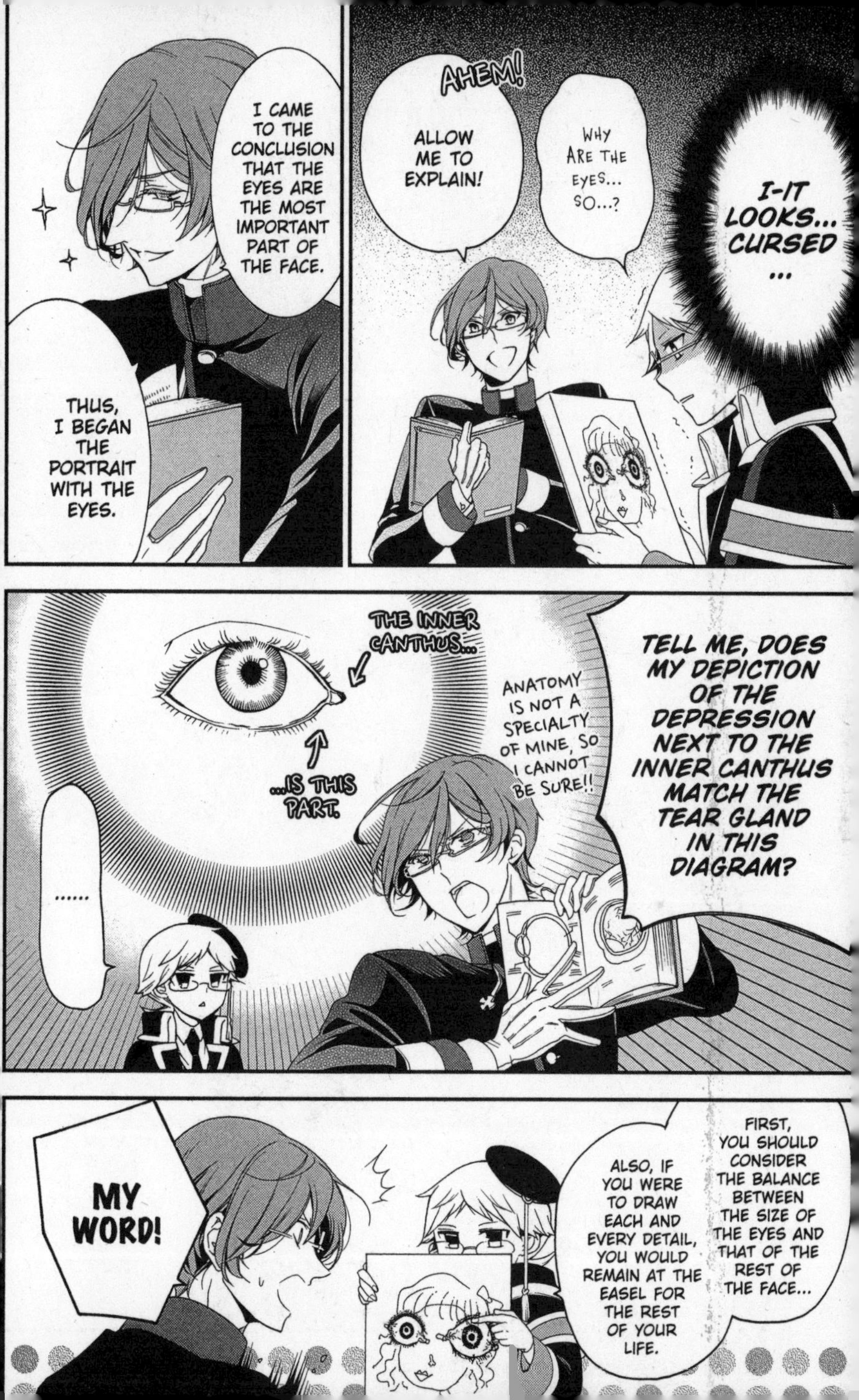
I-IT LOOKS... CURSED...
WHY ARE THE EYES... SO...?
AHEM!
ALLOW ME TO EXPLAIN!
I CAME TO THE CONCLUSION THAT THE EYES ARE THE MOST IMPORTANT PART OF THE FACE.
THUS, I BEGAN THE PORTRAIT WITH THE EYES.
TELL ME, DOES MY DEPICTION OF THE DEPRESSION NEXT TO THE INNER CANTHUS MATCH THE TEAR GLAND IN THIS DIAGRAM?
ANATOMY IS NOT A SPECIALTY OF MINE, SO I CANNOT BE SURE!!
THE INNER CANTHUS...
...IS THIS PART.
......
FIRST, YOU SHOULD CONSIDER THE BALANCE BETWEEN THE SIZE OF THE EYES AND THAT OF THE REST OF THE FACE...
ALSO, IF YOU WERE TO DRAW EACH AND EVERY DETAIL, YOU WOULD REMAIN AT THE EASEL FOR THE REST OF YOUR LIFE.
MY WORD!

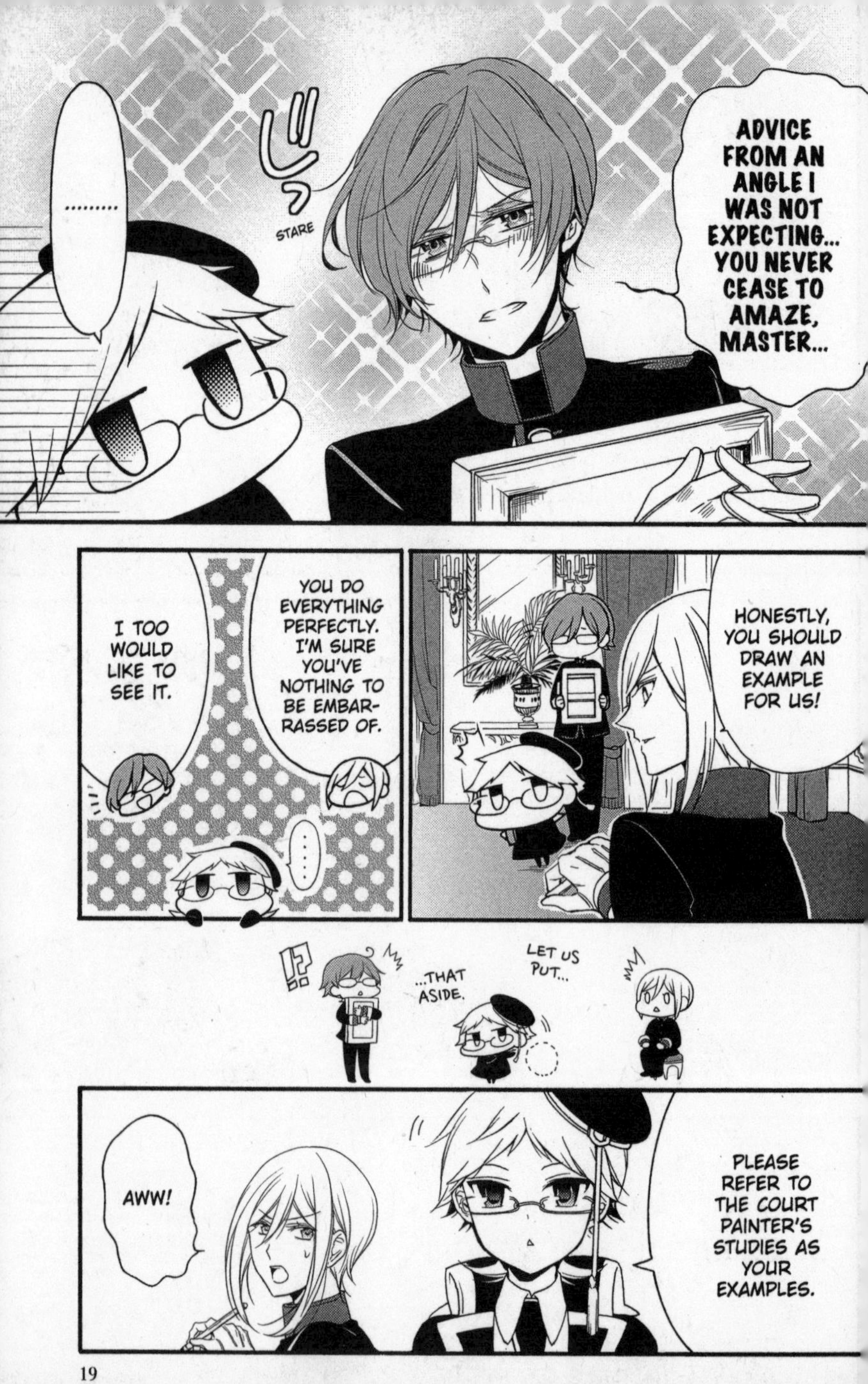
ADVICE FROM AN ANGLE I WAS NOT EXPECTING... YOU NEVER CEASE TO AMAZE, MASTER...
STARE
....
HONESTLY, YOU SHOULD DRAW AN EXAMPLE FOR US!
YOU DO EVERYTHING PERFECTLY. I'M SURE YOU'VE NOTHING TO BE EMBAR-RASSED OF.
I TOO WOULD LIKE TO SEE IT.
......
LET US PUT...
...THAT ASIDE.
PLEASE REFER TO THE COURT PAINTER'S STUDIES AS YOUR EXAMPLES.
AWW!

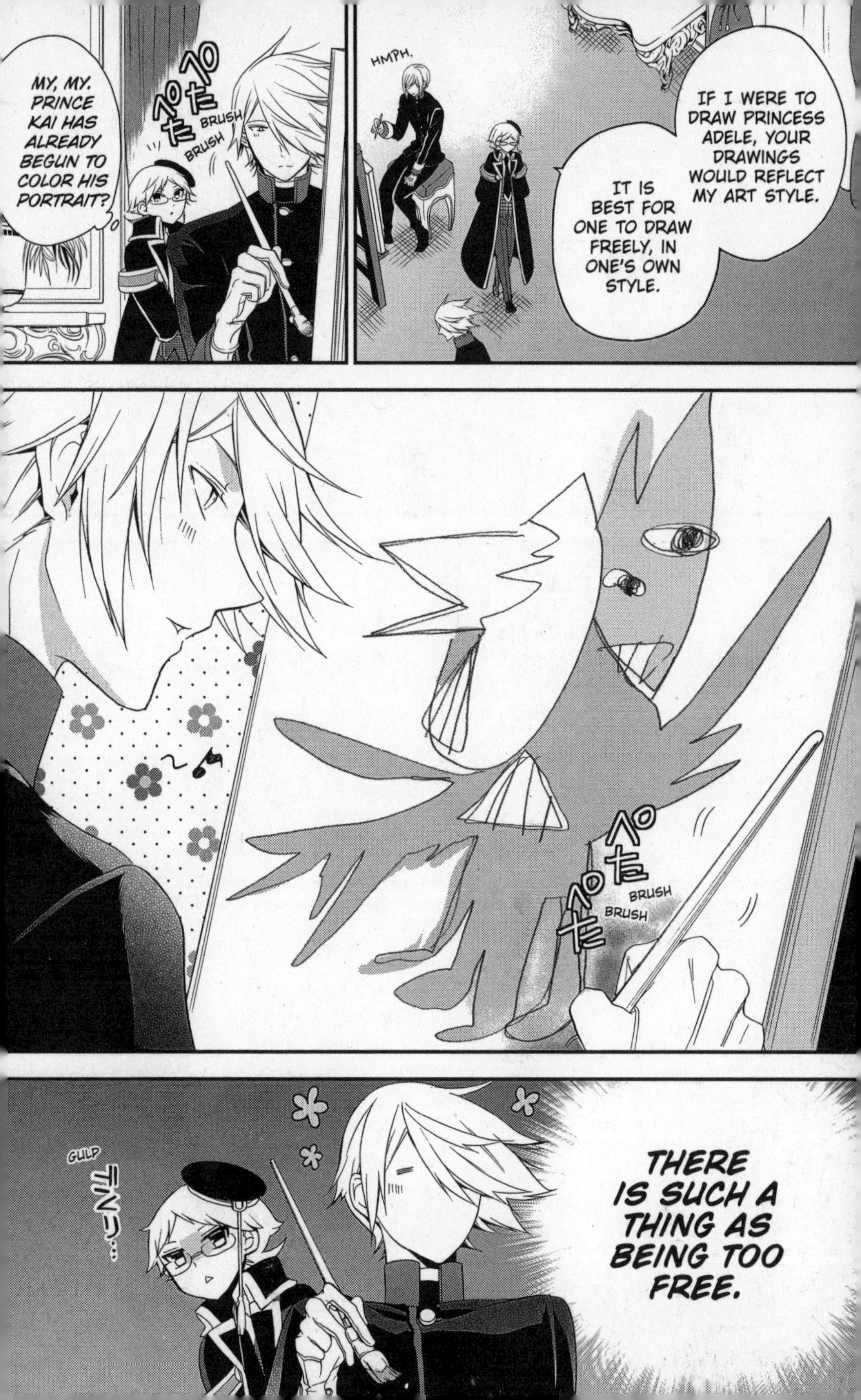
IF I WERE TO DRAW PRINCESS ADELE, YOUR DRAWINGS WOULD REFLECT MY ART STYLE.
IT IS BEST FOR ONE TO DRAW FREELY, IN ONE'S OWN STYLE.
HMPH.
MY, MY. PRINCE KAI HAS ALREADY BEGUN TO COLOR HIS PORTRAIT?
ぺたぺた
BRUSH BRUSH
ぺたぺた
BRUSH BRUSH
THERE IS SUCH A THING AS BEING TOO FREE.
GULP

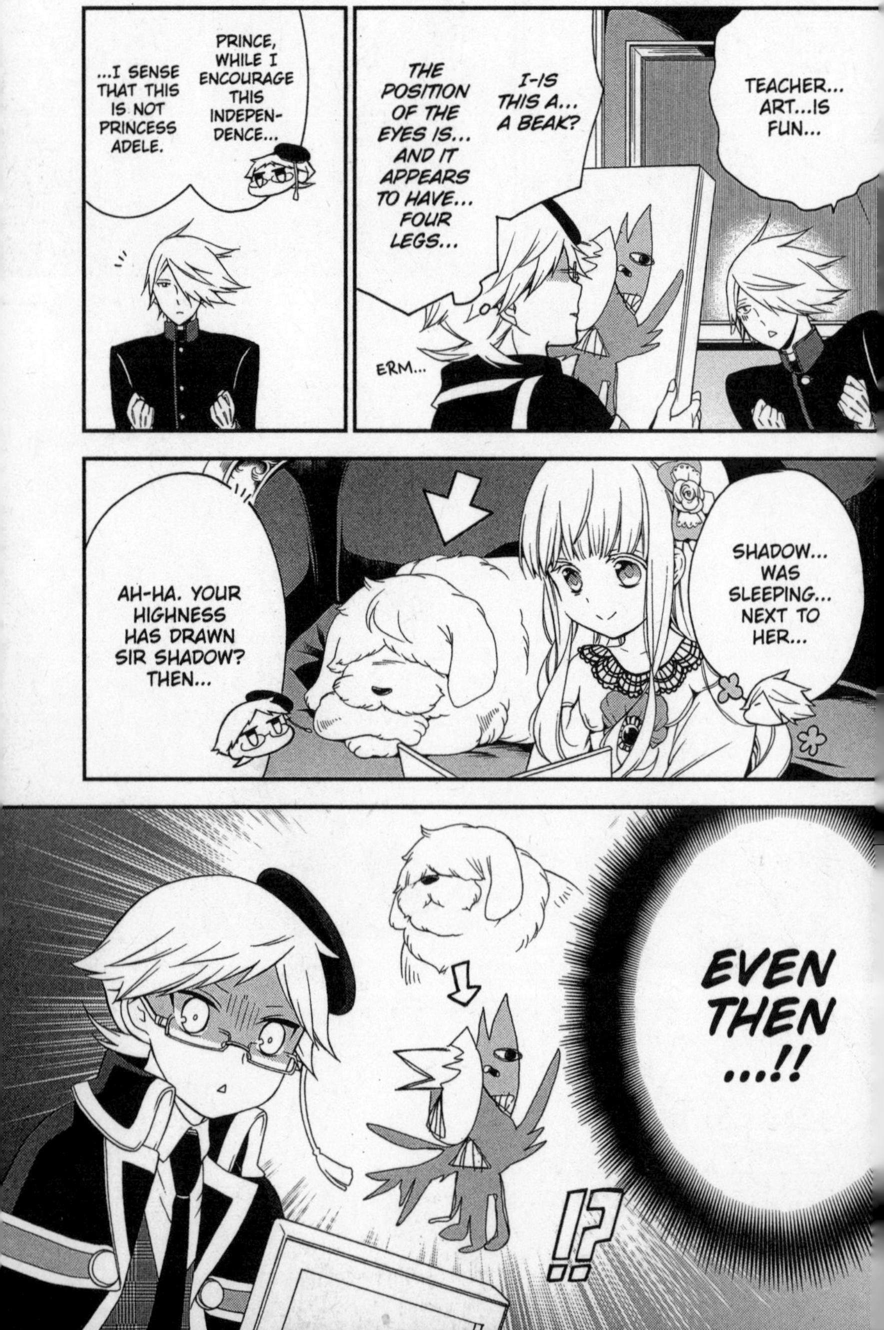
TEACHER... ART...IS FUN...
I-IS THIS A... A BEAK?
THE POSITION OF THE EYES IS... AND IT APPEARS TO HAVE... FOUR LEGS...
ERM...
PRINCE, WHILE I ENCOURAGE THIS INDEPEN-DENCE...
...I SENSE THAT THIS IS NOT PRINCESS ADELE.
SHADOW... WAS SLEEPING... NEXT TO HER...
AH-HA. YOUR HIGHNESS HAS DRAWN SIR SHADOW? THEN...
EVEN THEN ...!!
!?

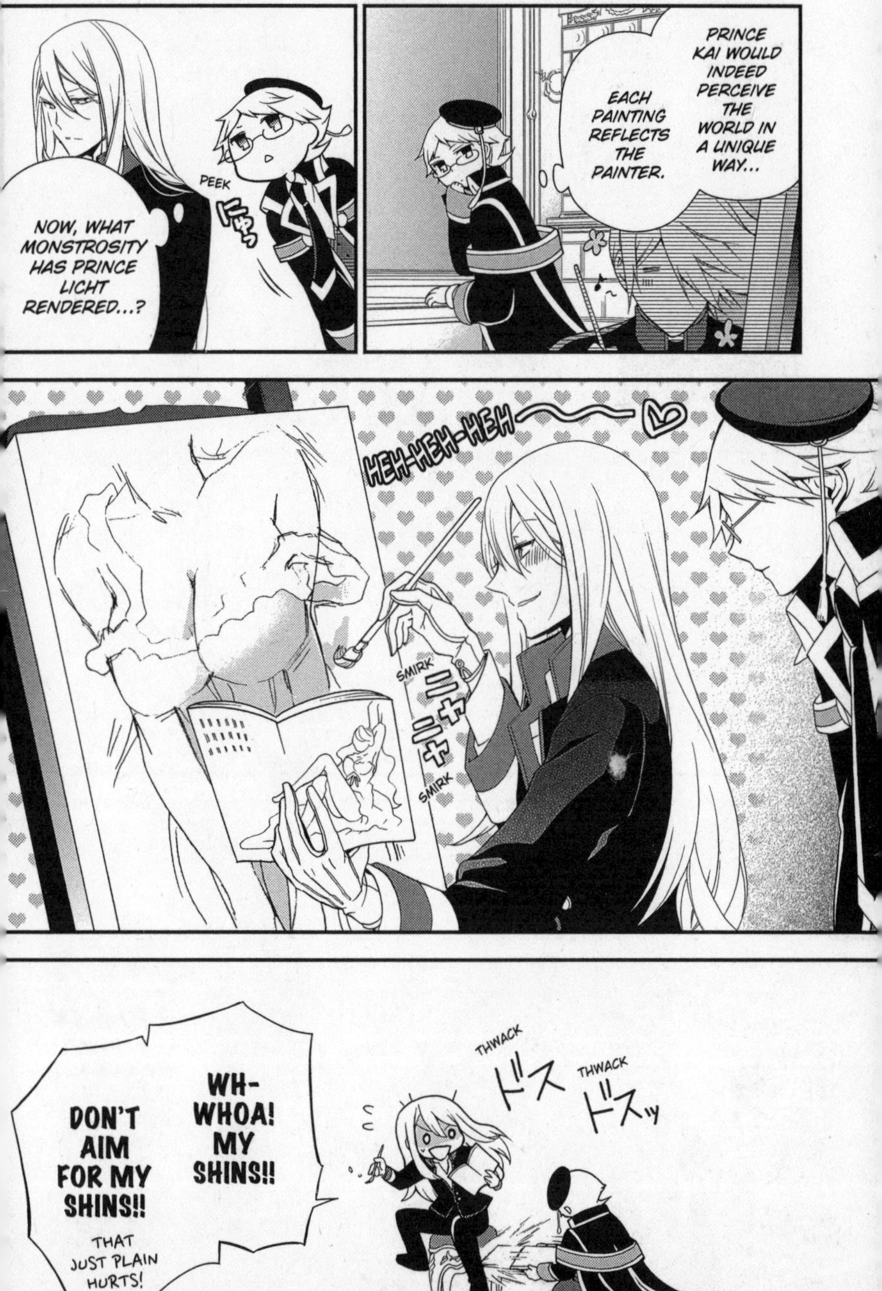
PRINCE KAI WOULD INDEED PERCEIVE THE WORLD IN A UNIQUE WAY...
EACH PAINTING REFLECTS THE PAINTER.
PEEK
にゅっ
NOW, WHAT MONSTROSITY HAS PRINCE LICHT RENDERED...?
HEH-HEH-HEH
SMIRK
ニャ
ニャ
SMIRK
THWACK
ドス
THWACK
ドスッ
WH-WHOA! MY SHINS!!
DON'T AIM FOR MY SHINS!!
THAT JUST PLAIN HURTS!

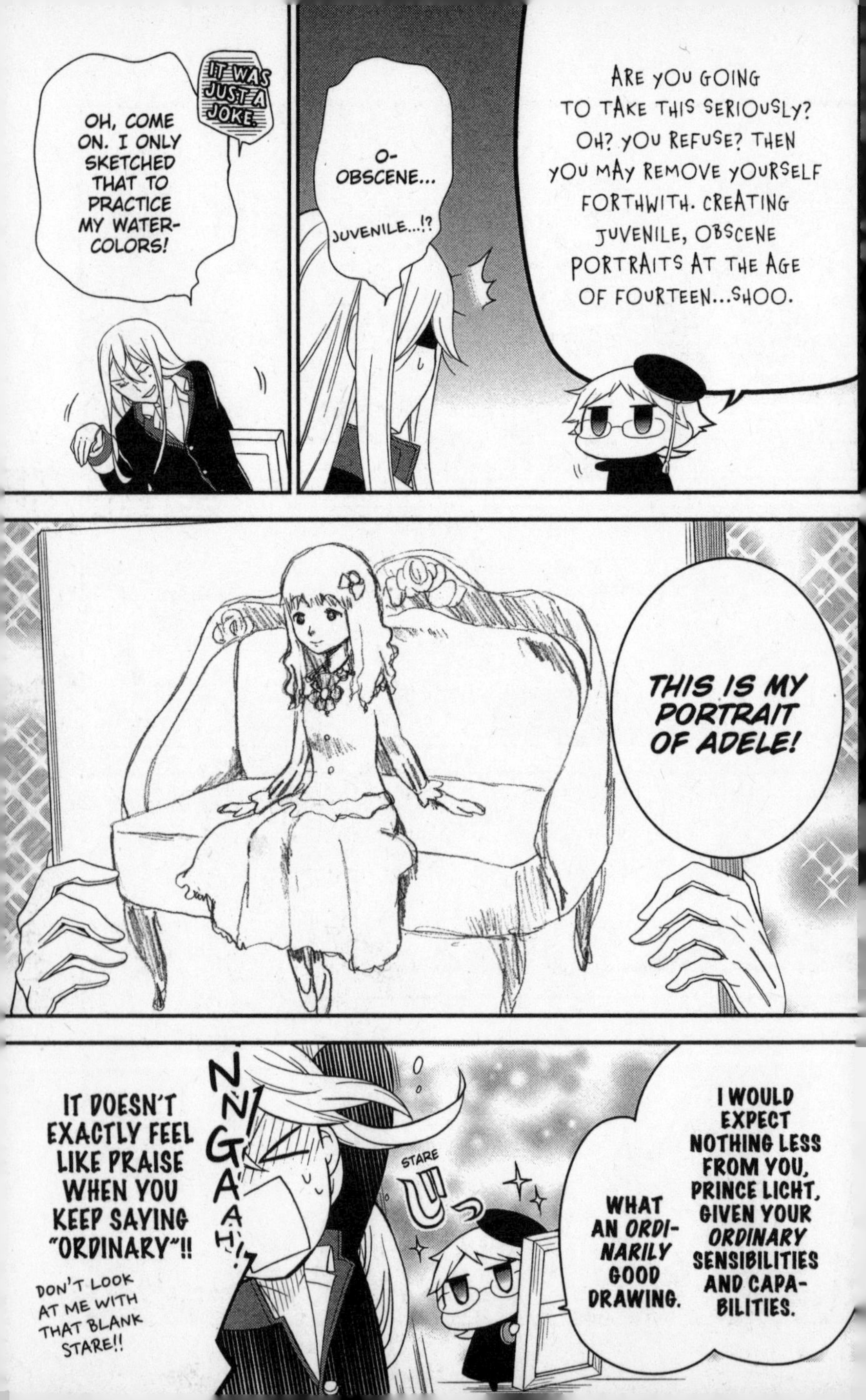
ARE YOU GOING TO TAKE THIS SERIOUSLY? OH? YOU REFUSE? THEN YOU MAY REMOVE YOURSELF FORTHWITH. CREATING JUVENILE, OBSCENE PORTRAITS AT THE AGE OF FOURTEEN...SHOO.
O-OBSCENE...
JUVENILE...!?
IT WAS JUST A JOKE.
OH, COME ON. I ONLY SKETCHED THAT TO PRACTICE MY WATER-COLORS!
THIS IS MY PORTRAIT OF ADELE!
I WOULD EXPECT NOTHING LESS FROM YOU, PRINCE LICHT, GIVEN YOUR *ORDINARY* SENSIBILITIES AND CAPA-BILITIES.
WHAT AN *ORDI-NARILY* GOOD DRAWING.
STARE
NNGAAH!!
IT DOESN'T EXACTLY FEEL LIKE PRAISE WHEN YOU KEEP SAYING "ORDINARY"!!
DON'T LOOK AT ME WITH THAT BLANK STARE!!

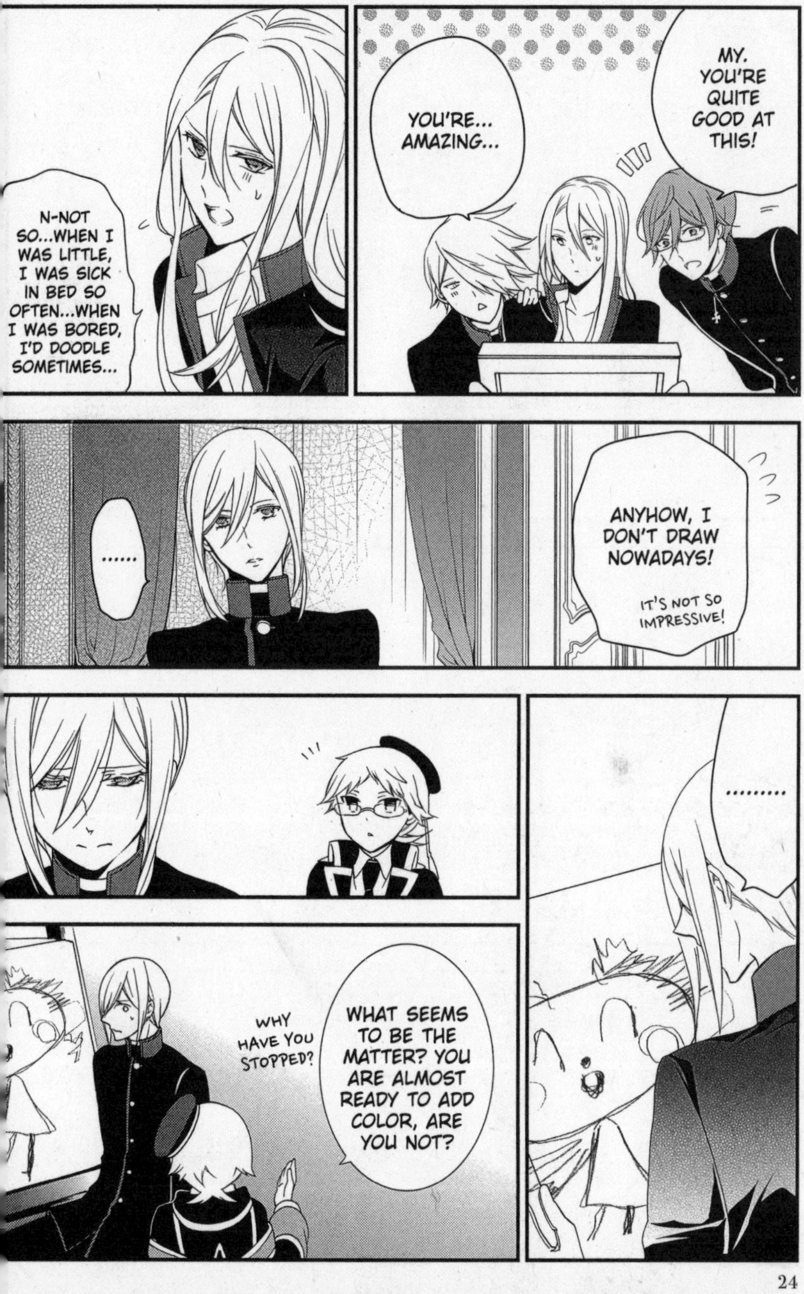
MY. YOU'RE QUITE GOOD AT THIS!
YOU'RE... AMAZING...
N-NOT SO...WHEN I WAS LITTLE, I WAS SICK IN BED SO OFTEN...WHEN I WAS BORED, I'D DOODLE SOMETIMES...
ANYHOW, I DON'T DRAW NOWADAYS!
IT'S NOT SO IMPRESSIVE!
......
....
WHAT SEEMS TO BE THE MATTER? YOU ARE ALMOST READY TO ADD COLOR, ARE YOU NOT?
WHY HAVE YOU STOPPED?

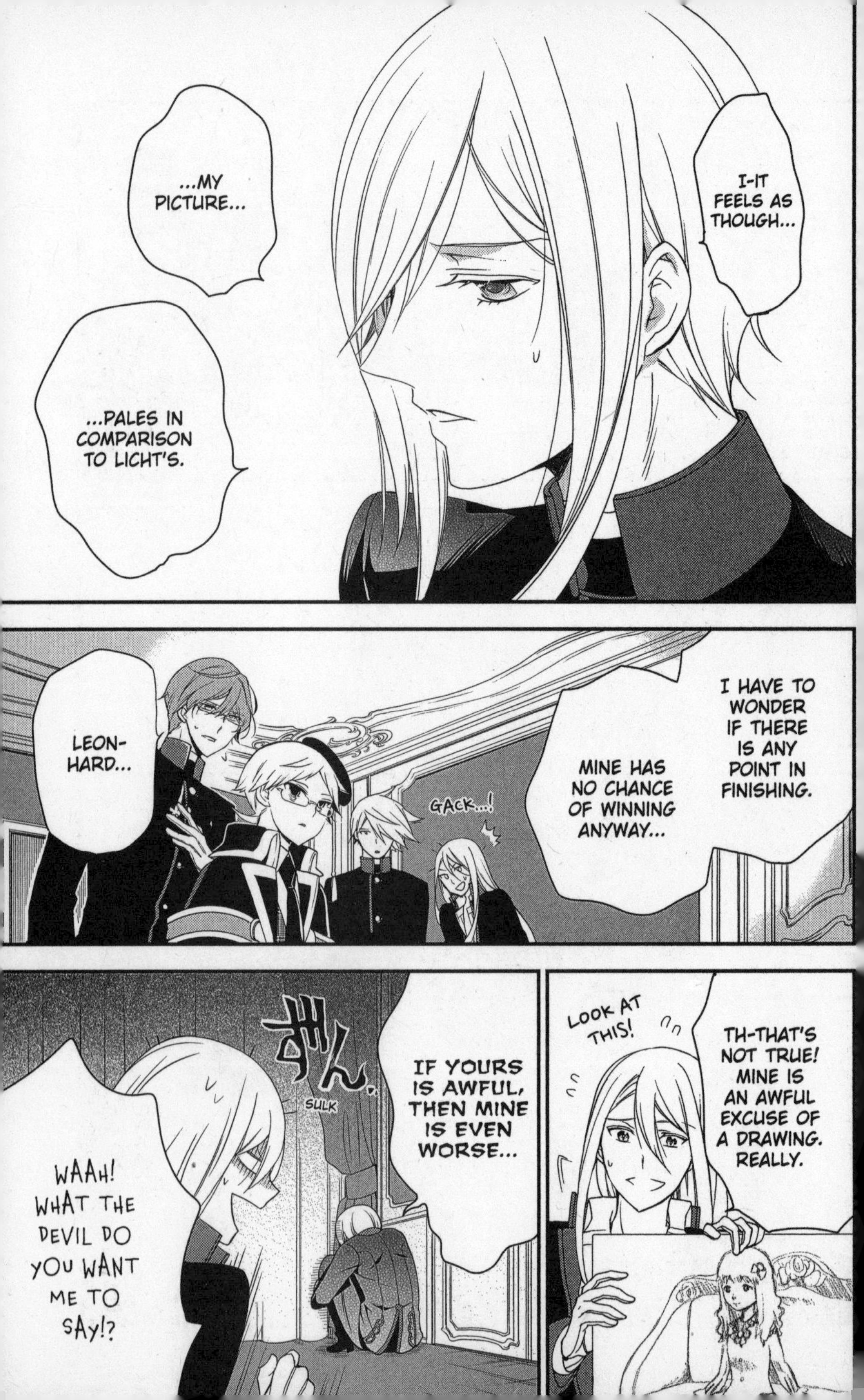
I-IT FEELS AS THOUGH...
...MY PICTURE...
...PALES IN COMPARISON TO LICHT'S.
I HAVE TO WONDER IF THERE IS ANY POINT IN FINISHING.
MINE HAS NO CHANCE OF WINNING ANYWAY...
GACK...!
LEON-HARD...
TH-THAT'S NOT TRUE! MINE IS AN AWFUL EXCUSE OF A DRAWING. REALLY.
LOOK AT THIS!
IF YOURS IS AWFUL, THEN MINE IS EVEN WORSE...
ずん
SULK
WAAH! WHAT THE DEVIL DO YOU WANT ME TO SAY!?

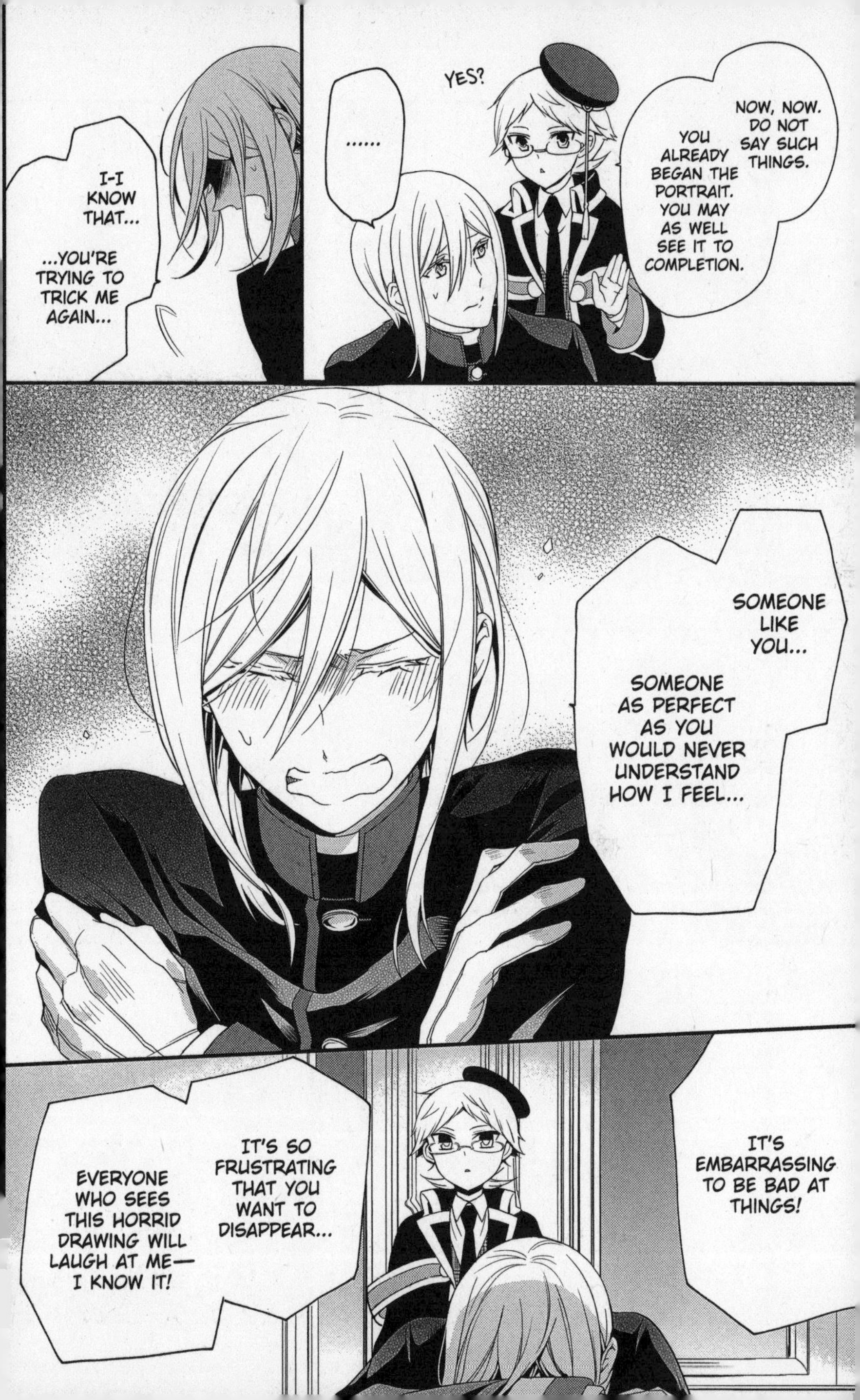
NOW, NOW. DO NOT SAY SUCH THINGS.
YOU ALREADY BEGAN THE PORTRAIT. YOU MAY AS WELL SEE IT TO COMPLETION.
YES?
......
I-I KNOW THAT...
...YOU'RE TRYING TO TRICK ME AGAIN...
SOMEONE LIKE YOU...
SOMEONE AS PERFECT AS YOU WOULD NEVER UNDERSTAND HOW I FEEL...
IT'S EMBARRASSING TO BE BAD AT THINGS!
IT'S SO FRUSTRATING THAT YOU WANT TO DISAPPEAR...
EVERYONE WHO SEES THIS HORRID DRAWING WILL LAUGH AT ME—I KNOW IT!

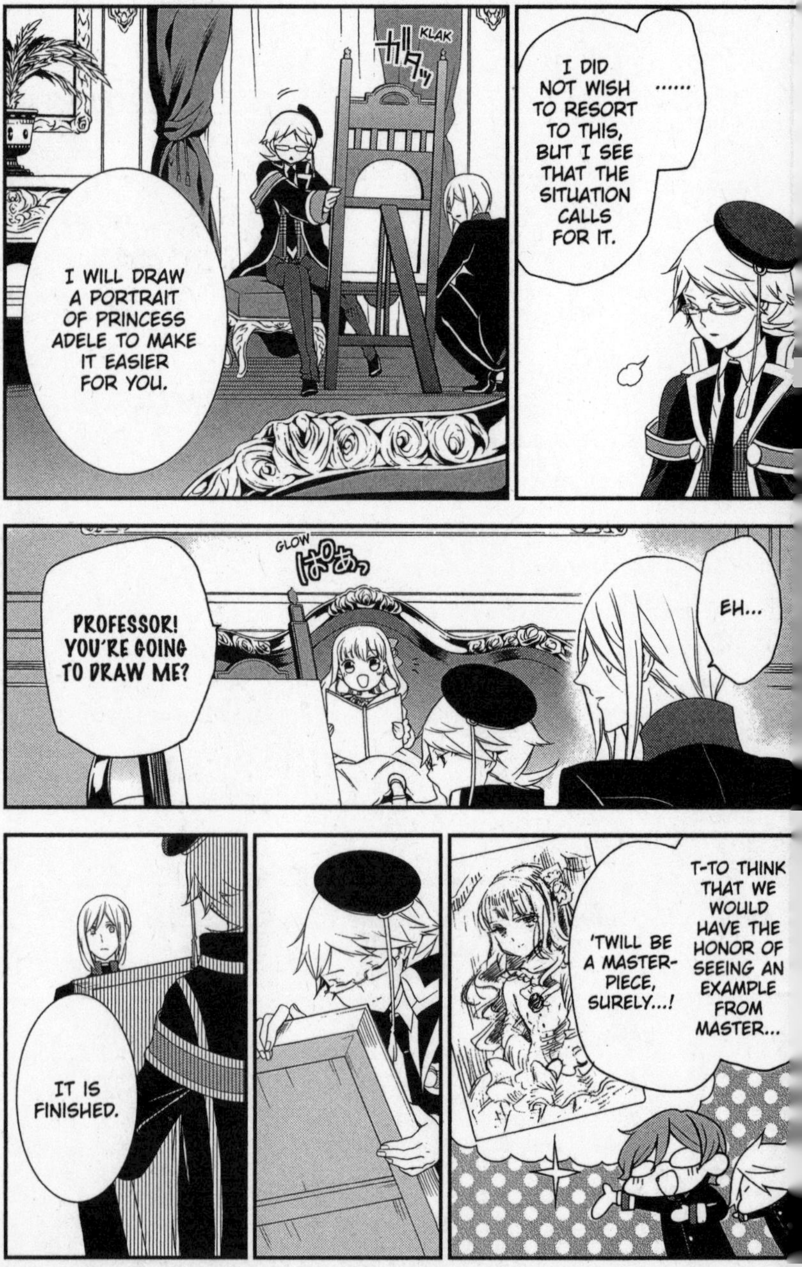
......
I DID NOT WISH TO RESORT TO THIS, BUT I SEE THAT THE SITUATION CALLS FOR IT.
KLAK
I WILL DRAW A PORTRAIT OF PRINCESS ADELE TO MAKE IT EASIER FOR YOU.
EH...
GLOW
PROFESSOR! YOU'RE GOING TO DRAW ME?
T-TO THINK THAT WE WOULD HAVE THE HONOR OF SEEING AN EXAMPLE FROM MASTER...
'TWILL BE A MASTER-PIECE, SURELY...!
IT IS FINISHED.

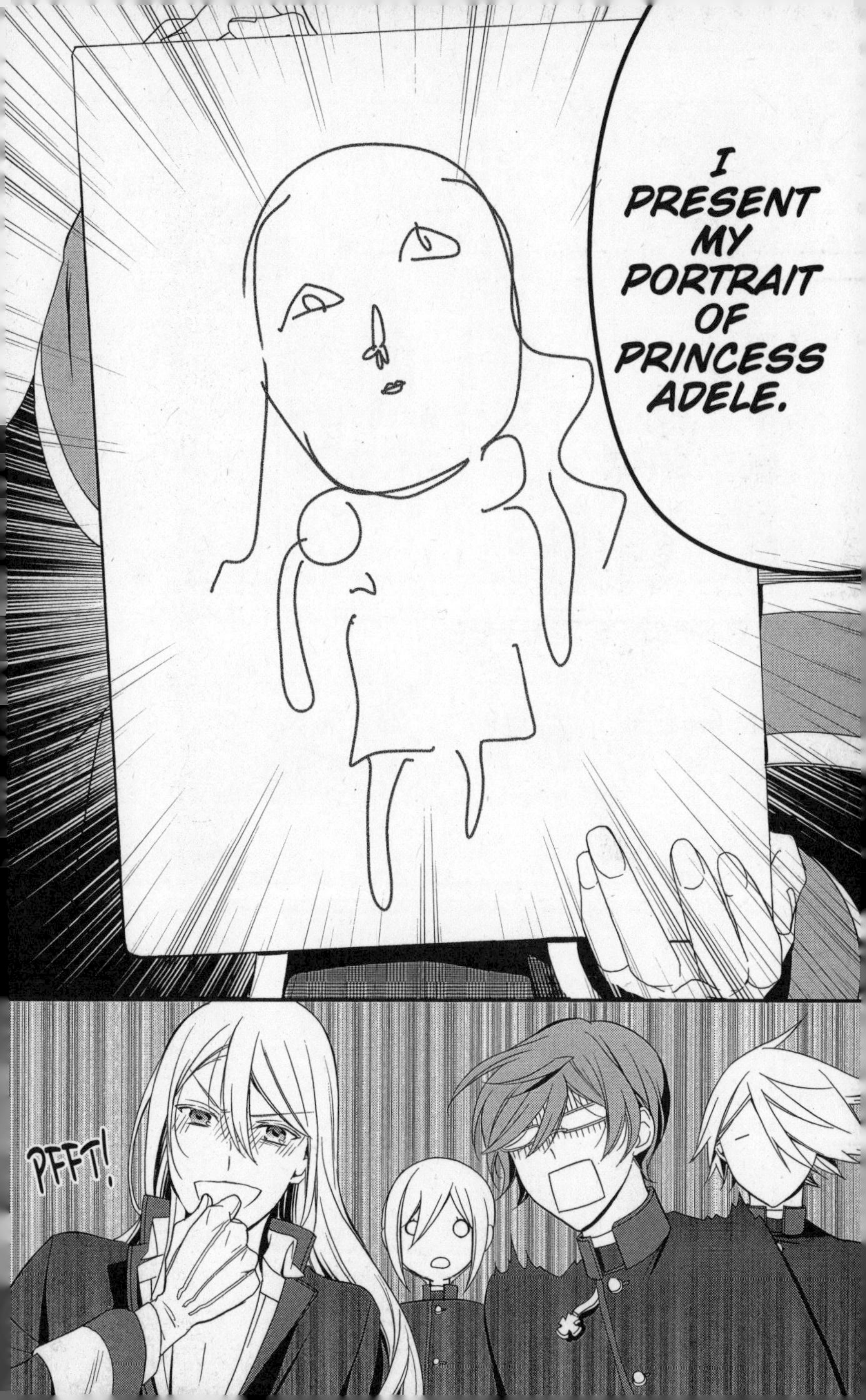
I PRESENT MY PORTRAIT OF PRINCESS ADELE.
PFFT!

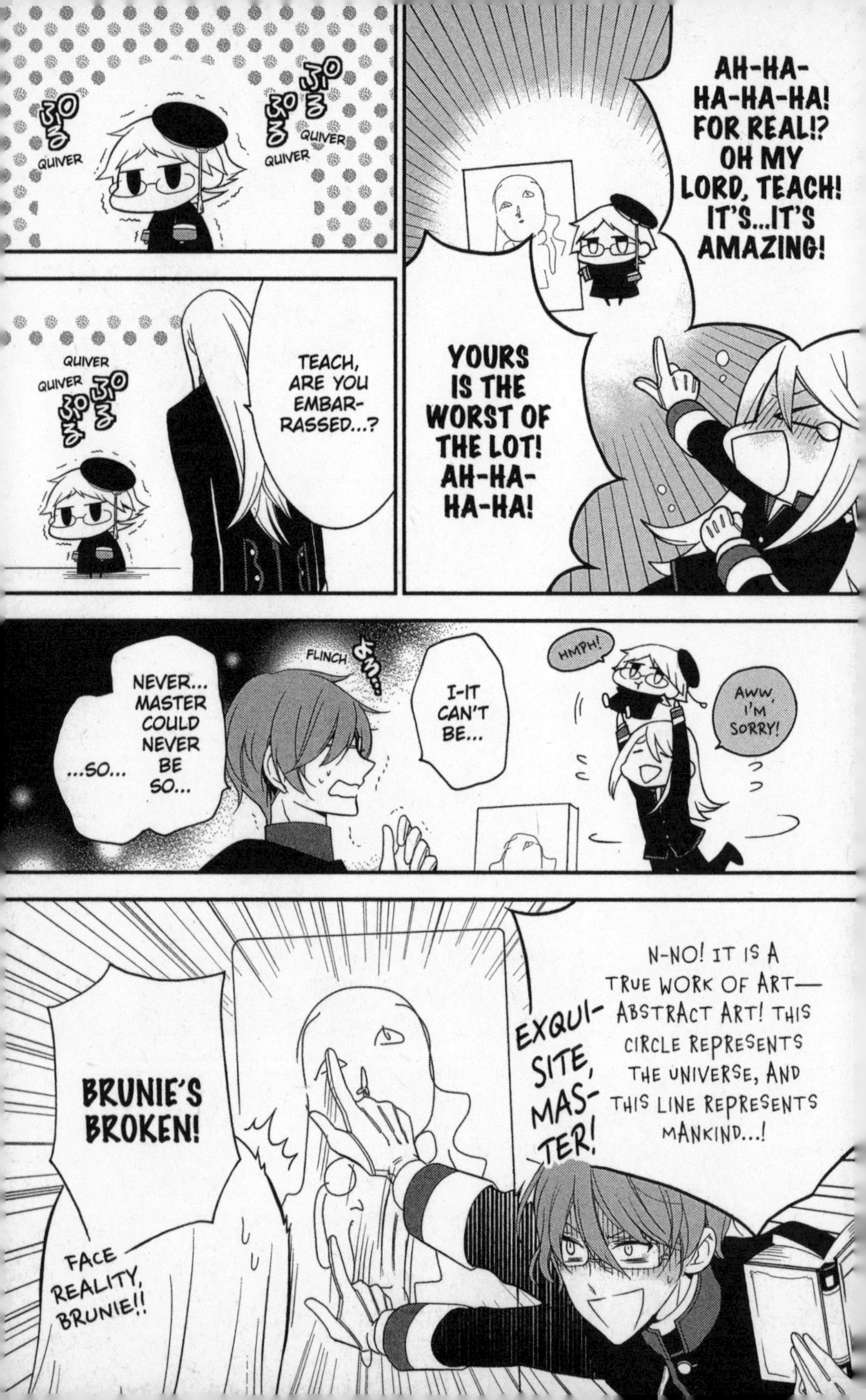
AH-HA-HA-HA-HA! FOR REAL!? OH MY LORD, TEACH! IT'S...IT'S AMAZING!
YOURS IS THE WORST OF THE LOT! AH-HA-HA-HA!
ぷるぷる QUIVER QUIVER
ぷるぷる QUIVER
ぷるぷる QUIVER QUIVER
TEACH, ARE YOU EMBARRASSED...?
AWW, I'M SORRY!
HMPH!
I-IT CAN'T BE...
FLINCH
NEVER... MASTER COULD NEVER BE SO...
...SO...
N-NO! IT IS A TRUE WORK OF ART—ABSTRACT ART! THIS CIRCLE REPRESENTS THE UNIVERSE, AND THIS LINE REPRESENTS MANKIND...!
EXQUISITE, MASTER!
BRUNIE'S BROKEN!
FACE REALITY, BRUNIE!!

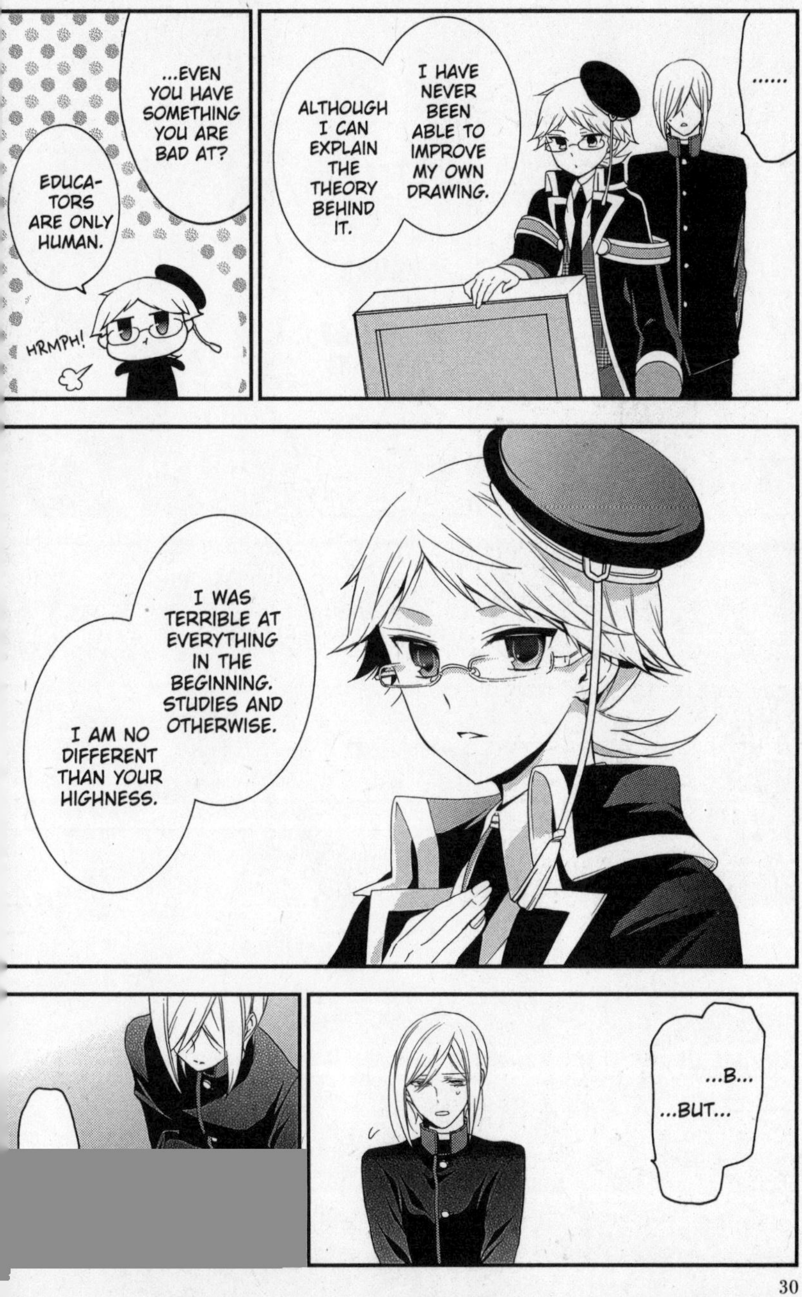
......
I HAVE NEVER BEEN ABLE TO IMPROVE MY OWN DRAWING.
ALTHOUGH I CAN EXPLAIN THE THEORY BEHIND IT.
...EVEN YOU HAVE SOMETHING YOU ARE BAD AT?
EDUCATORS ARE ONLY HUMAN.
HRMPH!
I WAS TERRIBLE AT EVERYTHING IN THE BEGINNING. STUDIES AND OTHERWISE.
I AM NO DIFFERENT THAN YOUR HIGHNESS.
...B...
...BUT...

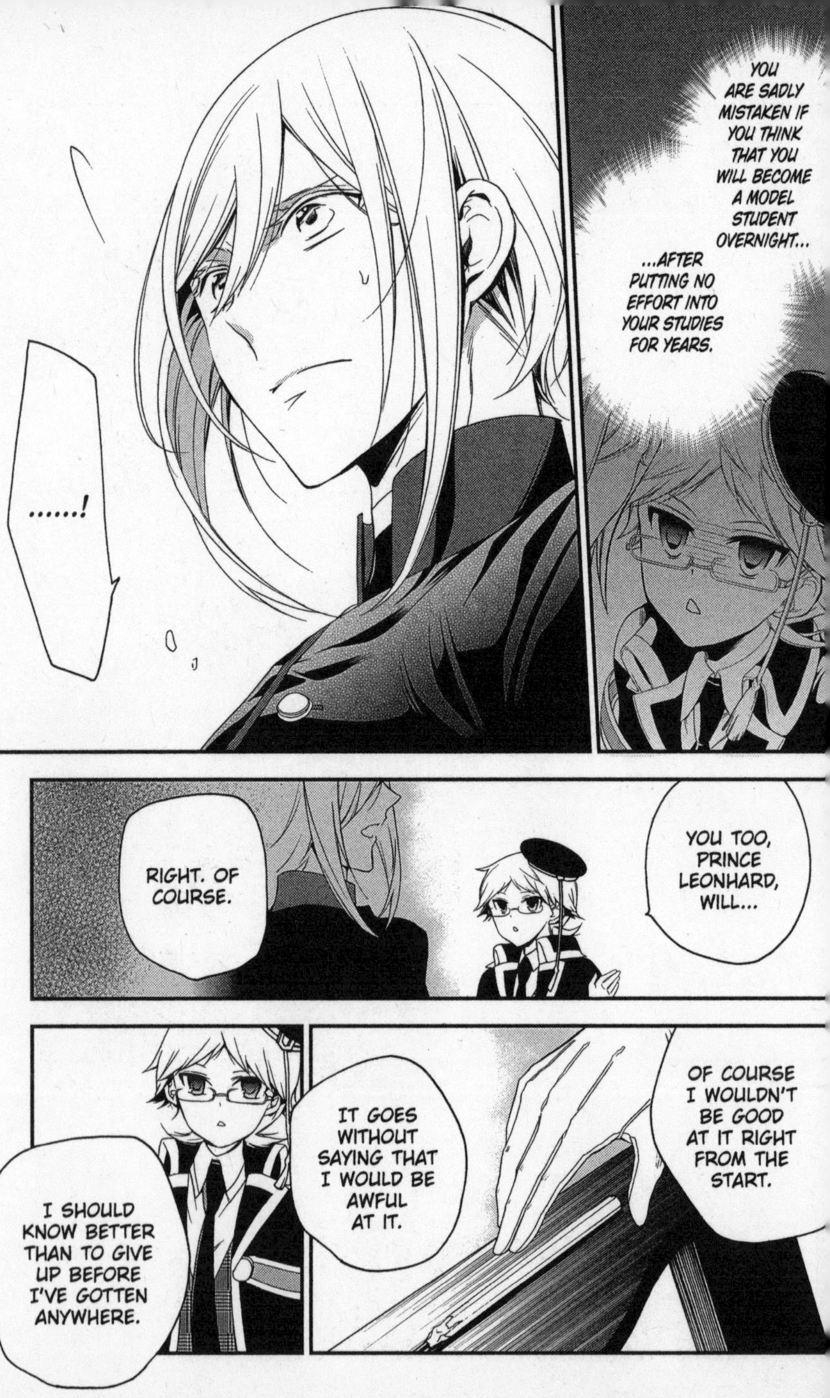
YOU ARE SADLY MISTAKEN IF YOU THINK THAT YOU WILL BECOME A MODEL STUDENT OVERNIGHT...
...AFTER PUTTING NO EFFORT INTO YOUR STUDIES FOR YEARS.
......!
YOU TOO, PRINCE LEONHARD, WILL...
RIGHT. OF COURSE.
OF COURSE I WOULDN'T BE GOOD AT IT RIGHT FROM THE START.
IT GOES WITHOUT SAYING THAT I WOULD BE AWFUL AT IT.
I SHOULD KNOW BETTER THAN TO GIVE UP BEFORE I'VE GOTTEN ANYWHERE.

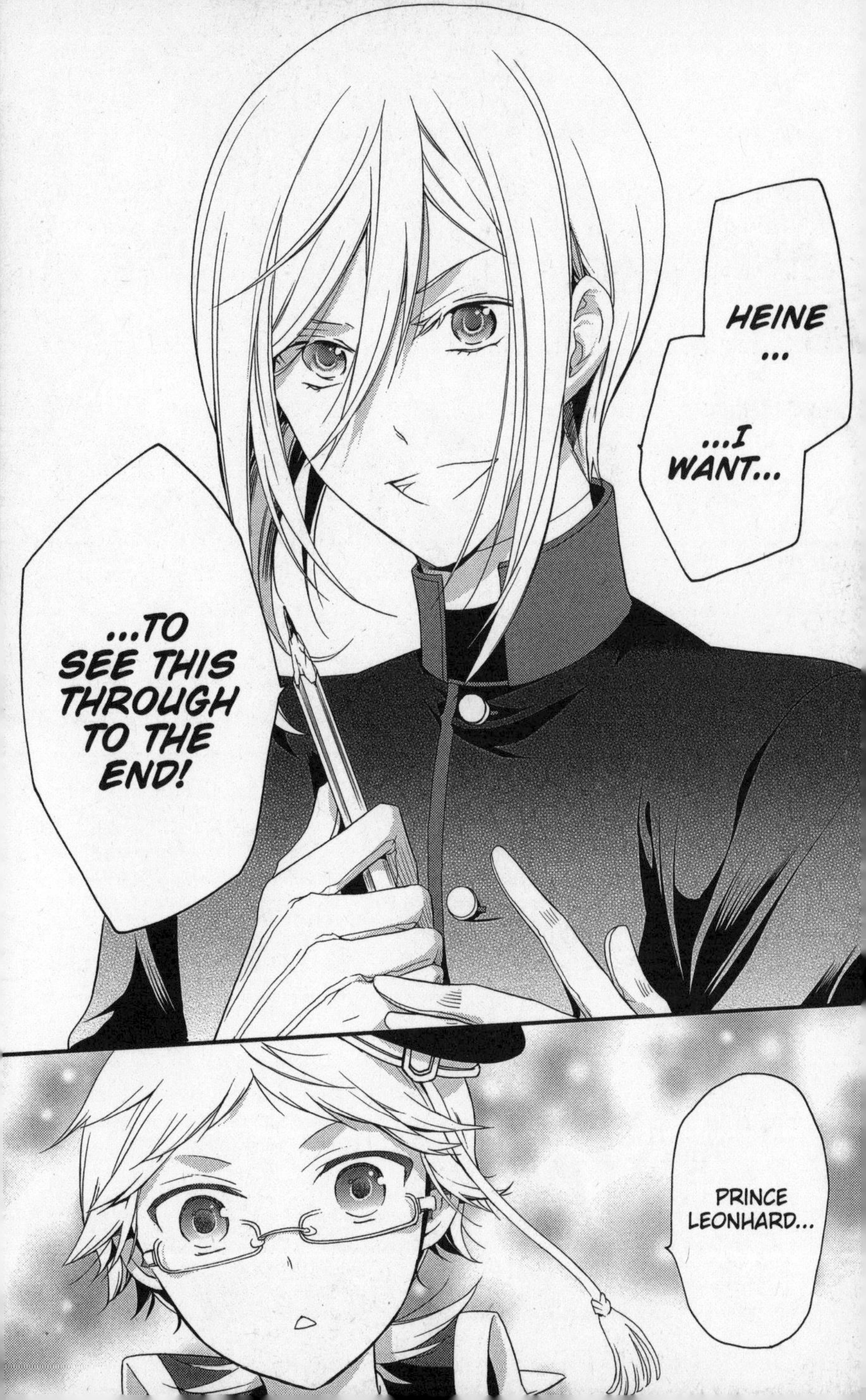
HEINE ...
...I WANT...
...TO SEE THIS THROUGH TO THE END!
PRINCE LEONHARD...

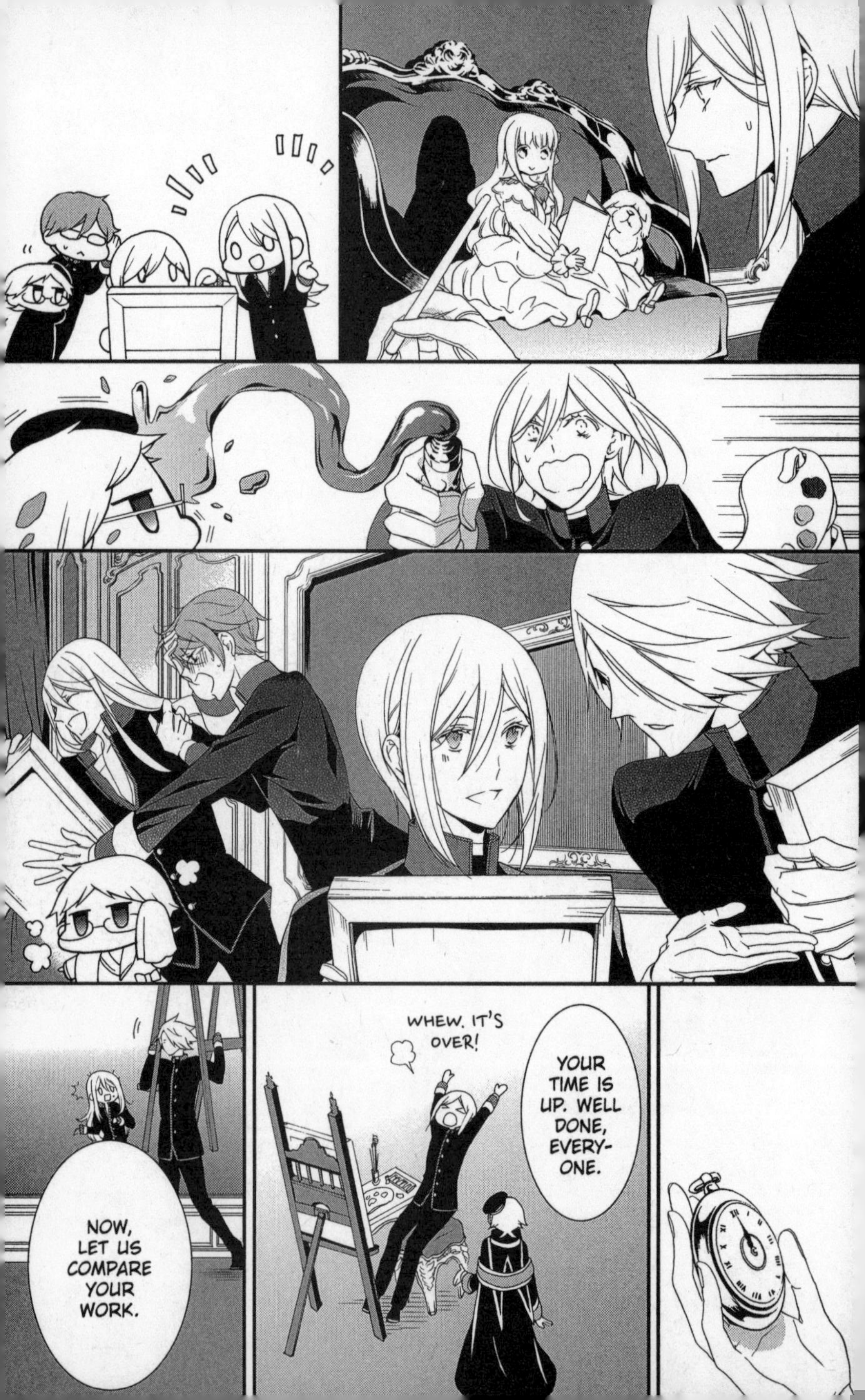
YOUR TIME IS UP. WELL DONE, EVERY-ONE.
WHEW. IT'S OVER!
NOW, LET US COMPARE YOUR WORK.

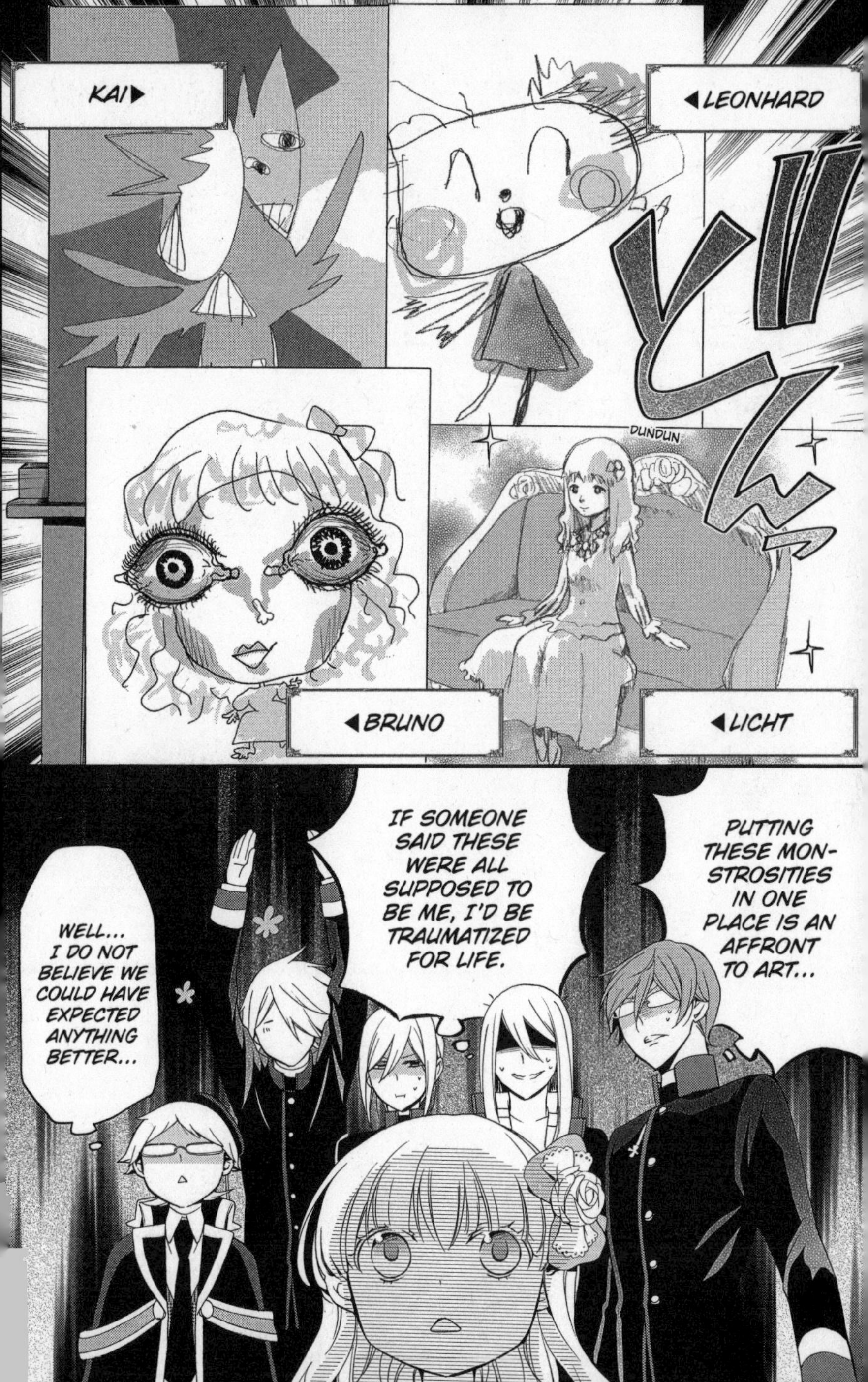

◀LEONHARD
KAI▶
DUNDUN
◀LICHT
◀BRUNO
PUTTING THESE MON-STROSITIES IN ONE PLACE IS AN AFFRONT TO ART...
IF SOMEONE SAID THESE WERE ALL SUPPOSED TO BE ME, I'D BE TRAUMATIZED FOR LIFE.
WELL... I DO NOT BELIEVE WE COULD HAVE EXPECTED ANYTHING BETTER...

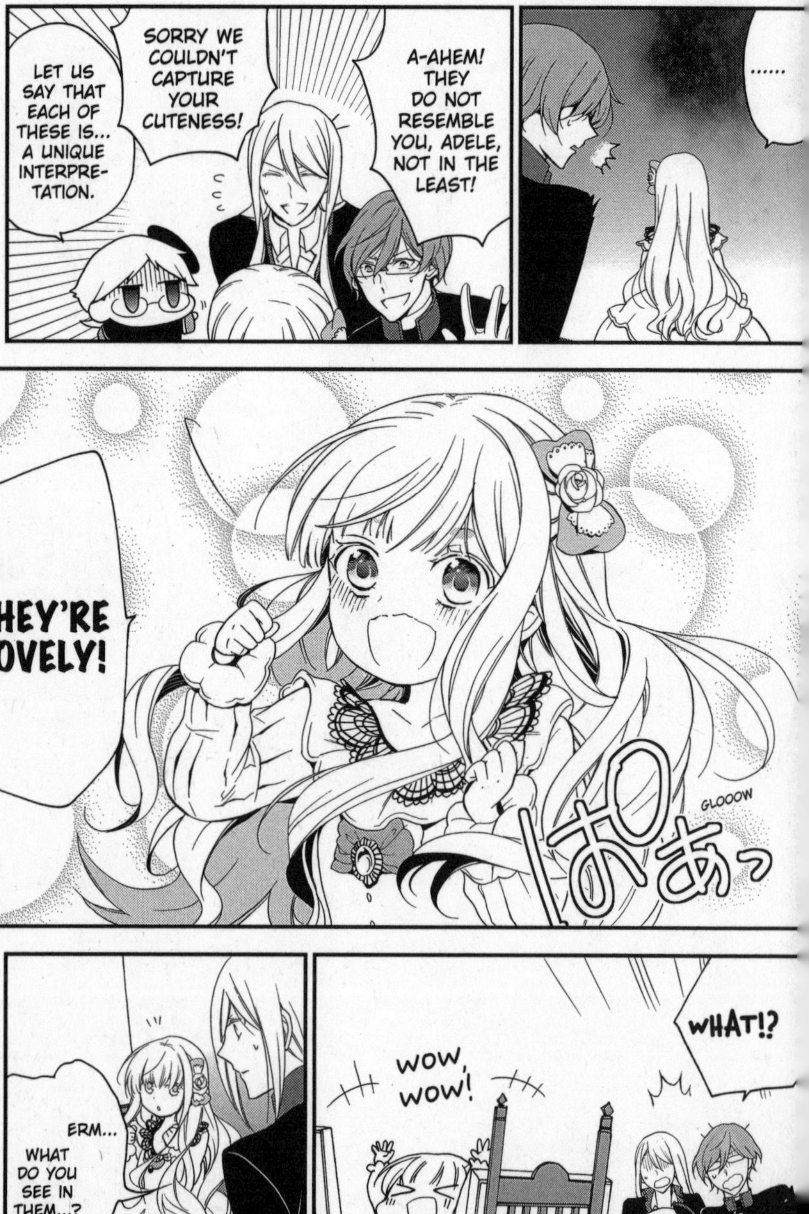
......
A-AHEM! THEY DO NOT RESEMBLE YOU, ADELE, NOT IN THE LEAST!
SORRY WE COULDN'T CAPTURE YOUR CUTENESS!
LET US SAY THAT EACH OF THESE IS... A UNIQUE INTERPRETATION.
THEY'RE LOVELY!
GLOOOW
WHAT!?
WOW, WOW!
ERM... WHAT DO YOU SEE IN THEM...?

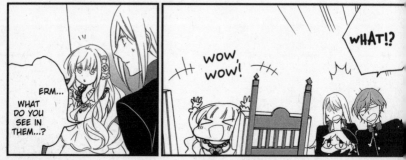

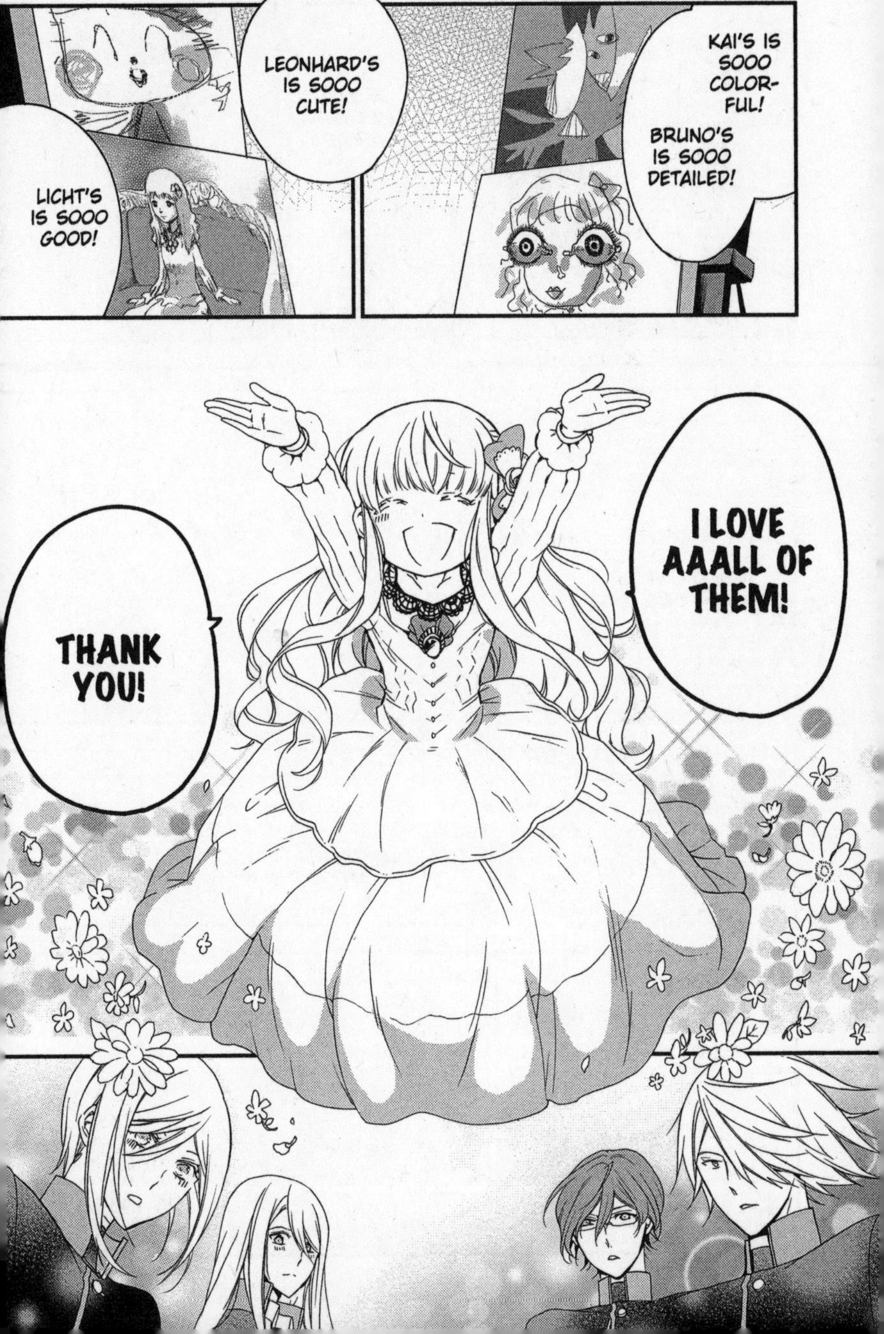
KAI'S IS SOOO COLOR-FUL!
BRUNO'S IS SOOO DETAILED!
LEONHARD'S IS SOOO CUTE!
LICHT'S IS SOOO GOOD!
I LOVE AAALL OF THEM!
THANK YOU!

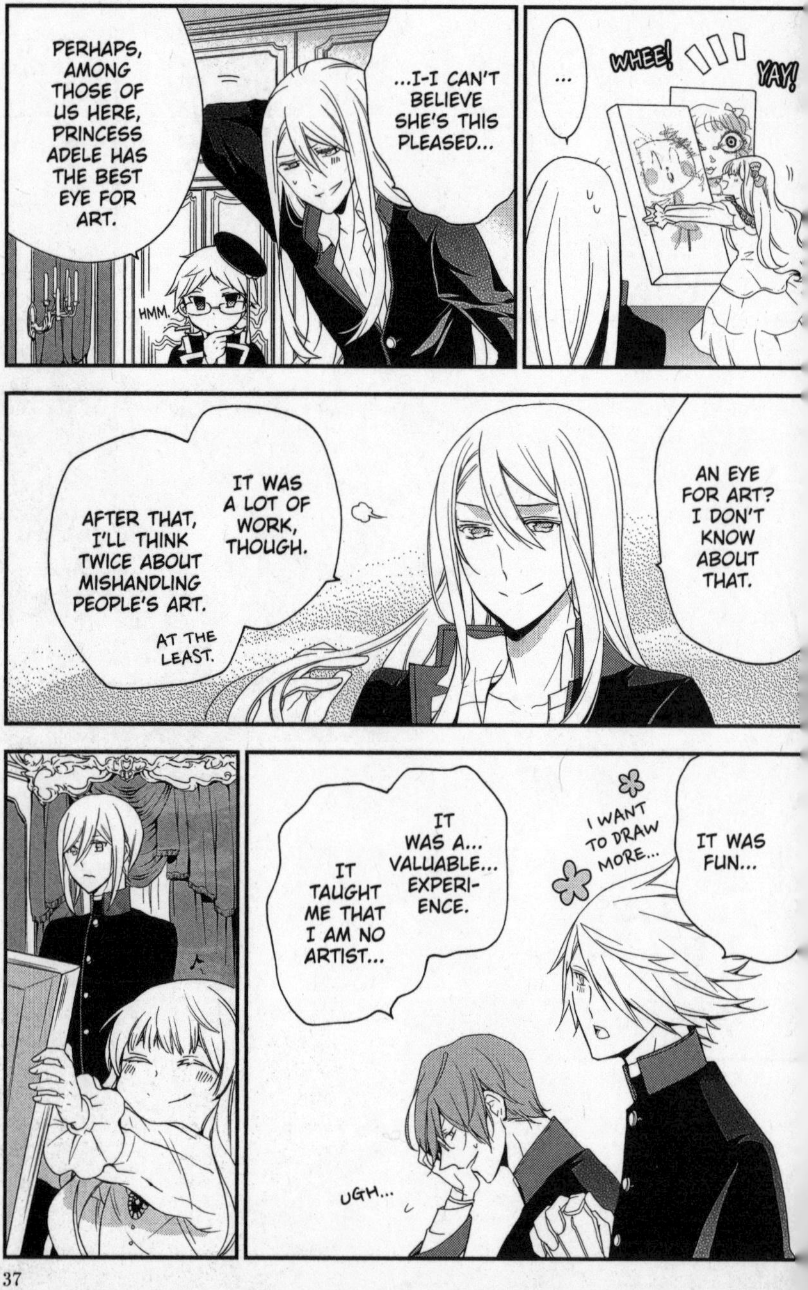
...
WHEE!
YAY!
...I-I CAN'T BELIEVE SHE'S THIS PLEASED...
PERHAPS, AMONG THOSE OF US HERE, PRINCESS ADELE HAS THE BEST EYE FOR ART.
HMM.
AN EYE FOR ART? I DON'T KNOW ABOUT THAT.
IT WAS A LOT OF WORK, THOUGH.
AFTER THAT, I'LL THINK TWICE ABOUT MISHANDLING PEOPLE'S ART.
AT THE LEAST.
IT WAS FUN...
I WANT TO DRAW MORE...
IT WAS A... VALUABLE... EXPERIENCE.
IT TAUGHT ME THAT I AM NO ARTIST...
UGH...

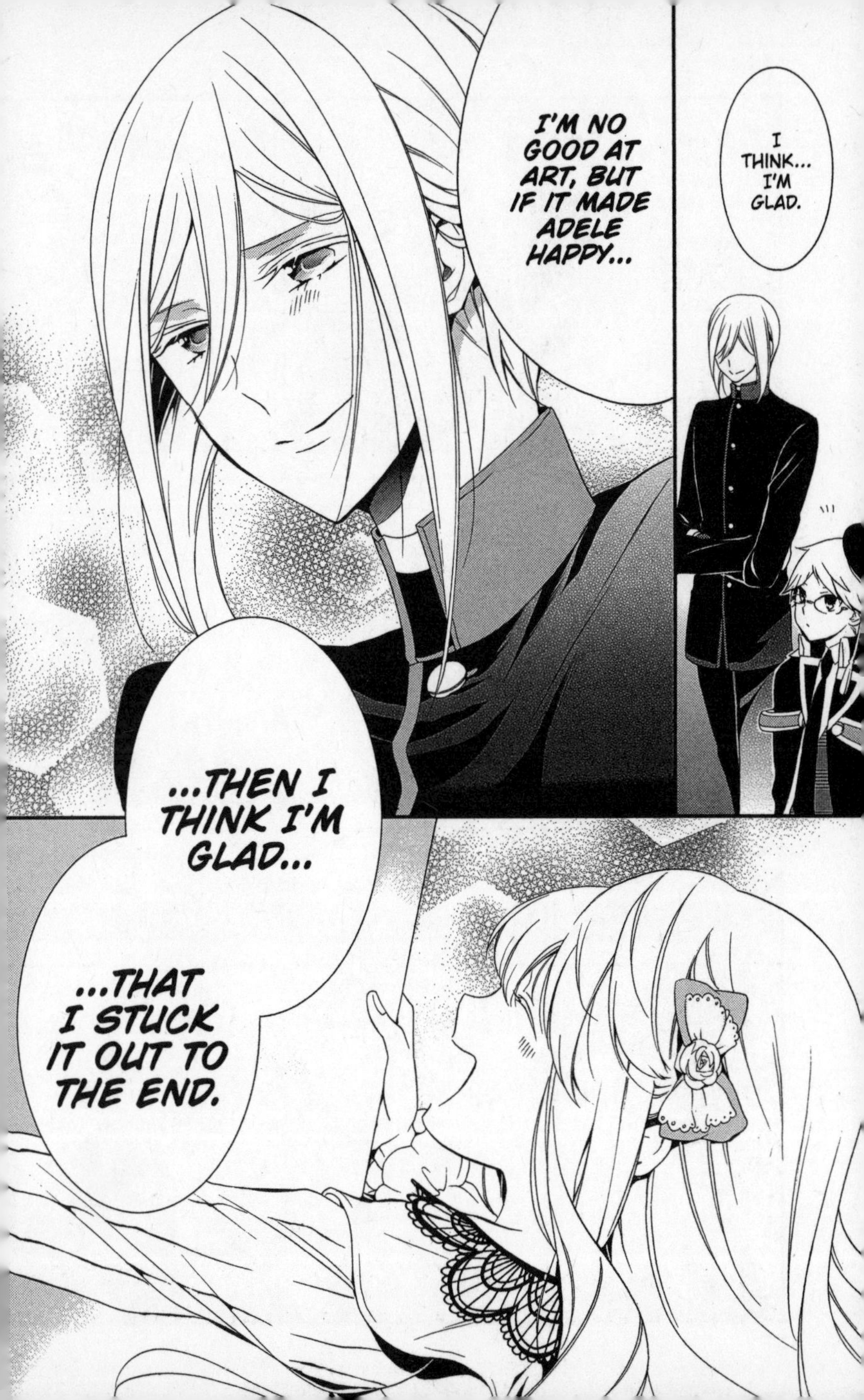
I THINK... I'M GLAD.
I'M NO GOOD AT ART, BUT IF IT MADE ADELE HAPPY...
...THEN I THINK I'M GLAD...
...THAT I STUCK IT OUT TO THE END.

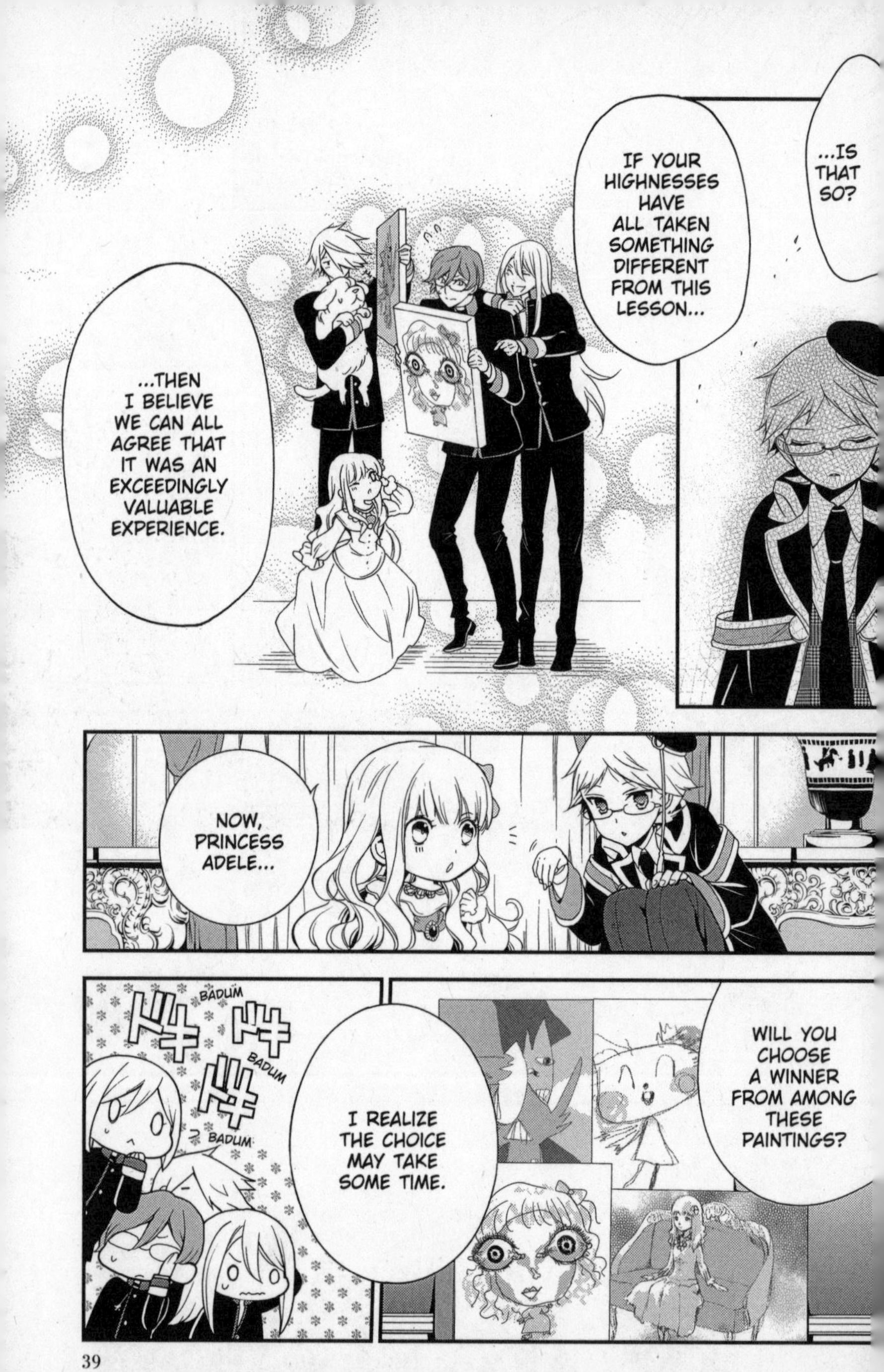
...IS THAT SO?
IF YOUR HIGHNESSES HAVE ALL TAKEN SOMETHING DIFFERENT FROM THIS LESSON...
...THEN I BELIEVE WE CAN ALL AGREE THAT IT WAS AN EXCEEDINGLY VALUABLE EXPERIENCE.
NOW, PRINCESS ADELE...
WILL YOU CHOOSE A WINNER FROM AMONG THESE PAINTINGS?
I REALIZE THE CHOICE MAY TAKE SOME TIME.
ドキ BADUM
ドキ BADUM
ドキ BADUM

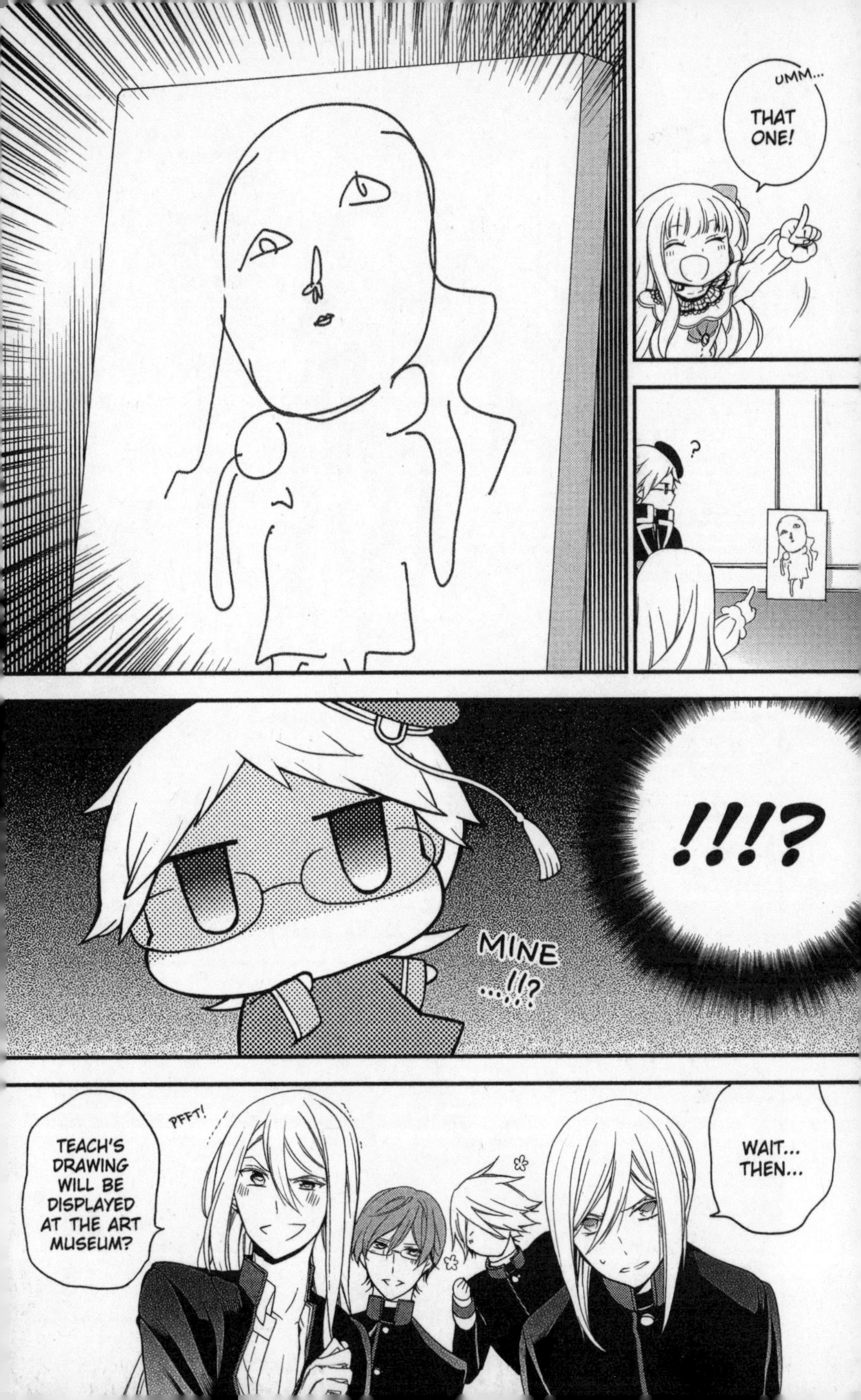
UMM...
THAT ONE!
?
!!!?
MINE ...!!?
WAIT... THEN...
PFFT!
TEACH'S DRAWING WILL BE DISPLAYED AT THE ART MUSEUM?

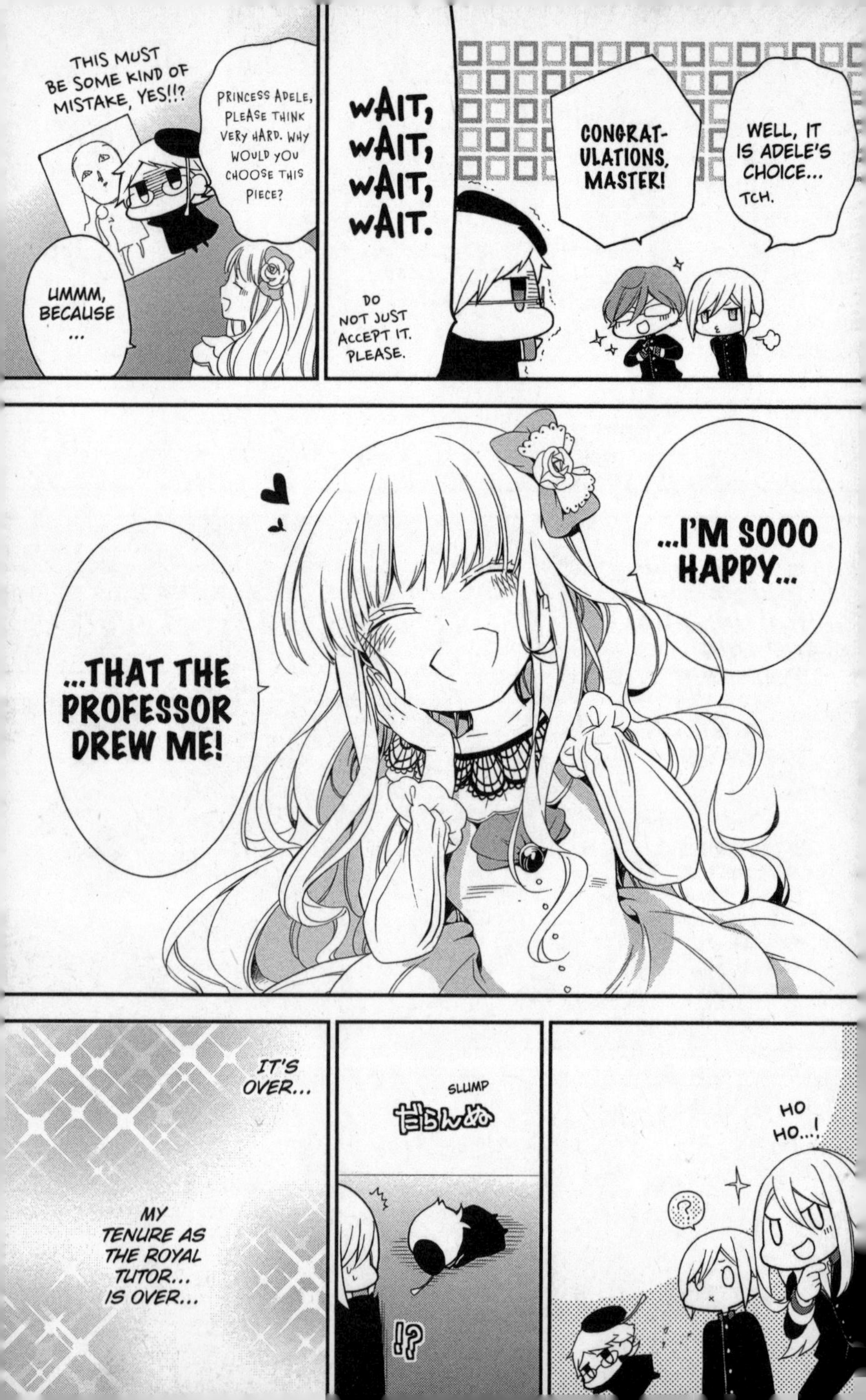
WELL, IT IS ADELE'S CHOICE...
TCH.
CONGRAT-ULATIONS, MASTER!
wAIT, wAIT, wAIT, wAIT.
DO NOT JUST ACCEPT IT. PLEASE.
THIS MUST BE SOME KIND OF MISTAKE, YES!!?
PRINCESS ADELE, PLEASE THINK VERY HARD. WHY WOULD YOU CHOOSE THIS PIECE?
UMMM, BECAUSE ...
...I'M SOOO HAPPY...
...THAT THE PROFESSOR DREW ME!
HO HO...!
?
SLUMP
だらんぬ
!?
IT'S OVER...
MY TENURE AS THE ROYAL TUTOR... IS OVER...

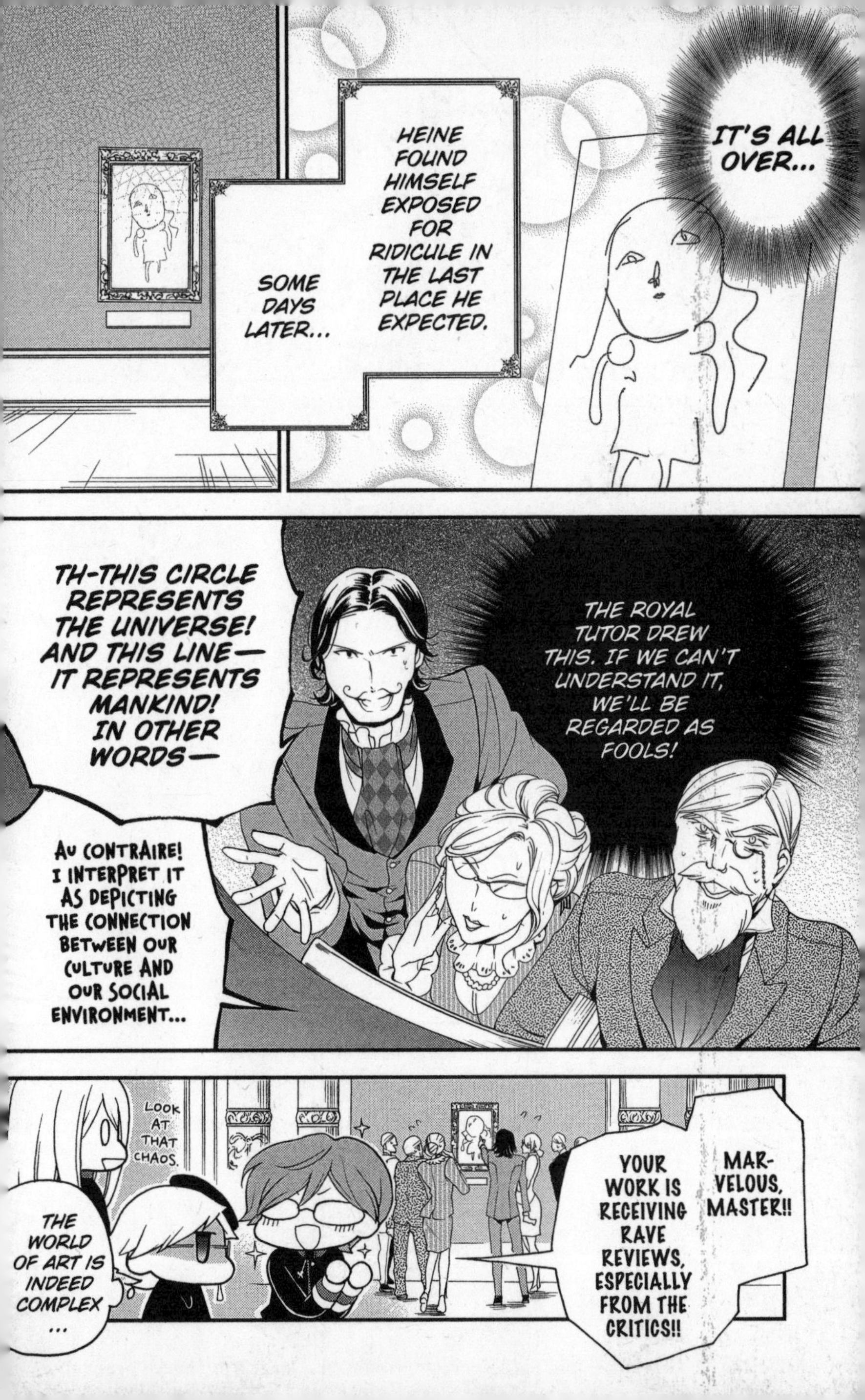
IT'S ALL OVER...
HEINE FOUND HIMSELF EXPOSED FOR RIDICULE IN THE LAST PLACE HE EXPECTED.
SOME DAYS LATER...
THE ROYAL TUTOR DREW THIS. IF WE CAN'T UNDERSTAND IT, WE'LL BE REGARDED AS FOOLS!
TH-THIS CIRCLE REPRESENTS THE UNIVERSE! AND THIS LINE—IT REPRESENTS MANKIND! IN OTHER WORDS—
AU CONTRAIRE! I INTERPRET IT AS DEPICTING THE CONNECTION BETWEEN OUR CULTURE AND OUR SOCIAL ENVIRONMENT...
MARVELOUS, MASTER!!
YOUR WORK IS RECEIVING RAVE REVIEWS, ESPECIALLY FROM THE CRITICS!!
LOOK AT THAT CHAOS.
THE WORLD OF ART IS INDEED COMPLEX...

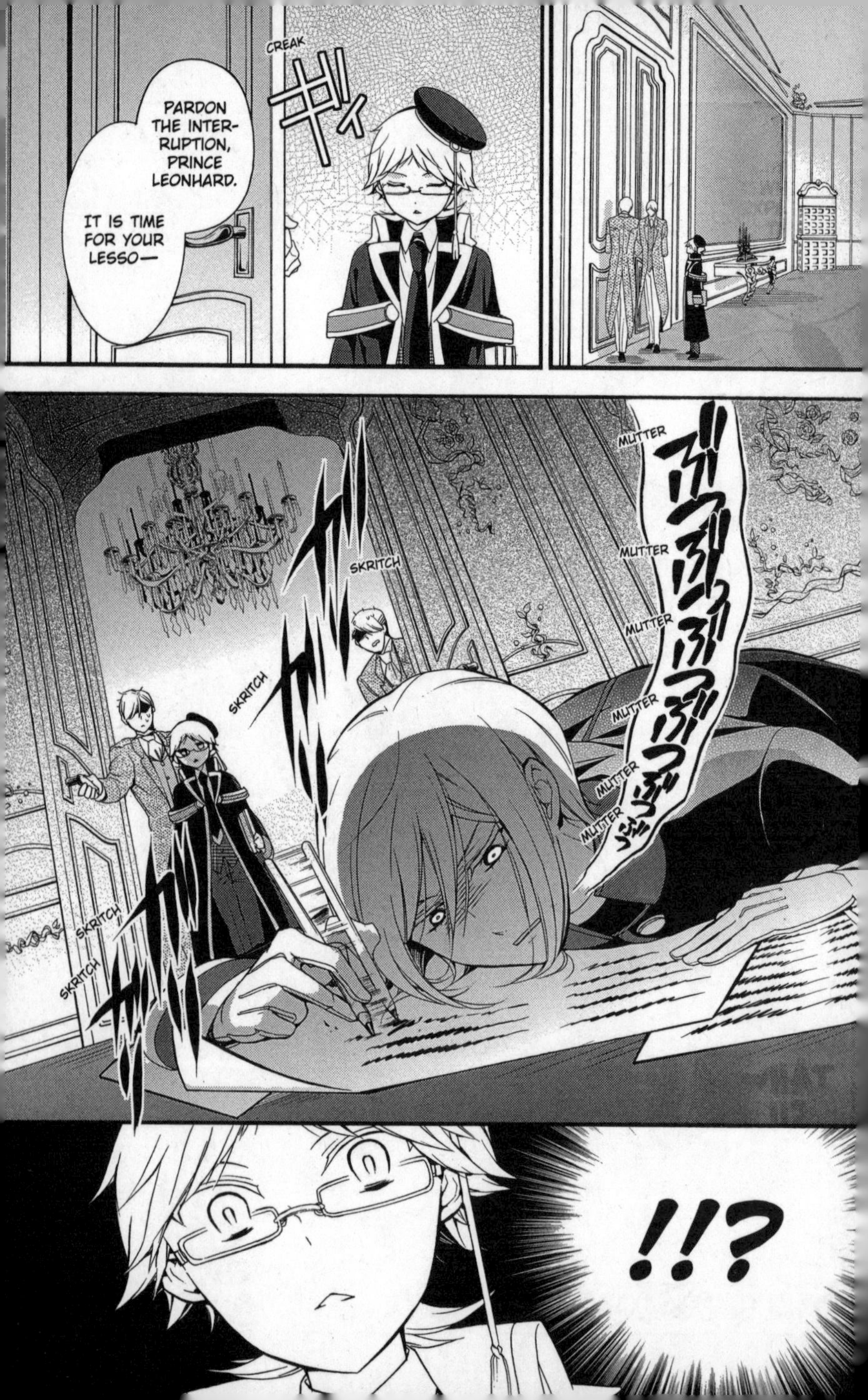
CREAK
PARDON THE INTER-RUPTION, PRINCE LEONHARD.
IT IS TIME FOR YOUR LESSO—
MUTTER
MUTTER
MUTTER
MUTTER
MUTTER
MUTTER
SKRITCH
SKRITCH
SKRITCH
SKRITCH
!!?

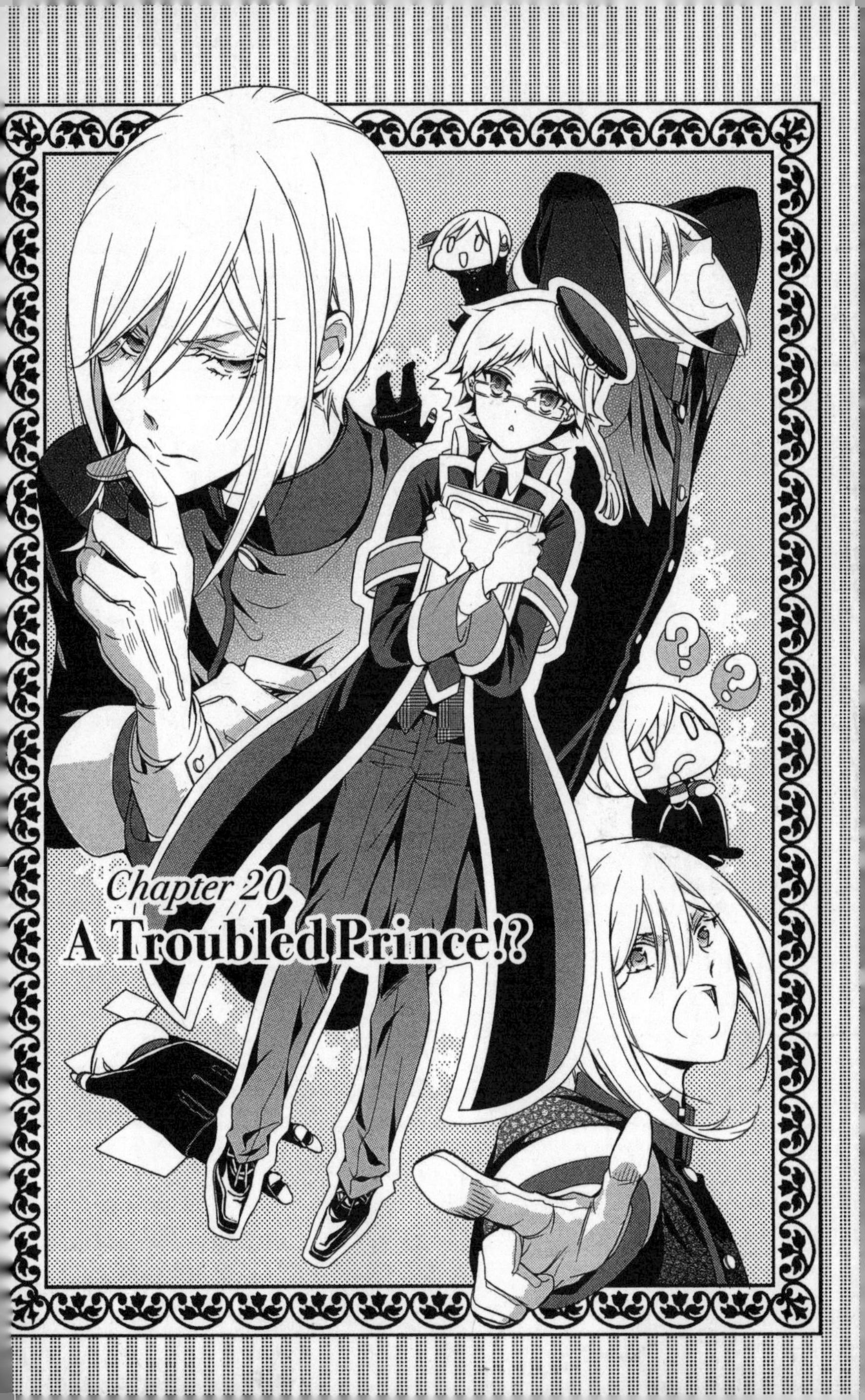
Chapter 20
A Troubled Prince!?

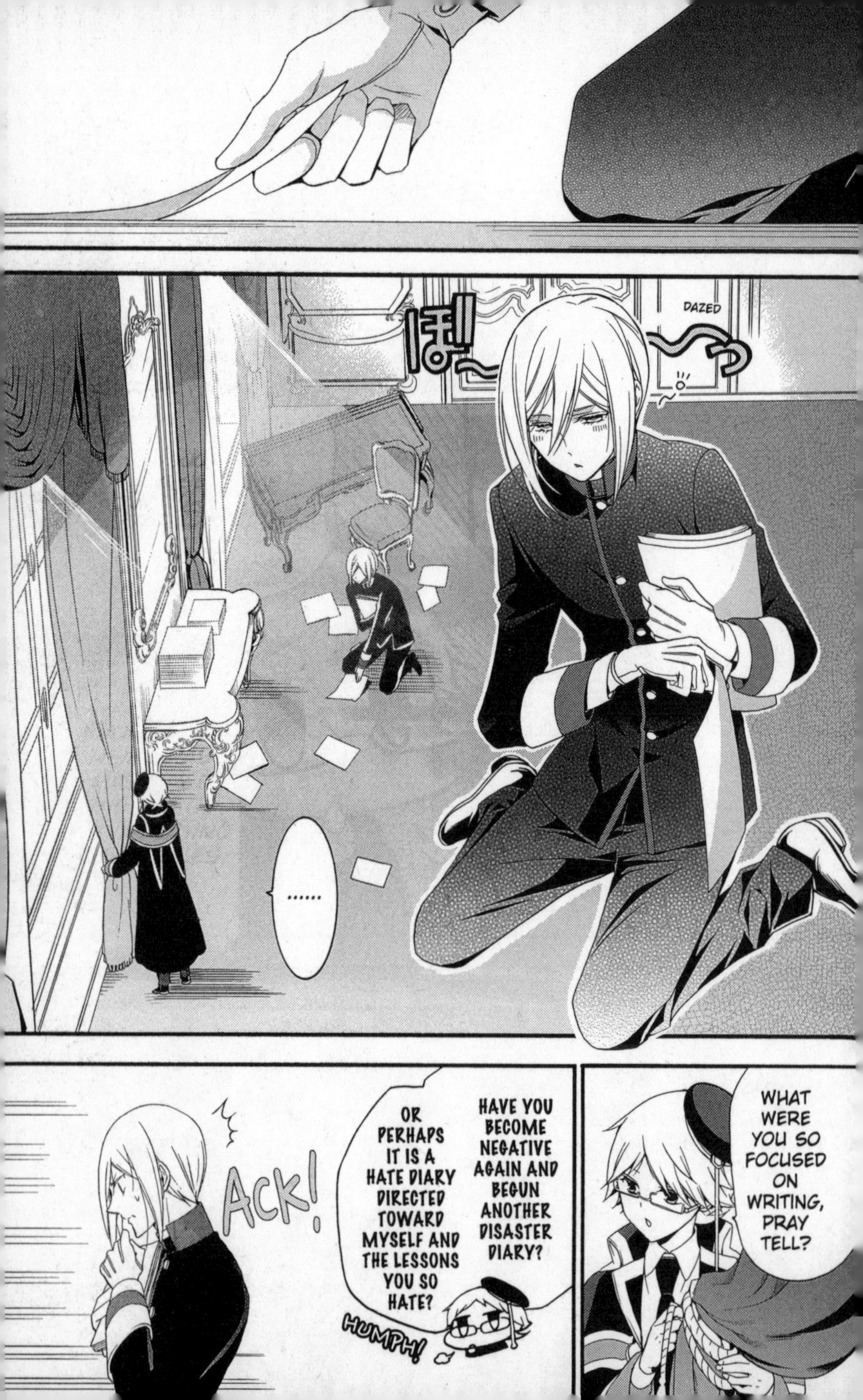
ぼ~~っ
DAZED
......
WHAT WERE YOU SO FOCUSED ON WRITING, PRAY TELL?
HAVE YOU BECOME NEGATIVE AGAIN AND BEGUN ANOTHER DISASTER DIARY?
OR PERHAPS IT IS A HATE DIARY DIRECTED TOWARD MYSELF AND THE LESSONS YOU SO HATE?
HUMPH!
ACK!

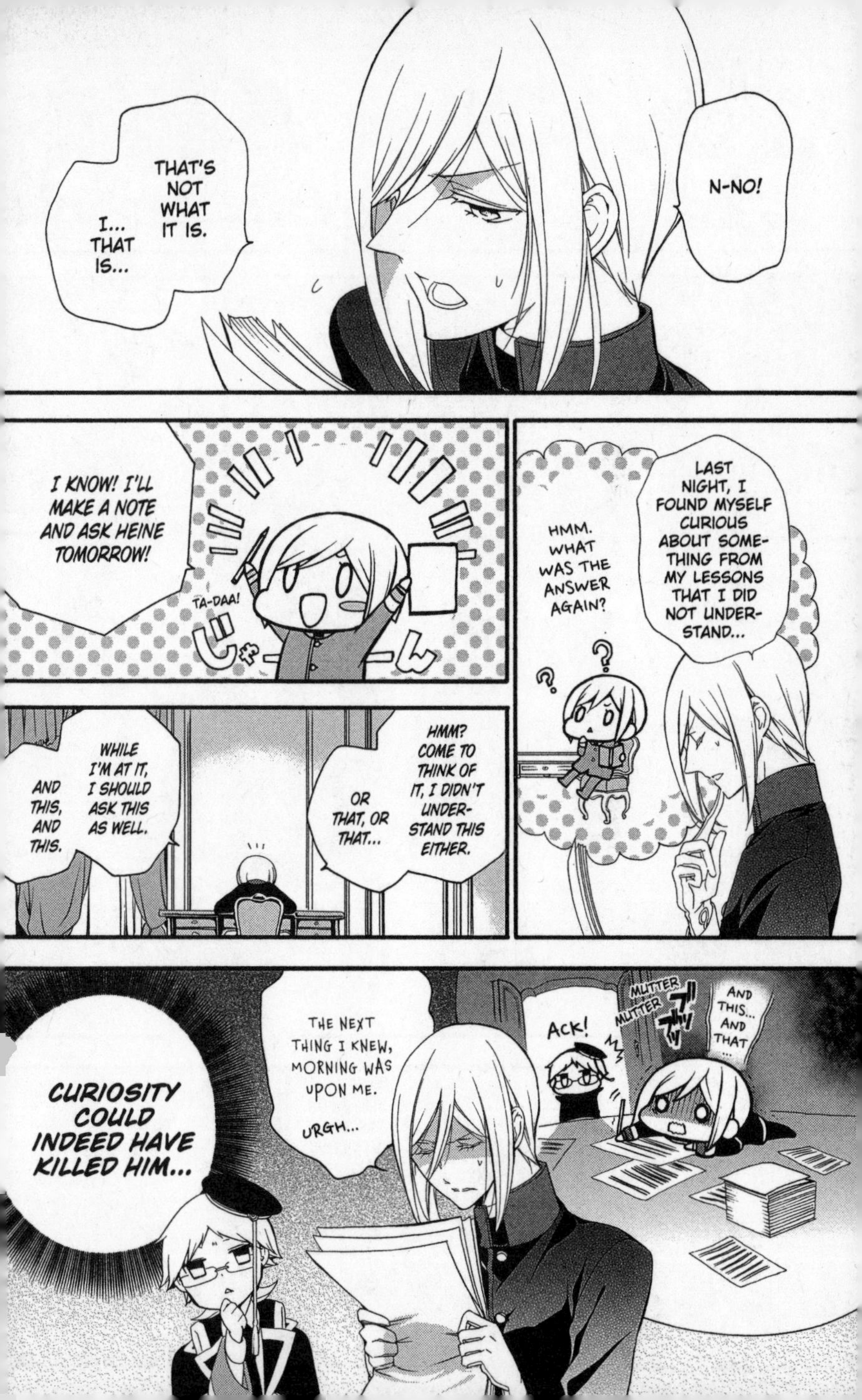

N-NO!
I... THAT IS... THAT'S NOT WHAT IT IS.
LAST NIGHT, I FOUND MYSELF CURIOUS ABOUT SOMETHING FROM MY LESSONS THAT I DID NOT UNDERSTAND...
HMM. WHAT WAS THE ANSWER AGAIN?
I KNOW! I'LL MAKE A NOTE AND ASK HEINE TOMORROW!
TA-DAA!
HMM? COME TO THINK OF IT, I DIDN'T UNDERSTAND THIS EITHER.
OR THAT, OR THAT...
WHILE I'M AT IT, I SHOULD ASK THIS AS WELL.
AND THIS, AND THIS.
AND THIS... AND THAT...
MUTTER MUTTER
ACK!
THE NEXT THING I KNEW, MORNING WAS UPON ME.
URGH...
CURIOSITY COULD INDEED HAVE KILLED HIM...

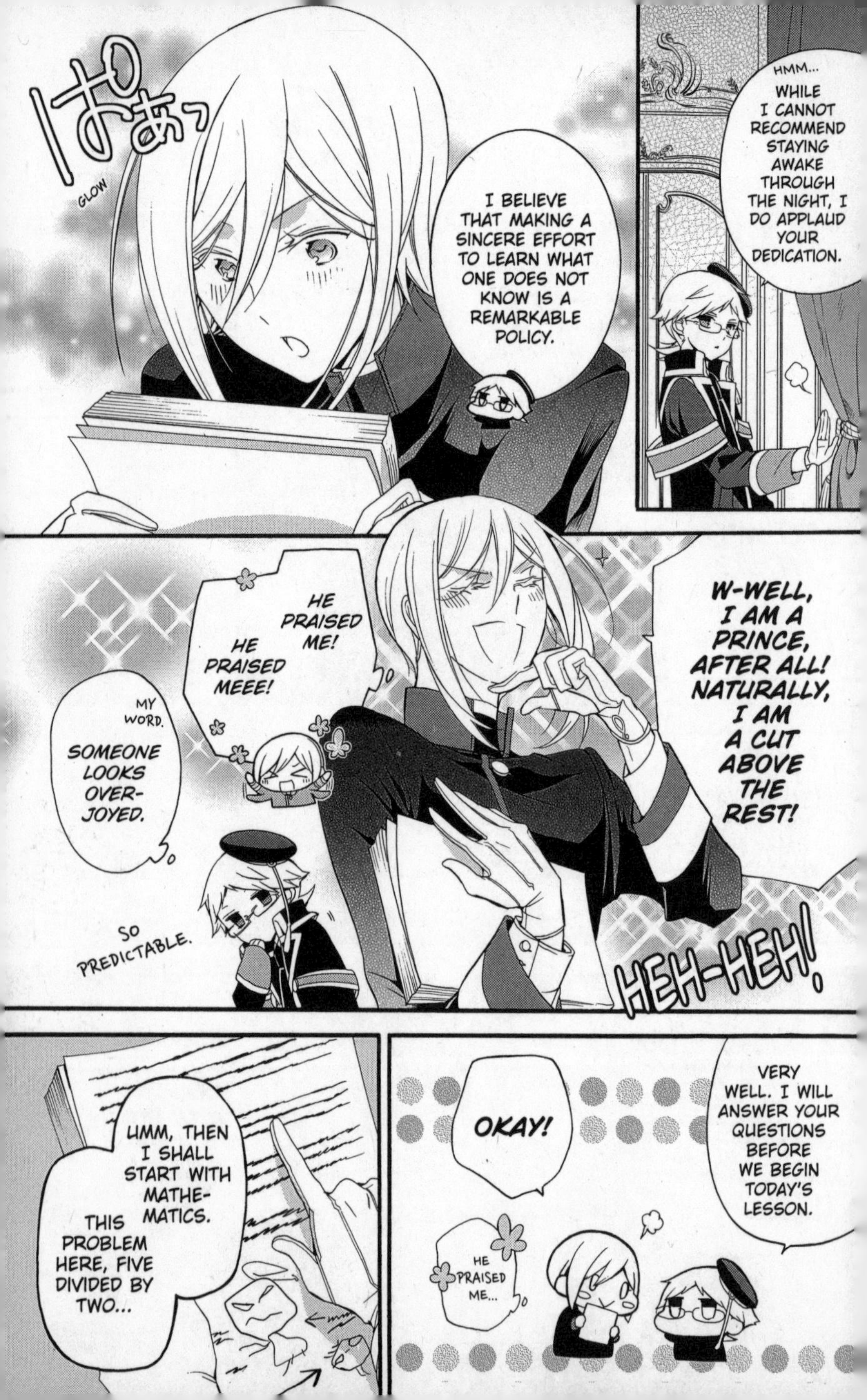
HMM... WHILE I CANNOT RECOMMEND STAYING AWAKE THROUGH THE NIGHT, I DO APPLAUD YOUR DEDICATION.
ぱあっ
GLOW
I BELIEVE THAT MAKING A SINCERE EFFORT TO LEARN WHAT ONE DOES NOT KNOW IS A REMARKABLE POLICY.
W-WELL, I AM A PRINCE, AFTER ALL! NATURALLY, I AM A CUT ABOVE THE REST!
HE PRAISED ME!
HE PRAISED MEEE!
MY WORD.
SOMEONE LOOKS OVER-JOYED.
HEH-HEH!
SO PREDICTABLE.
VERY WELL. I WILL ANSWER YOUR QUESTIONS BEFORE WE BEGIN TODAY'S LESSON.
OKAY!
HE PRAISED ME...
UMM, THEN I SHALL START WITH MATHE-MATICS.
THIS PROBLEM HERE, FIVE DIVIDED BY TWO...

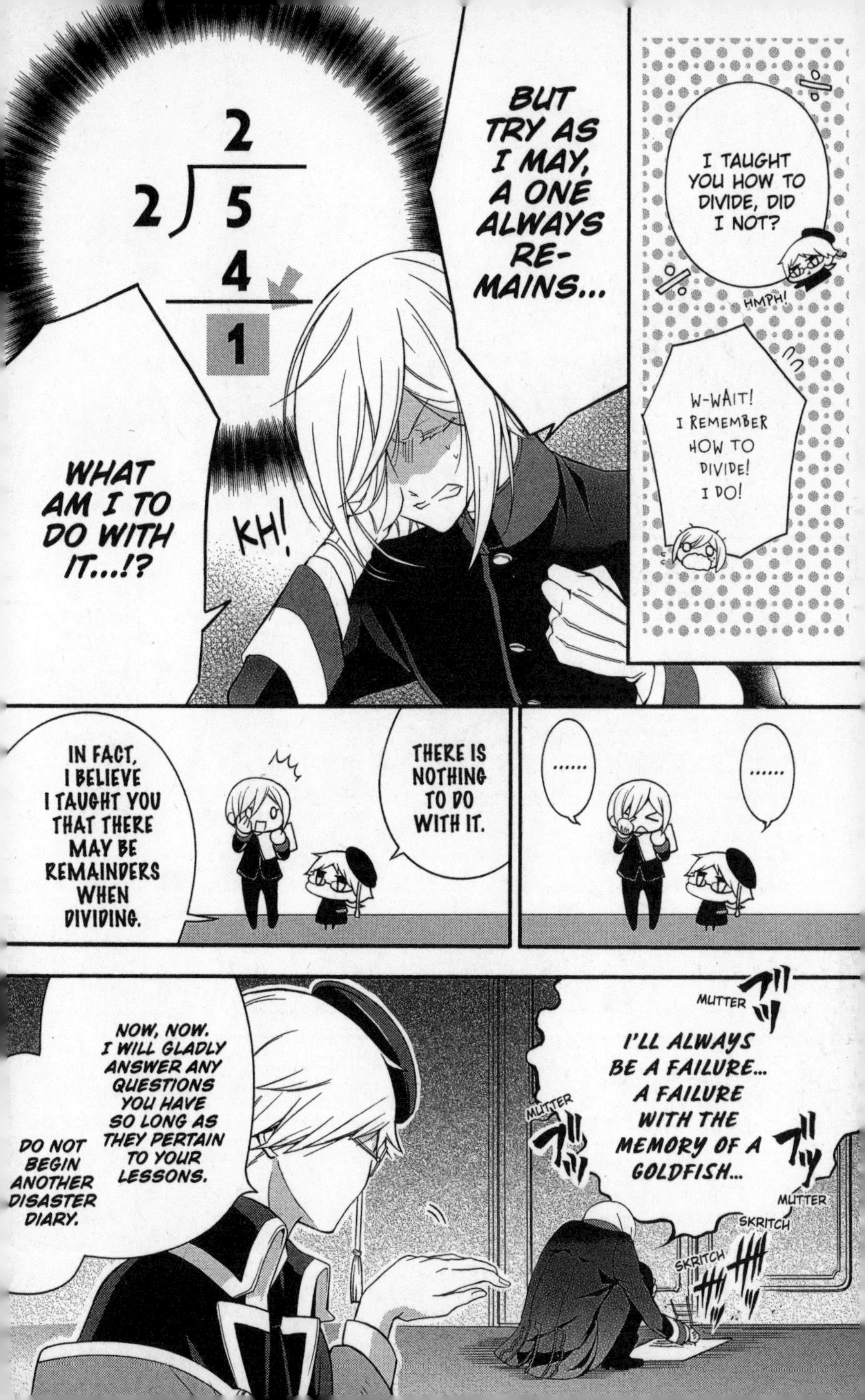
I TAUGHT YOU HOW TO DIVIDE, DID I NOT?
HMPH!
W-WAIT! I REMEMBER HOW TO DIVIDE! I DO!
BUT TRY AS I MAY, A ONE ALWAYS RE-MAINS...
2
2) 5
4
1
KH!
WHAT AM I TO DO WITH IT...!?
......
......
THERE IS NOTHING TO DO WITH IT.
IN FACT, I BELIEVE I TAUGHT YOU THAT THERE MAY BE REMAINDERS WHEN DIVIDING.
MUTTER
I'LL ALWAYS BE A FAILURE... A FAILURE WITH THE MEMORY OF A GOLDFISH...
MUTTER
MUTTER
SKRITCH
SKRITCH
NOW, NOW. I WILL GLADLY ANSWER ANY QUESTIONS YOU HAVE SO LONG AS THEY PERTAIN TO YOUR LESSONS.
DO NOT BEGIN ANOTHER DISASTER DIARY.

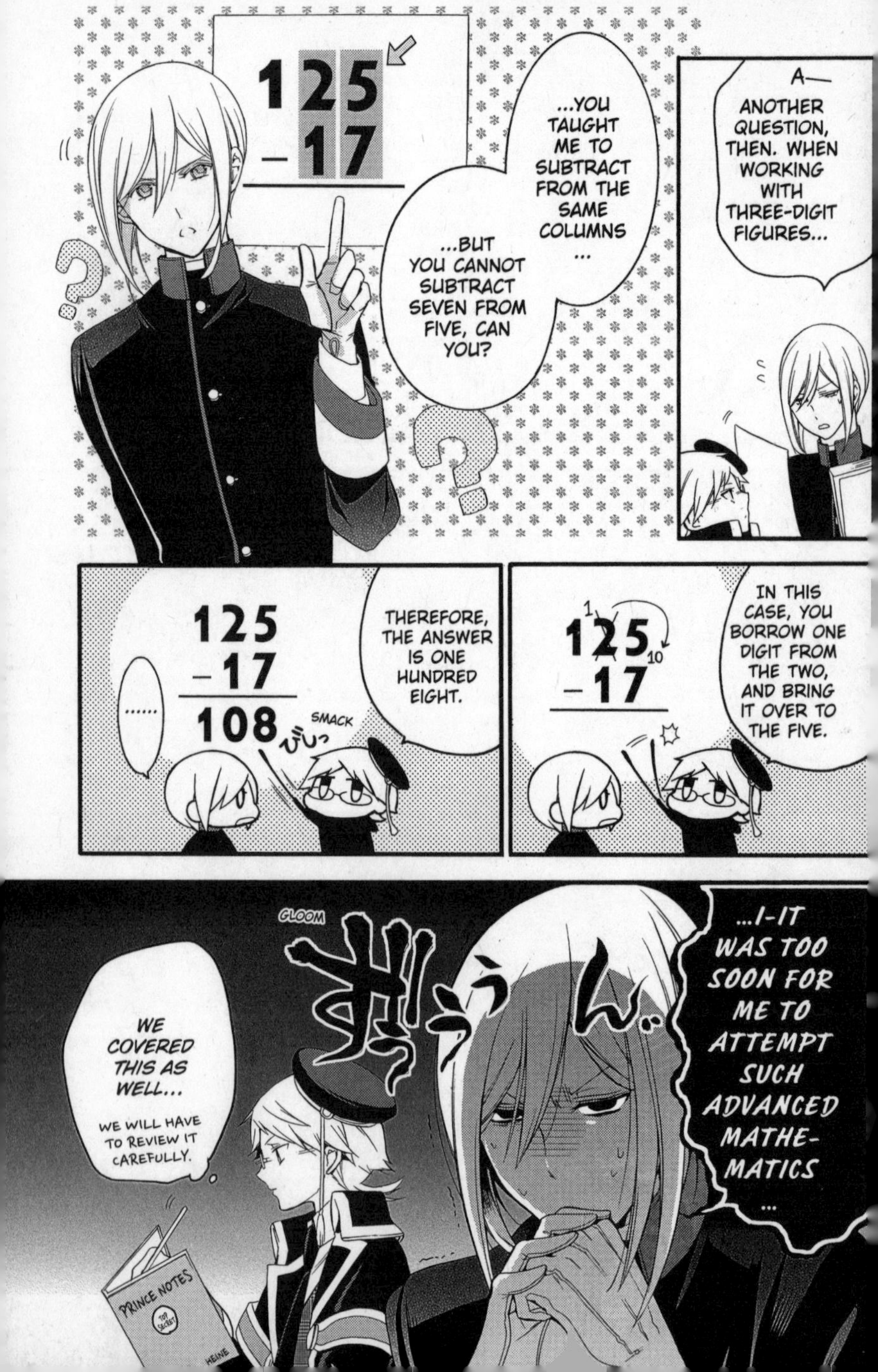
A— ANOTHER QUESTION, THEN. WHEN WORKING WITH THREE-DIGIT FIGURES...
125
− 17
...YOU TAUGHT ME TO SUBTRACT FROM THE SAME COLUMNS ...
...BUT YOU CANNOT SUBTRACT SEVEN FROM FIVE, CAN YOU?
IN THIS CASE, YOU BORROW ONE DIGIT FROM THE TWO, AND BRING IT OVER TO THE FIVE.
1
125
10
− 17
THEREFORE, THE ANSWER IS ONE HUNDRED EIGHT.
125
− 17
108
SMACK
......
...I-IT WAS TOO SOON FOR ME TO ATTEMPT SUCH ADVANCED MATHE-MATICS ...
GLOOM
WE COVERED THIS AS WELL...
WE WILL HAVE TO REVIEW IT CAREFULLY.
PRINCE NOTES
TOP SECRET
HEINE

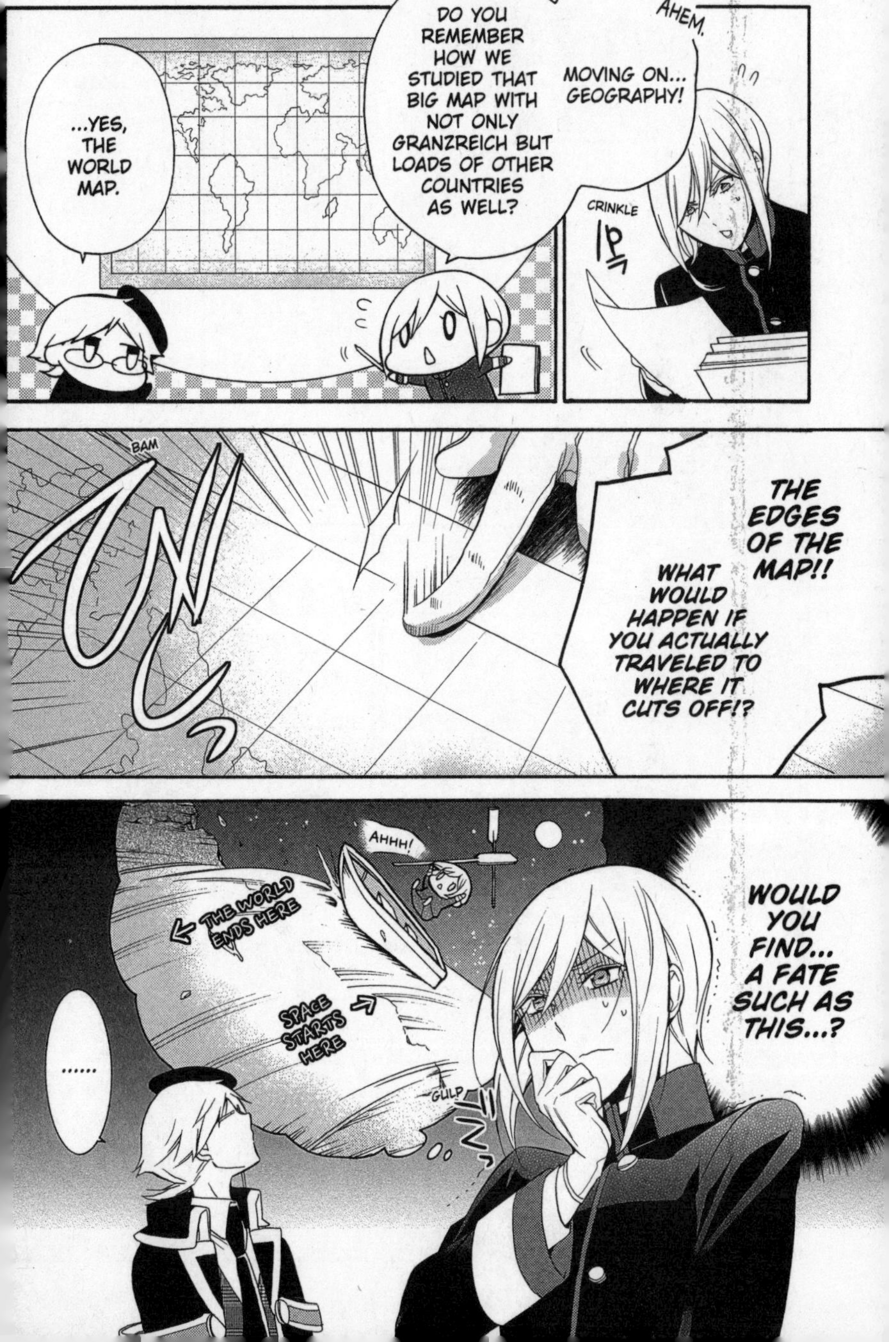
AHEM.
MOVING ON... GEOGRAPHY!
CRINKLE
DO YOU REMEMBER HOW WE STUDIED THAT BIG MAP WITH NOT ONLY GRANZREICH BUT LOADS OF OTHER COUNTRIES AS WELL?
...YES, THE WORLD MAP.
THE EDGES OF THE MAP!!
WHAT WOULD HAPPEN IF YOU ACTUALLY TRAVELED TO WHERE IT CUTS OFF!?
BAM
WOULD YOU FIND... A FATE SUCH AS THIS...?
AHHH!
THE WORLD ENDS HERE
SPACE STARTS HERE
GULP
......

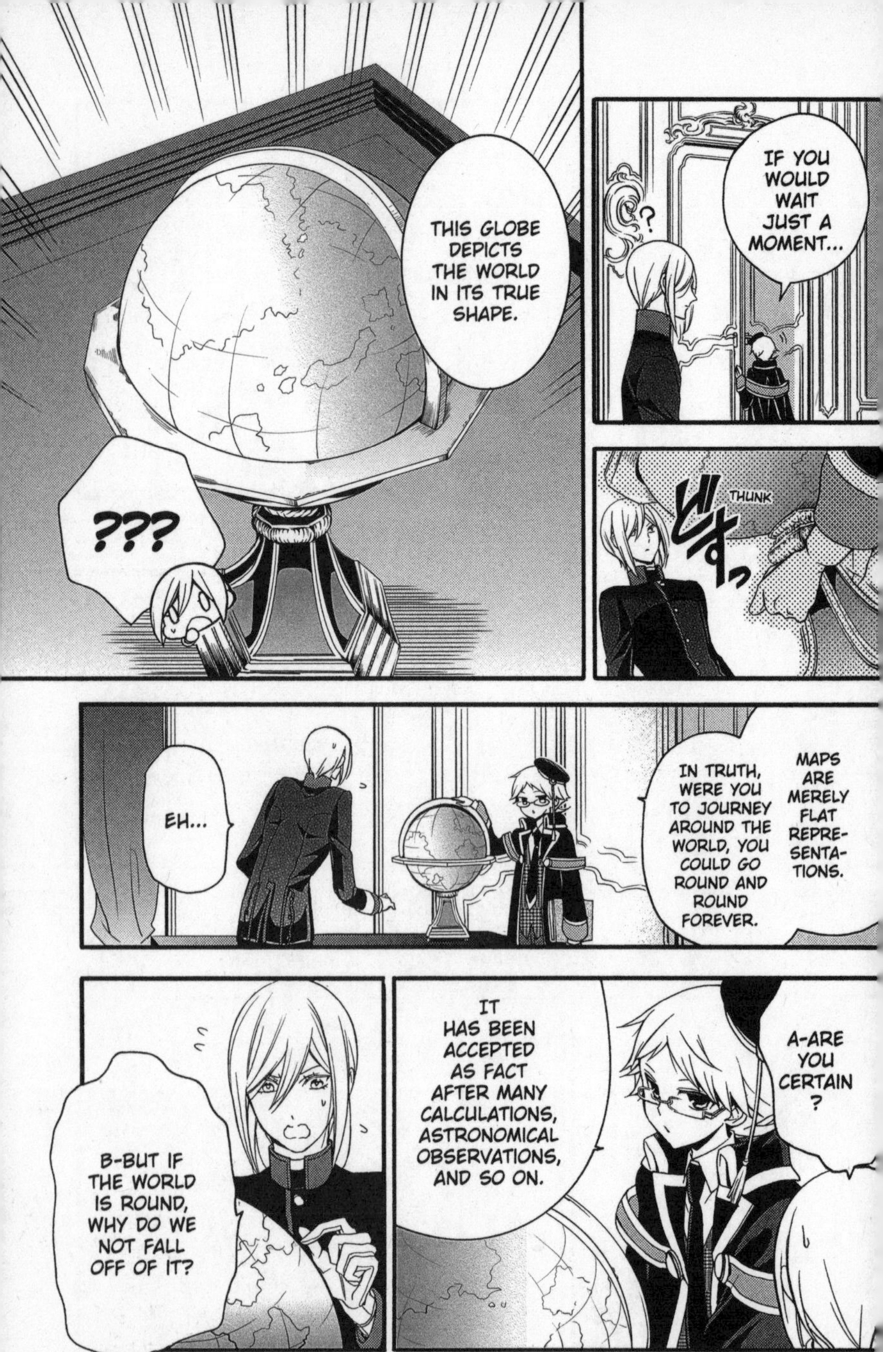
IF YOU WOULD WAIT JUST A MOMENT...
?
THUNK
どすっ
THIS GLOBE DEPICTS THE WORLD IN ITS TRUE SHAPE.
???
MAPS ARE MERELY FLAT REPRE-SENTA-TIONS.
IN TRUTH, WERE YOU TO JOURNEY AROUND THE WORLD, YOU COULD GO ROUND AND ROUND FOREVER.
EH...
A-ARE YOU CERTAIN?
IT HAS BEEN ACCEPTED AS FACT AFTER MANY CALCULATIONS, ASTRONOMICAL OBSERVATIONS, AND SO ON.
B-BUT IF THE WORLD IS ROUND, WHY DO WE NOT FALL OFF OF IT?

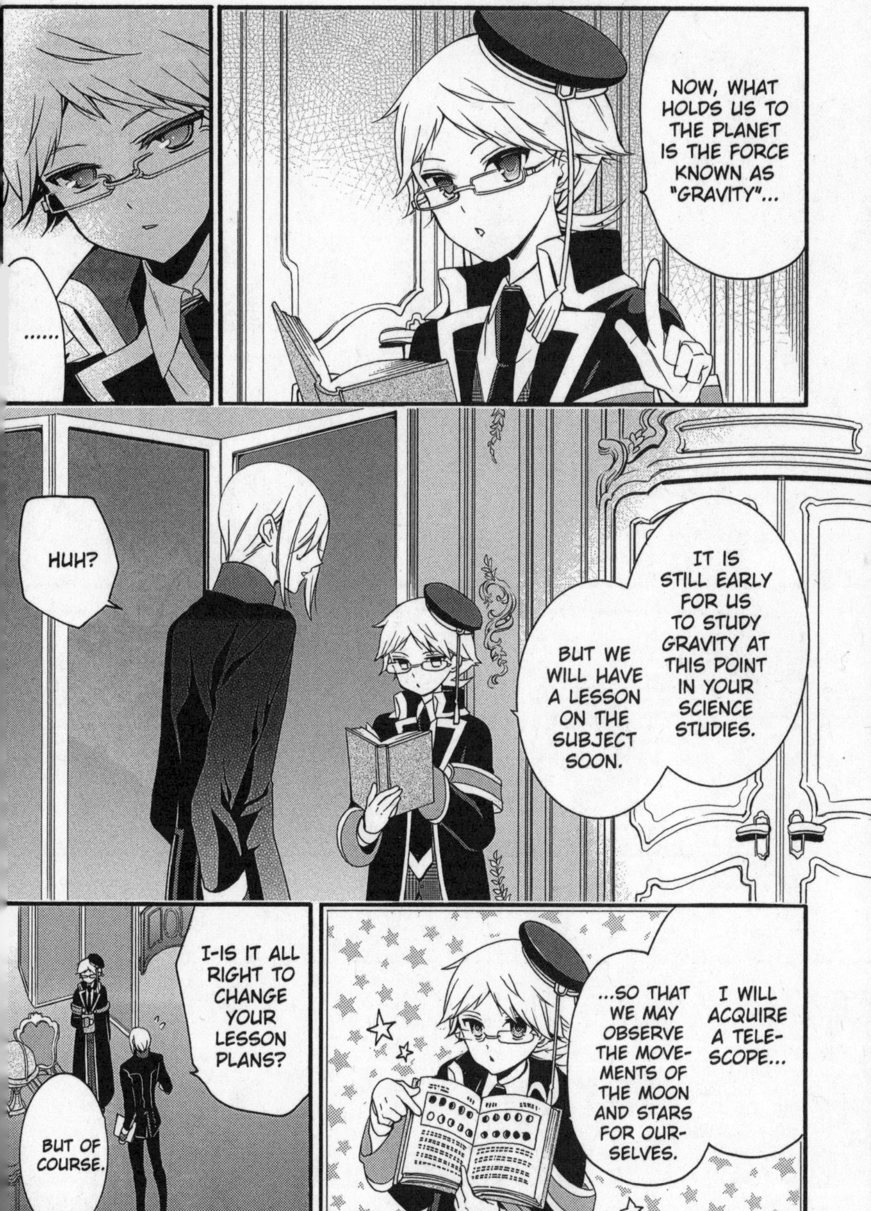
NOW, WHAT HOLDS US TO THE PLANET IS THE FORCE KNOWN AS "GRAVITY"...
......
IT IS STILL EARLY FOR US TO STUDY GRAVITY AT THIS POINT IN YOUR SCIENCE STUDIES.
BUT WE WILL HAVE A LESSON ON THE SUBJECT SOON.
HUH?
I WILL ACQUIRE A TELE-SCOPE...
...SO THAT WE MAY OBSERVE THE MOVE-MENTS OF THE MOON AND STARS FOR OUR-SELVES.
I-IS IT ALL RIGHT TO CHANGE YOUR LESSON PLANS?
BUT OF COURSE.

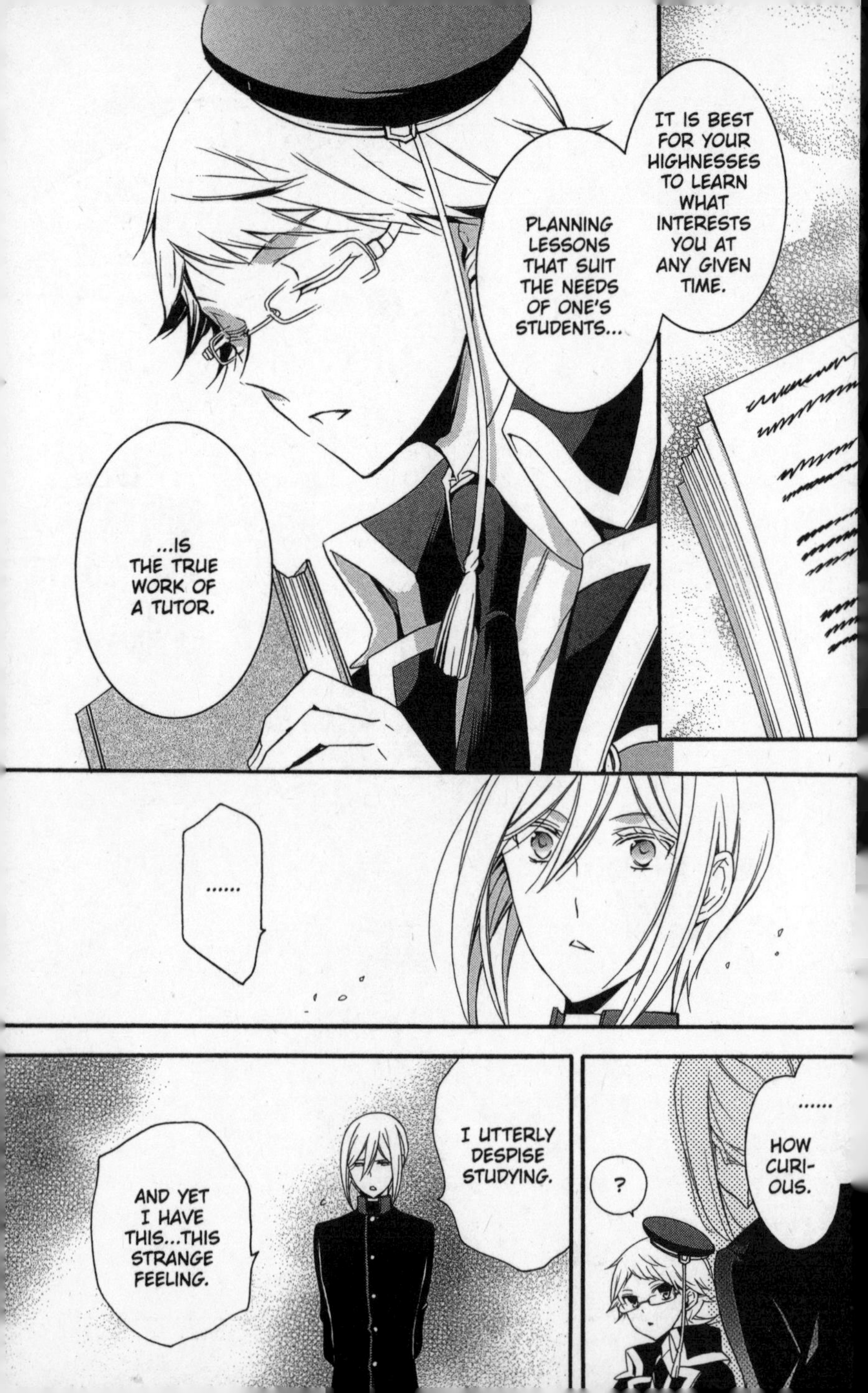
IT IS BEST FOR YOUR HIGHNESSES TO LEARN WHAT INTERESTS YOU AT ANY GIVEN TIME.
PLANNING LESSONS THAT SUIT THE NEEDS OF ONE'S STUDENTS...
...IS THE TRUE WORK OF A TUTOR.
......
...... HOW CURI- OUS.
?
I UTTERLY DESPISE STUDYING.
AND YET I HAVE THIS...THIS STRANGE FEELING.

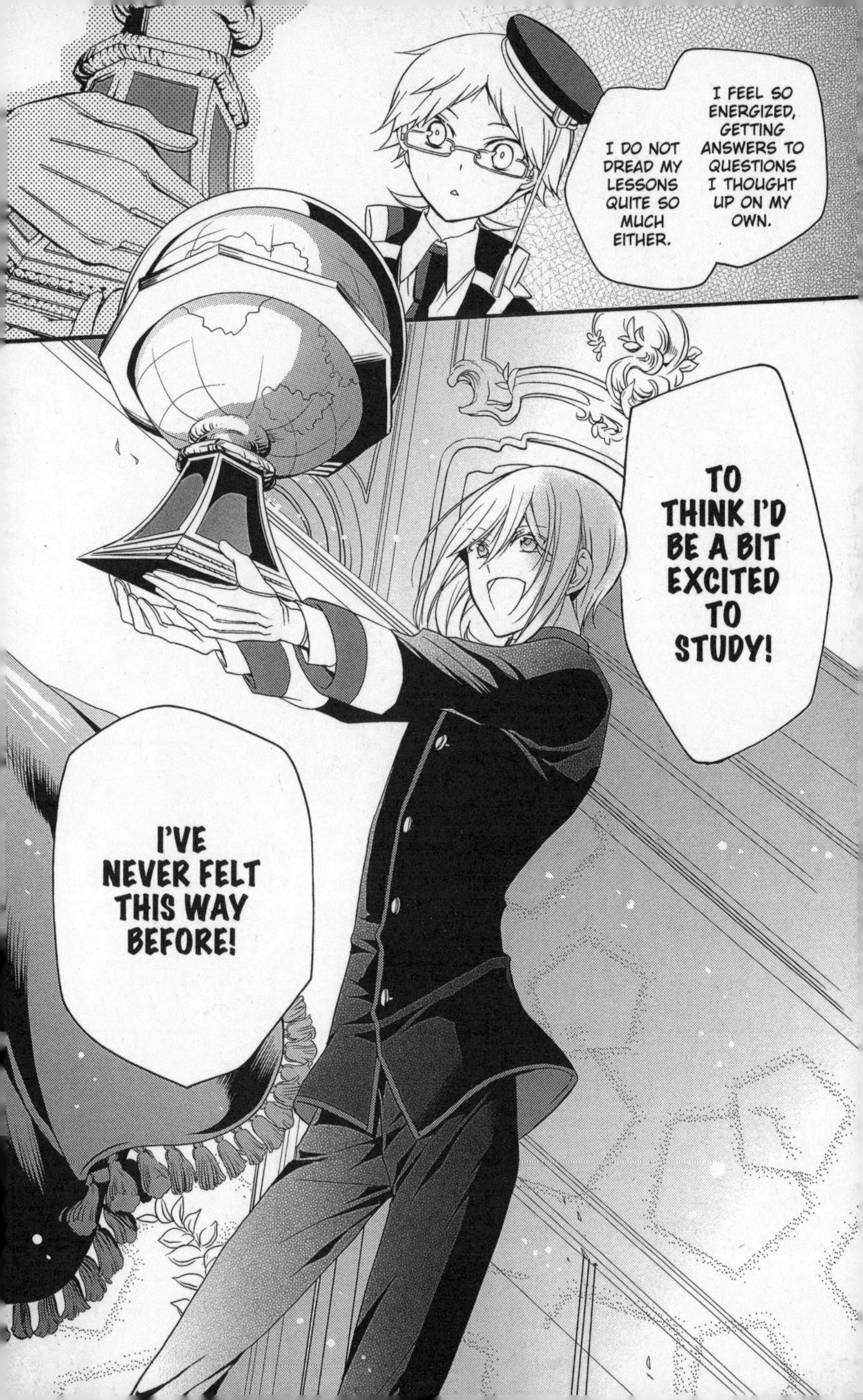
I FEEL SO ENERGIZED, GETTING ANSWERS TO QUESTIONS I THOUGHT UP ON MY OWN.
I DO NOT DREAD MY LESSONS QUITE SO MUCH EITHER.
TO THINK I'D BE A BIT EXCITED TO STUDY!
I'VE NEVER FELT THIS WAY BEFORE!

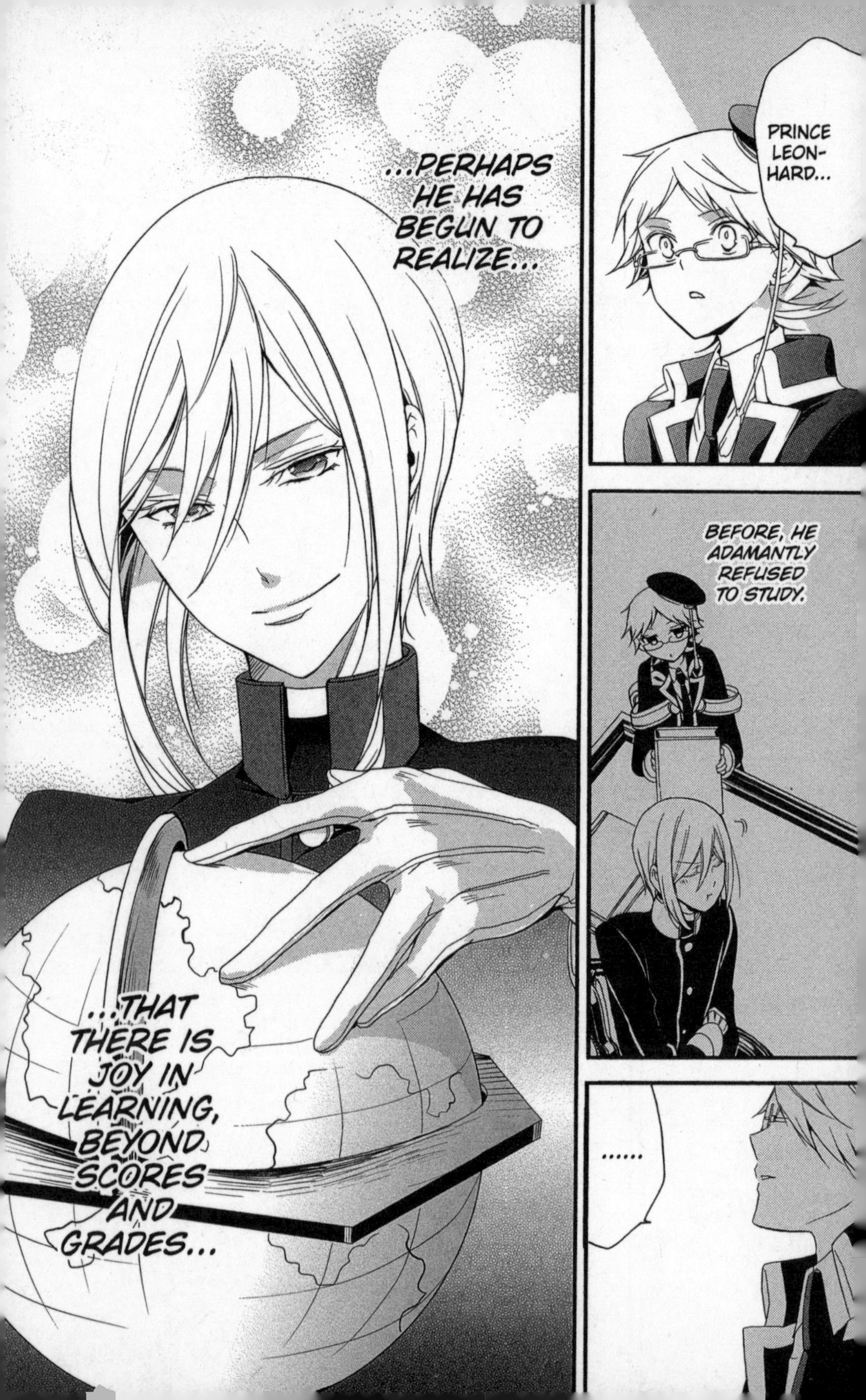
PRINCE LEON-HARD...
BEFORE, HE ADAMANTLY REFUSED TO STUDY.
......
...PERHAPS HE HAS BEGUN TO REALIZE...
...THAT THERE IS JOY IN LEARNING, BEYOND SCORES AND GRADES...

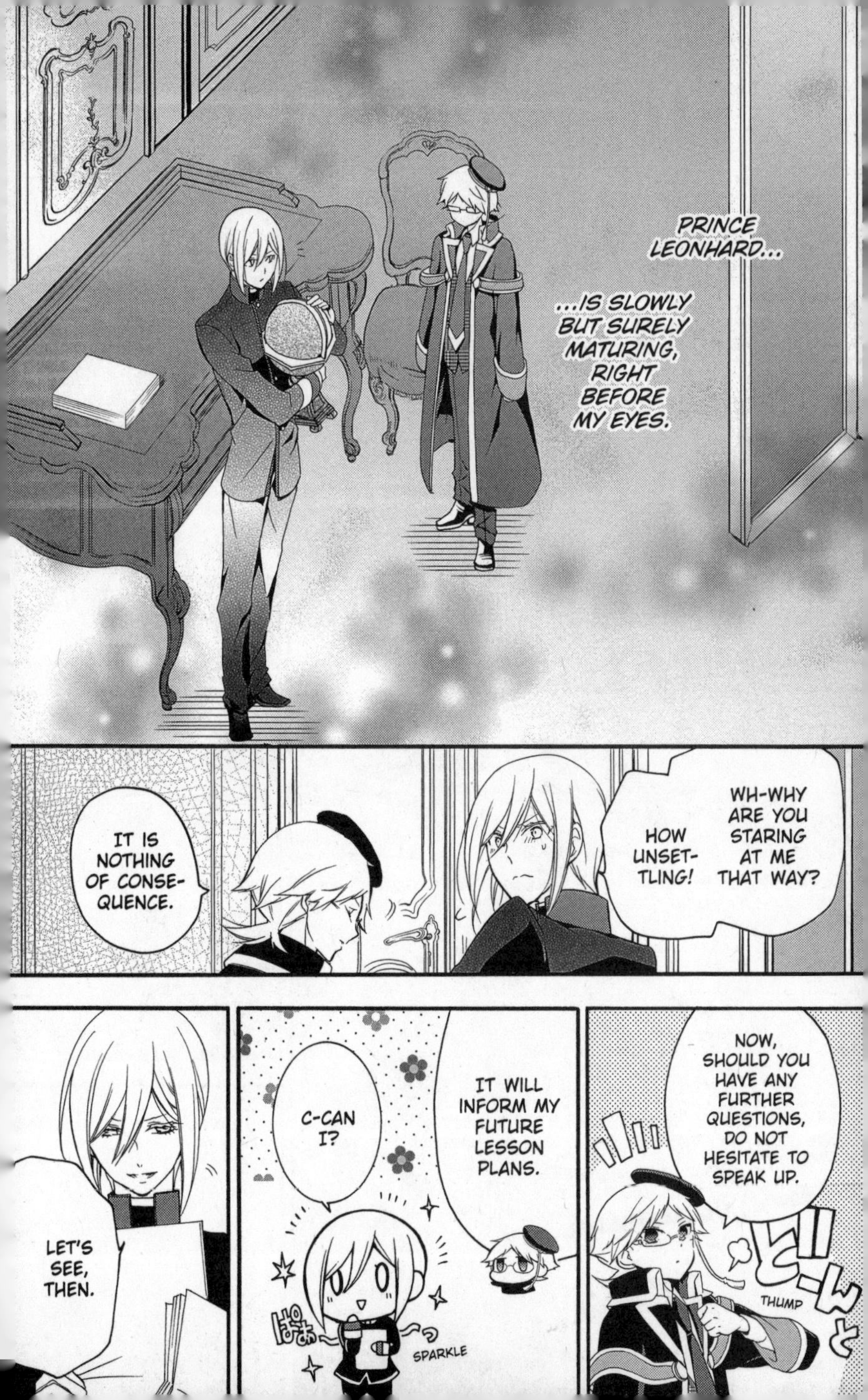
PRINCE LEONHARD...
...IS SLOWLY BUT SURELY MATURING, RIGHT BEFORE MY EYES.
WH-WHY ARE YOU STARING AT ME THAT WAY?
HOW UNSET-TLING!
IT IS NOTHING OF CONSE-QUENCE.
NOW, SHOULD YOU HAVE ANY FURTHER QUESTIONS, DO NOT HESITATE TO SPEAK UP.
THUMP
IT WILL INFORM MY FUTURE LESSON PLANS.
C-CAN I?
SPARKLE
LET'S SEE, THEN.

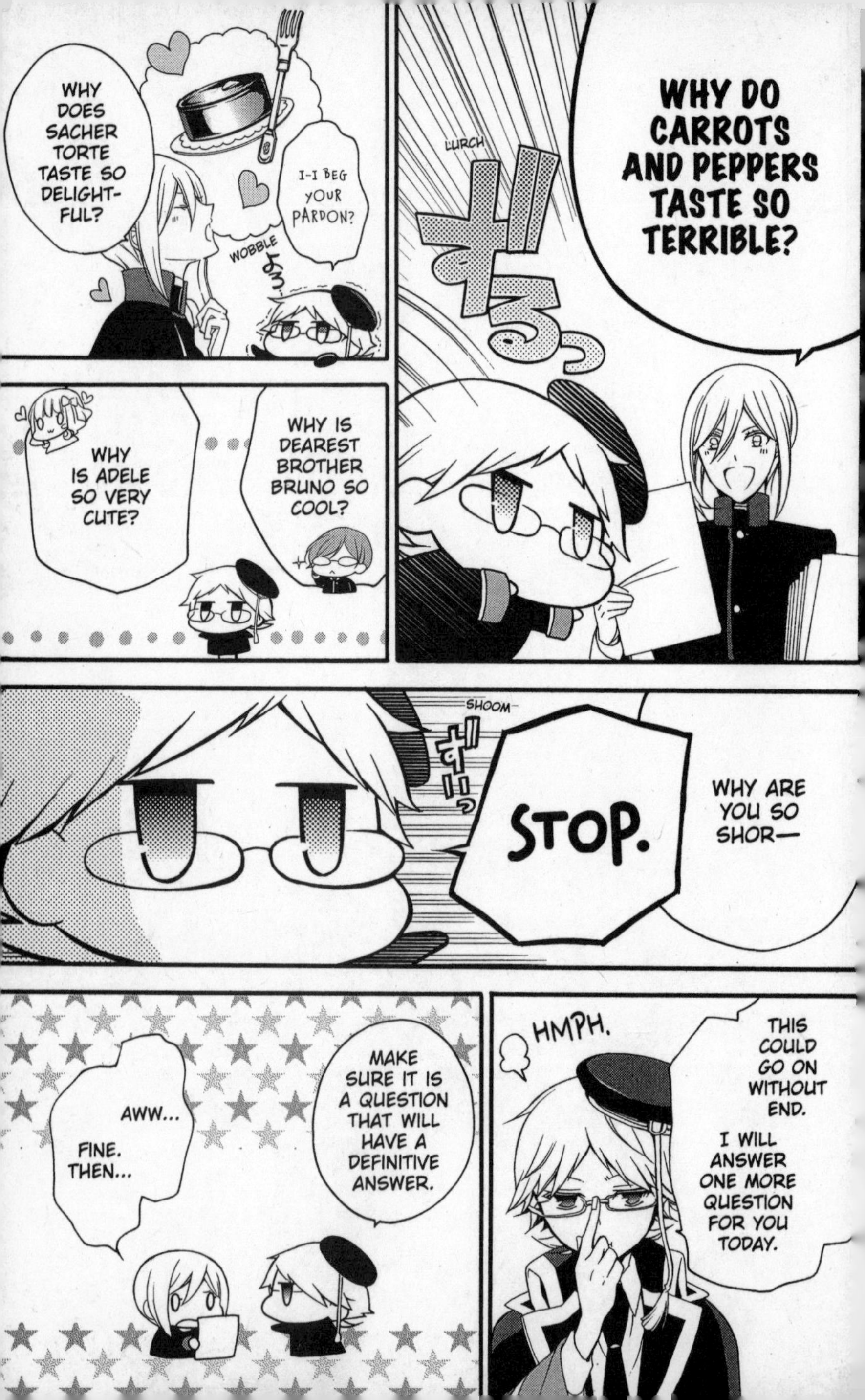
WHY DO CARROTS AND PEPPERS TASTE SO TERRIBLE?
LURCH
WHY DOES SACHER TORTE TASTE SO DELIGHTFUL?
I-I BEG YOUR PARDON?
WOBBLE
WHY IS DEAREST BROTHER BRUNO SO COOL?
WHY IS ADELE SO VERY CUTE?
WHY ARE YOU SO SHOR—
SHOOM
STOP.
HMPH.
THIS COULD GO ON WITHOUT END.
I WILL ANSWER ONE MORE QUESTION FOR YOU TODAY.
MAKE SURE IT IS A QUESTION THAT WILL HAVE A DEFINITIVE ANSWER.
AWW...
FINE. THEN...

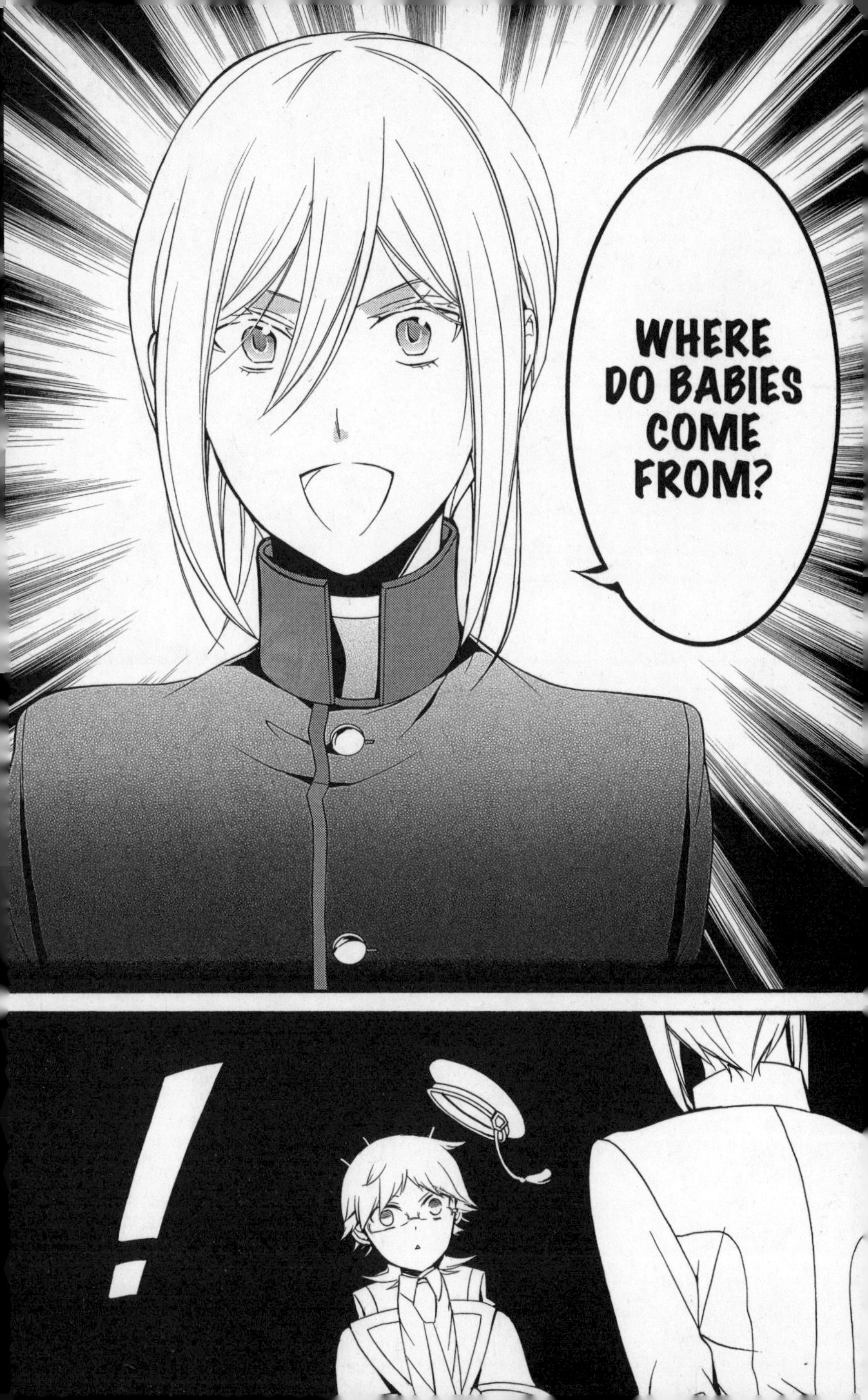
WHERE DO BABIES COME FROM?
!

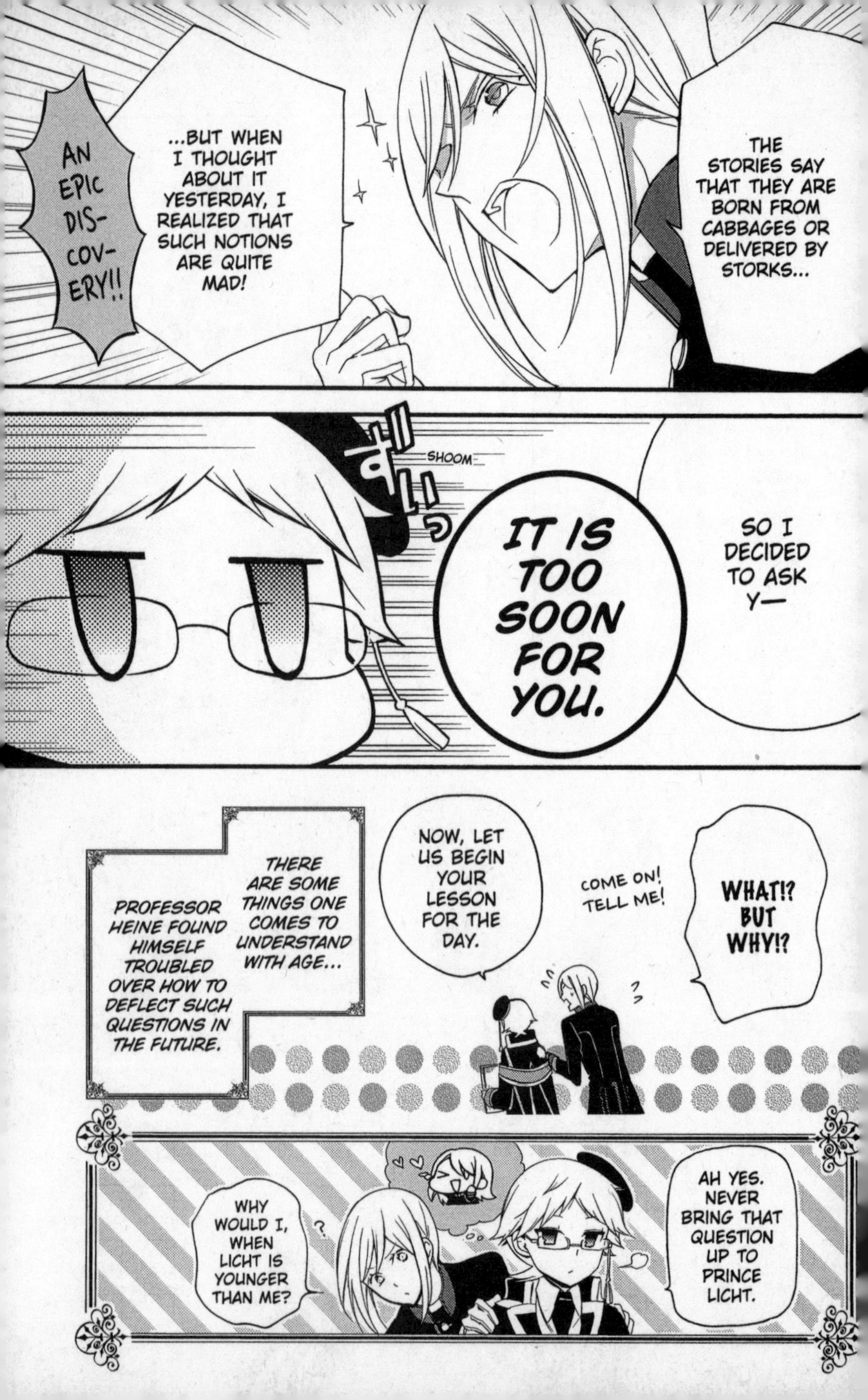
THE STORIES SAY THAT THEY ARE BORN FROM CABBAGES OR DELIVERED BY STORKS...
...BUT WHEN I THOUGHT ABOUT IT YESTERDAY, I REALIZED THAT SUCH NOTIONS ARE QUITE MAD!
AN EPIC DIS-COV-ERY!!
SO I DECIDED TO ASK Y—
IT IS TOO SOON FOR YOU.
ずいっ
SHOOM
WHAT!? BUT WHY!?
COME ON! TELL ME!
NOW, LET US BEGIN YOUR LESSON FOR THE DAY.
THERE ARE SOME THINGS ONE COMES TO UNDERSTAND WITH AGE...
PROFESSOR HEINE FOUND HIMSELF TROUBLED OVER HOW TO DEFLECT SUCH QUESTIONS IN THE FUTURE.
AH YES. NEVER BRING THAT QUESTION UP TO PRINCE LICHT.
WHY WOULD I, WHEN LICHT IS YOUNGER THAN ME?

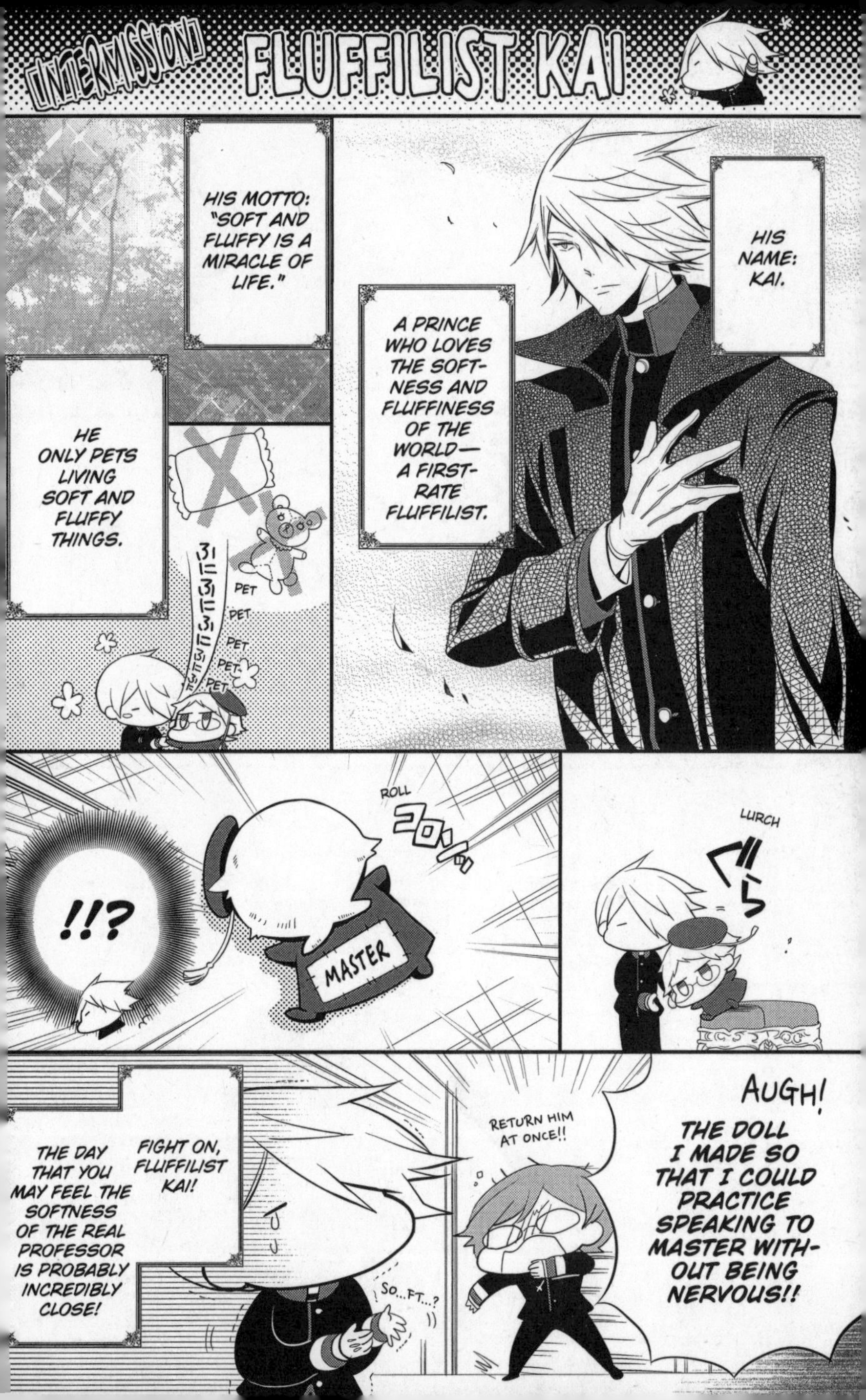
[INTERMISSION]
FLUFFILIST KAI
HIS NAME: KAI.
A PRINCE WHO LOVES THE SOFT-NESS AND FLUFFINESS OF THE WORLD— A FIRST-RATE FLUFFILIST.
HIS MOTTO: "SOFT AND FLUFFY IS A MIRACLE OF LIFE."
HE ONLY PETS LIVING SOFT AND FLUFFY THINGS.
PET
PET
PET
PET
PET
LURCH
ROLL
MASTER
!!?
AUGH!
THE DOLL I MADE SO THAT I COULD PRACTICE SPEAKING TO MASTER WITH-OUT BEING NERVOUS!!
RETURN HIM AT ONCE!!
SO...FT...?
FIGHT ON, FLUFFILIST KAI!
THE DAY THAT YOU MAY FEEL THE SOFTNESS OF THE REAL PROFESSOR IS PROBABLY INCREDIBLY CLOSE!

Chapter 21
Café Break Game

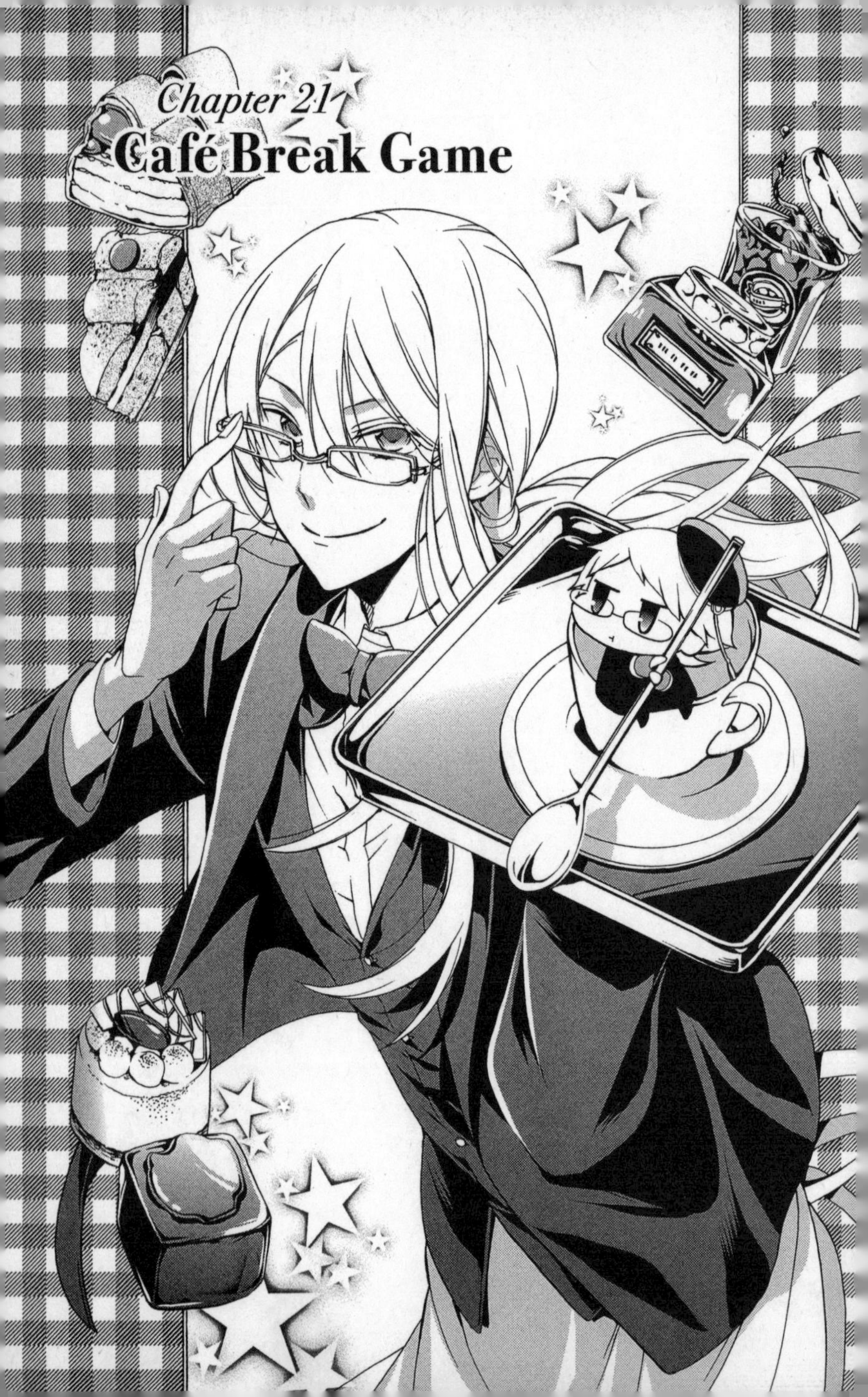

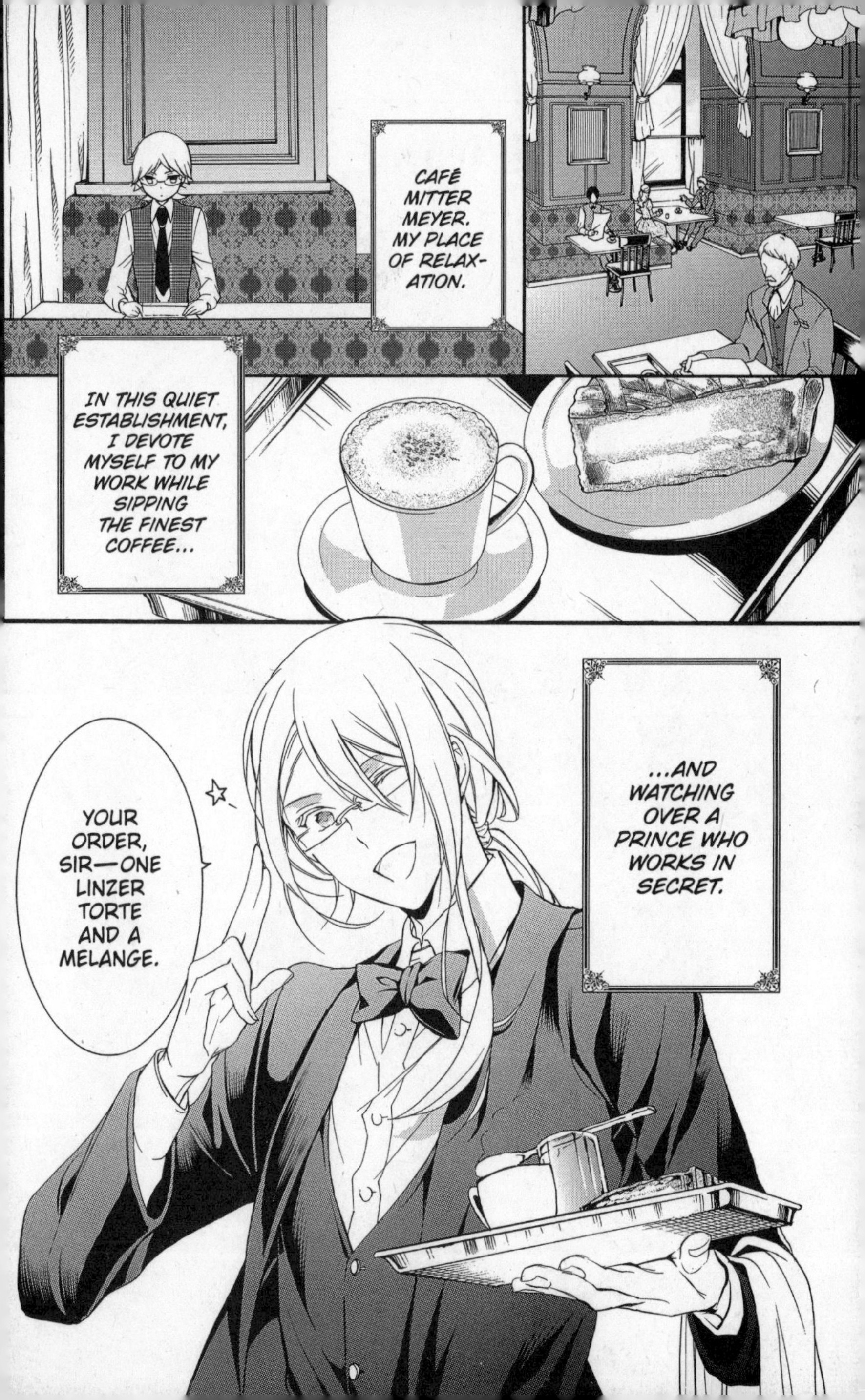
CAFÉ MITTER MEYER. MY PLACE OF RELAX-ATION.
IN THIS QUIET ESTABLISHMENT, I DEVOTE MYSELF TO MY WORK WHILE SIPPING THE FINEST COFFEE...
...AND WATCHING OVER A PRINCE WHO WORKS IN SECRET.
YOUR ORDER, SIR—ONE LINZER TORTE AND A MELANGE.

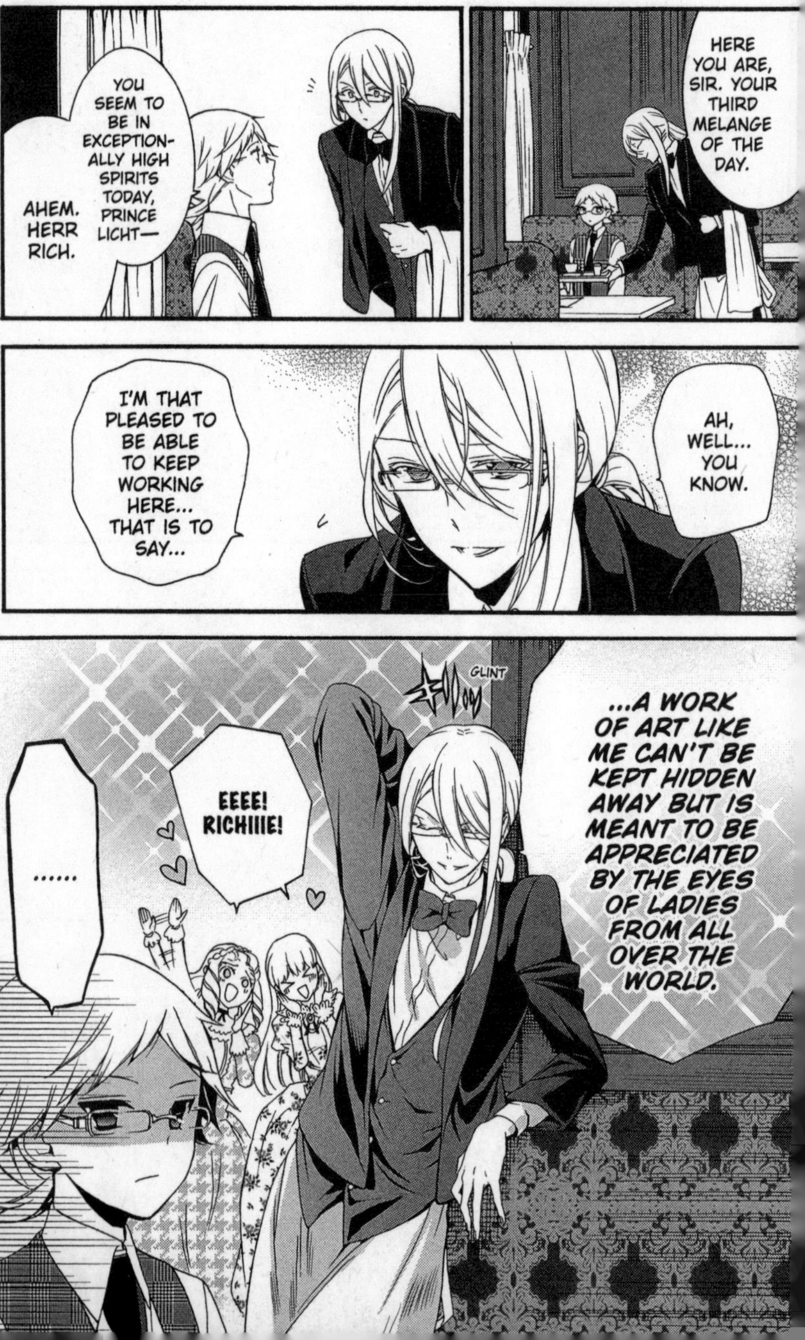
HERE YOU ARE, SIR. YOUR THIRD MELANGE OF THE DAY.
YOU SEEM TO BE IN EXCEPTION-ALLY HIGH SPIRITS TODAY, PRINCE LICHT—
AHEM. HERR RICH.
AH, WELL... YOU KNOW.
I'M THAT PLEASED TO BE ABLE TO KEEP WORKING HERE... THAT IS TO SAY...
GLINT
...A WORK OF ART LIKE ME CAN'T BE KEPT HIDDEN AWAY BUT IS MEANT TO BE APPRECIATED BY THE EYES OF LADIES FROM ALL OVER THE WORLD.
EEEE! RICHIIIE!
......

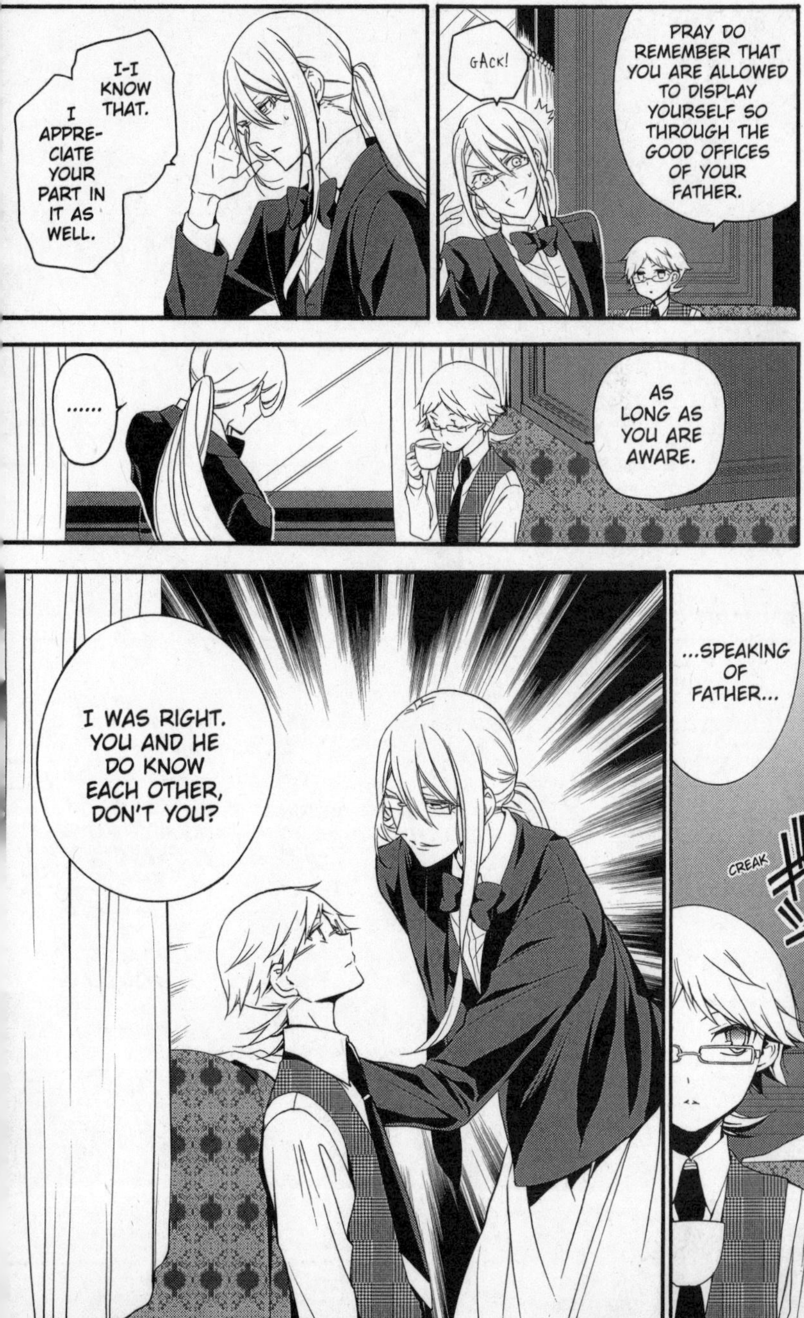
PRAY DO REMEMBER THAT YOU ARE ALLOWED TO DISPLAY YOURSELF SO THROUGH THE GOOD OFFICES OF YOUR FATHER.
GACK!
I-I KNOW THAT.
I APPRECIATE YOUR PART IN IT AS WELL.
AS LONG AS YOU ARE AWARE.
......
...SPEAKING OF FATHER...
CREAK
I WAS RIGHT. YOU AND HE DO KNOW EACH OTHER, DON'T YOU?

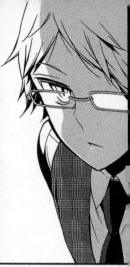

...WHAT MAKES YOU SAY THAT?
STILL GOING TO PLAY DUMB?
THAT WON'T DO.
I SPIED YOU TWO CHATTING LIKE OLD FRIENDS WHEN HE WAS HERE.
THEN YOU MISINTER-PRETED.
I AM BUT A COMMONER. HOW, PRAY TELL, WOULD I HAVE BECOME "FRIENDS" WITH HIS MAJESTY THE KING?
ひょい!
YOINK
KLAK
NOW, NOW!

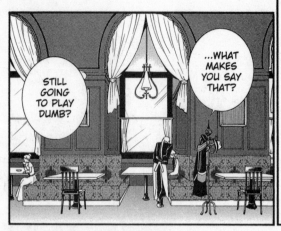

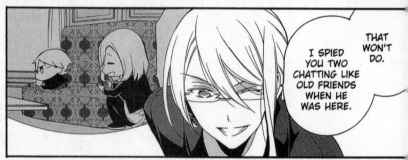

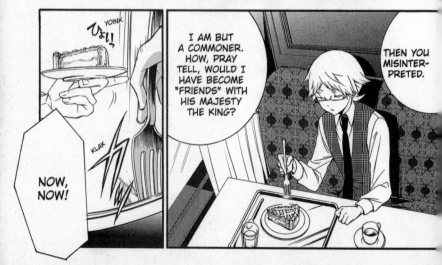

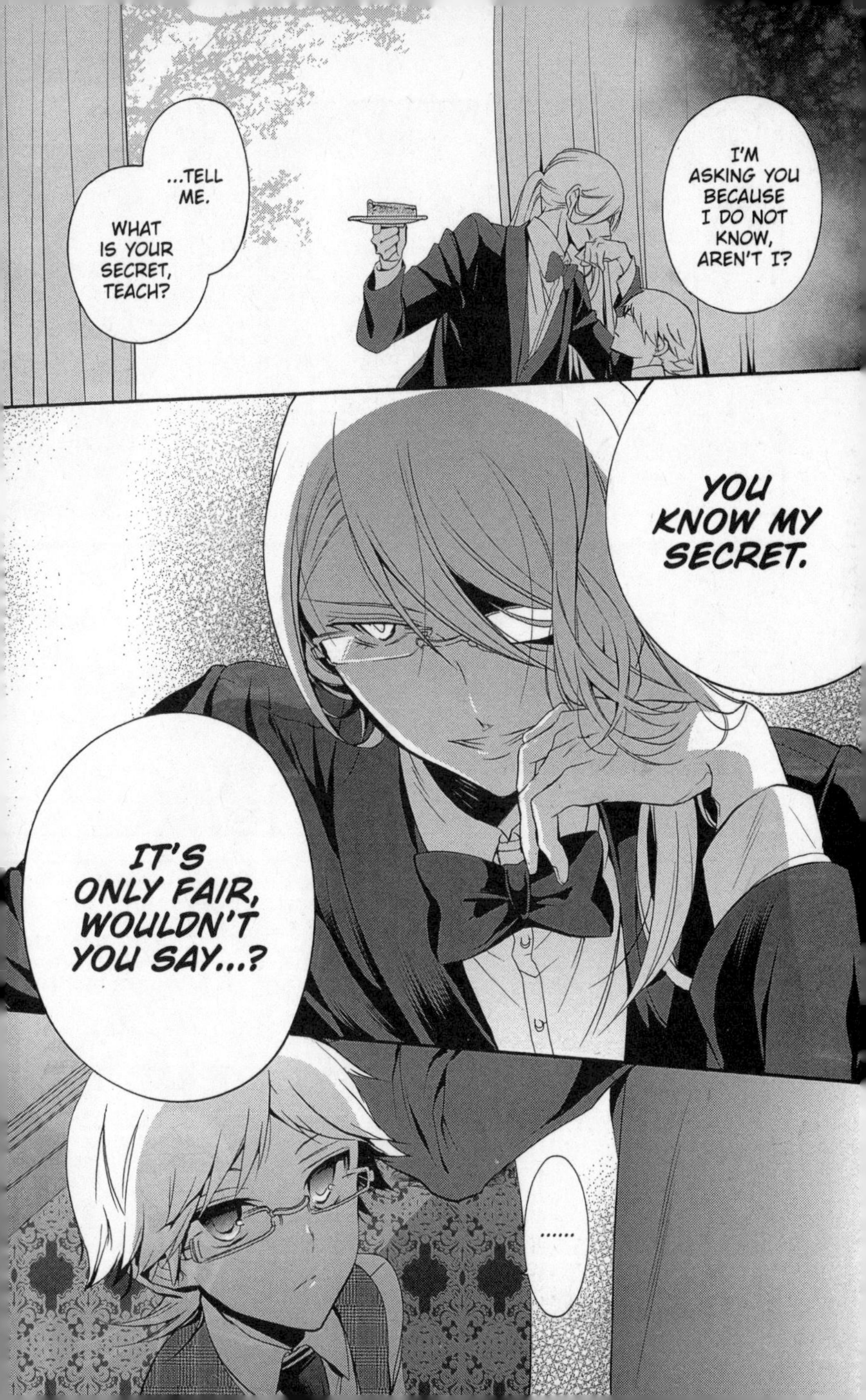
I'M ASKING YOU BECAUSE I DO NOT KNOW, AREN'T I?
...TELL ME.
WHAT IS YOUR SECRET, TEACH?
YOU KNOW MY SECRET.
IT'S ONLY FAIR, WOULDN'T YOU SAY...?
......

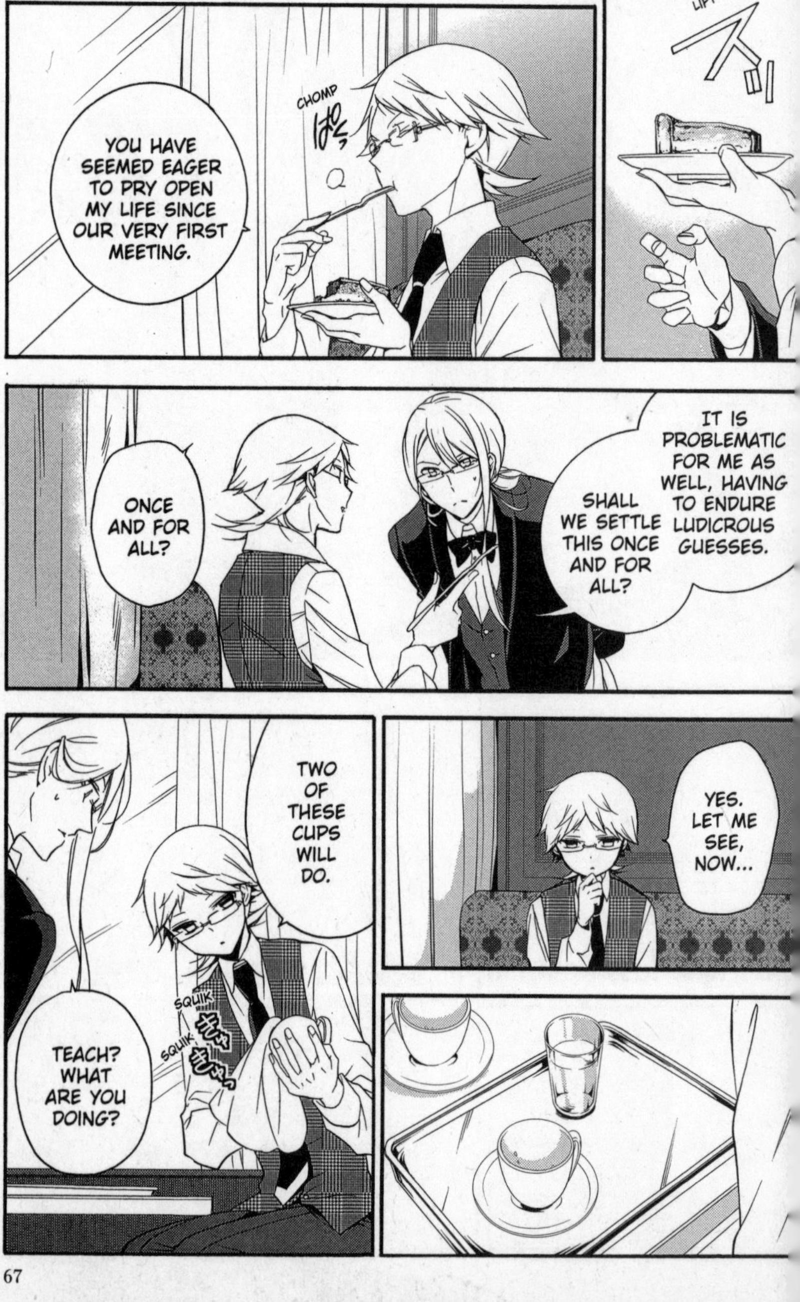
LIFT
CHOMP
YOU HAVE SEEMED EAGER TO PRY OPEN MY LIFE SINCE OUR VERY FIRST MEETING.
IT IS PROBLEMATIC FOR ME AS WELL, HAVING TO ENDURE LUDICROUS GUESSES.
SHALL WE SETTLE THIS ONCE AND FOR ALL?
ONCE AND FOR ALL?
YES. LET ME SEE, NOW...
TWO OF THESE CUPS WILL DO.
SQUIK SQUIK
TEACH? WHAT ARE YOU DOING?

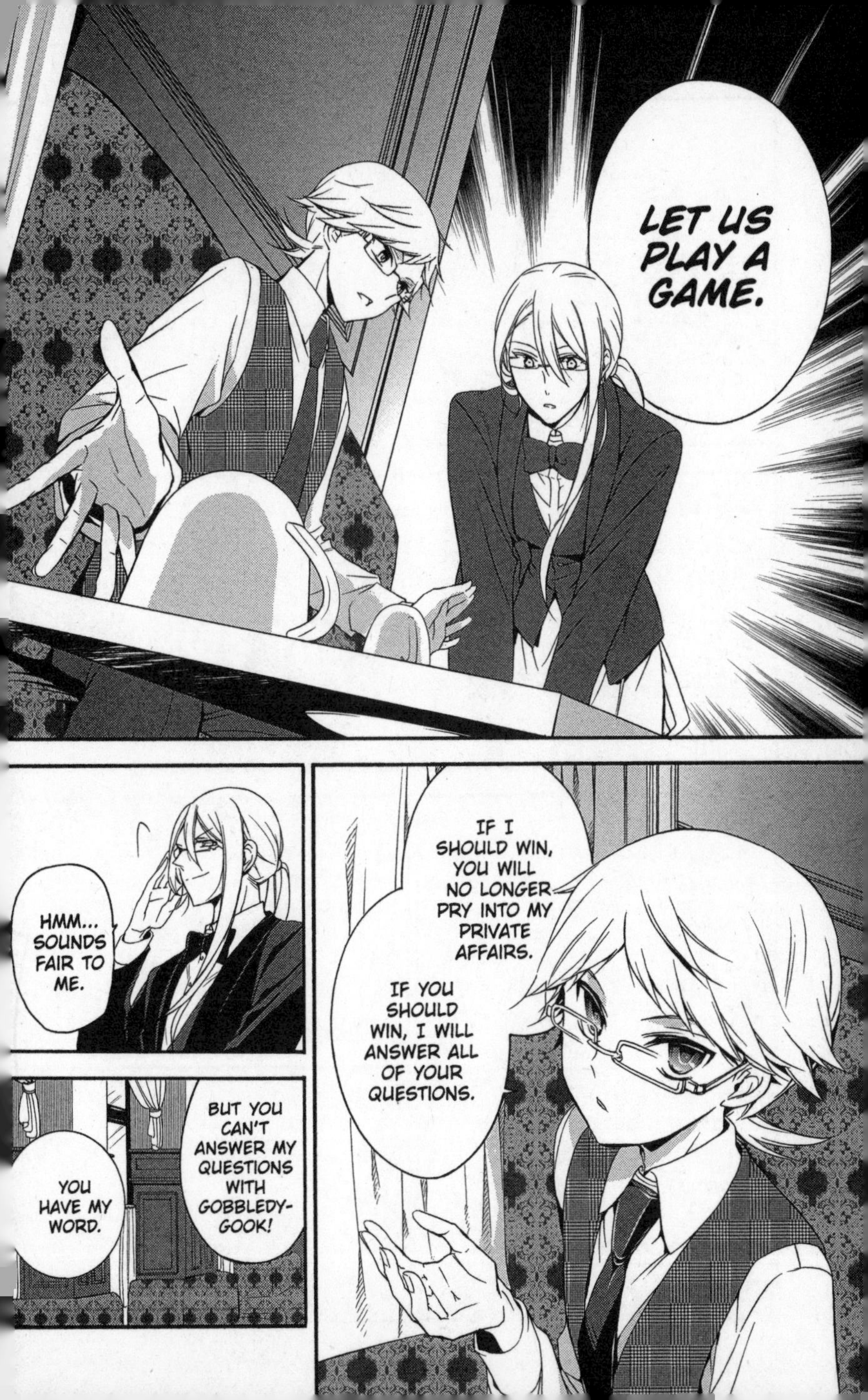
LET US PLAY A GAME.
IF I SHOULD WIN, YOU WILL NO LONGER PRY INTO MY PRIVATE AFFAIRS.
IF YOU SHOULD WIN, I WILL ANSWER ALL OF YOUR QUESTIONS.
HMM... SOUNDS FAIR TO ME.
BUT YOU CAN'T ANSWER MY QUESTIONS WITH GOBBLEDY-GOOK!
YOU HAVE MY WORD.

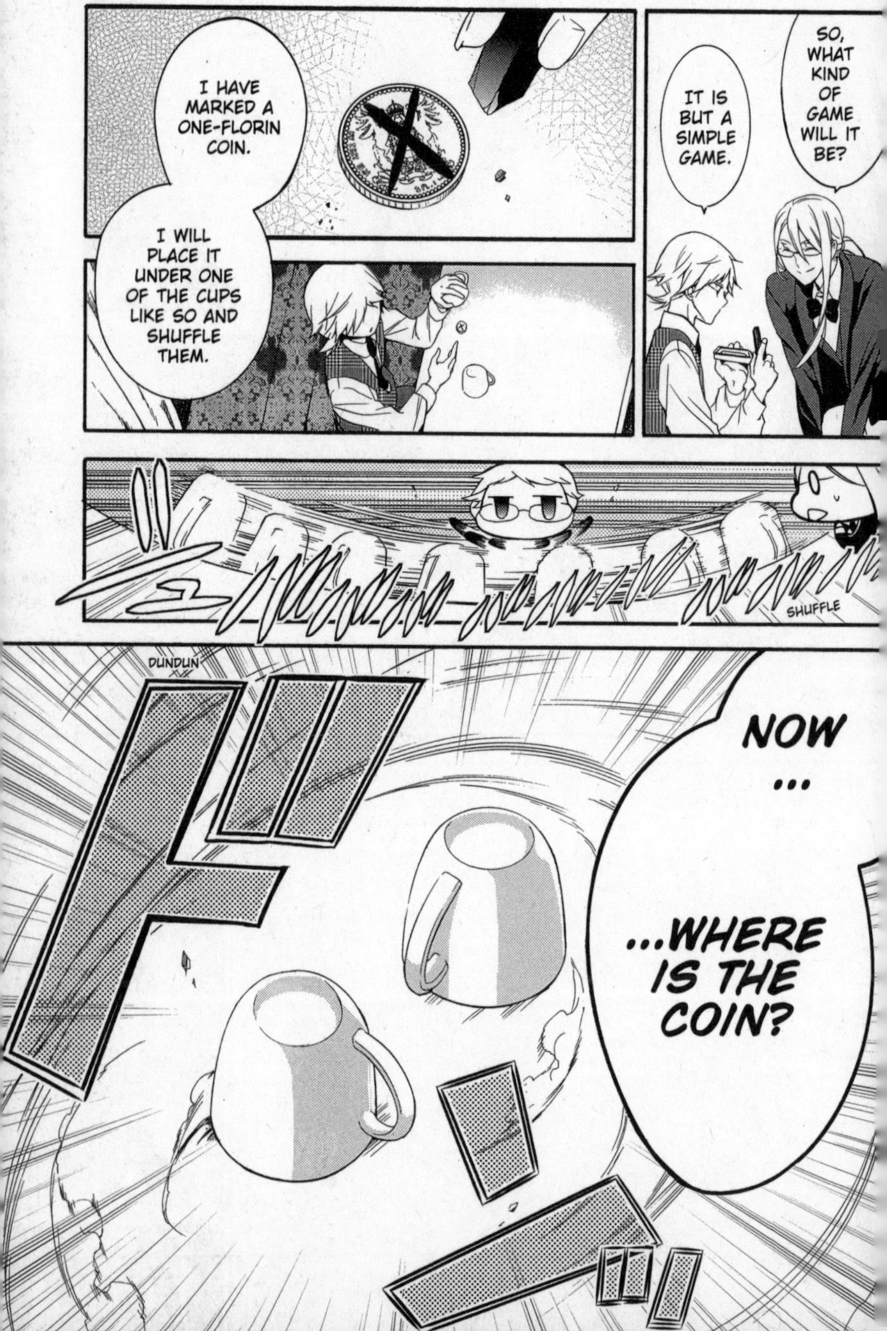
SO, WHAT KIND OF GAME WILL IT BE?
IT IS BUT A SIMPLE GAME.
I HAVE MARKED A ONE-FLORIN COIN.
I WILL PLACE IT UNDER ONE OF THE CUPS LIKE SO AND SHUFFLE THEM.
SHUFFLE
NOW ...
...WHERE IS THE COIN?
DUNDUN

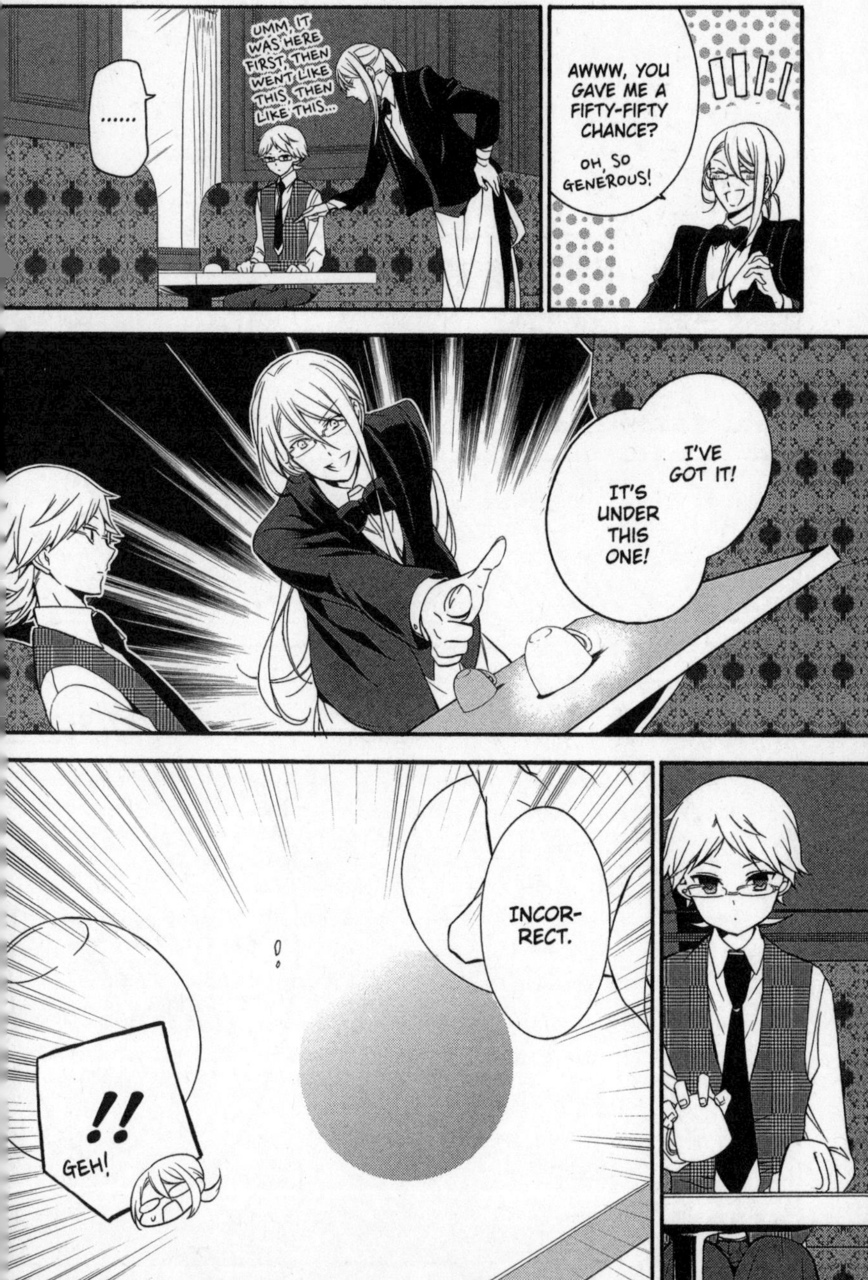
AWWW, YOU GAVE ME A FIFTY-FIFTY CHANCE?
OH, SO GENEROUS!
UMM, IT WAS HERE FIRST, THEN WENT LIKE THIS, THEN LIKE THIS...
......
I'VE GOT IT!
IT'S UNDER THIS ONE!
INCOR-RECT.
!
!!
GEH!

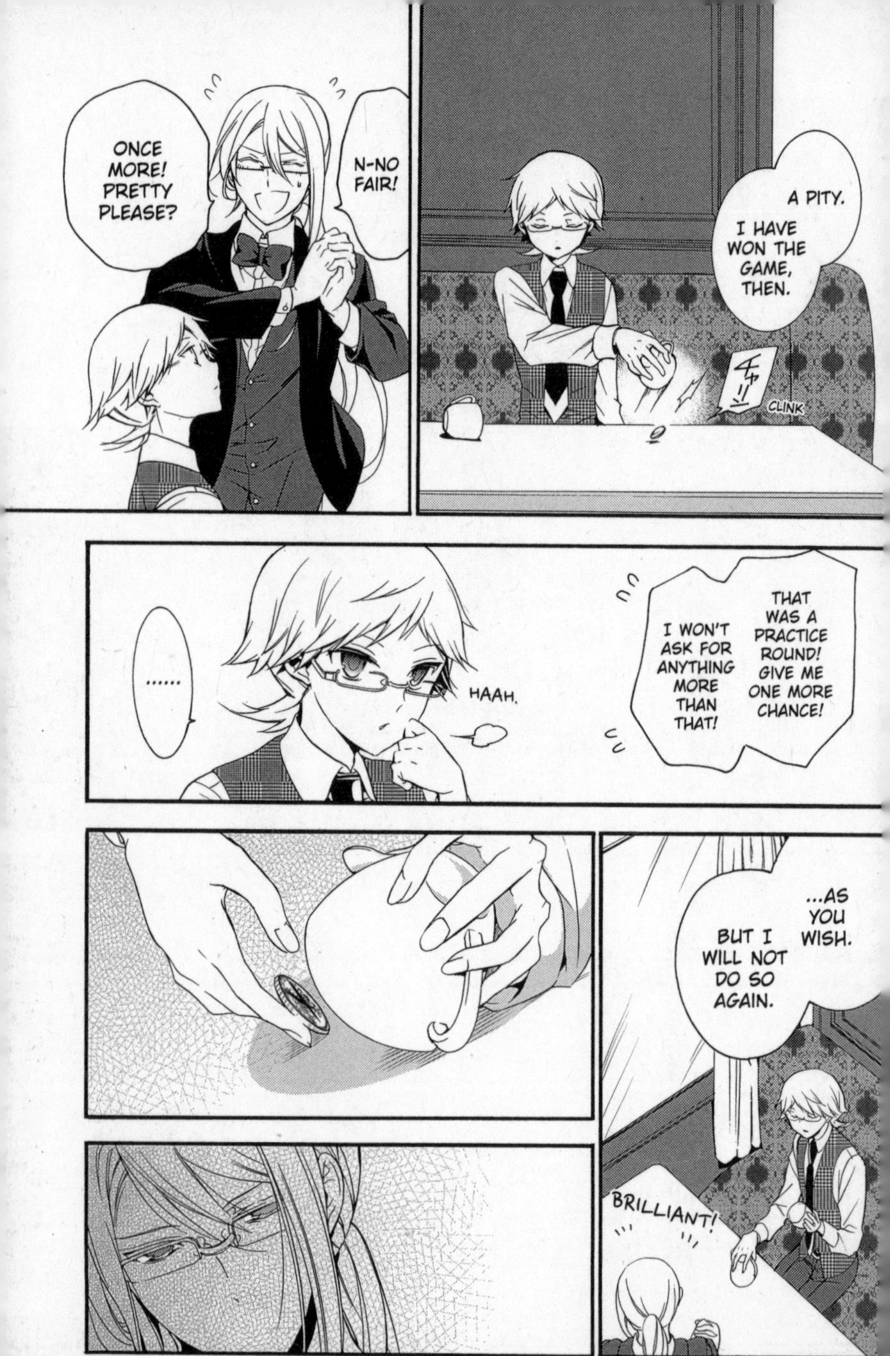
A PITY.
I HAVE WON THE GAME, THEN.
CLINK
N-NO FAIR!
ONCE MORE! PRETTY PLEASE?
THAT WAS A PRACTICE ROUND! GIVE ME ONE MORE CHANCE!
I WON'T ASK FOR ANYTHING MORE THAN THAT!
HAAH.
......
...AS YOU WISH.
BUT I WILL NOT DO SO AGAIN.
BRILLIANT!

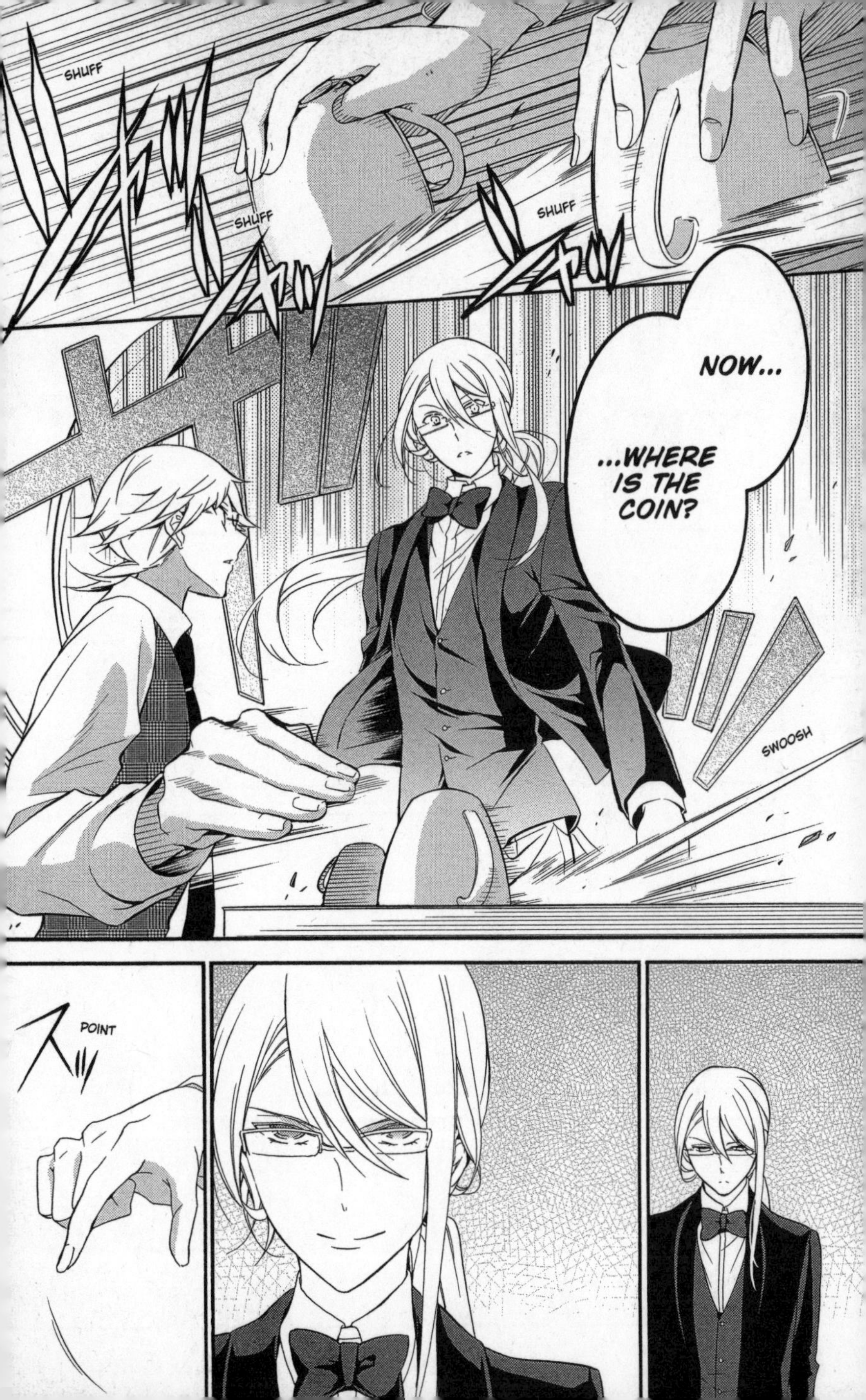
SHUFF
SHUFF
SHUFF
NOW...
...WHERE IS THE COIN?
SWOOSH
POINT

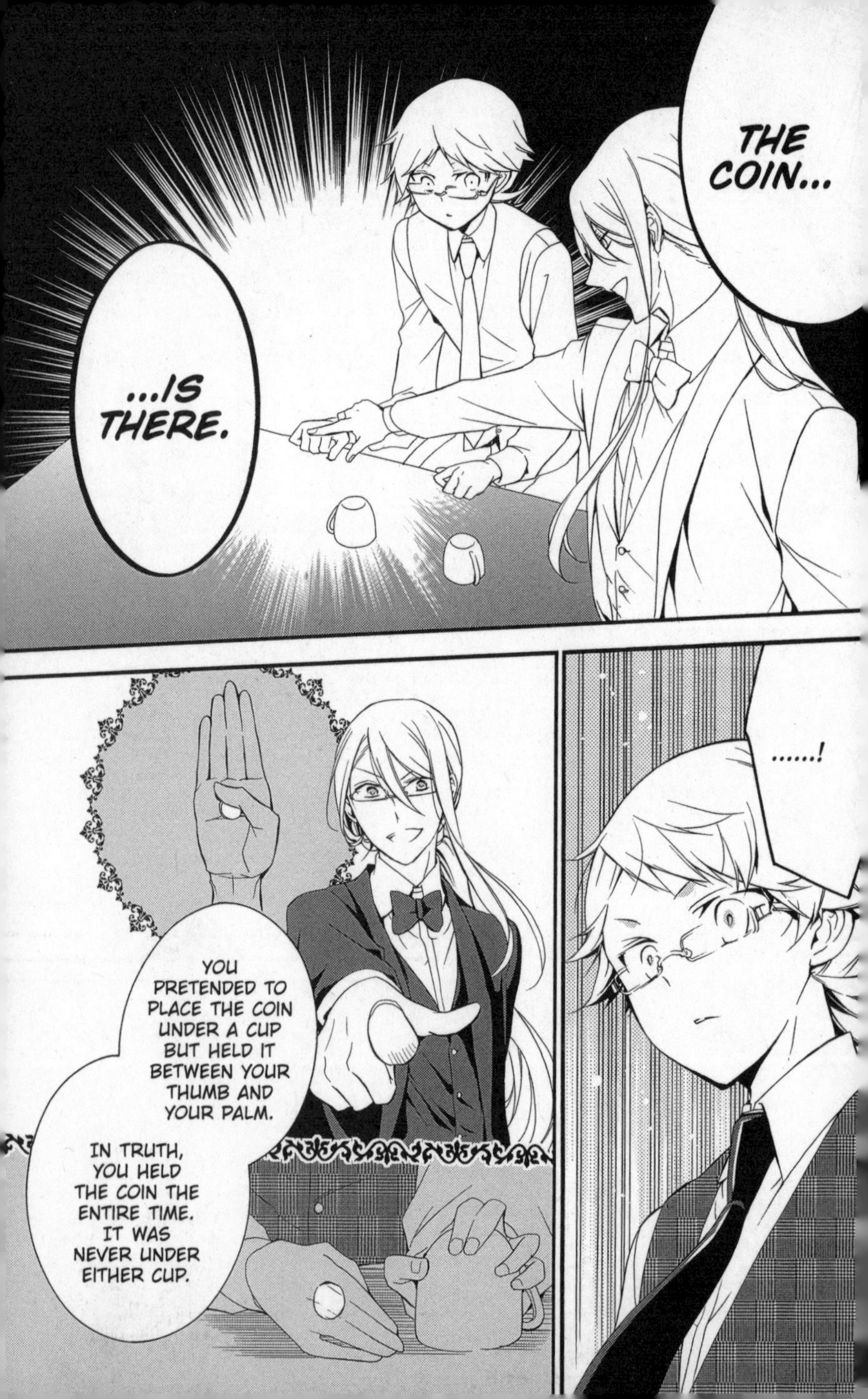
THE COIN...
...IS THERE.
......!
YOU PRETENDED TO PLACE THE COIN UNDER A CUP BUT HELD IT BETWEEN YOUR THUMB AND YOUR PALM.
IN TRUTH, YOU HELD THE COIN THE ENTIRE TIME. IT WAS NEVER UNDER EITHER CUP.

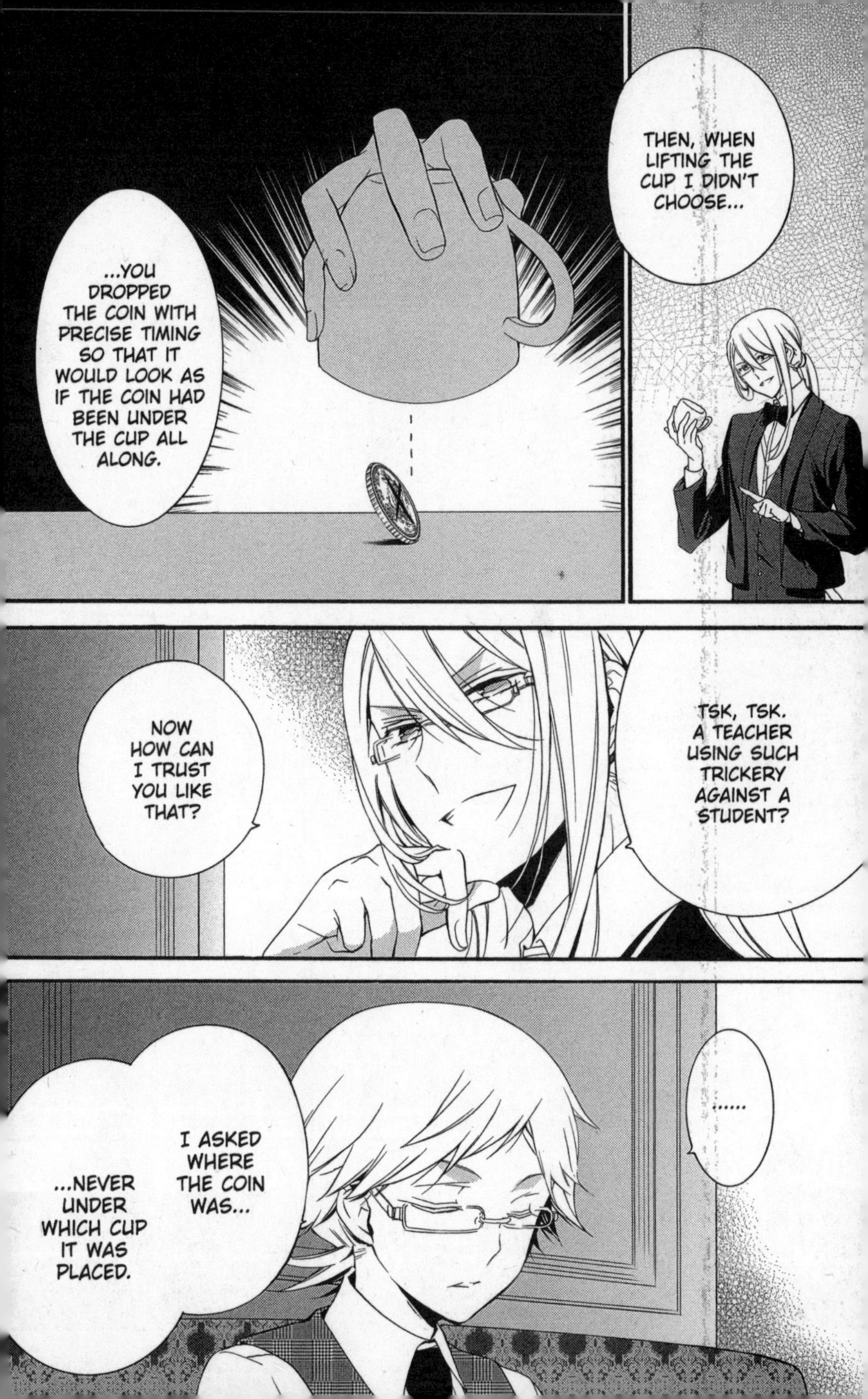
THEN, WHEN LIFTING THE CUP I DIDN'T CHOOSE...
...YOU DROPPED THE COIN WITH PRECISE TIMING SO THAT IT WOULD LOOK AS IF THE COIN HAD BEEN UNDER THE CUP ALL ALONG.
TSK, TSK. A TEACHER USING SUCH TRICKERY AGAINST A STUDENT?
NOW HOW CAN I TRUST YOU LIKE THAT?
......
I ASKED WHERE THE COIN WAS...
...NEVER UNDER WHICH CUP IT WAS PLACED.

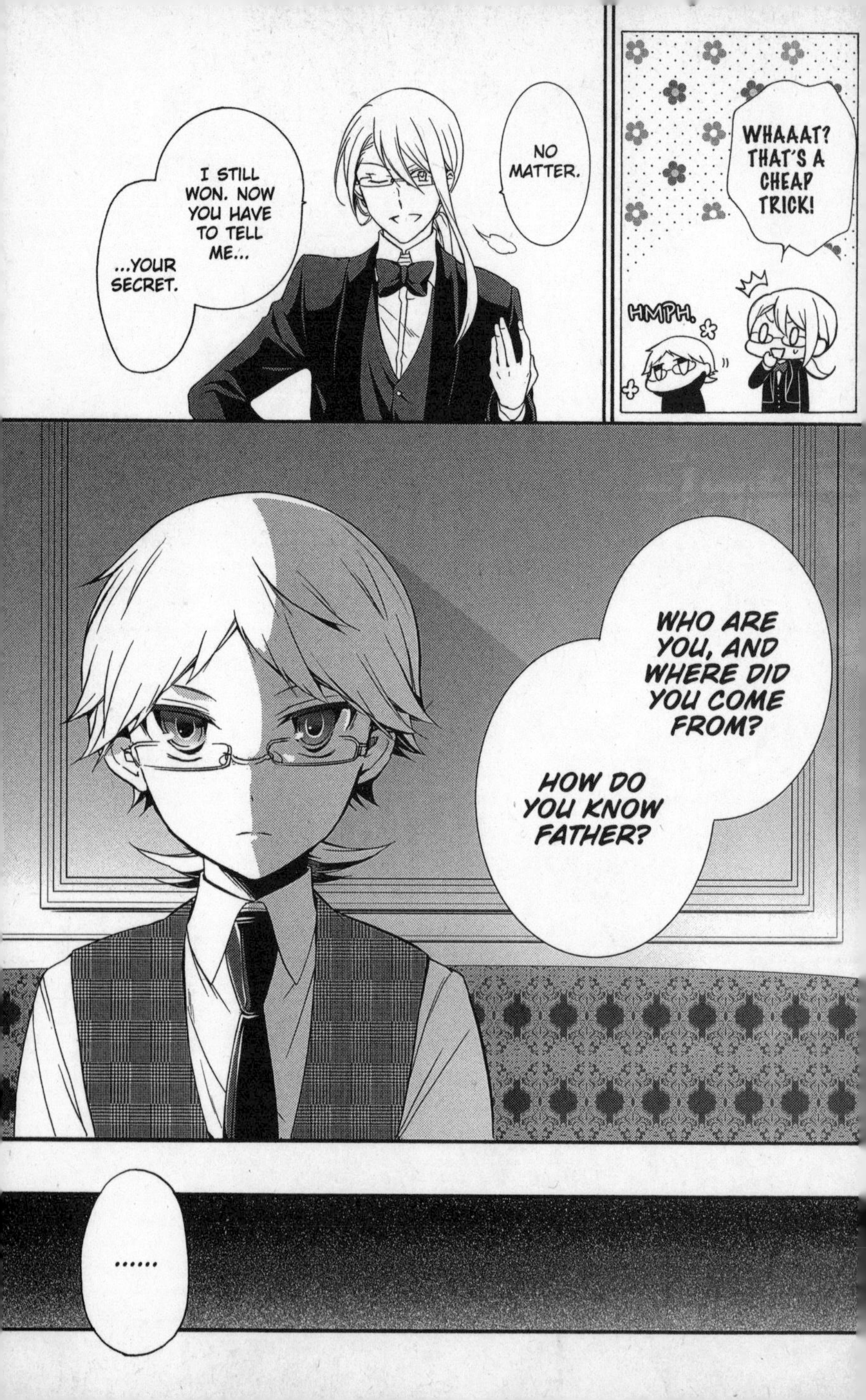
WHAAAT? THAT'S A CHEAP TRICK!
HMPH.
NO MATTER.
I STILL WON. NOW YOU HAVE TO TELL ME... ...YOUR SECRET.
WHO ARE YOU, AND WHERE DID YOU COME FROM?
HOW DO YOU KNOW FATHER?
......

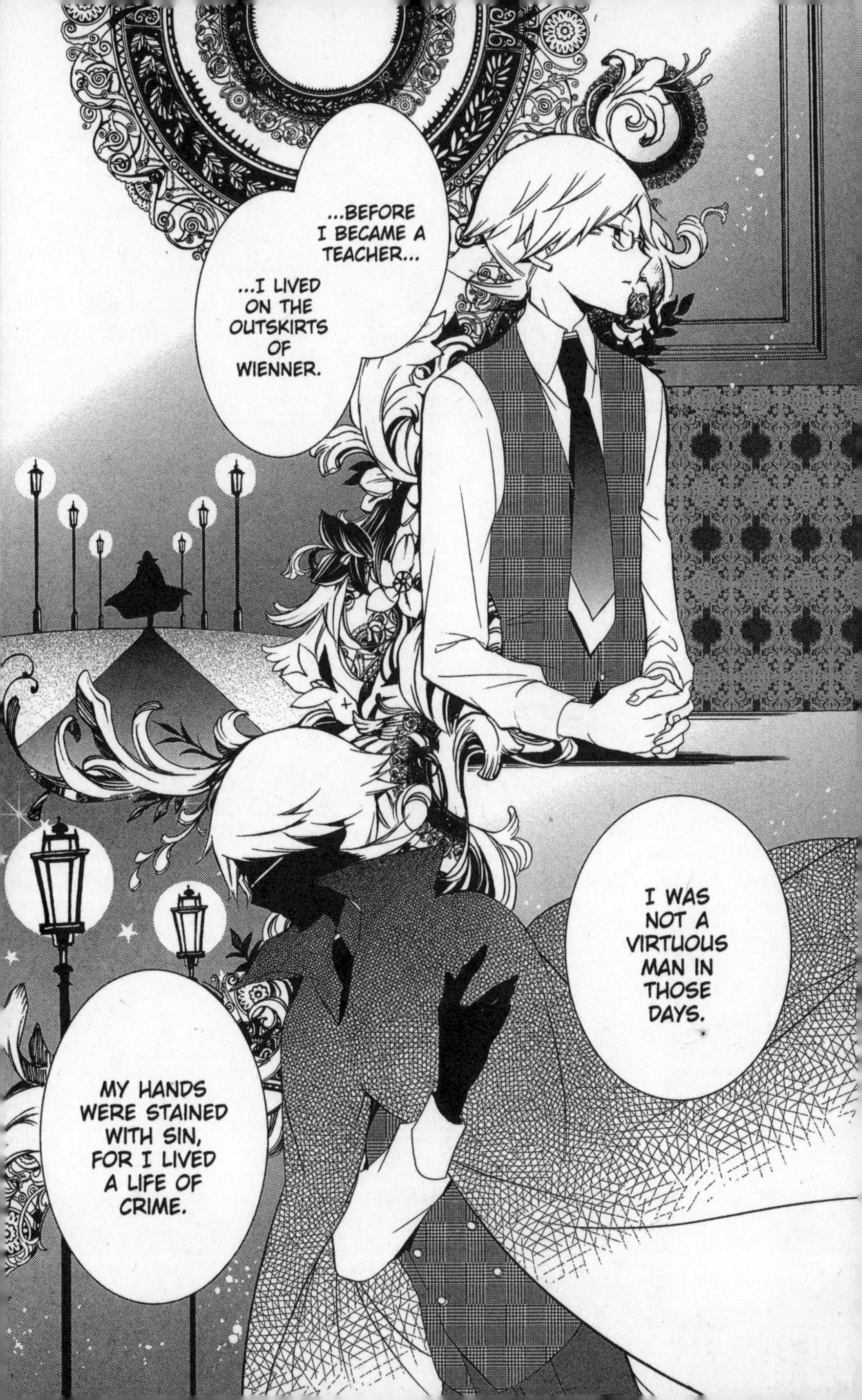
...BEFORE I BECAME A TEACHER...
...I LIVED ON THE OUTSKIRTS OF WIENNER.
I WAS NOT A VIRTUOUS MAN IN THOSE DAYS.
MY HANDS WERE STAINED WITH SIN, FOR I LIVED A LIFE OF CRIME.

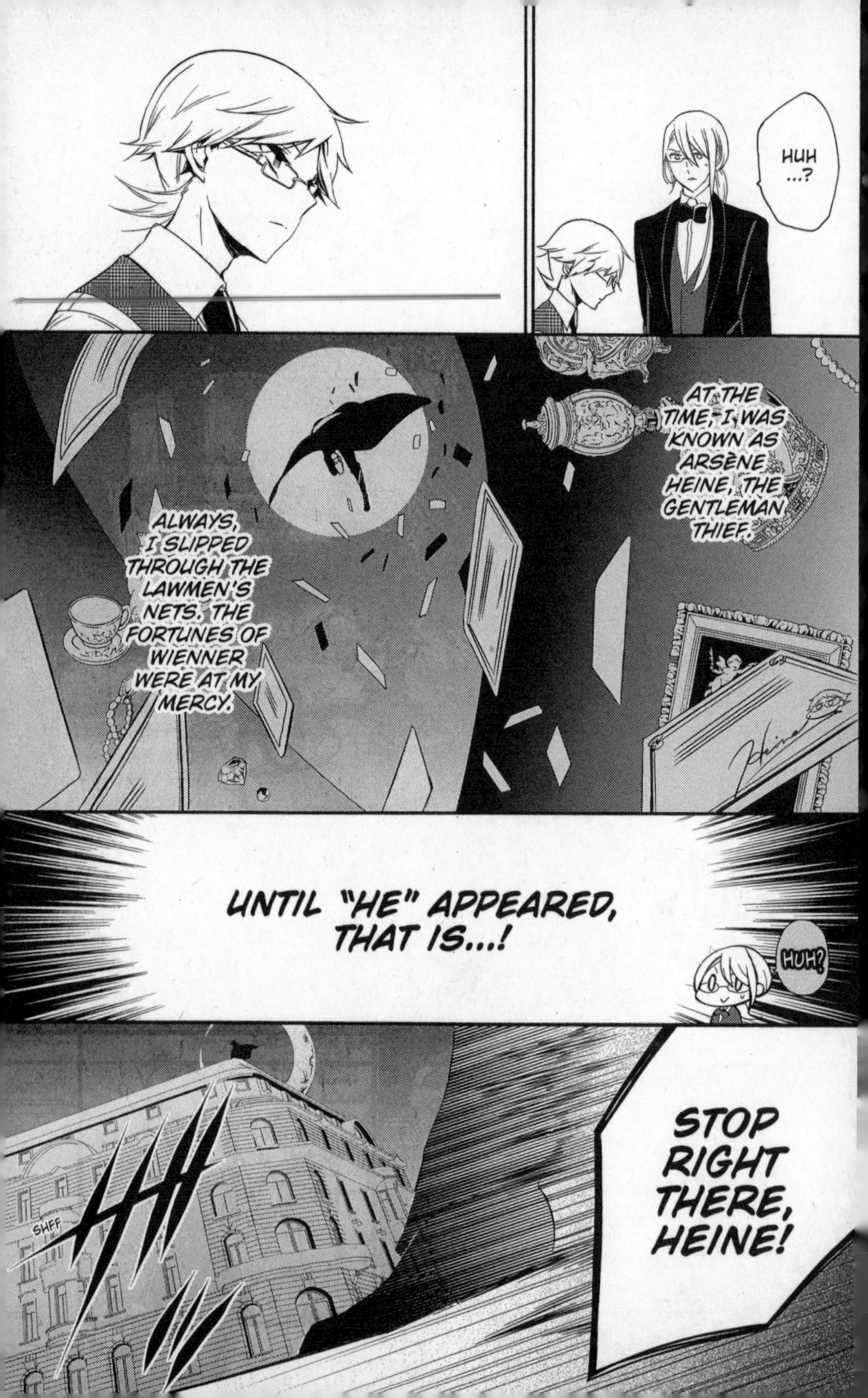
HUH ...?
AT THE TIME, I WAS KNOWN AS ARSÈNE HEINE, THE GENTLEMAN THIEF.
ALWAYS, I SLIPPED THROUGH THE LAWMEN'S NETS. THE FORTUNES OF WIENNER WERE AT MY MERCY.
UNTIL "HE" APPEARED, THAT IS...!
HUH?
STOP RIGHT THERE, HEINE!
SHFF

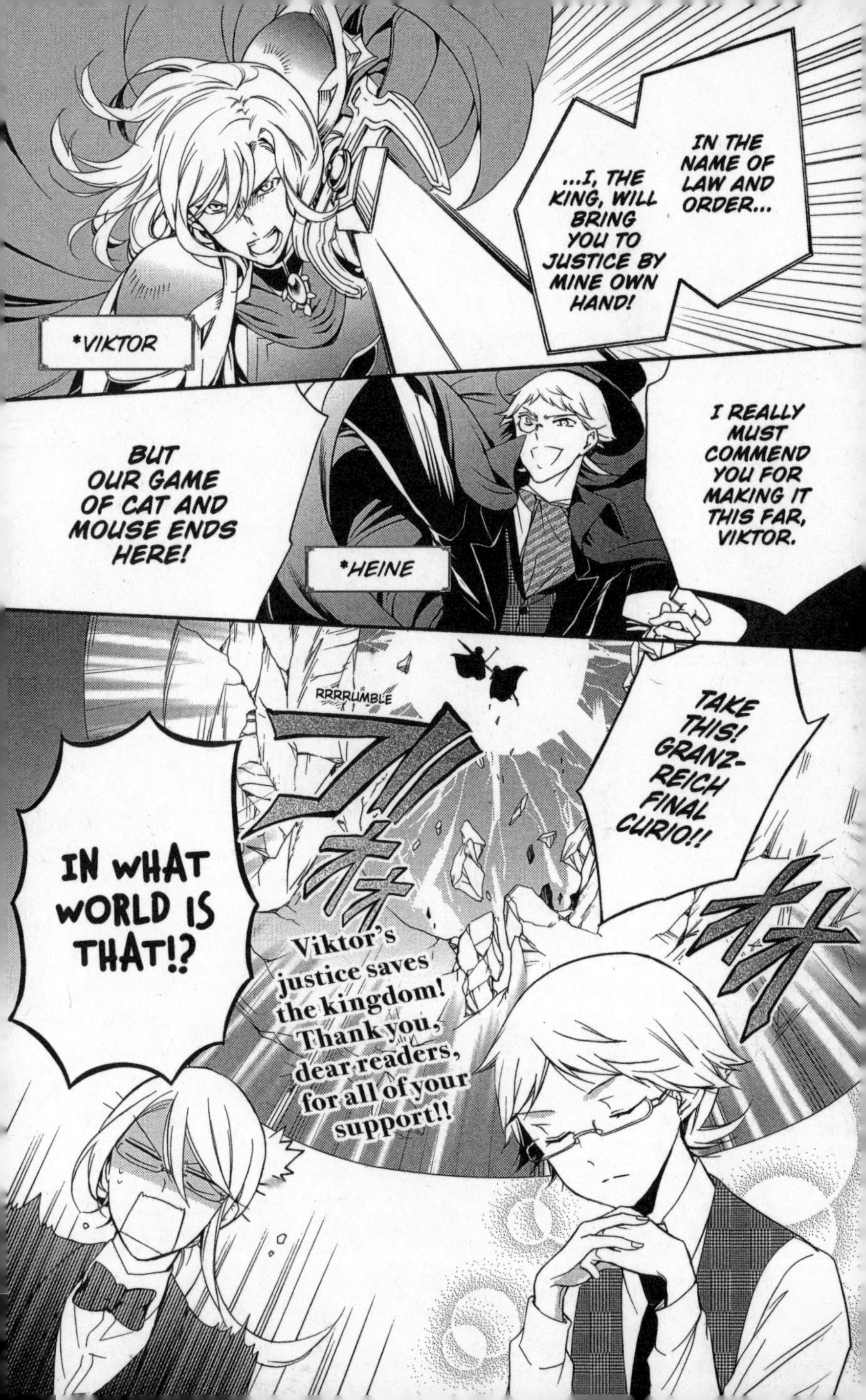
IN THE NAME OF LAW AND ORDER...
...I, THE KING, WILL BRING YOU TO JUSTICE BY MINE OWN HAND!
*VIKTOR
I REALLY MUST COMMEND YOU FOR MAKING IT THIS FAR, VIKTOR.
*HEINE
BUT OUR GAME OF CAT AND MOUSE ENDS HERE!
RRRUMBLE
ゴオォ
オオ
TAKE THIS! GRANZ-REICH FINAL CURIO!!
IN WHAT WORLD IS THAT!?
Viktor's justice saves the kingdom! Thank you, dear readers, for all of your support!!

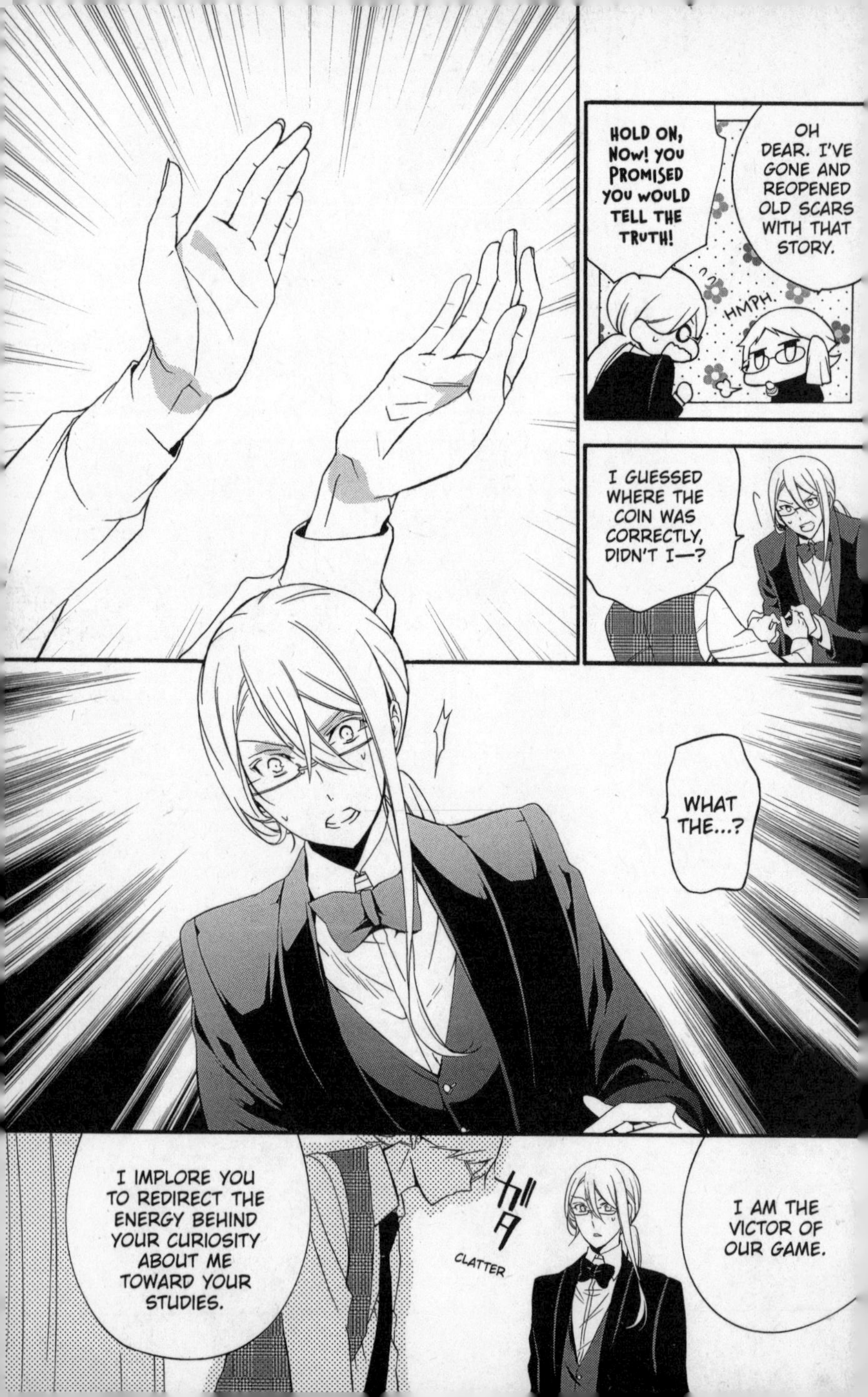

OH DEAR. I'VE GONE AND REOPENED OLD SCARS WITH THAT STORY.
HOLD ON, NOW! YOU PROMISED YOU WOULD TELL THE TRUTH!
HMPH.
I GUESSED WHERE THE COIN WAS CORRECTLY, DIDN'T I—?
WHAT THE...?
I AM THE VICTOR OF OUR GAME.
ガタ
CLATTER
I IMPLORE YOU TO REDIRECT THE ENERGY BEHIND YOUR CURIOSITY ABOUT ME TOWARD YOUR STUDIES.

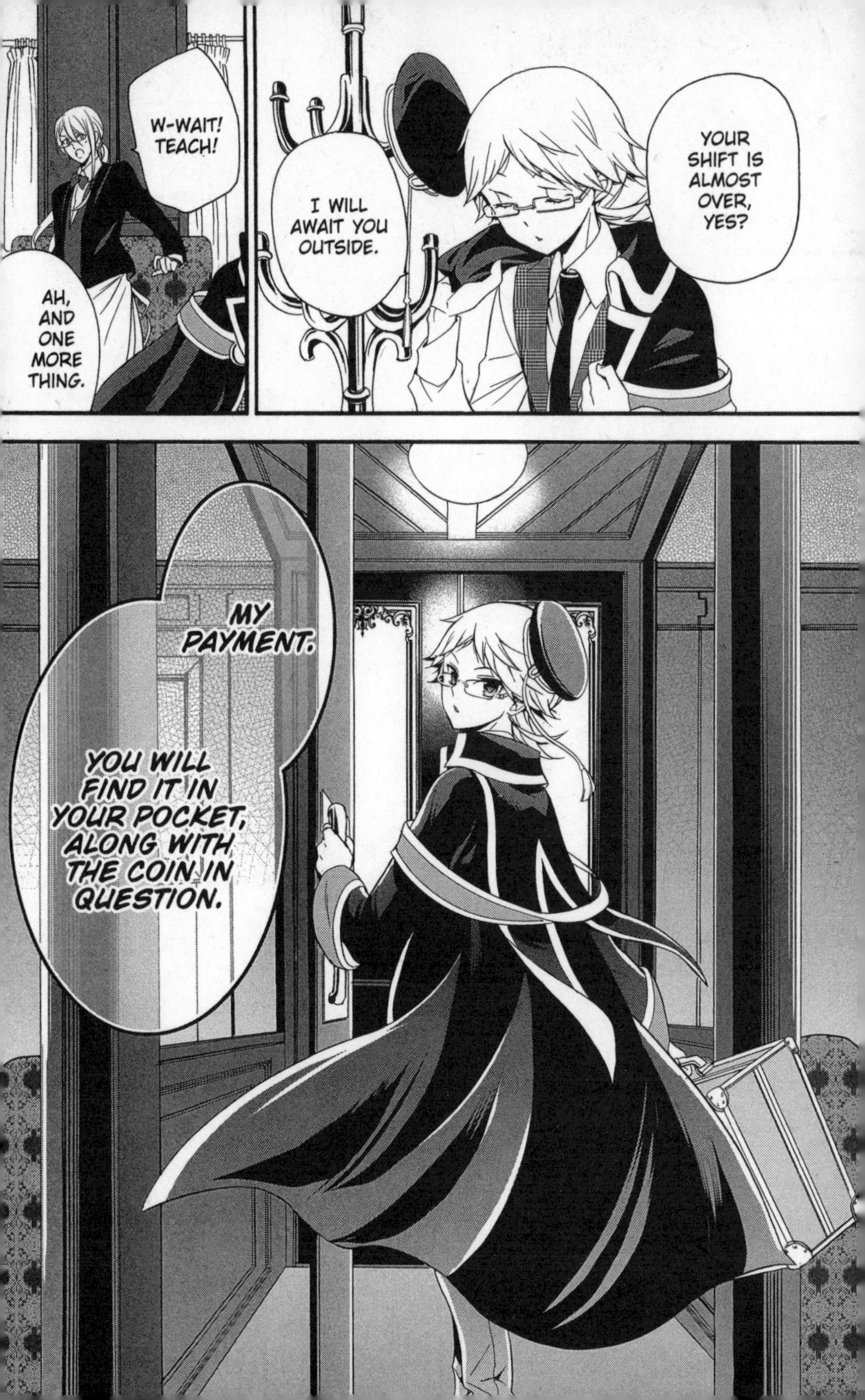
YOUR SHIFT IS ALMOST OVER, YES?
I WILL AWAIT YOU OUTSIDE.
W-WAIT! TEACH!
AH, AND ONE MORE THING.
MY PAYMENT.
YOU WILL FIND IT IN YOUR POCKET, ALONG WITH THE COIN IN QUESTION.

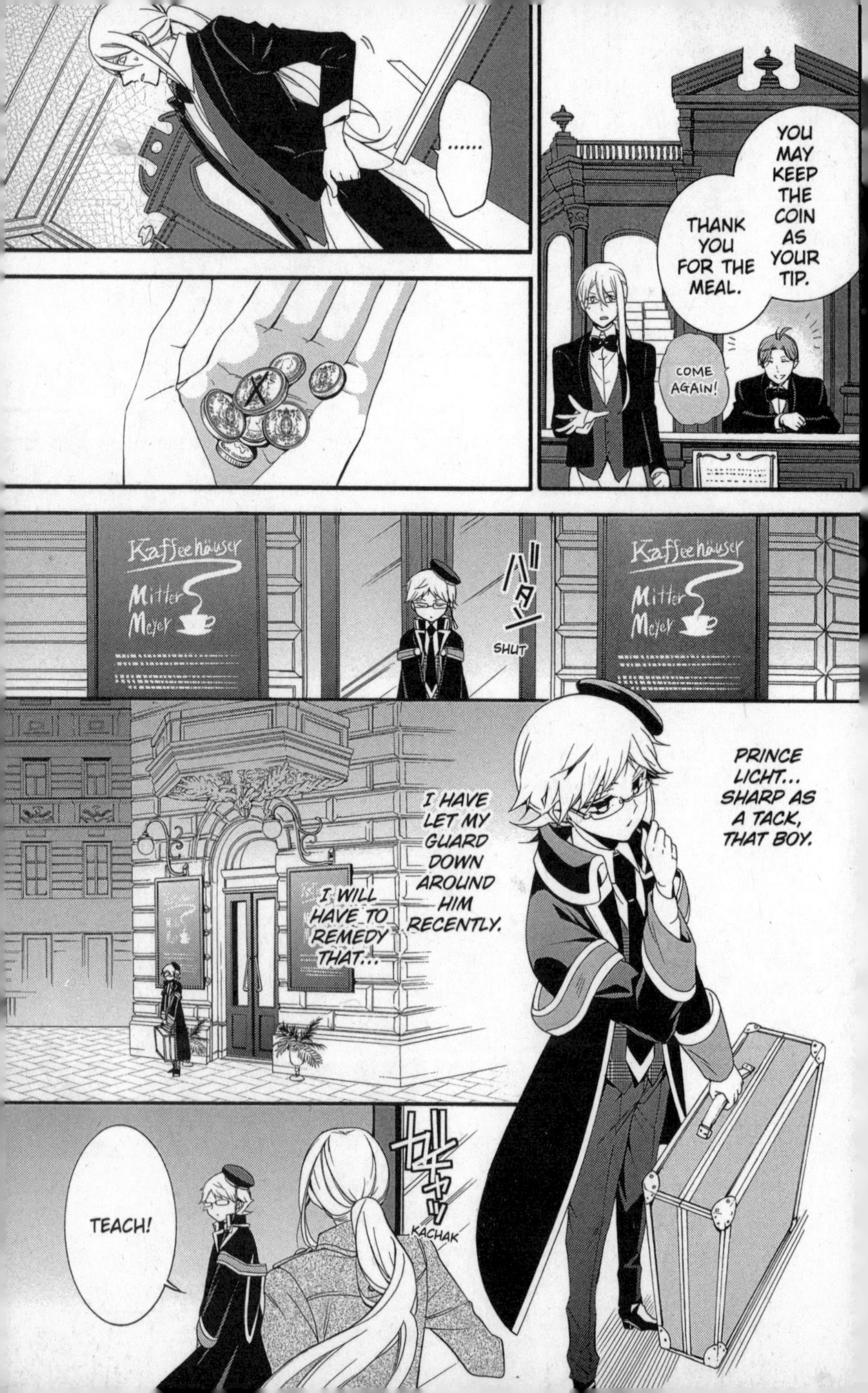
YOU MAY KEEP THE COIN AS YOUR TIP.
THANK YOU FOR THE MEAL.
COME AGAIN!
......
Kaffeehäuser Mitter Meyer
バタン
SHUT
PRINCE LICHT... SHARP AS A TACK, THAT BOY.
I HAVE LET MY GUARD DOWN AROUND HIM RECENTLY.
I WILL HAVE TO REMEDY THAT...
ガチャッ
KACHAK
TEACH!

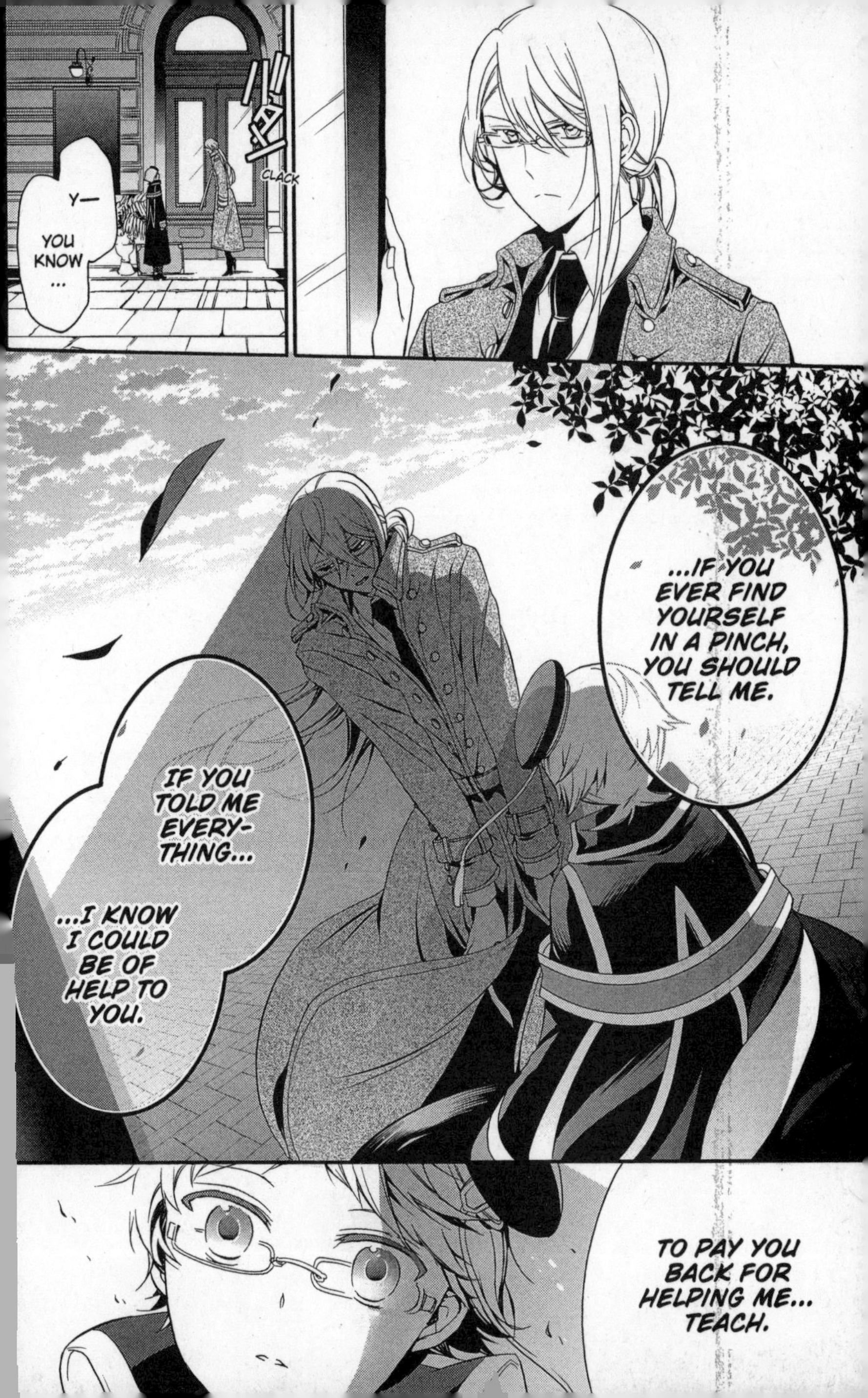
CLACK
Y— YOU KNOW ...
...IF YOU EVER FIND YOURSELF IN A PINCH, YOU SHOULD TELL ME.
IF YOU TOLD ME EVERY-THING...
...I KNOW I COULD BE OF HELP TO YOU.
TO PAY YOU BACK FOR HELPING ME... TEACH.

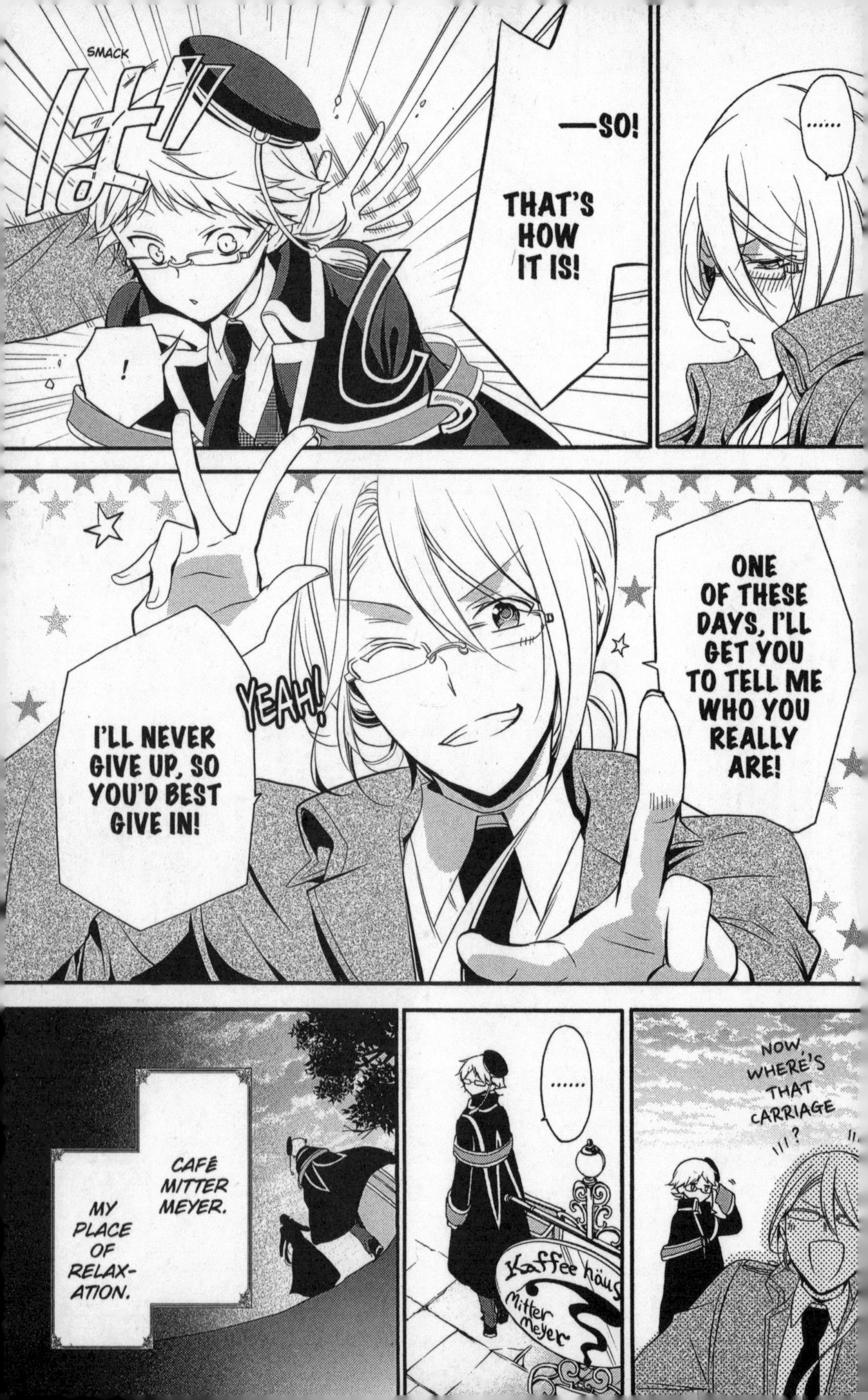
……
—SO!
THAT'S HOW IT IS!
SMACK
!
ONE OF THESE DAYS, I'LL GET YOU TO TELL ME WHO YOU REALLY ARE!
YEAH!
I'LL NEVER GIVE UP, SO YOU'D BEST GIVE IN!
NOW, WHERE'S THAT CARRIAGE ?
……
Kaffee häus Mitter meyer
CAFÉ MITTER MEYER.
MY PLACE OF RELAXATION.

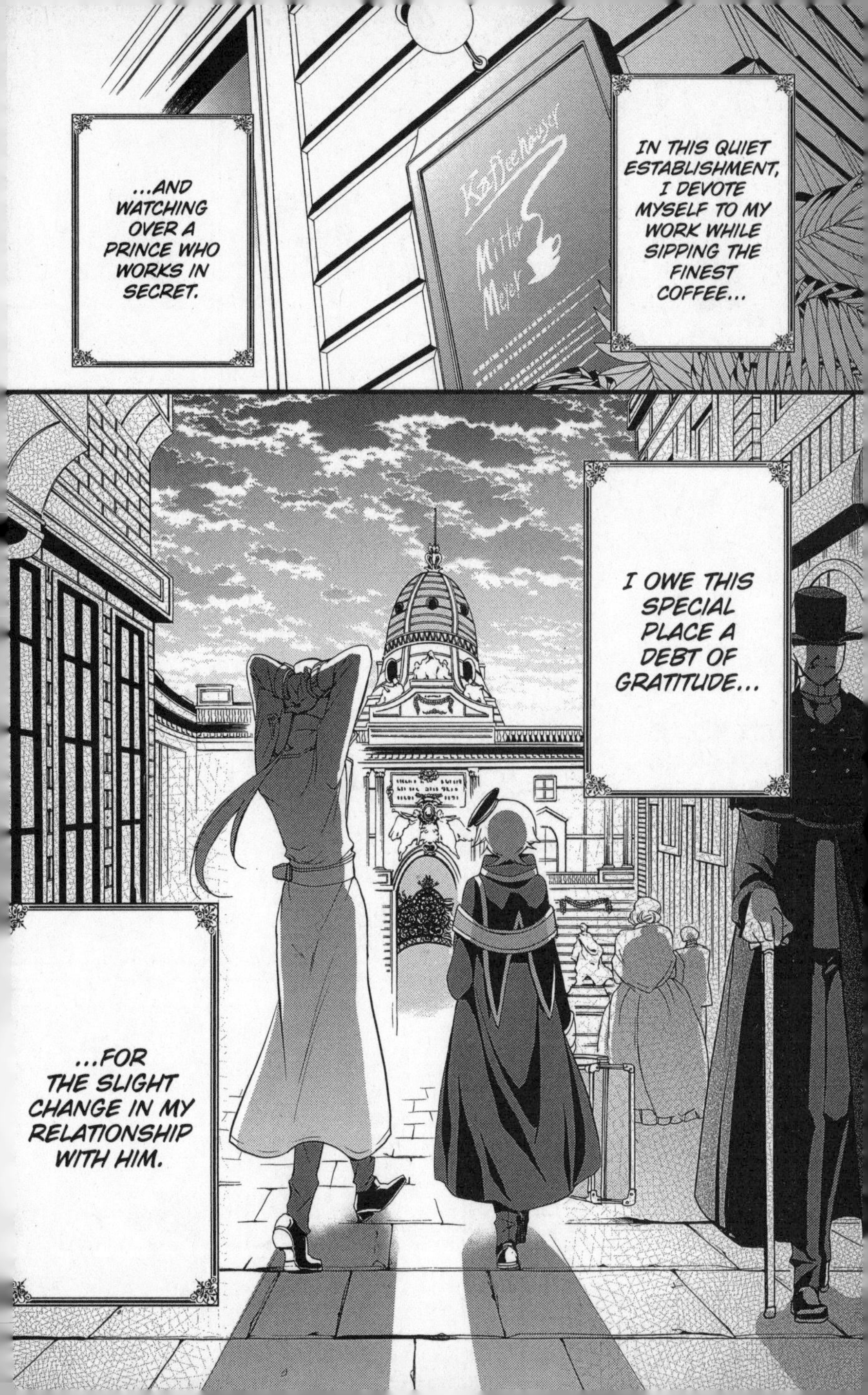
IN THIS QUIET ESTABLISHMENT, I DEVOTE MYSELF TO MY WORK WHILE SIPPING THE FINEST COFFEE...
...AND WATCHING OVER A PRINCE WHO WORKS IN SECRET.
I OWE THIS SPECIAL PLACE A DEBT OF GRATITUDE...
...FOR THE SLIGHT CHANGE IN MY RELATIONSHIP WITH HIM.

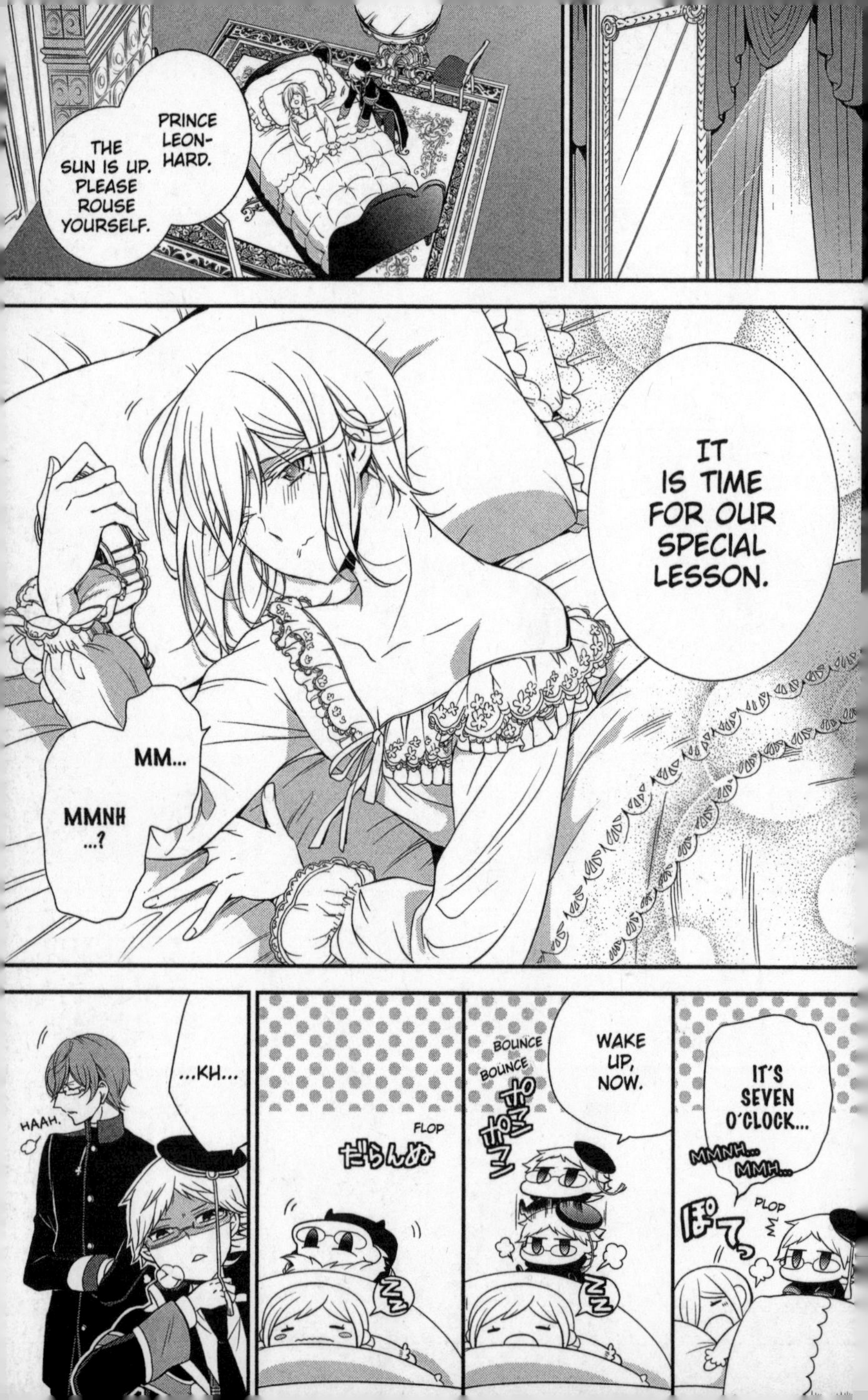
PRINCE LEONHARD.
THE SUN IS UP. PLEASE ROUSE YOURSELF.
IT IS TIME FOR OUR SPECIAL LESSON.
MM...
MMNH ...?
IT'S SEVEN O'CLOCK...
MMNH... MMH...
PLOP
ぽてっ
WAKE UP, NOW.
BOUNCE BOUNCE
ポフポフ
FLOP
だらんぬ
...KH...
HAAH.

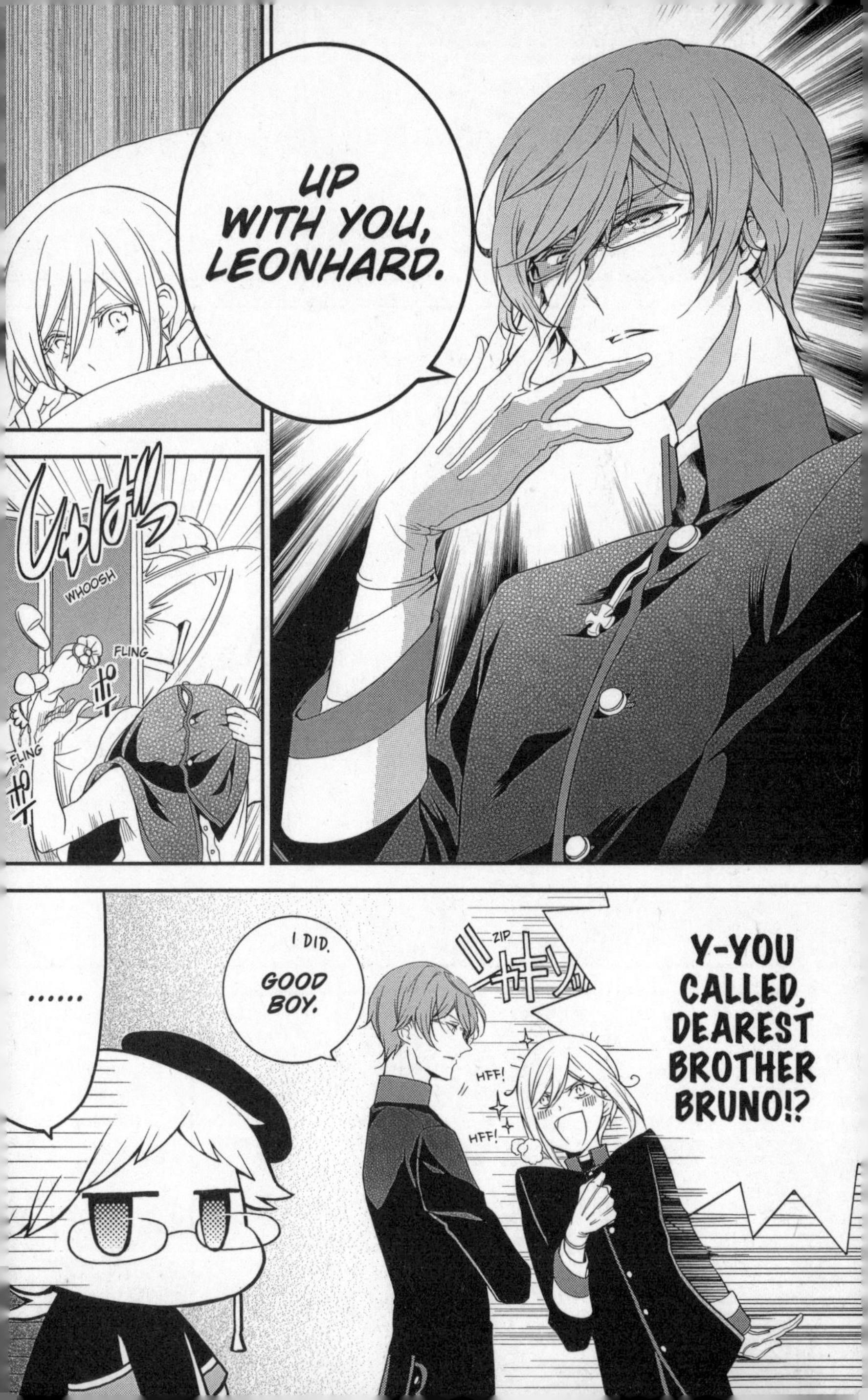
UP WITH YOU, LEONHARD.
WHOOSH
FLING
ポイ
FLING
ポイ
Y-YOU CALLED, DEAREST BROTHER BRUNO!?
ZIP
シャキーン
HFF!
HFF!
I DID.
GOOD BOY.
......

Chapter 22

Assistants to the King

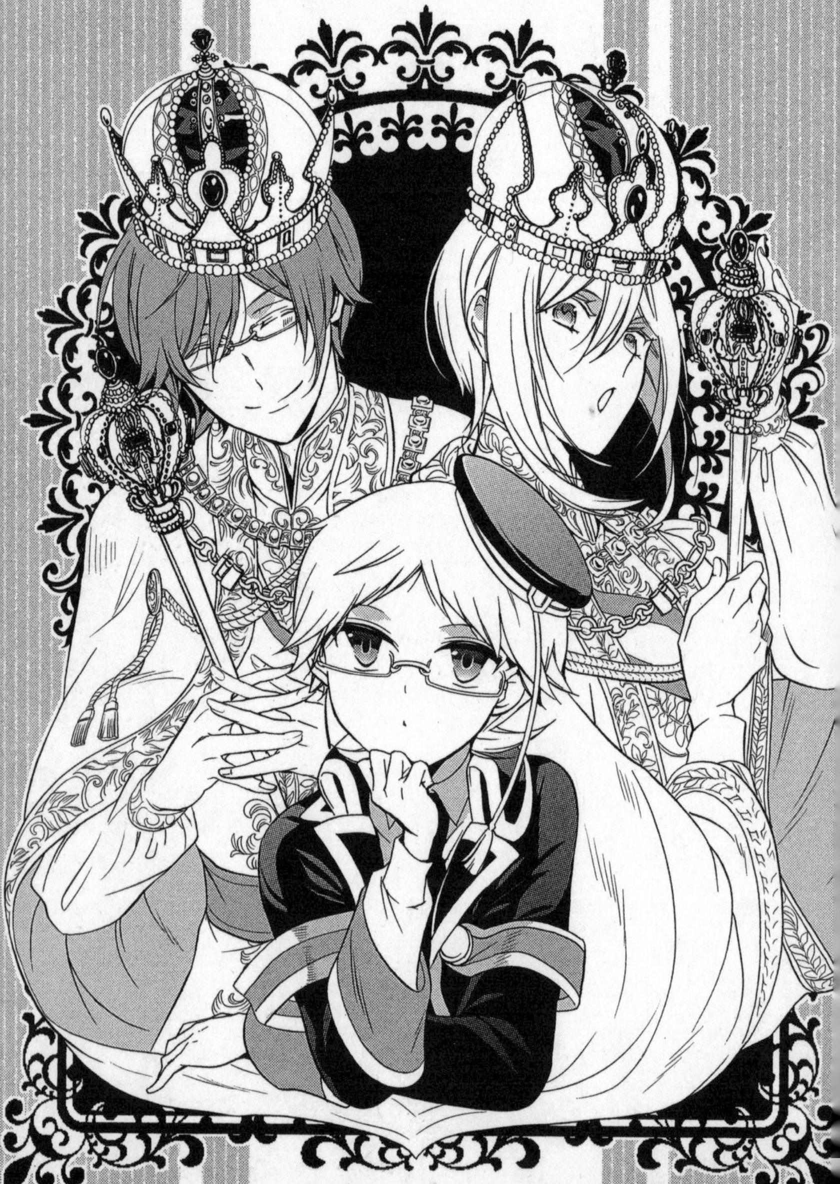

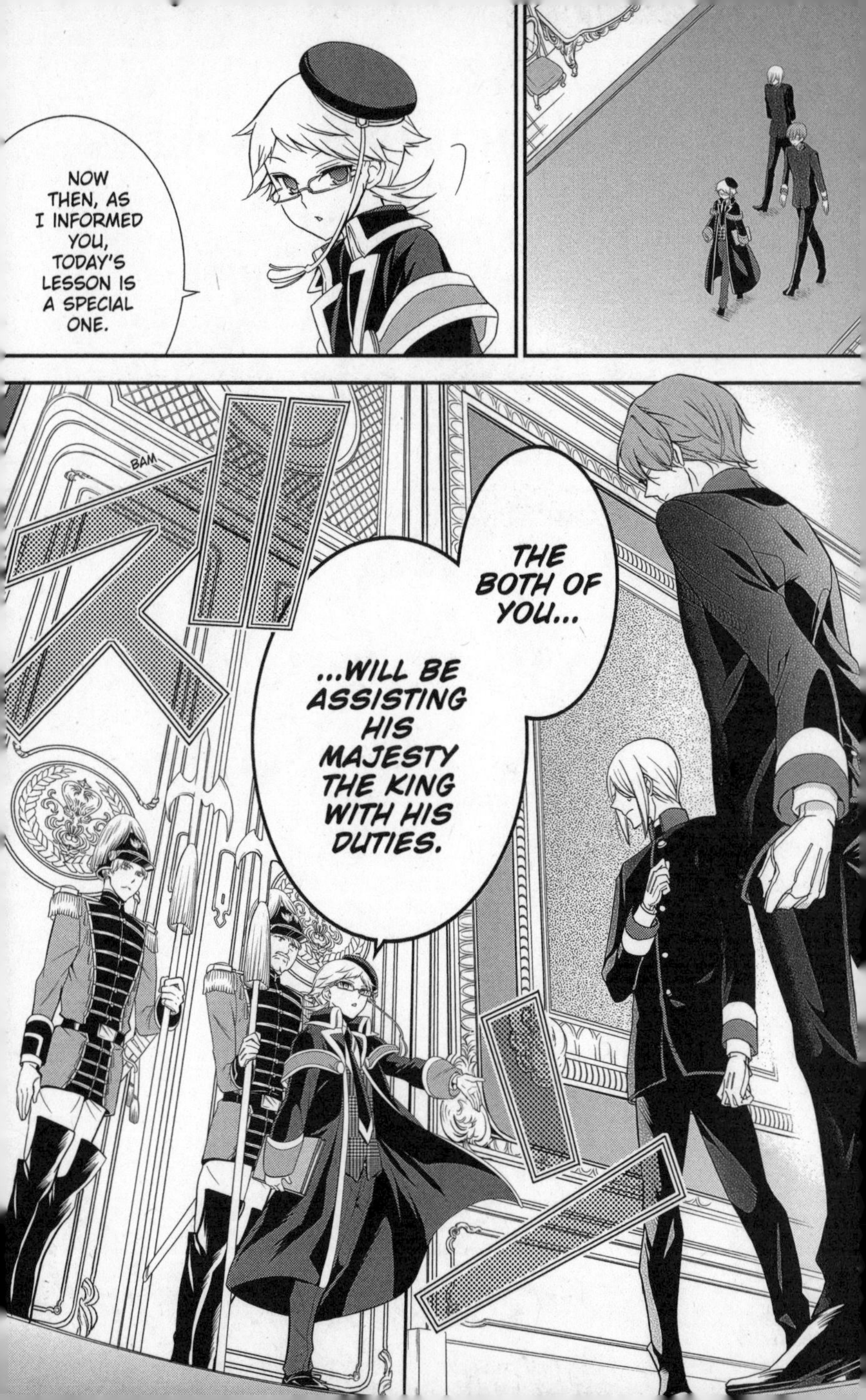
NOW THEN, AS I INFORMED YOU, TODAY'S LESSON IS A SPECIAL ONE.
THE BOTH OF YOU... ...WILL BE ASSISTING HIS MAJESTY THE KING WITH HIS DUTIES.
BAM

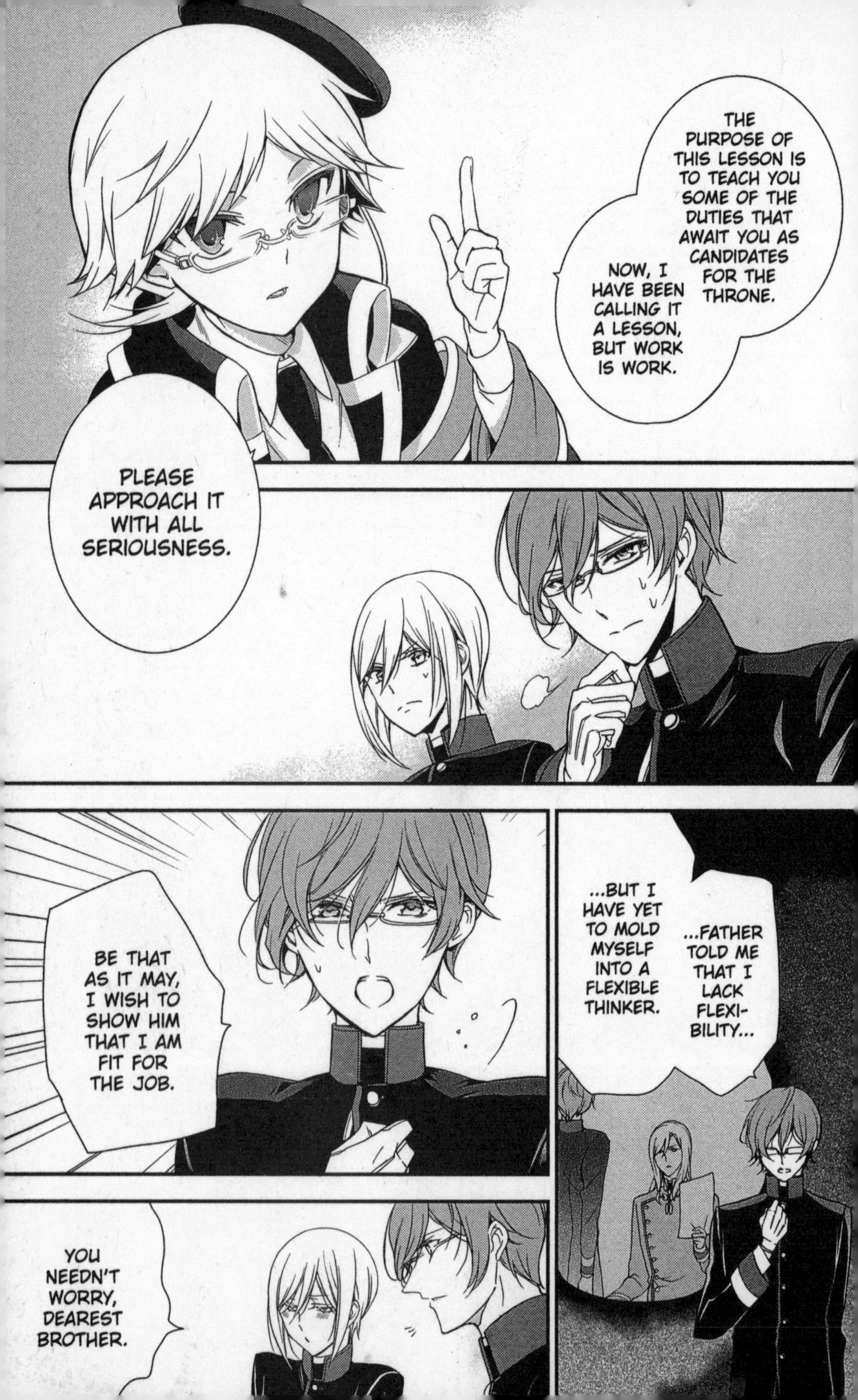
THE PURPOSE OF THIS LESSON IS TO TEACH YOU SOME OF THE DUTIES THAT AWAIT YOU AS CANDIDATES FOR THE THRONE.
NOW, I HAVE BEEN CALLING IT A LESSON, BUT WORK IS WORK.
PLEASE APPROACH IT WITH ALL SERIOUSNESS.
...FATHER TOLD ME THAT I LACK FLEXI-BILITY...
...BUT I HAVE YET TO MOLD MYSELF INTO A FLEXIBLE THINKER.
BE THAT AS IT MAY, I WISH TO SHOW HIM THAT I AM FIT FOR THE JOB.
YOU NEEDN'T WORRY, DEAREST BROTHER.

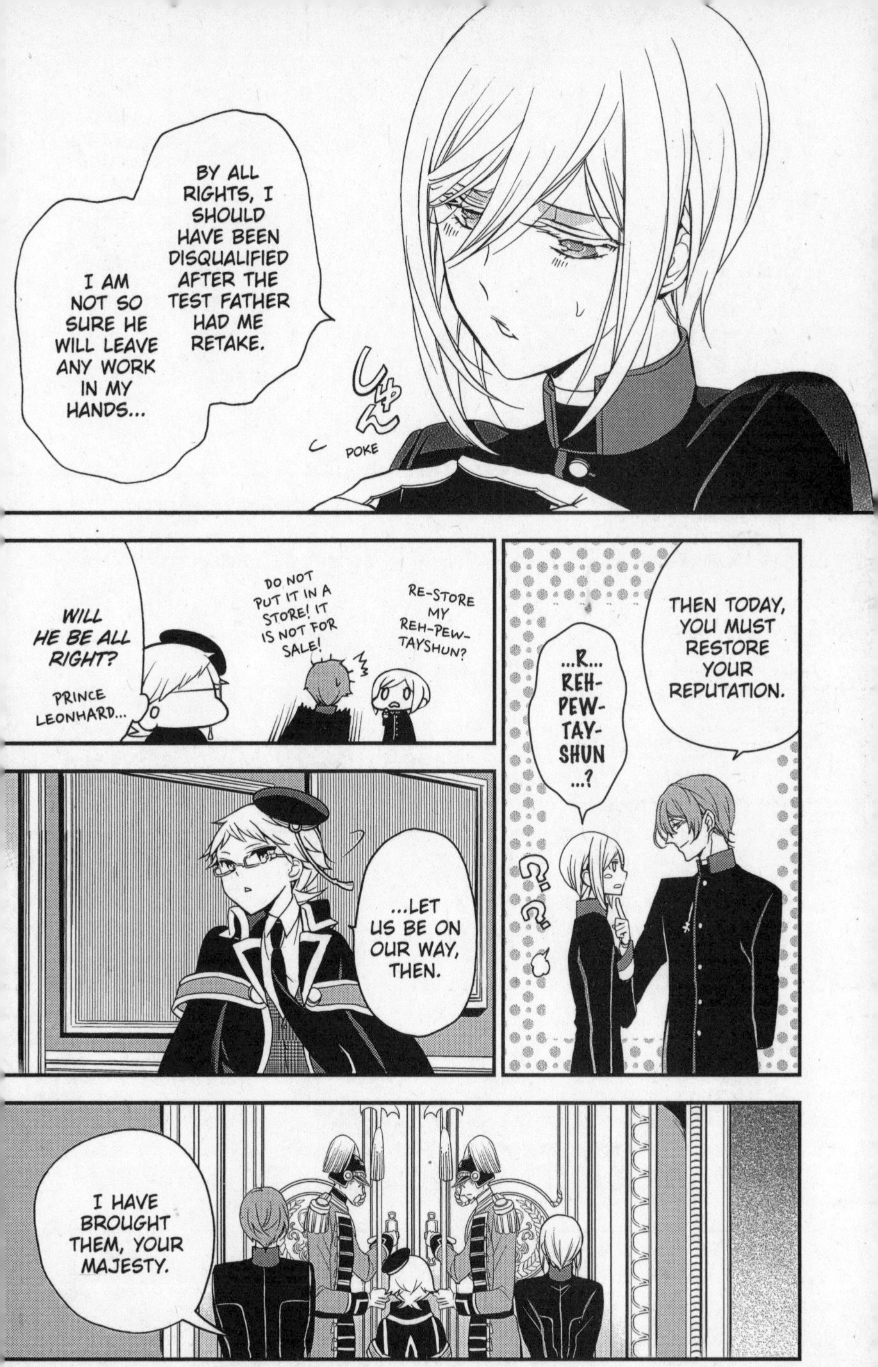
BY ALL RIGHTS, I SHOULD HAVE BEEN DISQUALIFIED AFTER THE TEST FATHER HAD ME RETAKE.
I AM NOT SO SURE HE WILL LEAVE ANY WORK IN MY HANDS...
しゅん
POKE
THEN TODAY, YOU MUST RESTORE YOUR REPUTATION.
...R... REH-PEW-TAY-SHUN...?
RE-STORE MY REH-PEW-TAYSHUN?
DO NOT PUT IT IN A STORE! IT IS NOT FOR SALE!
WILL HE BE ALL RIGHT?
PRINCE LEONHARD...
...LET US BE ON OUR WAY, THEN.
I HAVE BROUGHT THEM, YOUR MAJESTY.

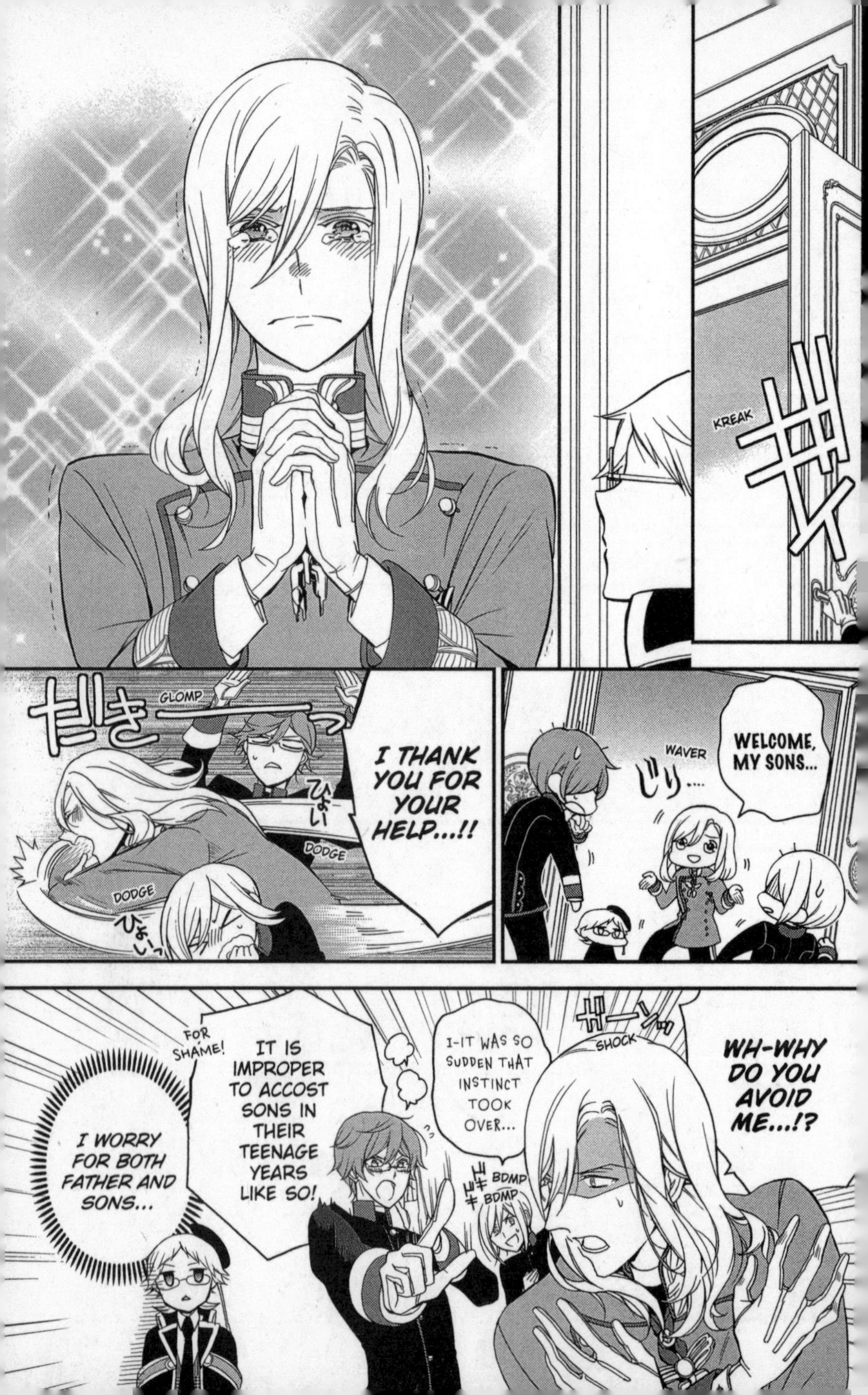
KREAK
WAVER
じり....
WELCOME, MY SONS...
GLOMP
I THANK YOU FOR YOUR HELP...!!
ひょい
DODGE
DODGE
WH-WHY DO YOU AVOID ME...!?
SHOCK
I-IT WAS SO SUDDEN THAT INSTINCT TOOK OVER...
BDMP
BDMP
IT IS IMPROPER TO ACCOST SONS IN THEIR TEENAGE YEARS LIKE SO!
FOR SHAME!
I WORRY FOR BOTH FATHER AND SONS...

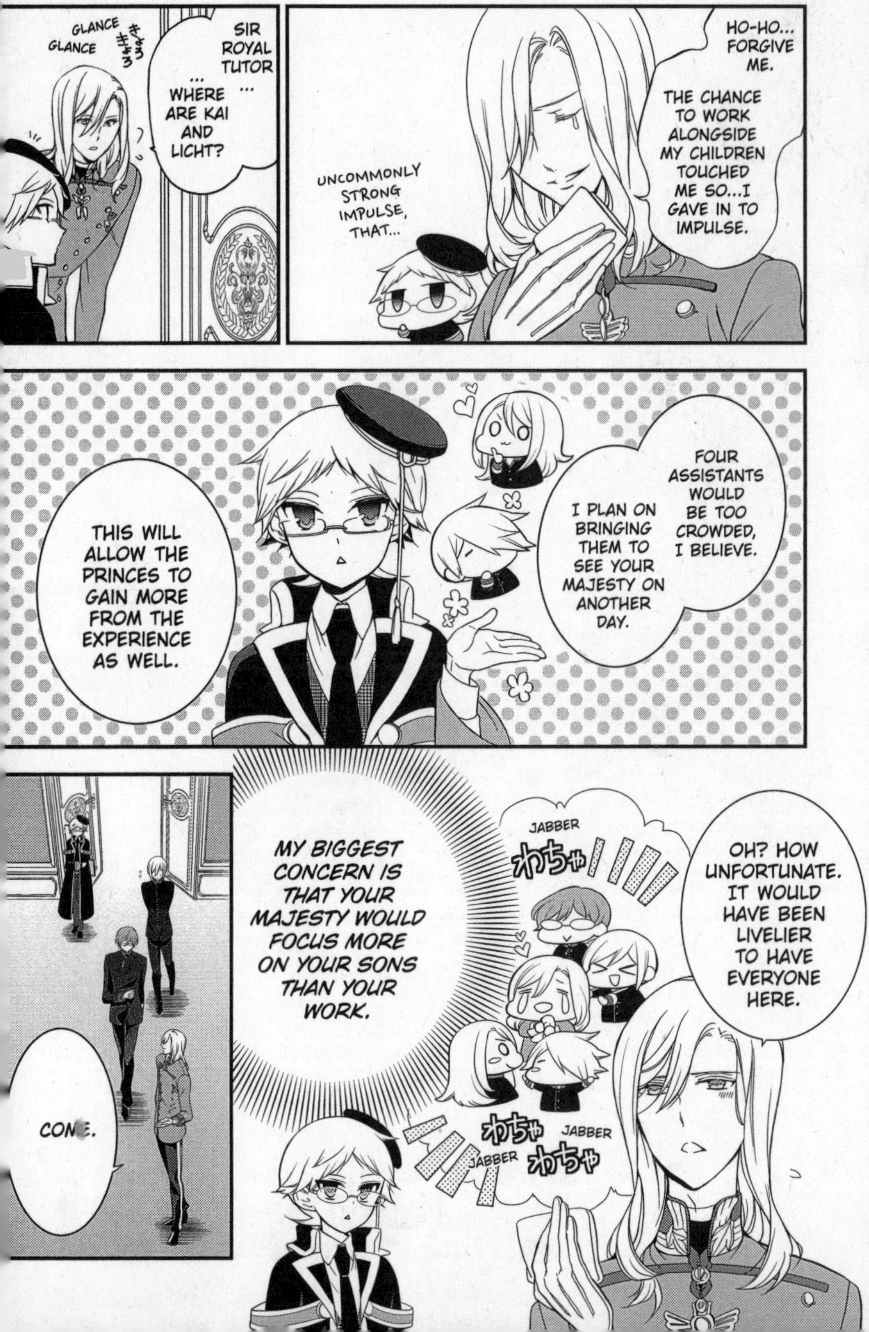
HO-HO... FORGIVE ME.
THE CHANCE TO WORK ALONGSIDE MY CHILDREN TOUCHED ME SO...I GAVE IN TO IMPULSE.
UNCOMMONLY STRONG IMPULSE, THAT...
GLANCE GLANCE
きょろきょろ
SIR ROYAL TUTOR... ...WHERE ARE KAI AND LICHT?
FOUR ASSISTANTS WOULD BE TOO CROWDED, I BELIEVE.
I PLAN ON BRINGING THEM TO SEE YOUR MAJESTY ON ANOTHER DAY.
THIS WILL ALLOW THE PRINCES TO GAIN MORE FROM THE EXPERIENCE AS WELL.
OH? HOW UNFORTUNATE. IT WOULD HAVE BEEN LIVELIER TO HAVE EVERYONE HERE.
JABBER
わちゃ
JABBER
わちゃ
JABBER
わちゃ
MY BIGGEST CONCERN IS THAT YOUR MAJESTY WOULD FOCUS MORE ON YOUR SONS THAN YOUR WORK.
COME.

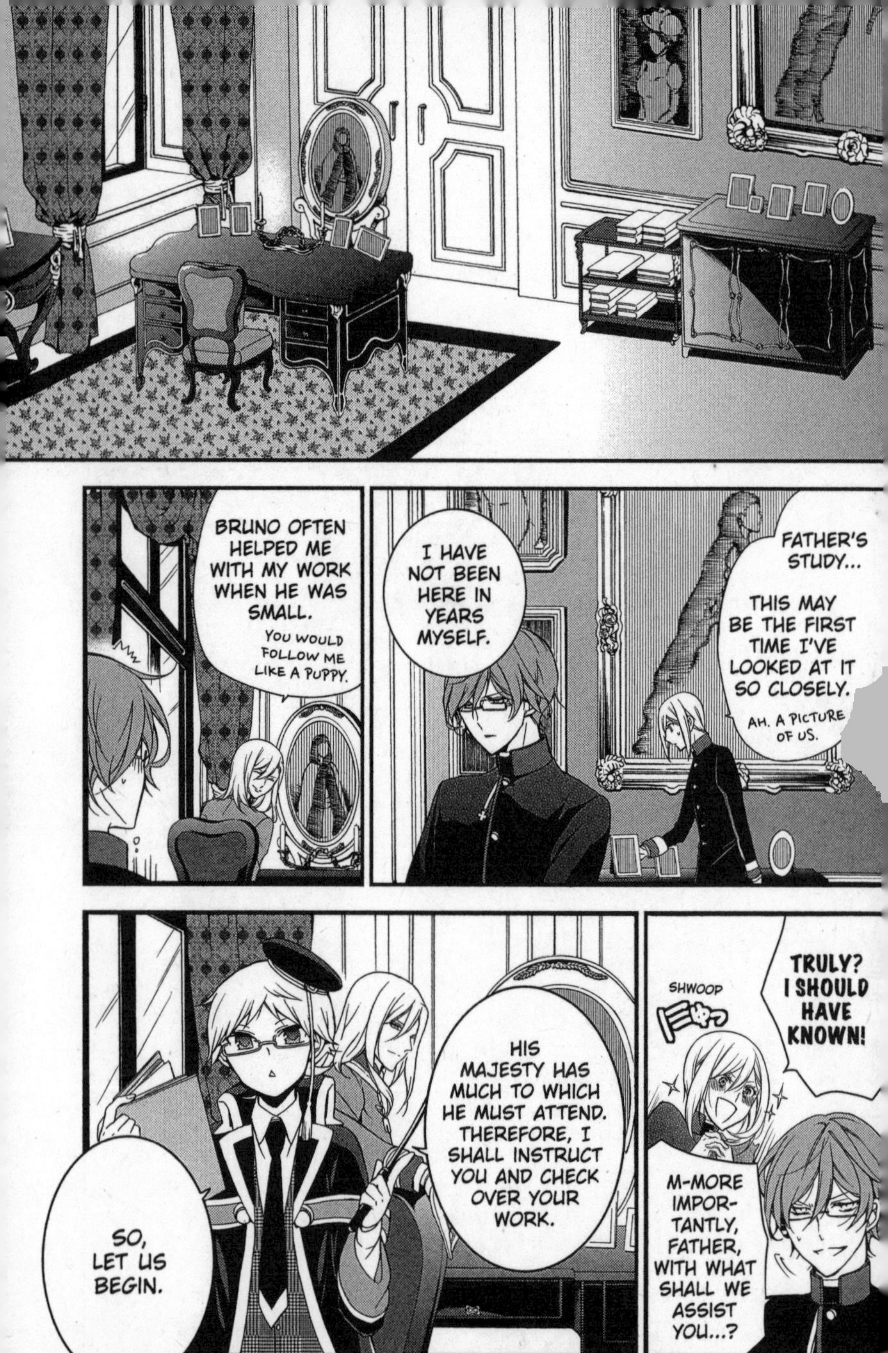
FATHER'S STUDY...
THIS MAY BE THE FIRST TIME I'VE LOOKED AT IT SO CLOSELY.
AH. A PICTURE OF US.
I HAVE NOT BEEN HERE IN YEARS MYSELF.
BRUNO OFTEN HELPED ME WITH MY WORK WHEN HE WAS SMALL.
YOU WOULD FOLLOW ME LIKE A PUPPY.
TRULY? I SHOULD HAVE KNOWN!
SHWOOP
M-MORE IMPOR-TANTLY, FATHER, WITH WHAT SHALL WE ASSIST YOU...?
HIS MAJESTY HAS MUCH TO WHICH HE MUST ATTEND. THEREFORE, I SHALL INSTRUCT YOU AND CHECK OVER YOUR WORK.
SO, LET US BEGIN.

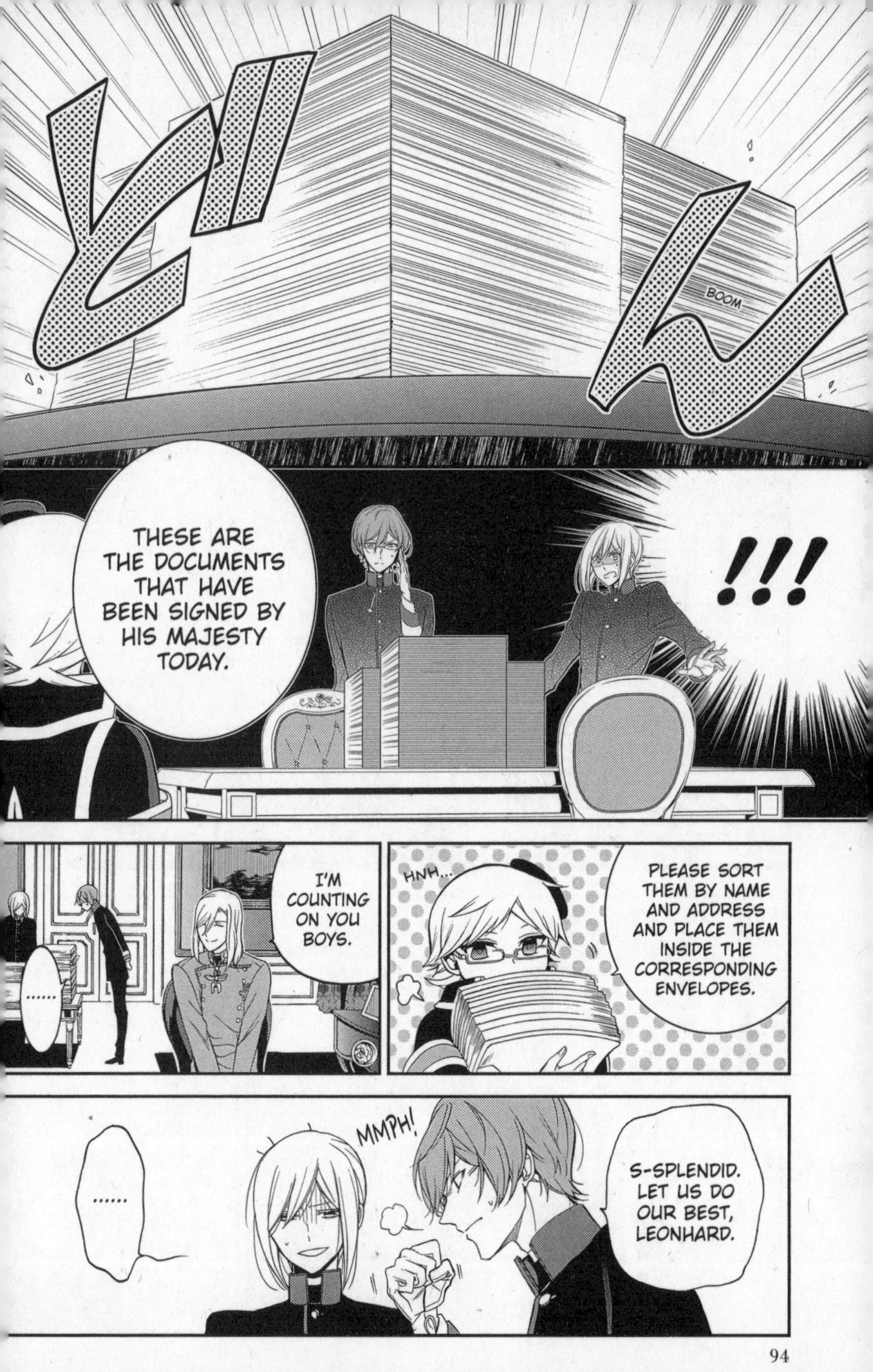
BOOM
!!!
THESE ARE THE DOCUMENTS THAT HAVE BEEN SIGNED BY HIS MAJESTY TODAY.
PLEASE SORT THEM BY NAME AND ADDRESS AND PLACE THEM INSIDE THE CORRESPONDING ENVELOPES.
HNH...
I'M COUNTING ON YOU BOYS.
......
S-SPLENDID. LET US DO OUR BEST, LEONHARD.
MMPH!
......

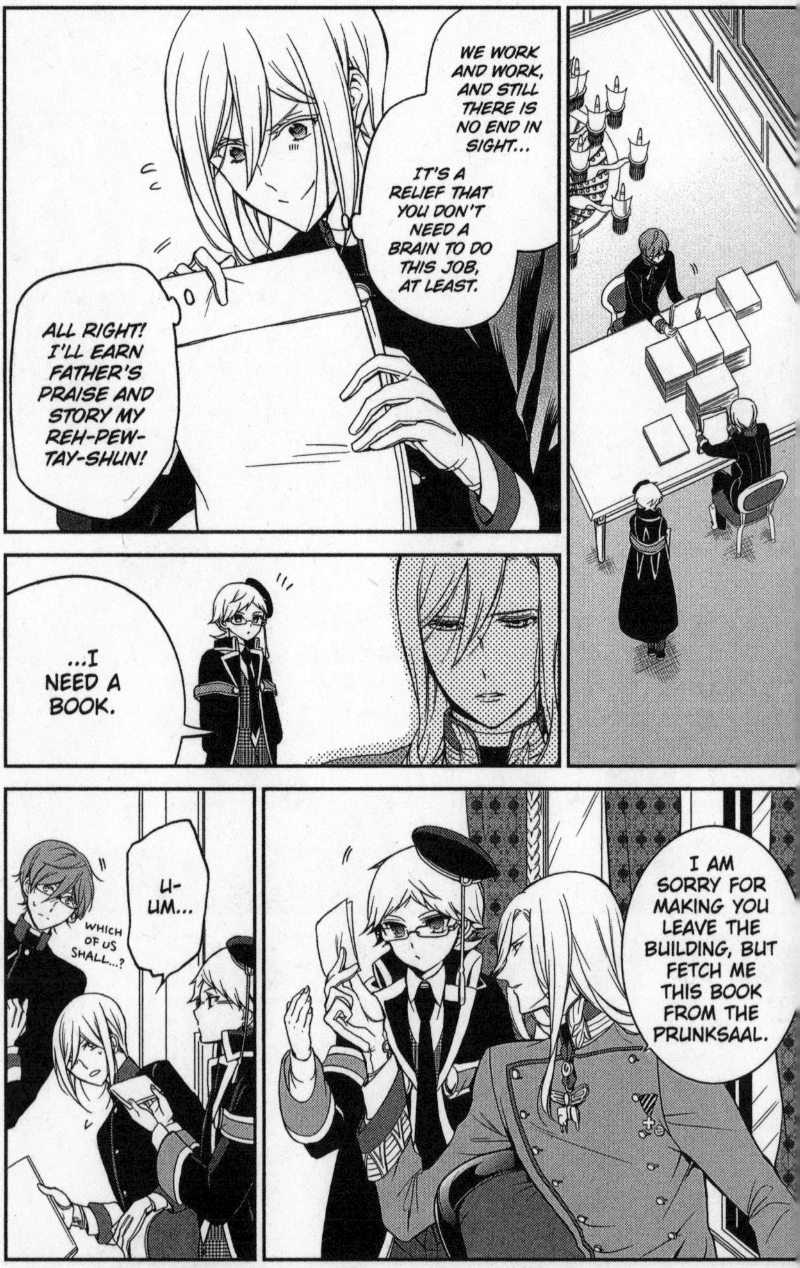
WE WORK AND WORK, AND STILL THERE IS NO END IN SIGHT...
IT'S A RELIEF THAT YOU DON'T NEED A BRAIN TO DO THIS JOB, AT LEAST.
ALL RIGHT! I'LL EARN FATHER'S PRAISE AND STORY MY REH-PEW-TAY-SHUN!
...I NEED A BOOK.
I AM SORRY FOR MAKING YOU LEAVE THE BUILDING, BUT FETCH ME THIS BOOK FROM THE PRUNKSAAL.
U-UM...
WHICH OF US SHALL...?

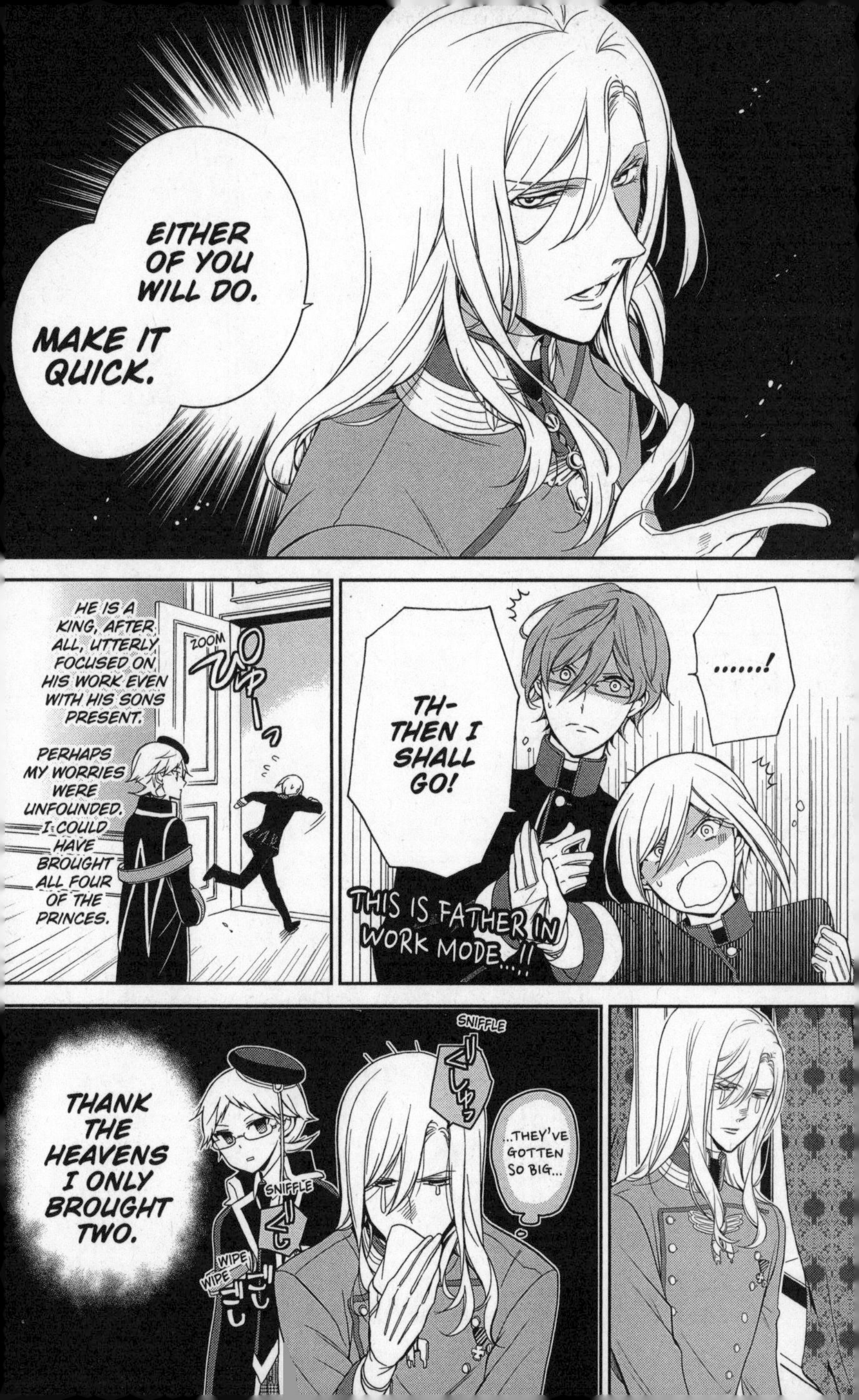
EITHER OF YOU WILL DO.
MAKE IT QUICK.
......!
TH- THEN I SHALL GO!
THIS IS FATHER IN WORK MODE...!!
ZOOM
HE IS A KING, AFTER ALL, UTTERLY FOCUSED ON HIS WORK EVEN WITH HIS SONS PRESENT.
PERHAPS MY WORRIES WERE UNFOUNDED. I COULD HAVE BROUGHT ALL FOUR OF THE PRINCES.
SNIFFLE
...THEY'VE GOTTEN SO BIG...
THANK THE HEAVENS I ONLY BROUGHT TWO.
SNIFFLE
WIPE
WIPE

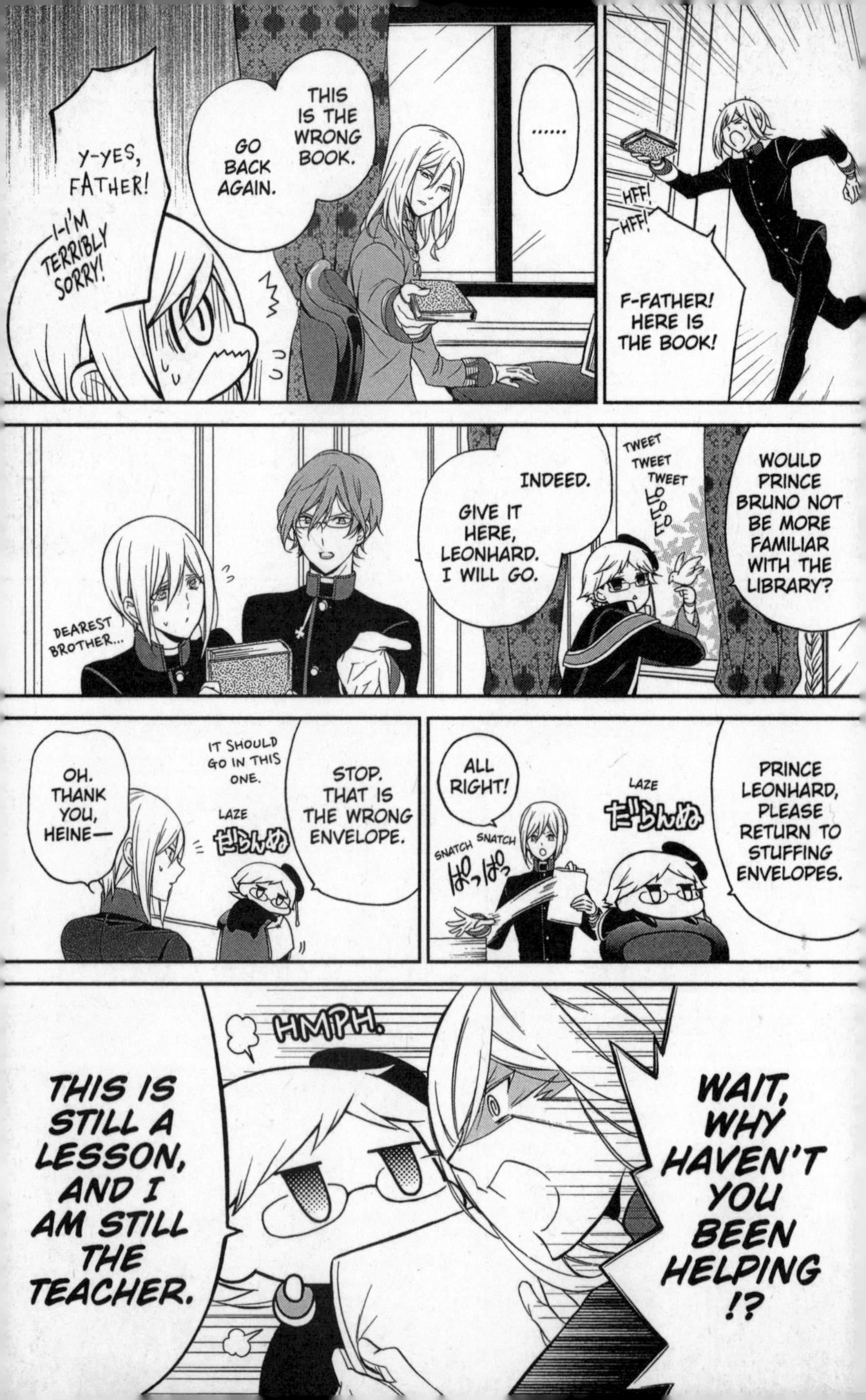
HFF! HFF!
F-FATHER! HERE IS THE BOOK!
......
THIS IS THE WRONG BOOK.
GO BACK AGAIN.
Y-YES, FATHER!
I-I'M TERRIBLY SORRY!
WOULD PRINCE BRUNO NOT BE MORE FAMILIAR WITH THE LIBRARY?
TWEET TWEET TWEET
ピピピ
INDEED.
GIVE IT HERE, LEONHARD. I WILL GO.
DEAREST BROTHER...
PRINCE LEONHARD, PLEASE RETURN TO STUFFING ENVELOPES.
LAZE
だらんぬ
ALL RIGHT!
SNATCH SNATCH
ぱっぱっ
STOP. THAT IS THE WRONG ENVELOPE.
IT SHOULD GO IN THIS ONE.
LAZE
だらんぬ
OH. THANK YOU, HEINE—
WAIT, WHY HAVEN'T YOU BEEN HELPING!?
HMPH.
THIS IS STILL A LESSON, AND I AM STILL THE TEACHER.

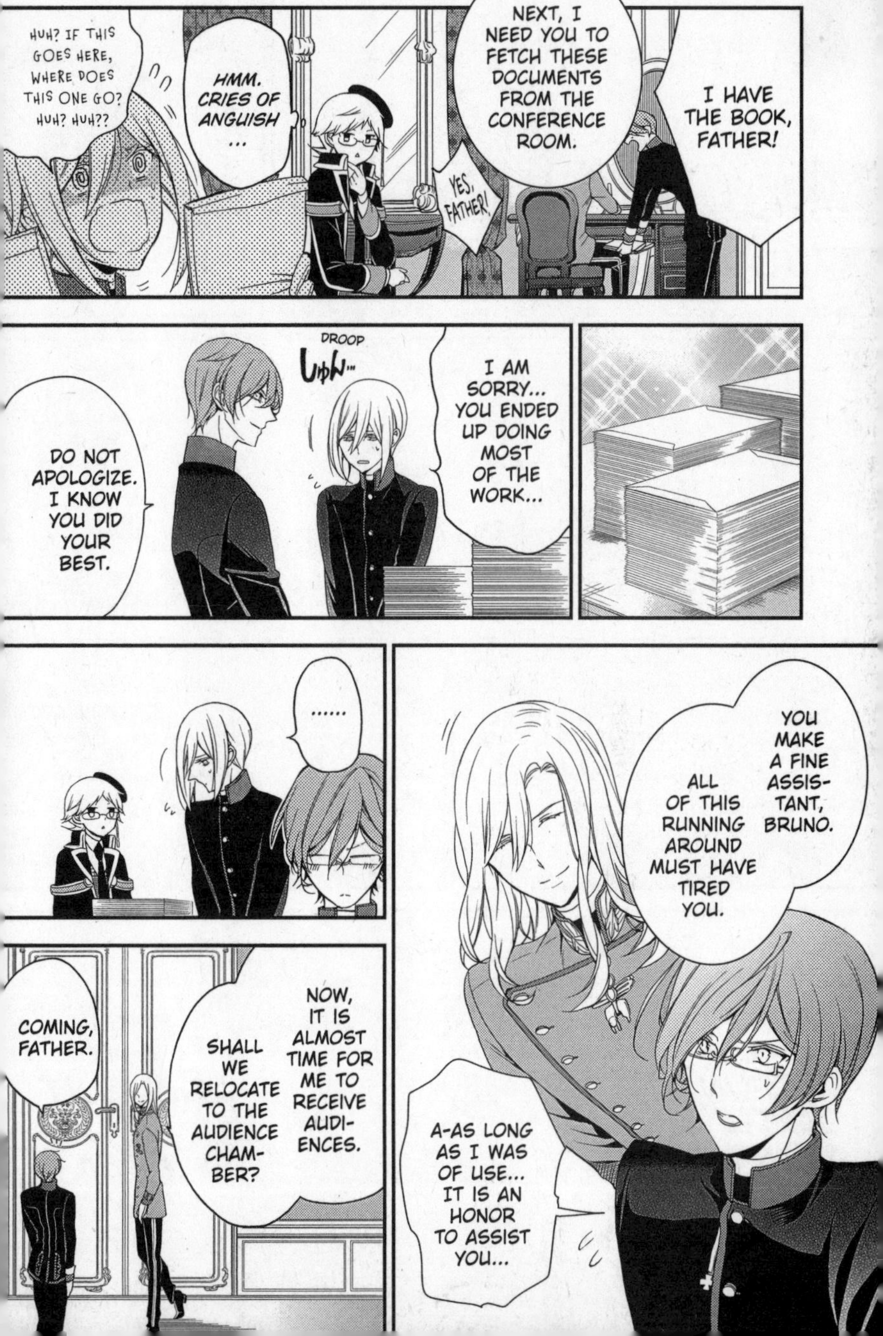
I HAVE THE BOOK, FATHER!
NEXT, I NEED YOU TO FETCH THESE DOCUMENTS FROM THE CONFERENCE ROOM.
YES, FATHER!
HMM. CRIES OF ANGUISH ...
HUH? IF THIS GOES HERE, WHERE DOES THIS ONE GO? HUH? HUH??
I AM SORRY... YOU ENDED UP DOING MOST OF THE WORK...
DROOP
しゅん…
DO NOT APOLOGIZE. I KNOW YOU DID YOUR BEST.
YOU MAKE A FINE ASSIS-TANT, BRUNO.
ALL OF THIS RUNNING AROUND MUST HAVE TIRED YOU.
A-AS LONG AS I WAS OF USE... IT IS AN HONOR TO ASSIST YOU...
......
NOW, IT IS ALMOST TIME FOR ME TO RECEIVE AUDI-ENCES.
SHALL WE RELOCATE TO THE AUDIENCE CHAM-BER?
COMING, FATHER.

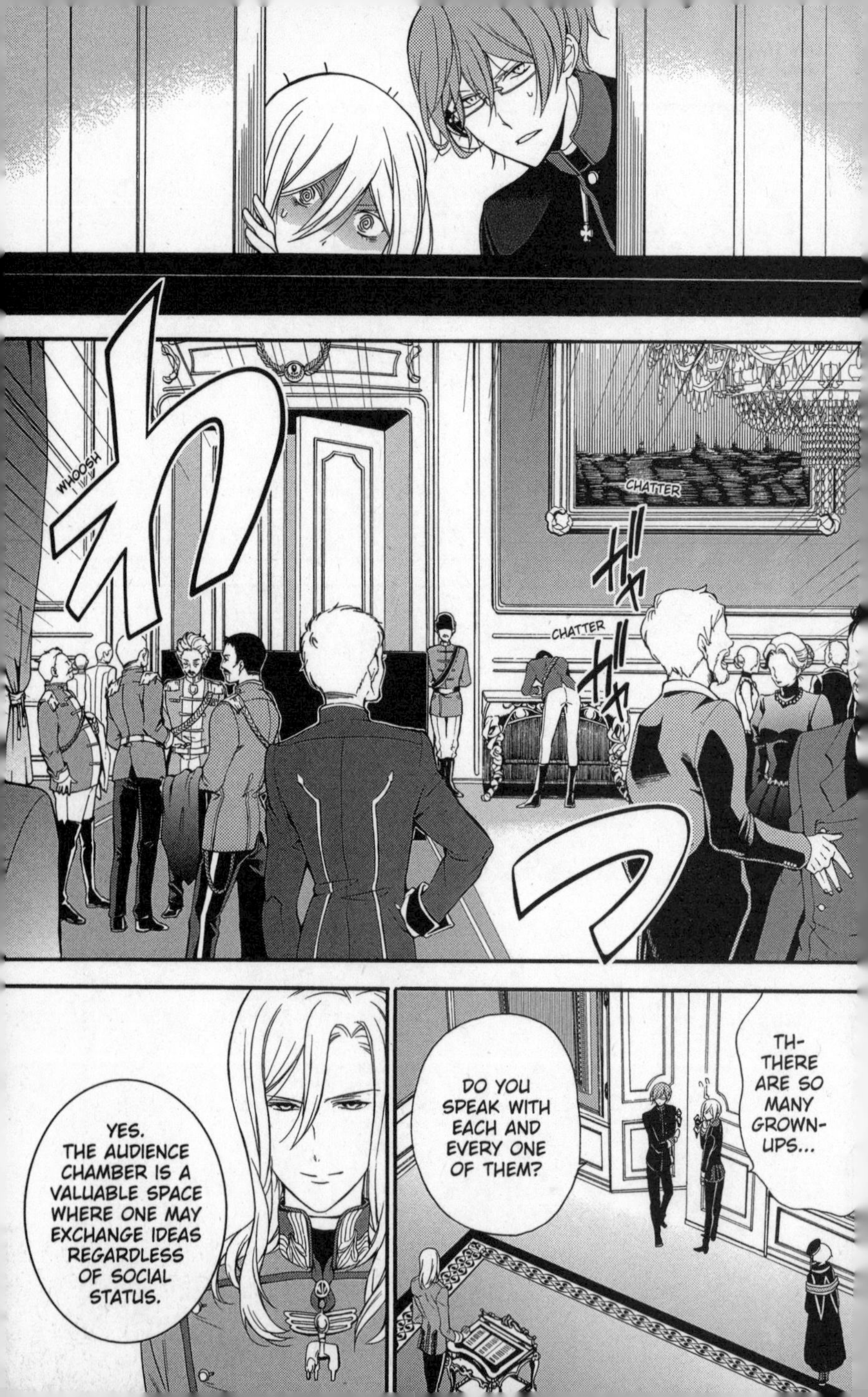
CHATTER
CHATTER
ガヤ
ガヤ
WHOOSH
TH- THERE ARE SO MANY GROWN-UPS...
DO YOU SPEAK WITH EACH AND EVERY ONE OF THEM?
YES. THE AUDIENCE CHAMBER IS A VALUABLE SPACE WHERE ONE MAY EXCHANGE IDEAS REGARDLESS OF SOCIAL STATUS.

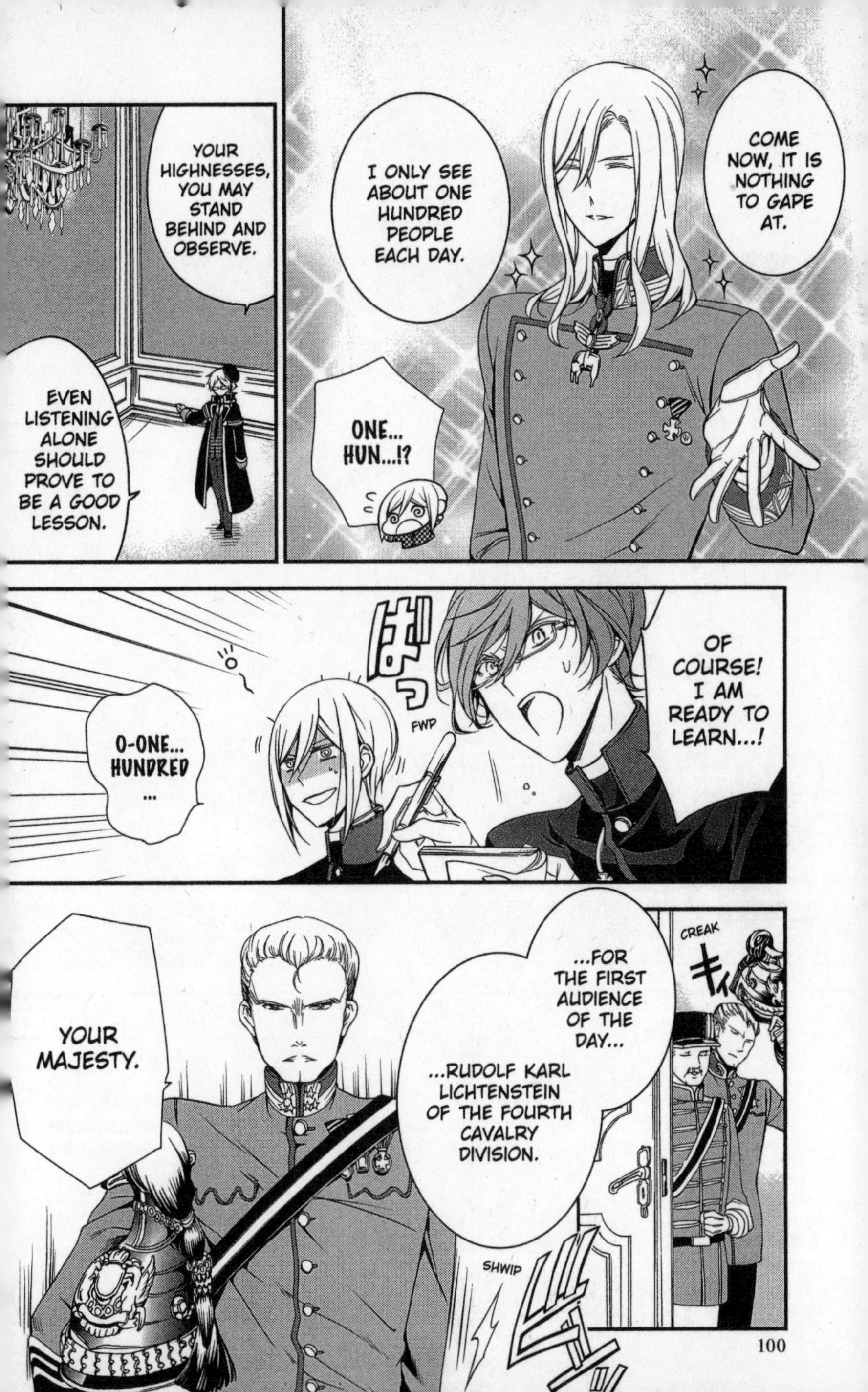
COME NOW, IT IS NOTHING TO GAPE AT.
I ONLY SEE ABOUT ONE HUNDRED PEOPLE EACH DAY.
ONE... HUN...!?
YOUR HIGHNESSES, YOU MAY STAND BEHIND AND OBSERVE.
EVEN LISTENING ALONE SHOULD PROVE TO BE A GOOD LESSON.
OF COURSE! I AM READY TO LEARN...!
ぱっ
FWP
O-ONE... HUNDRED ...
CREAK
キィ
...FOR THE FIRST AUDIENCE OF THE DAY...
...RUDOLF KARL LICHTENSTEIN OF THE FOURTH CAVALRY DIVISION.
SHWIP
YOUR MAJESTY.

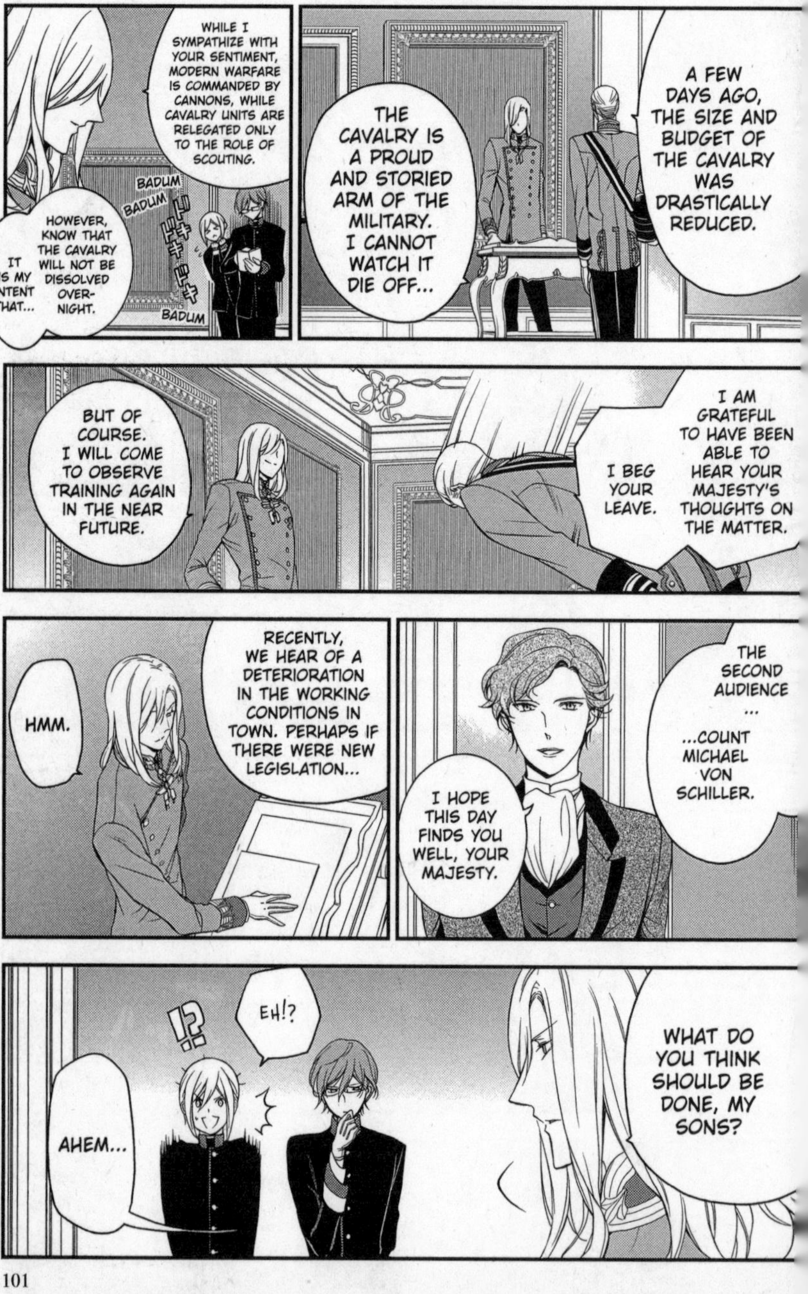
A FEW DAYS AGO, THE SIZE AND BUDGET OF THE CAVALRY WAS DRASTICALLY REDUCED.
THE CAVALRY IS A PROUD AND STORIED ARM OF THE MILITARY. I CANNOT WATCH IT DIE OFF...
WHILE I SYMPATHIZE WITH YOUR SENTIMENT, MODERN WARFARE IS COMMANDED BY CANNONS, WHILE CAVALRY UNITS ARE RELEGATED ONLY TO THE ROLE OF SCOUTING.
BADUM BADUM
BADUM
HOWEVER, KNOW THAT THE CAVALRY WILL NOT BE DISSOLVED OVER-NIGHT.
IT IS MY INTENT THAT...
I AM GRATEFUL TO HAVE BEEN ABLE TO HEAR YOUR MAJESTY'S THOUGHTS ON THE MATTER.
I BEG YOUR LEAVE.
BUT OF COURSE. I WILL COME TO OBSERVE TRAINING AGAIN IN THE NEAR FUTURE.
THE SECOND AUDIENCE ...
...COUNT MICHAEL VON SCHILLER.
I HOPE THIS DAY FINDS YOU WELL, YOUR MAJESTY.
RECENTLY, WE HEAR OF A DETERIORATION IN THE WORKING CONDITIONS IN TOWN. PERHAPS IF THERE WERE NEW LEGISLATION...
HMM.
WHAT DO YOU THINK SHOULD BE DONE, MY SONS?
EH!?
!?
AHEM...

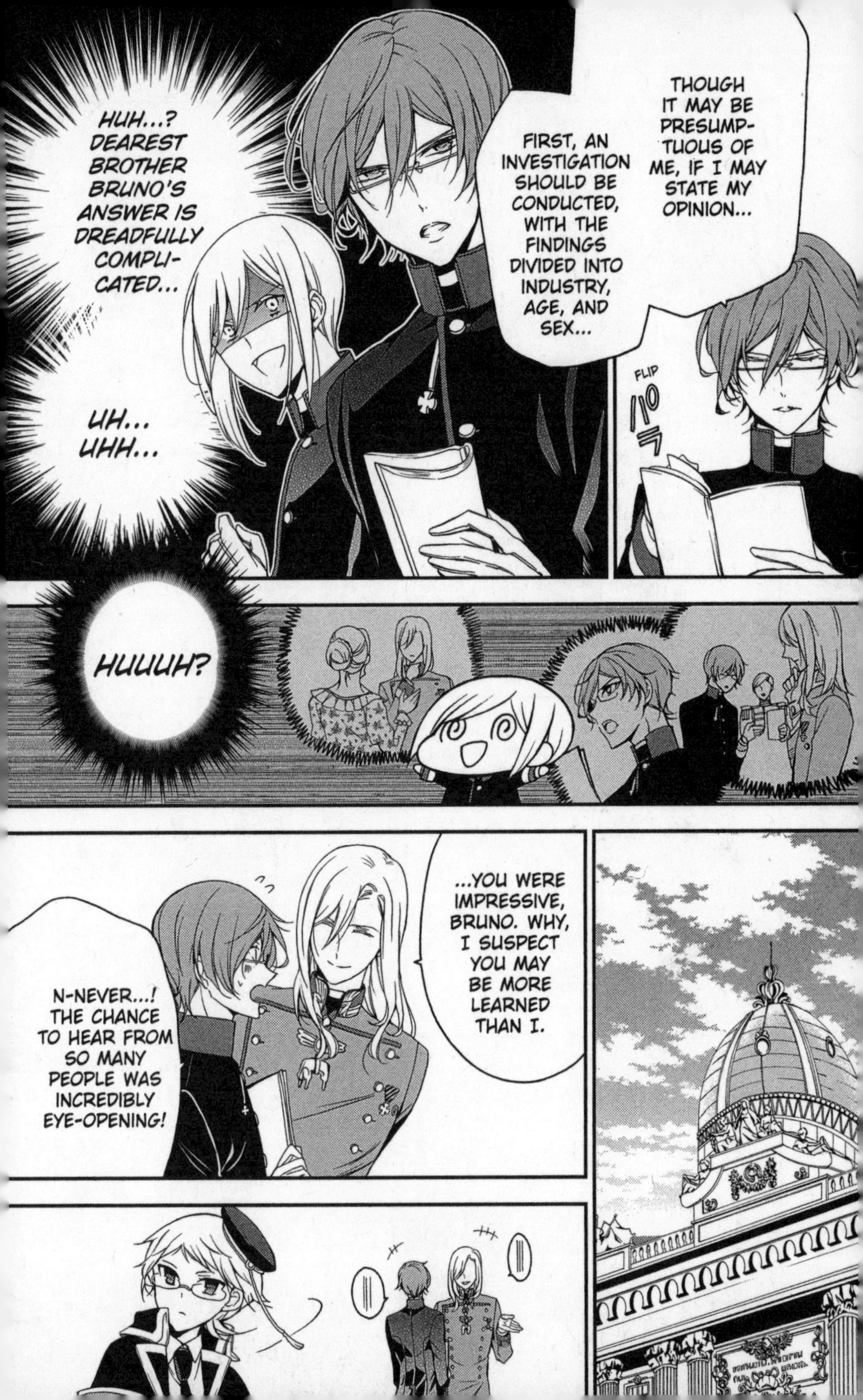
THOUGH IT MAY BE PRESUMPTUOUS OF ME, IF I MAY STATE MY OPINION...
FLIP
FIRST, AN INVESTIGATION SHOULD BE CONDUCTED, WITH THE FINDINGS DIVIDED INTO INDUSTRY, AGE, AND SEX...
HUH...? DEAREST BROTHER BRUNO'S ANSWER IS DREADFULLY COMPLICATED...
UH... UHH...
HUUUH?
...YOU WERE IMPRESSIVE, BRUNO. WHY, I SUSPECT YOU MAY BE MORE LEARNED THAN I.
N-NEVER...! THE CHANCE TO HEAR FROM SO MANY PEOPLE WAS INCREDIBLY EYE-OPENING!

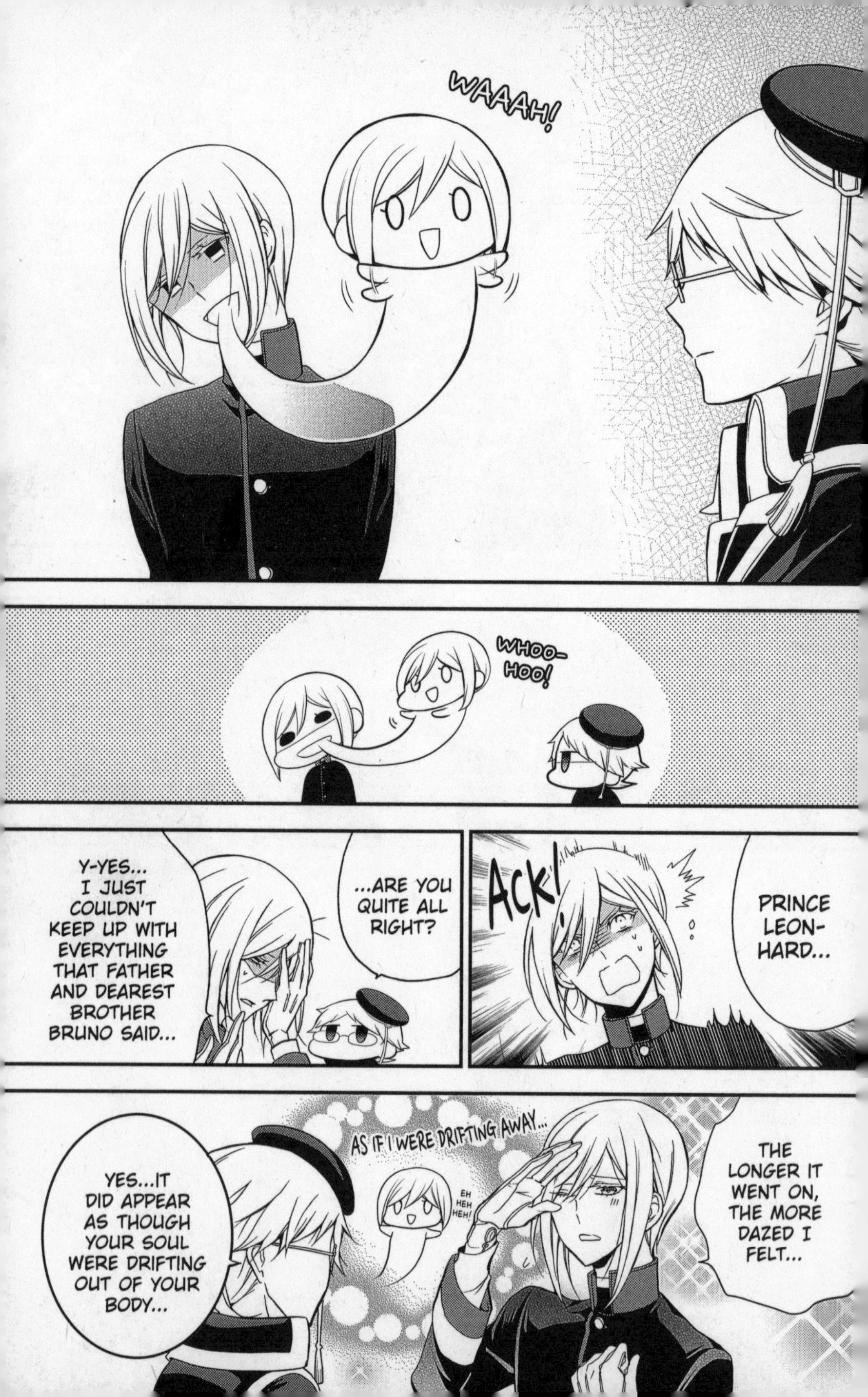
WAAAH!
WHOO-HOO!
PRINCE LEON-HARD...
ACK!
...ARE YOU QUITE ALL RIGHT?
Y-YES... I JUST COULDN'T KEEP UP WITH EVERYTHING THAT FATHER AND DEAREST BROTHER BRUNO SAID...
THE LONGER IT WENT ON, THE MORE DAZED I FELT...
AS IF I WERE DRIFTING AWAY...
EH HEH HEH!
YES...IT DID APPEAR AS THOUGH YOUR SOUL WERE DRIFTING OUT OF YOUR BODY...

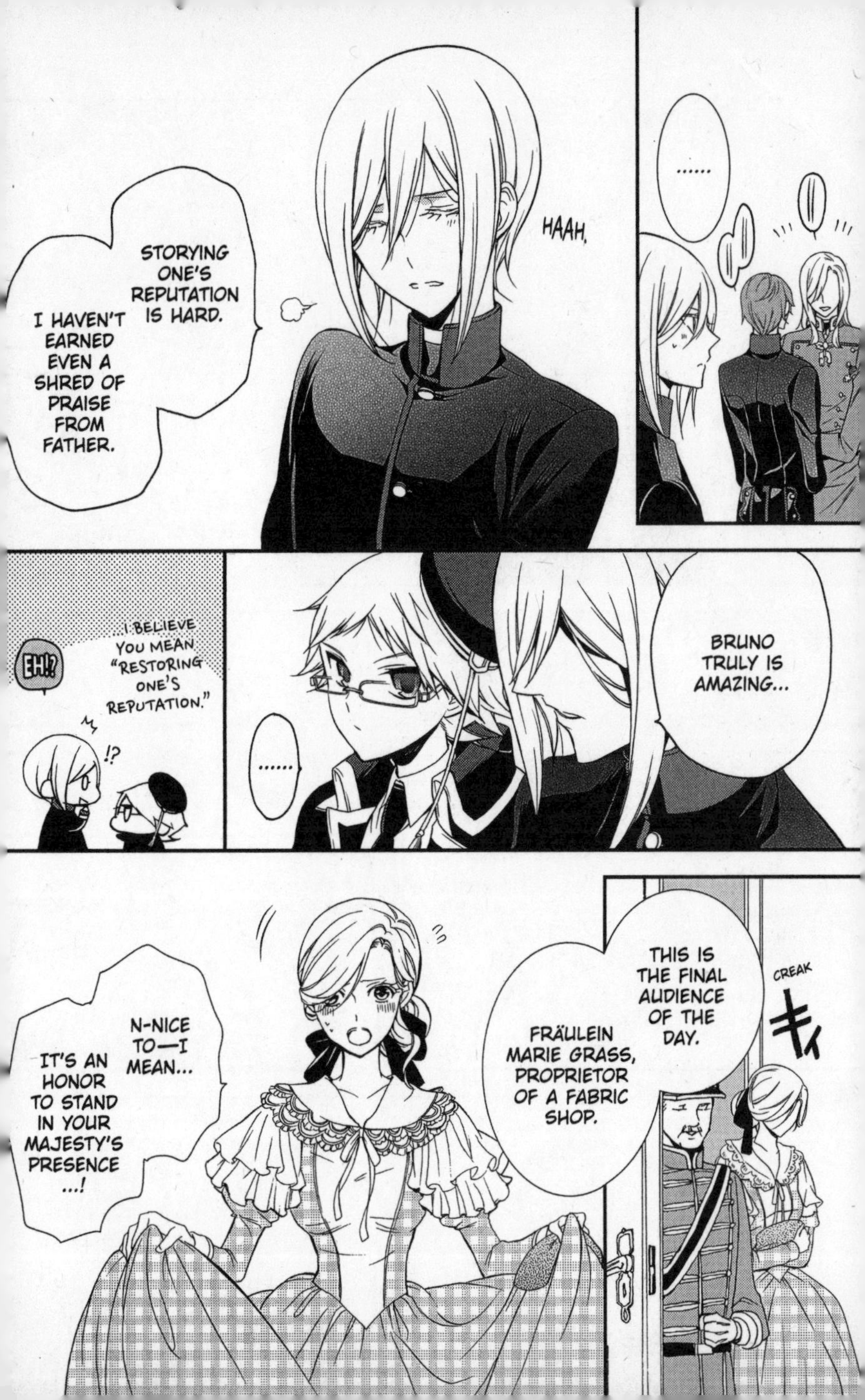
......
!
STORYING ONE'S REPUTATION IS HARD.
I HAVEN'T EARNED EVEN A SHRED OF PRAISE FROM FATHER.
HAAH
BRUNO TRULY IS AMAZING...
......
I BELIEVE YOU MEAN "RESTORING ONE'S REPUTATION."
EH!?
!?
CREAK
キィ
THIS IS THE FINAL AUDIENCE OF THE DAY.
FRÄULEIN MARIE GRASS, PROPRIETOR OF A FABRIC SHOP.
N-NICE TO—I MEAN...
IT'S AN HONOR TO STAND IN YOUR MAJESTY'S PRESENCE...!

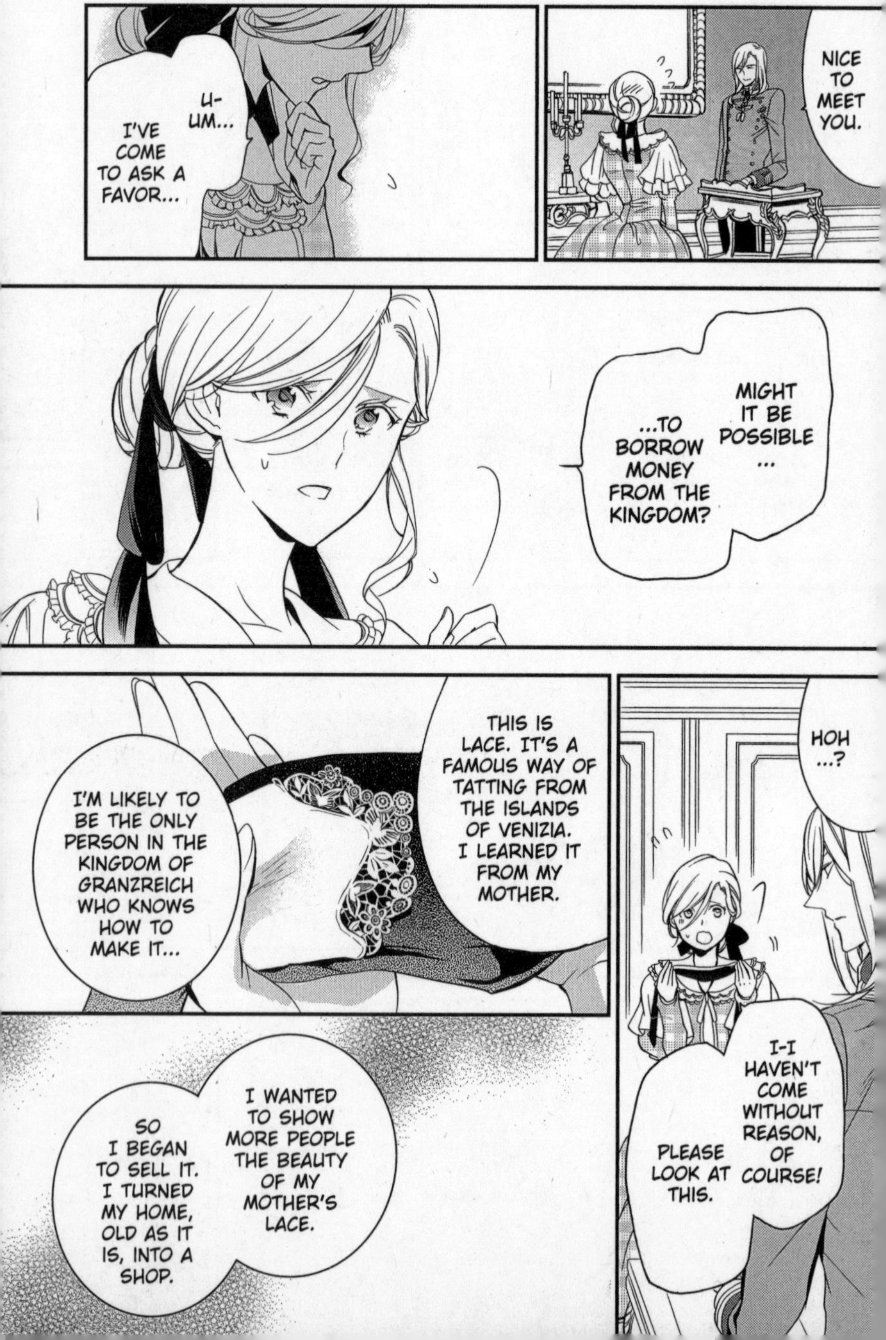
NICE TO MEET YOU.
U-UM...
I'VE COME TO ASK A FAVOR...
MIGHT IT BE POSSIBLE ...
...TO BORROW MONEY FROM THE KINGDOM?
HOH ...?
I-I HAVEN'T COME WITHOUT REASON, OF COURSE!
PLEASE LOOK AT THIS.
THIS IS LACE. IT'S A FAMOUS WAY OF TATTING FROM THE ISLANDS OF VENIZIA. I LEARNED IT FROM MY MOTHER.
I'M LIKELY TO BE THE ONLY PERSON IN THE KINGDOM OF GRANZREICH WHO KNOWS HOW TO MAKE IT...
I WANTED TO SHOW MORE PEOPLE THE BEAUTY OF MY MOTHER'S LACE.
SO I BEGAN TO SELL IT. I TURNED MY HOME, OLD AS IT IS, INTO A SHOP.

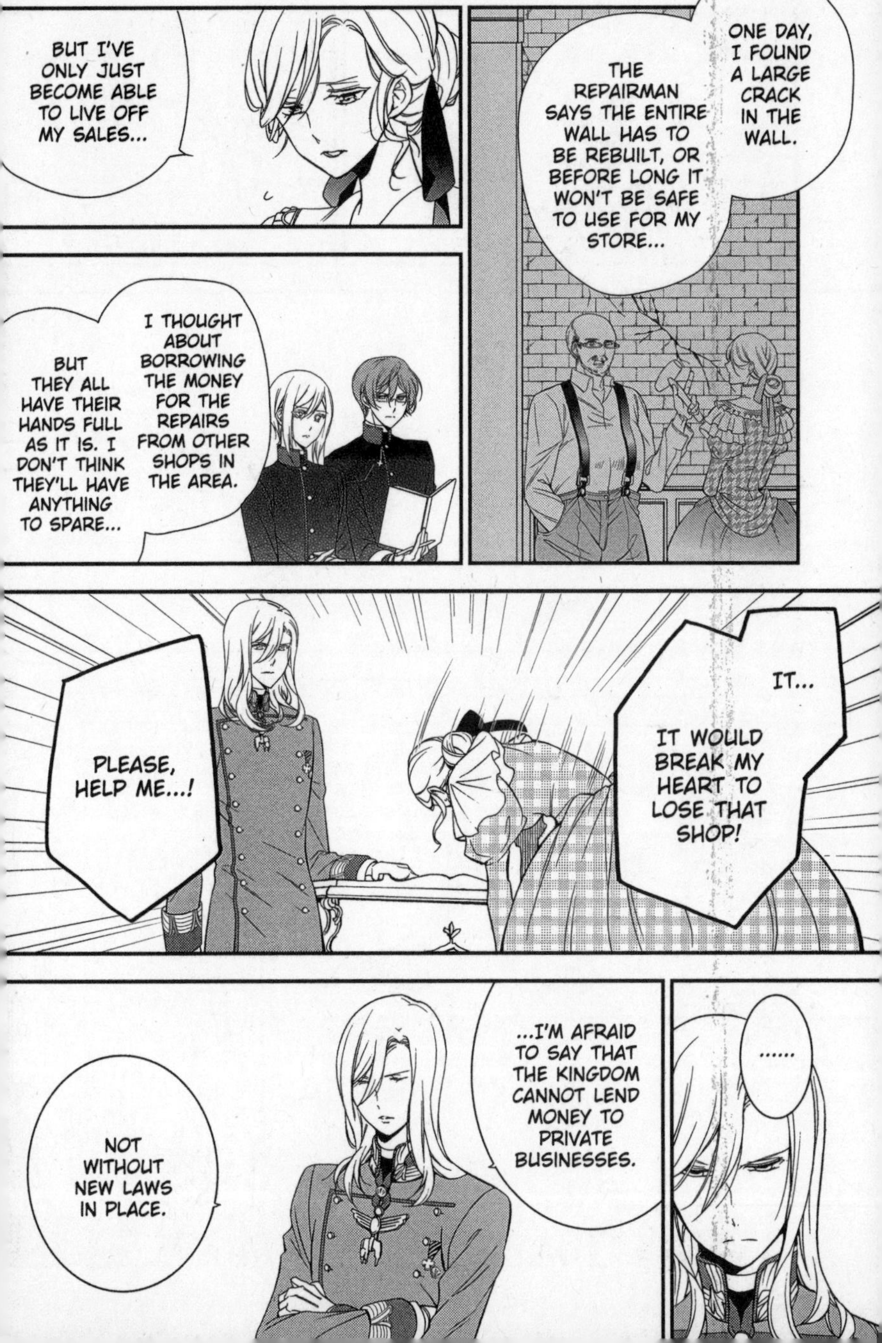

ONE DAY, I FOUND A LARGE CRACK IN THE WALL.
THE REPAIRMAN SAYS THE ENTIRE WALL HAS TO BE REBUILT, OR BEFORE LONG IT WON'T BE SAFE TO USE FOR MY STORE...
BUT I'VE ONLY JUST BECOME ABLE TO LIVE OFF MY SALES...
I THOUGHT ABOUT BORROWING THE MONEY FOR THE REPAIRS FROM OTHER SHOPS IN THE AREA.
BUT THEY ALL HAVE THEIR HANDS FULL AS IT IS. I DON'T THINK THEY'LL HAVE ANYTHING TO SPARE...
IT...
IT WOULD BREAK MY HEART TO LOSE THAT SHOP!
PLEASE, HELP ME...!
......
...I'M AFRAID TO SAY THAT THE KINGDOM CANNOT LEND MONEY TO PRIVATE BUSINESSES.
NOT WITHOUT NEW LAWS IN PLACE.

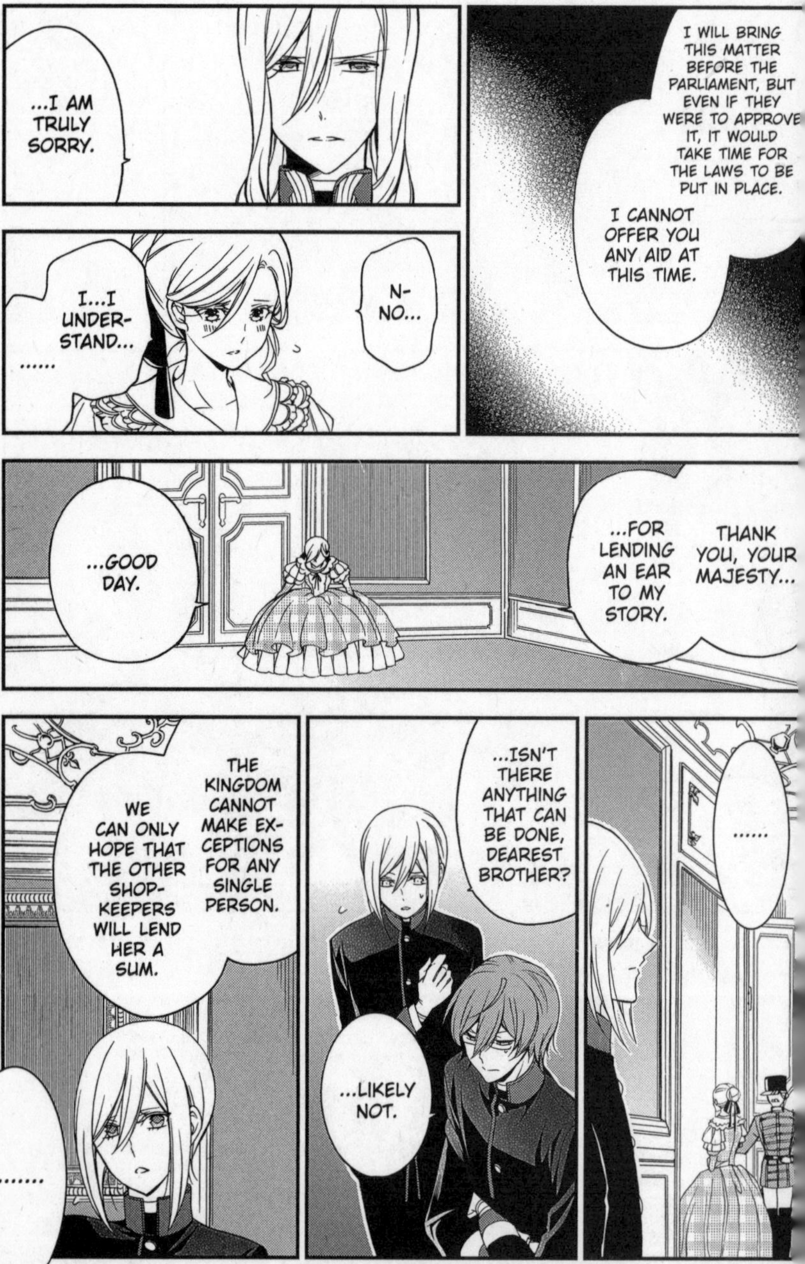
I WILL BRING THIS MATTER BEFORE THE PARLIAMENT, BUT EVEN IF THEY WERE TO APPROVE IT, IT WOULD TAKE TIME FOR THE LAWS TO BE PUT IN PLACE.
I CANNOT OFFER YOU ANY AID AT THIS TIME.
...I AM TRULY SORRY.
N-NO...
I...I UNDERSTAND...
......
THANK YOU, YOUR MAJESTY...
...FOR LENDING AN EAR TO MY STORY.
...GOOD DAY.
......
...ISN'T THERE ANYTHING THAT CAN BE DONE, DEAREST BROTHER?
...LIKELY NOT.
THE KINGDOM CANNOT MAKE EXCEPTIONS FOR ANY SINGLE PERSON.
WE CAN ONLY HOPE THAT THE OTHER SHOP-KEEPERS WILL LEND HER A SUM.
....

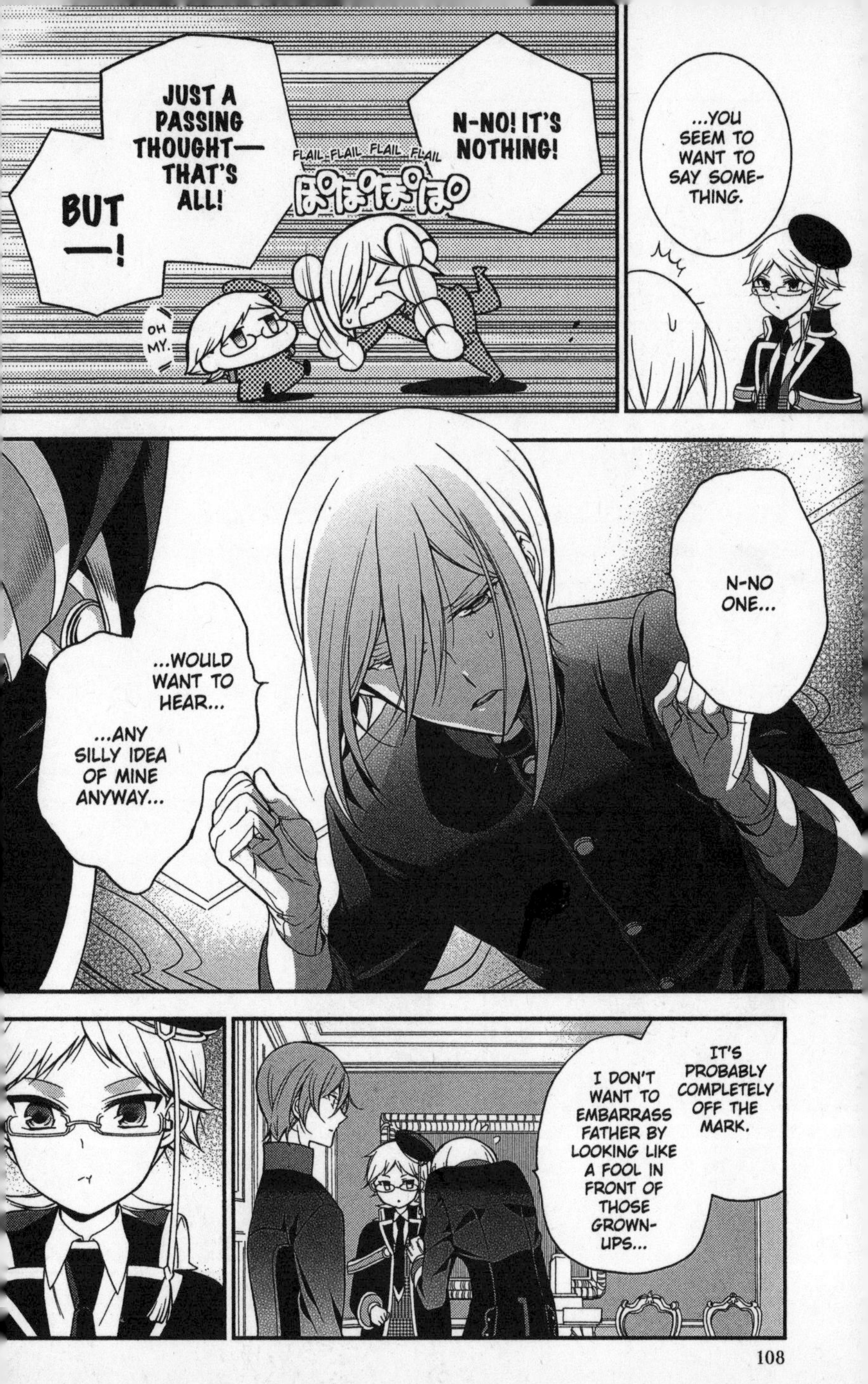
...YOU SEEM TO WANT TO SAY SOME-THING.
N-NO! IT'S NOTHING!
FLAIL FLAIL FLAIL FLAIL
JUST A PASSING THOUGHT— THAT'S ALL!
BUT —!
OH MY.
N-NO ONE...
...WOULD WANT TO HEAR...
...ANY SILLY IDEA OF MINE ANYWAY...
IT'S PROBABLY COMPLETELY OFF THE MARK.
I DON'T WANT TO EMBARRASS FATHER BY LOOKING LIKE A FOOL IN FRONT OF THOSE GROWN-UPS...

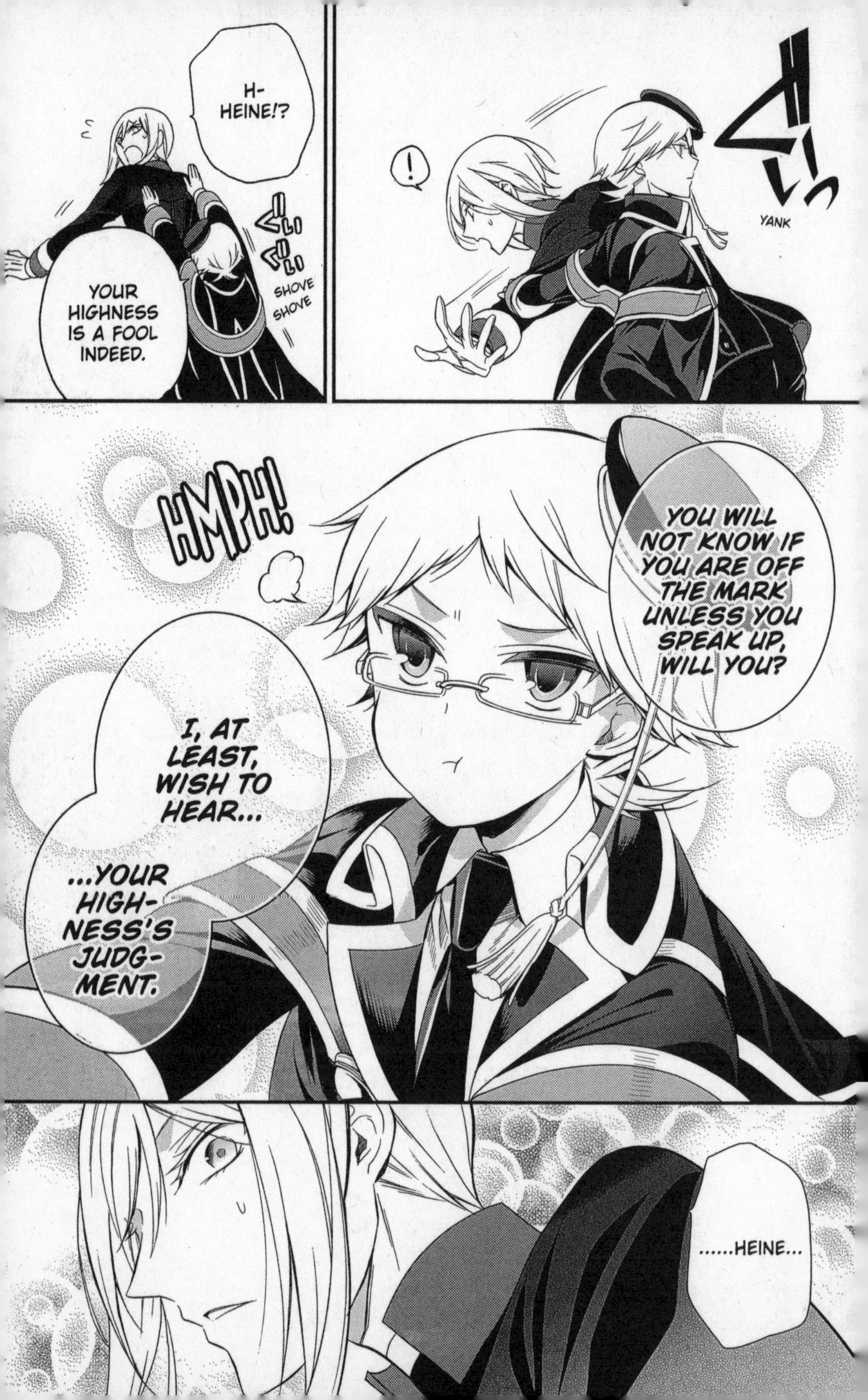
!
YANK
H-HEINE!?
SHOVE SHOVE
YOUR HIGHNESS IS A FOOL INDEED.
YOU WILL NOT KNOW IF YOU ARE OFF THE MARK UNLESS YOU SPEAK UP, WILL YOU?
HMPH!
I, AT LEAST, WISH TO HEAR...
...YOUR HIGH-NESS'S JUDG-MENT.
......HEINE...

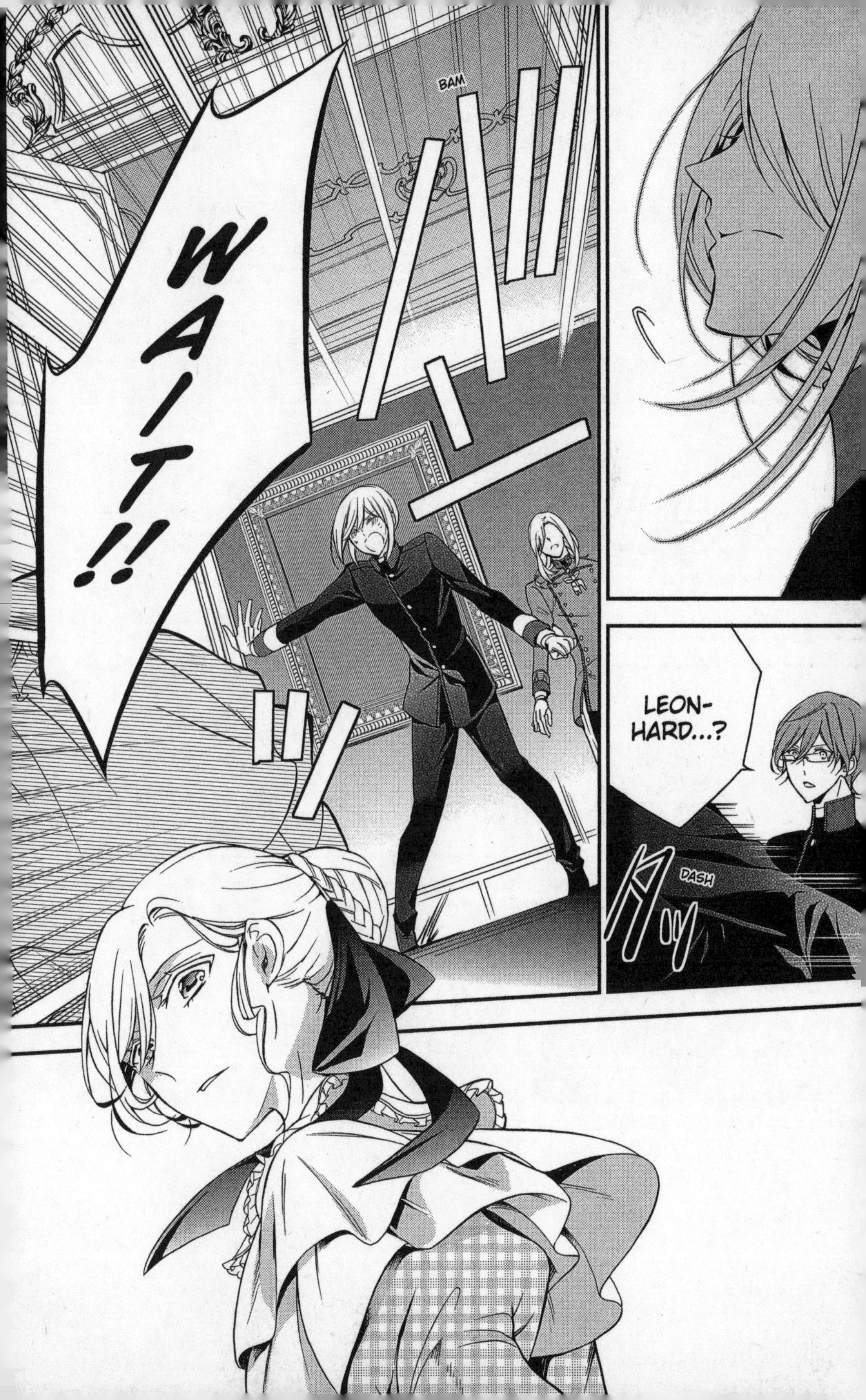
LEON-HARD...?
DASH
BAM
WAIT!!

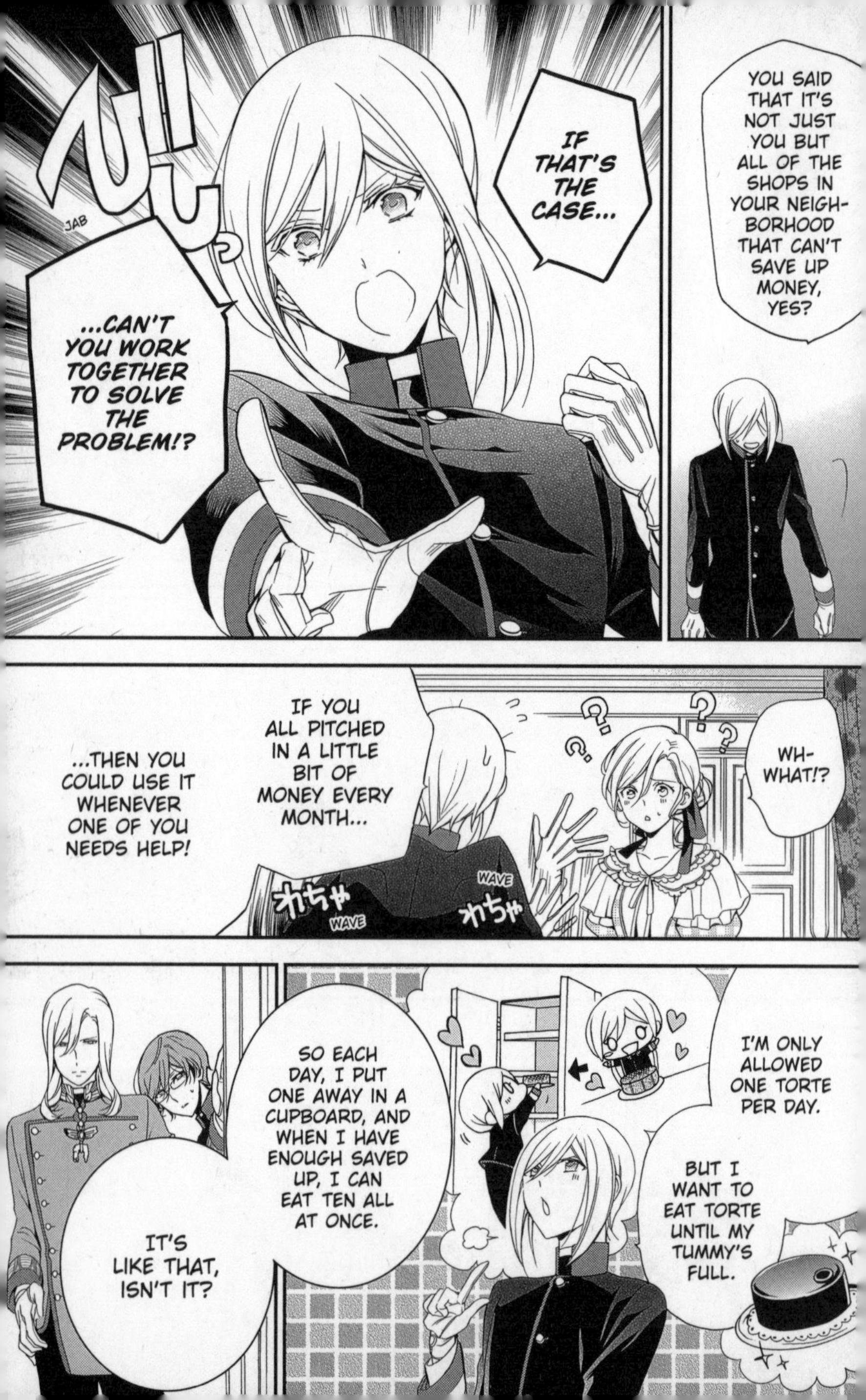
YOU SAID THAT IT'S NOT JUST YOU BUT ALL OF THE SHOPS IN YOUR NEIGHBORHOOD THAT CAN'T SAVE UP MONEY, YES?
IF THAT'S THE CASE...
JAB
...CAN'T YOU WORK TOGETHER TO SOLVE THE PROBLEM!?
WH-WHAT!?
WAVE
WAVE
IF YOU ALL PITCHED IN A LITTLE BIT OF MONEY EVERY MONTH...
...THEN YOU COULD USE IT WHENEVER ONE OF YOU NEEDS HELP!
I'M ONLY ALLOWED ONE TORTE PER DAY.
BUT I WANT TO EAT TORTE UNTIL MY TUMMY'S FULL.
SO EACH DAY, I PUT ONE AWAY IN A CUPBOARD, AND WHEN I HAVE ENOUGH SAVED UP, I CAN EAT TEN ALL AT ONCE.
IT'S LIKE THAT, ISN'T IT?

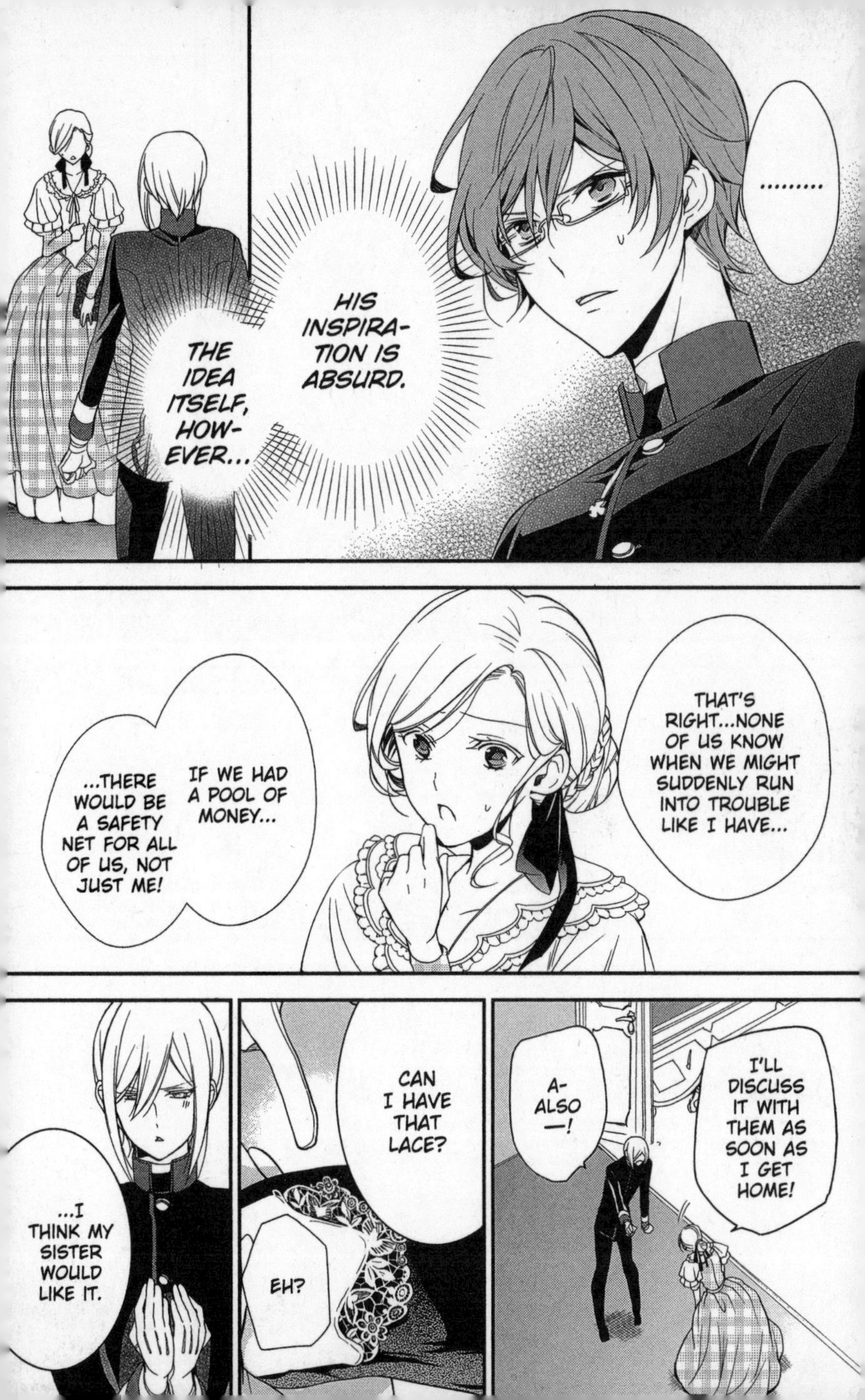
....
HIS INSPIRATION IS ABSURD.
THE IDEA ITSELF, HOWEVER...
THAT'S RIGHT...NONE OF US KNOW WHEN WE MIGHT SUDDENLY RUN INTO TROUBLE LIKE I HAVE...
IF WE HAD A POOL OF MONEY...
...THERE WOULD BE A SAFETY NET FOR ALL OF US, NOT JUST ME!
I'LL DISCUSS IT WITH THEM AS SOON AS I GET HOME!
A-ALSO—!
CAN I HAVE THAT LACE?
EH?
...I THINK MY SISTER WOULD LIKE IT.

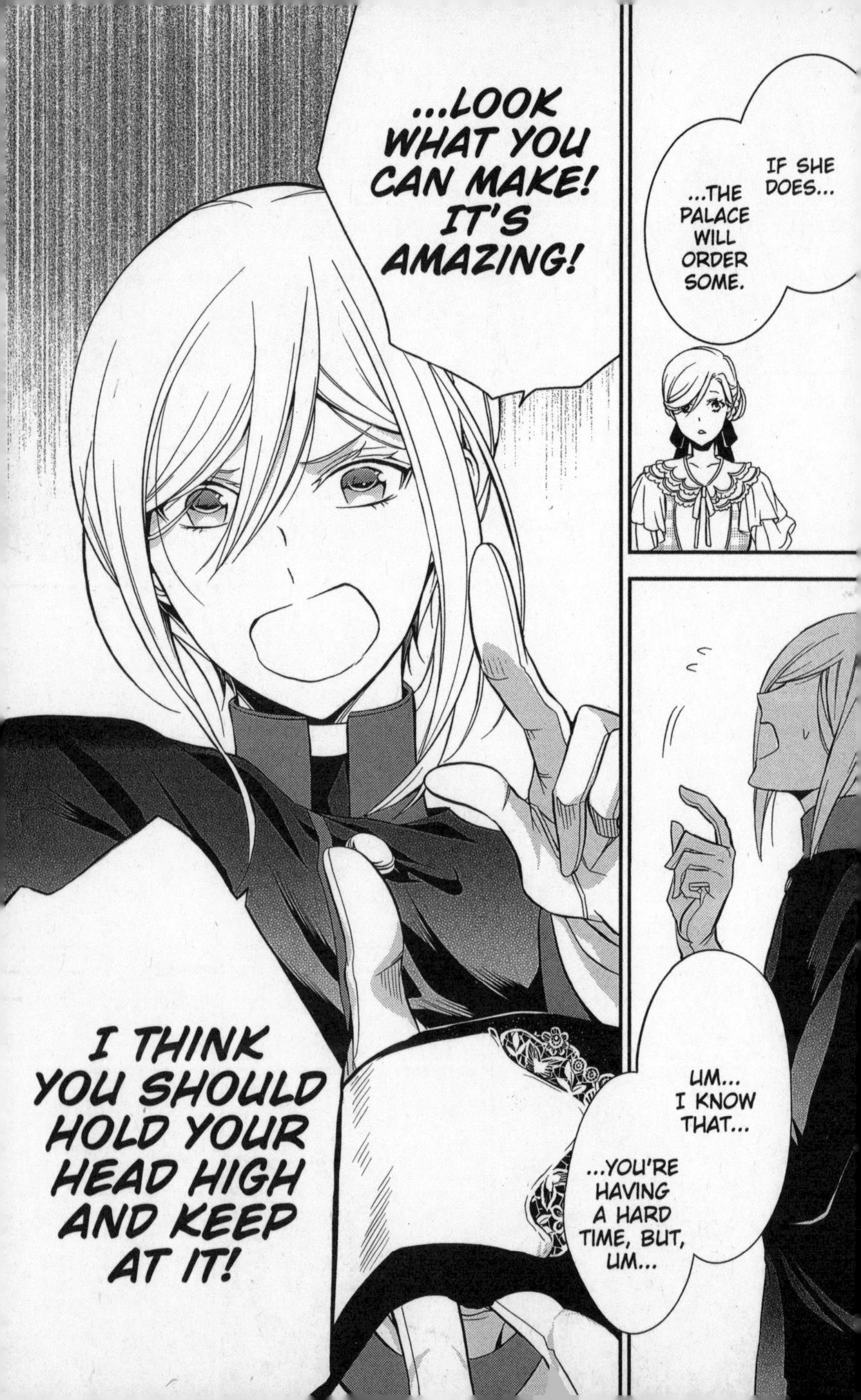
IF SHE DOES...
...THE PALACE WILL ORDER SOME.
UM... I KNOW THAT...
...YOU'RE HAVING A HARD TIME, BUT, UM...
...LOOK WHAT YOU CAN MAKE! IT'S AMAZING!
I THINK YOU SHOULD HOLD YOUR HEAD HIGH AND KEEP AT IT!

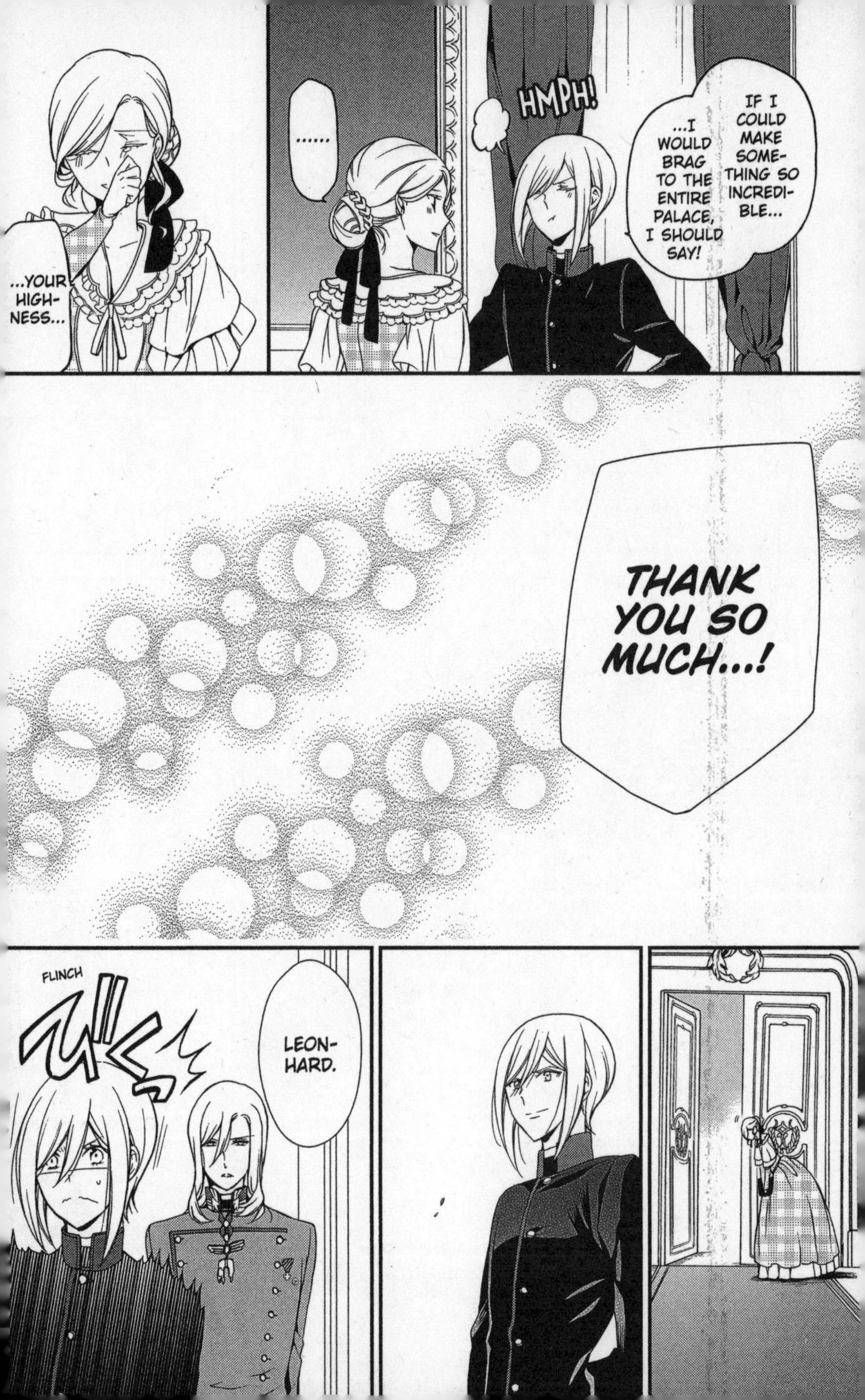
IF I COULD MAKE SOMETHING SO INCREDIBLE...
...I WOULD BRAG TO THE ENTIRE PALACE, I SHOULD SAY!
HMPH!
......
...YOUR HIGHNESS...
THANK YOU SO MUCH...!
LEON-HARD.
FLINCH

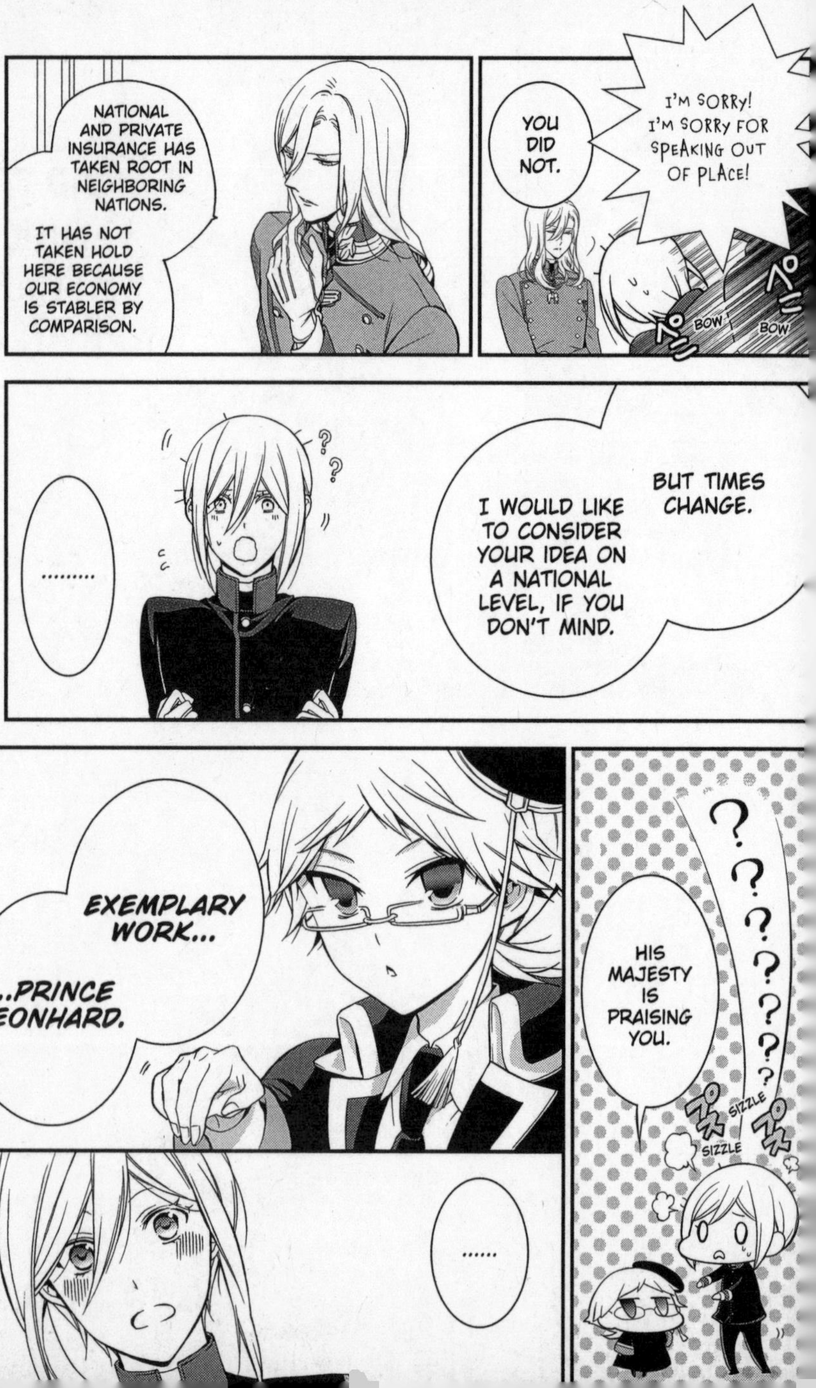
I'M SORRY! I'M SORRY FOR SPEAKING OUT OF PLACE!
YOU DID NOT.
BOW
BOW
NATIONAL AND PRIVATE INSURANCE HAS TAKEN ROOT IN NEIGHBORING NATIONS.
IT HAS NOT TAKEN HOLD HERE BECAUSE OUR ECONOMY IS STABLER BY COMPARISON.
BUT TIMES CHANGE.
I WOULD LIKE TO CONSIDER YOUR IDEA ON A NATIONAL LEVEL, IF YOU DON'T MIND.
....
HIS MAJESTY IS PRAISING YOU.
SIZZLE
SIZZLE
EXEMPLARY WORK...
...PRINCE LEONHARD.
......

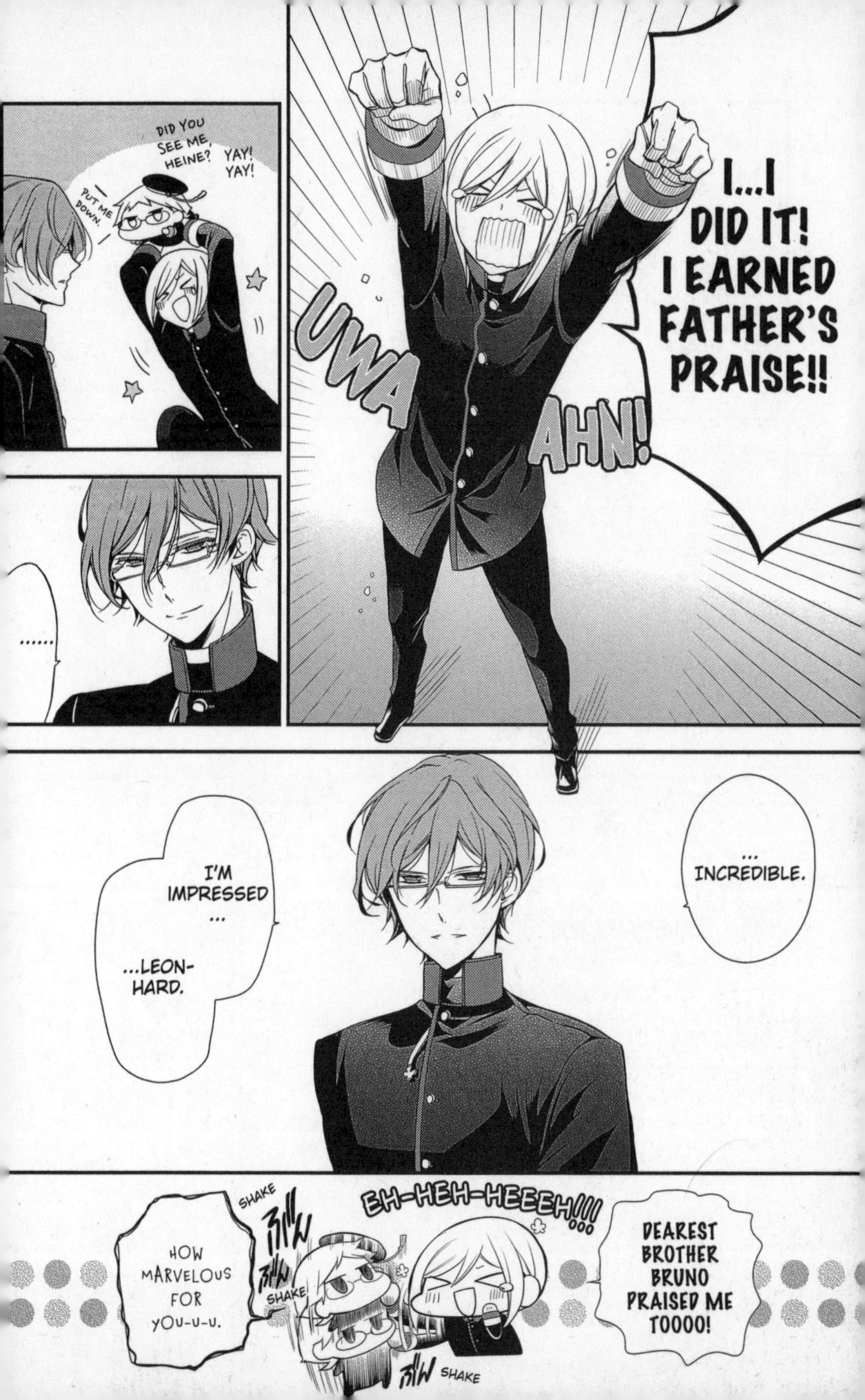
I...I DID IT! I EARNED FATHER'S PRAISE!!
UWAAHN!
DID YOU SEE ME, HEINE?
YAY! YAY!
PUT ME DOWN.
......
... INCREDIBLE.
I'M IMPRESSED ...
...LEON-HARD.
DEAREST BROTHER BRUNO PRAISED ME TOOOO!
EH-HEH-HEEEH!!!
SHAKE
SHAKE
SHAKE
HOW MARVELOUS FOR YOU-U-U.

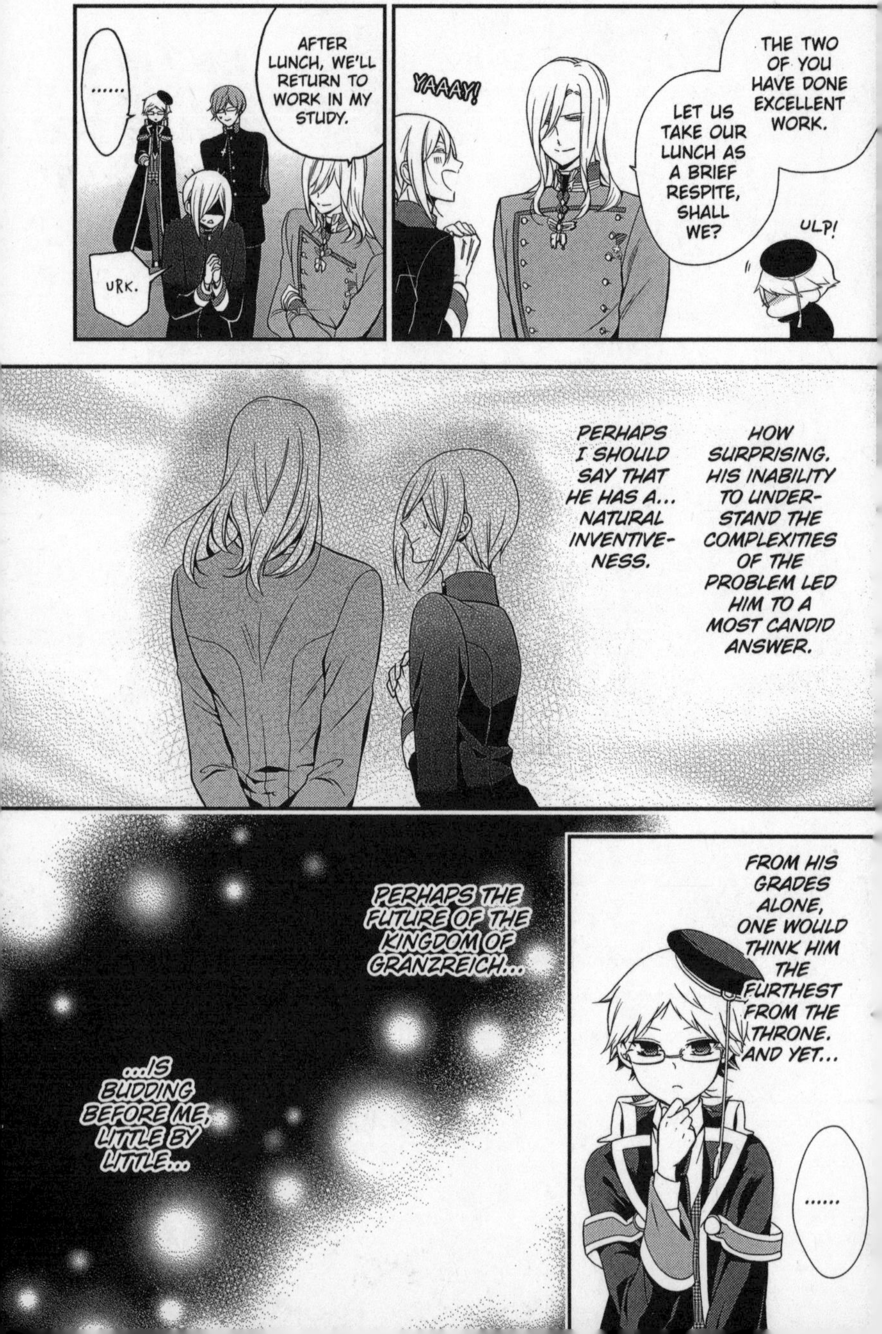
THE TWO OF YOU HAVE DONE EXCELLENT WORK.
LET US TAKE OUR LUNCH AS A BRIEF RESPITE, SHALL WE?
YAAAY!
ULP!
AFTER LUNCH, WE'LL RETURN TO WORK IN MY STUDY.
......
URK.
HOW SURPRISING. HIS INABILITY TO UNDER-STAND THE COMPLEXITIES OF THE PROBLEM LED HIM TO A MOST CANDID ANSWER.
PERHAPS I SHOULD SAY THAT HE HAS A... NATURAL INVENTIVE-NESS.
FROM HIS GRADES ALONE, ONE WOULD THINK HIM THE FURTHEST FROM THE THRONE. AND YET...
......
PERHAPS THE FUTURE OF THE KINGDOM OF GRANZREICH...
...IS BUDDING BEFORE ME, LITTLE BY LITTLE...

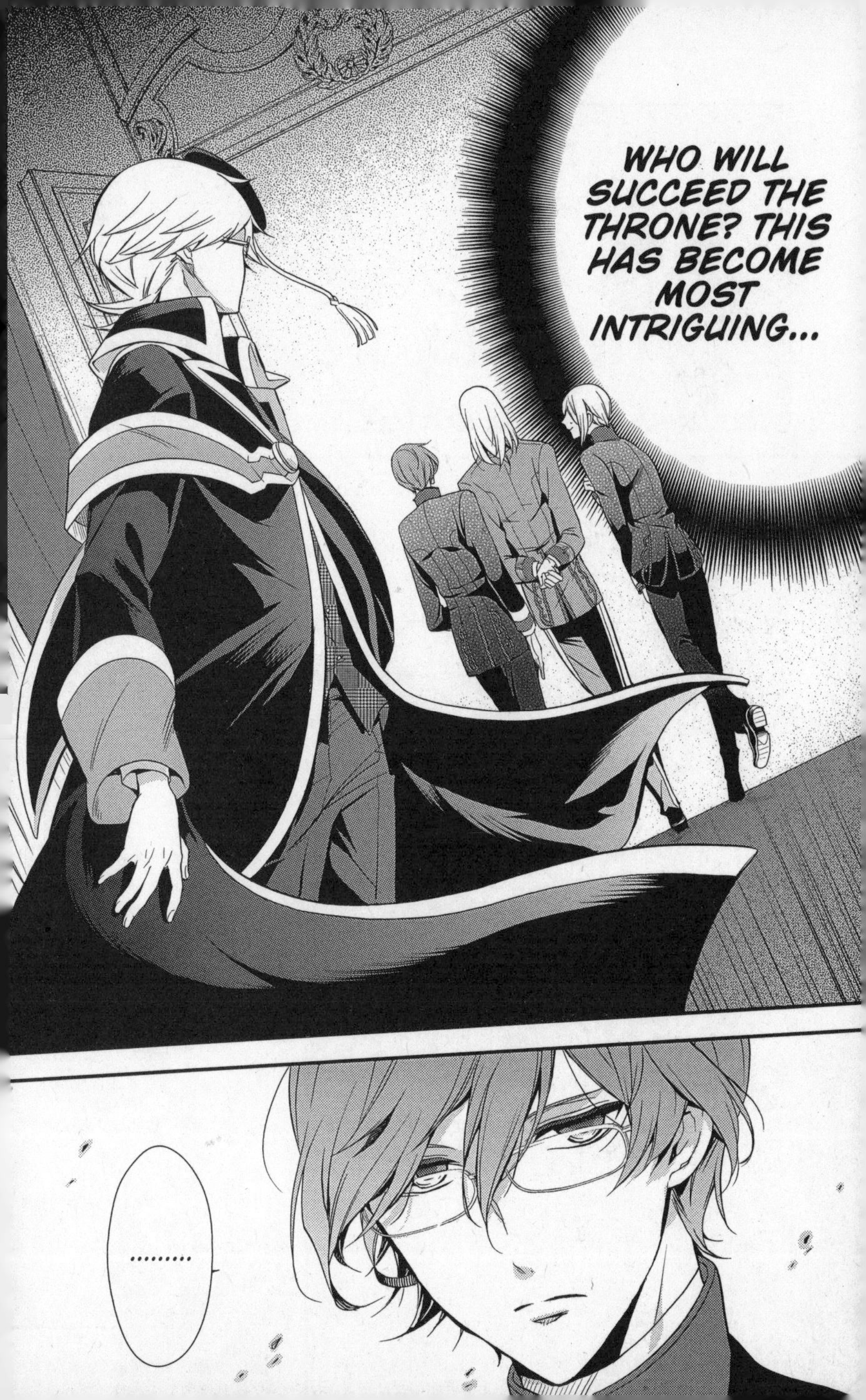
WHO WILL SUCCEED THE THRONE? THIS HAS BECOME MOST INTRIGUING...
....

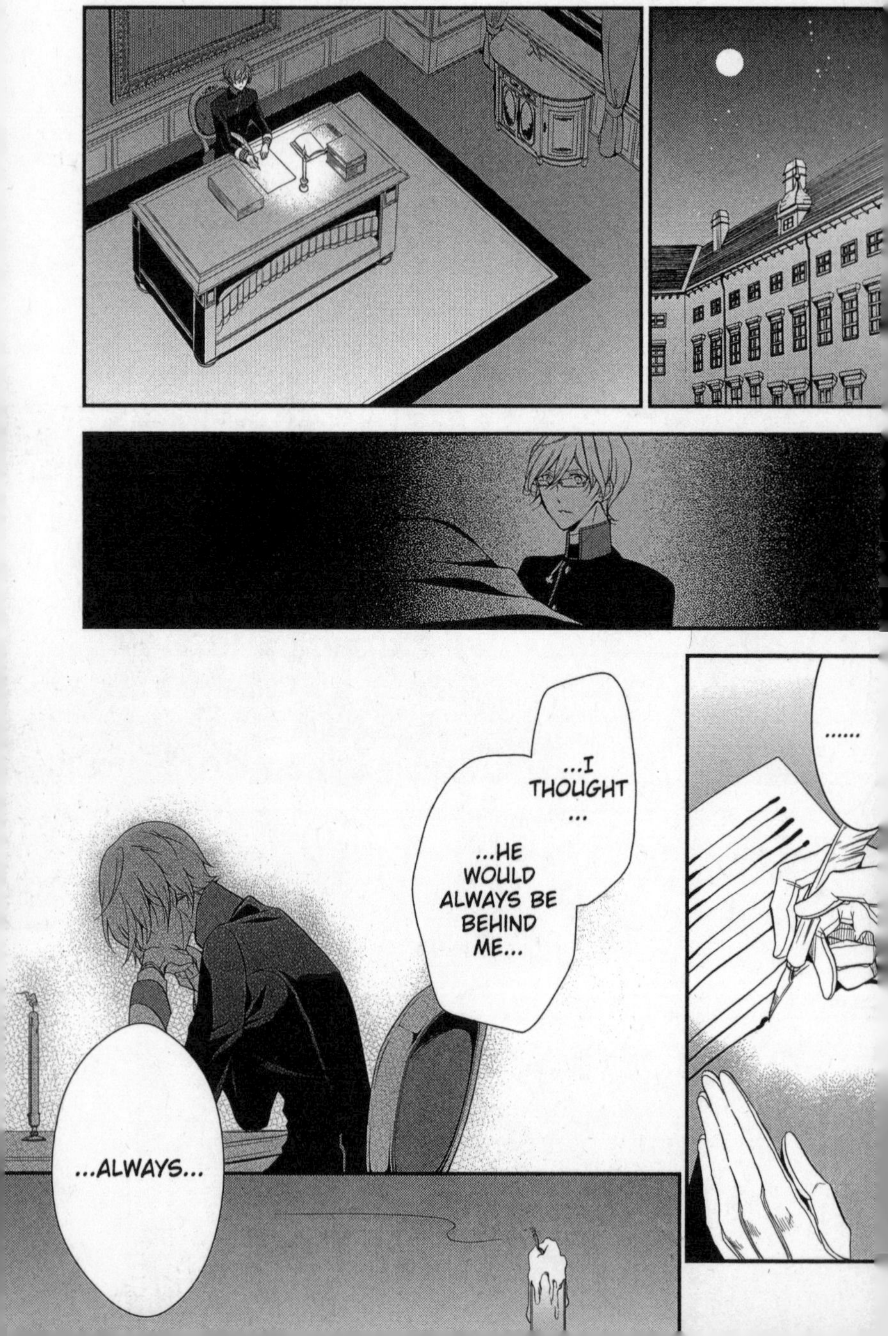
......
...I THOUGHT ...
...HE WOULD ALWAYS BE BEHIND ME...
...ALWAYS...

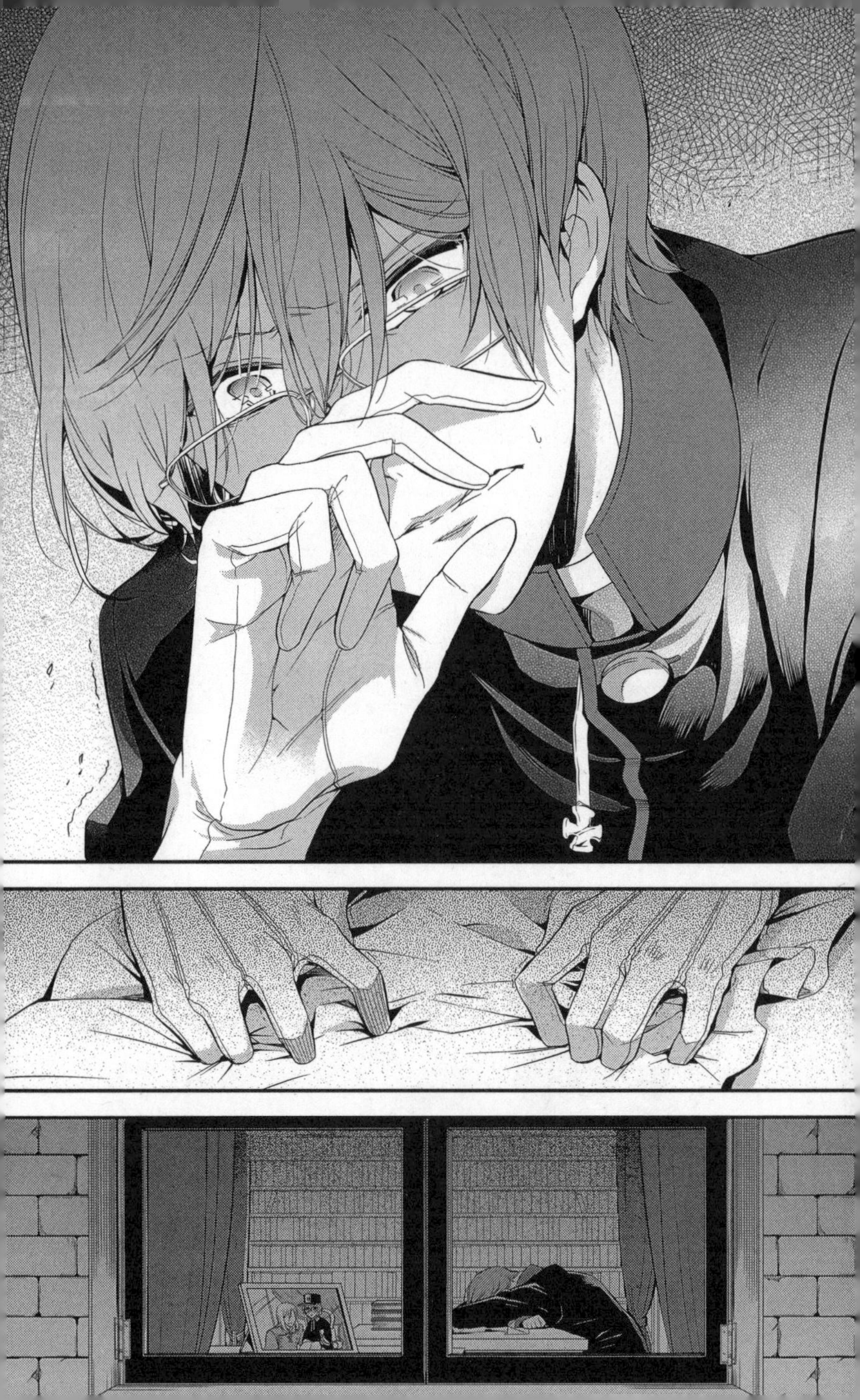

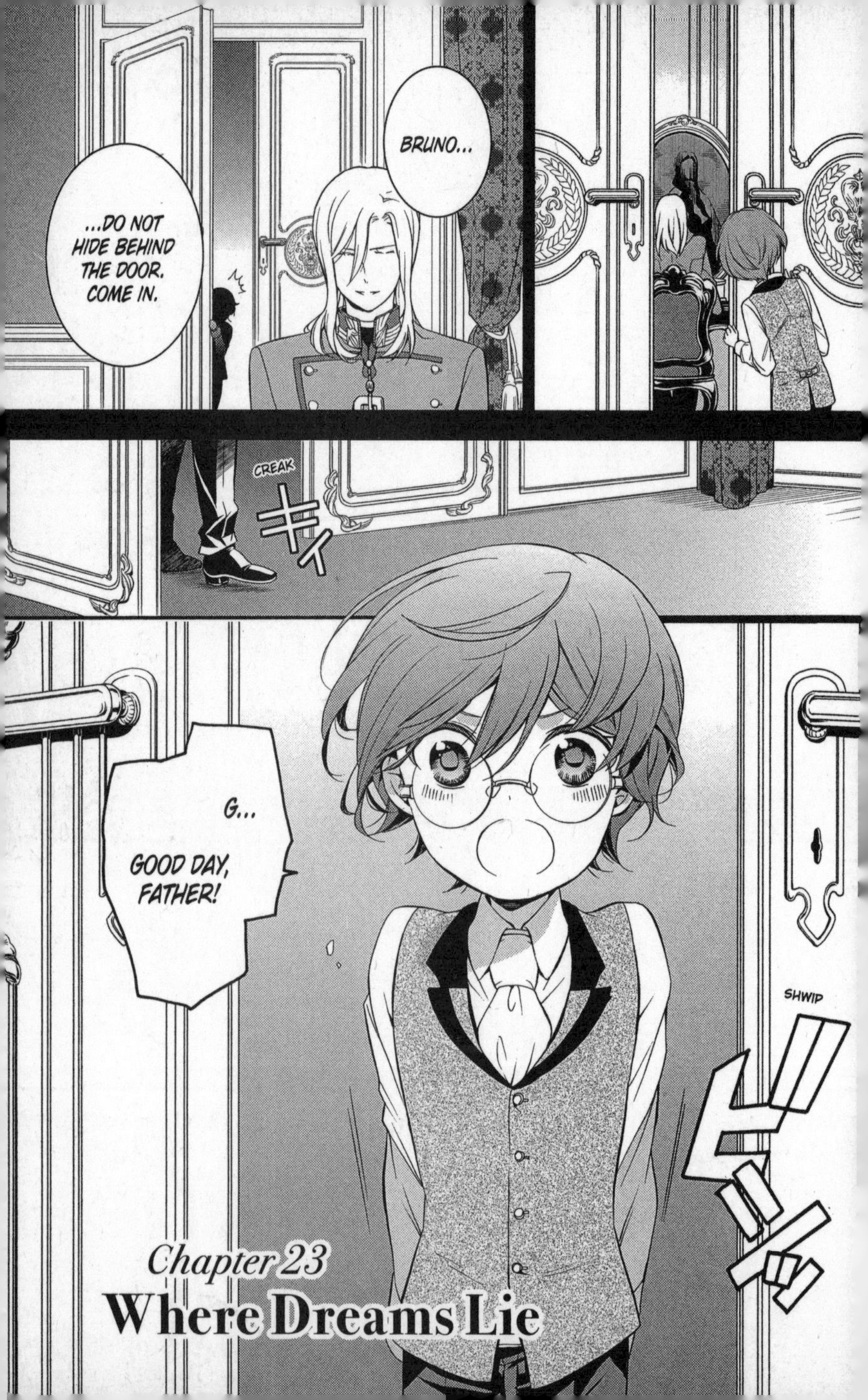
BRUNO...
...DO NOT HIDE BEHIND THE DOOR. COME IN.
CREAK
キィ
SHWIP
G...
GOOD DAY, FATHER!
Chapter 23
Where Dreams Lie

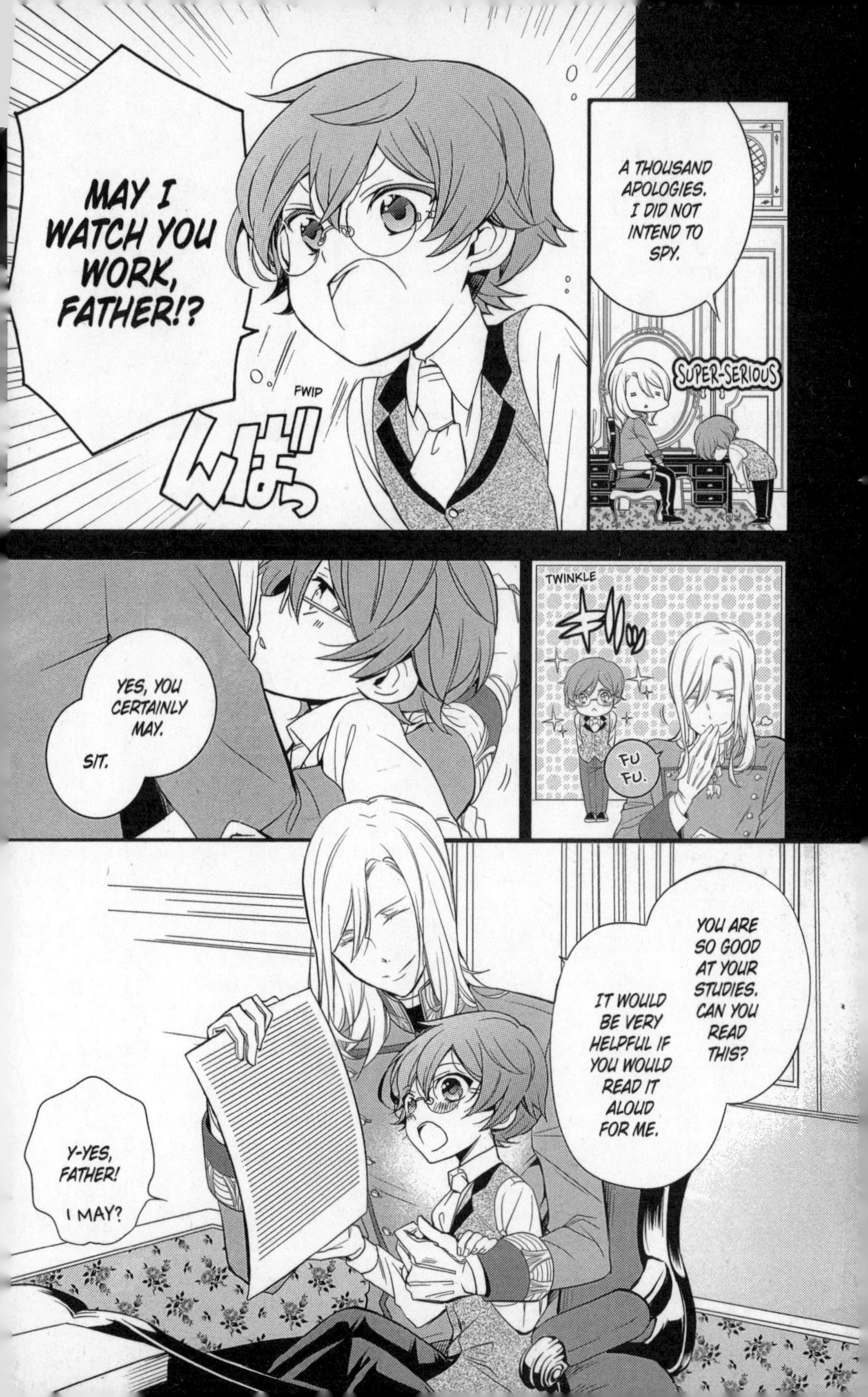
A THOUSAND APOLOGIES. I DID NOT INTEND TO SPY.
SUPER-SERIOUS
MAY I WATCH YOU WORK, FATHER!?
FWIP
んばっ
TWINKLE
キリッ
FU FU.
YES, YOU CERTAINLY MAY.
SIT.
YOU ARE SO GOOD AT YOUR STUDIES. CAN YOU READ THIS?
IT WOULD BE VERY HELPFUL IF YOU WOULD READ IT ALOUD FOR ME.
Y-YES, FATHER!
I MAY?

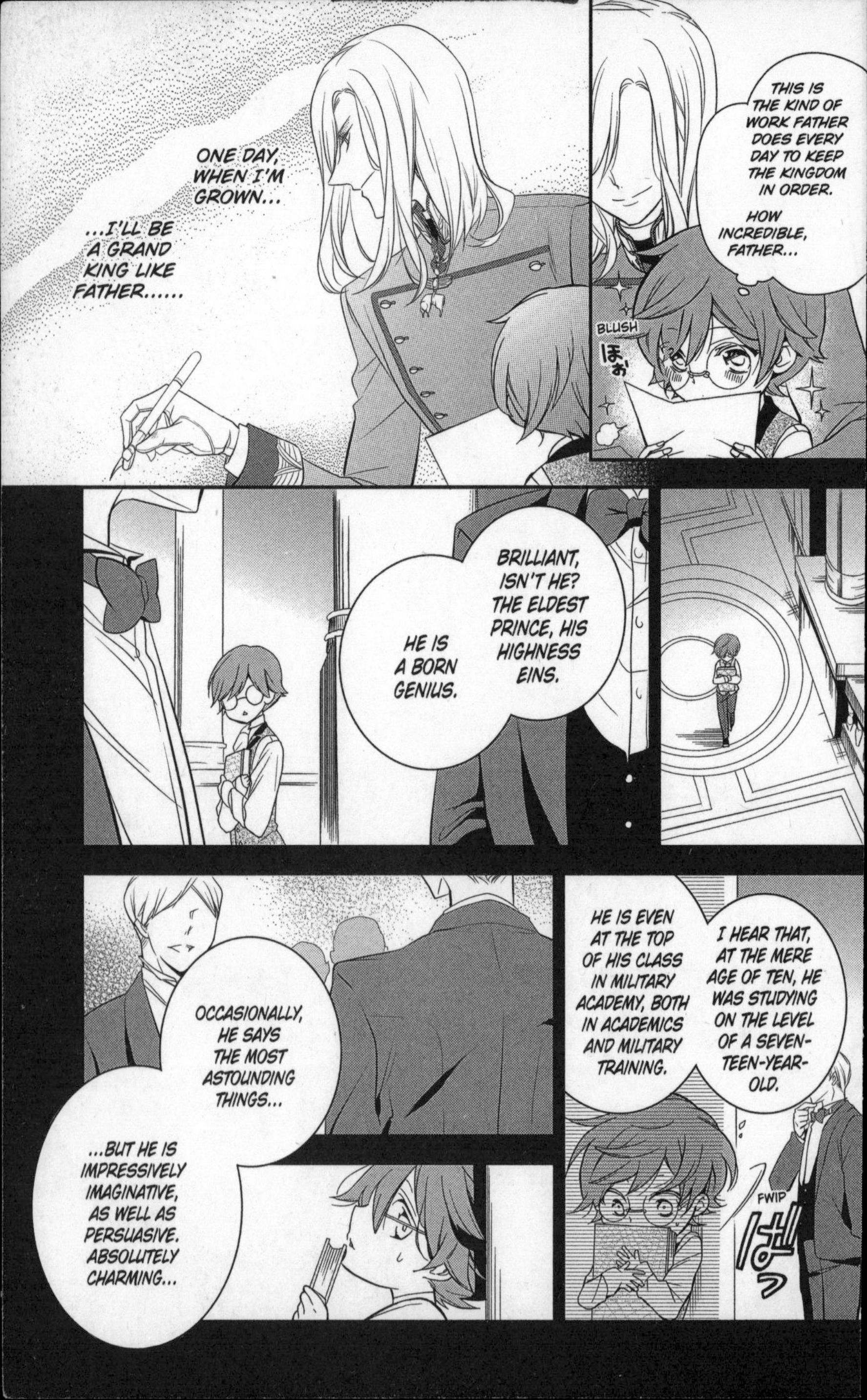

THIS IS THE KIND OF WORK FATHER DOES EVERY DAY TO KEEP THE KINGDOM IN ORDER.
HOW INCREDIBLE, FATHER...
BLUSH
ほぉ
ONE DAY, WHEN I'M GROWN...
...I'LL BE A GRAND KING LIKE FATHER......
BRILLIANT, ISN'T HE? THE ELDEST PRINCE, HIS HIGHNESS EINS.
HE IS A BORN GENIUS.
I HEAR THAT, AT THE MERE AGE OF TEN, HE WAS STUDYING ON THE LEVEL OF A SEVEN-TEEN-YEAR-OLD.
HE IS EVEN AT THE TOP OF HIS CLASS IN MILITARY ACADEMY, BOTH IN ACADEMICS AND MILITARY TRAINING.
FWIP
はっ
OCCASIONALLY, HE SAYS THE MOST ASTOUNDING THINGS...
...BUT HE IS IMPRESSIVELY IMAGINATIVE, AS WELL AS PERSUASIVE. ABSOLUTELY CHARMING...

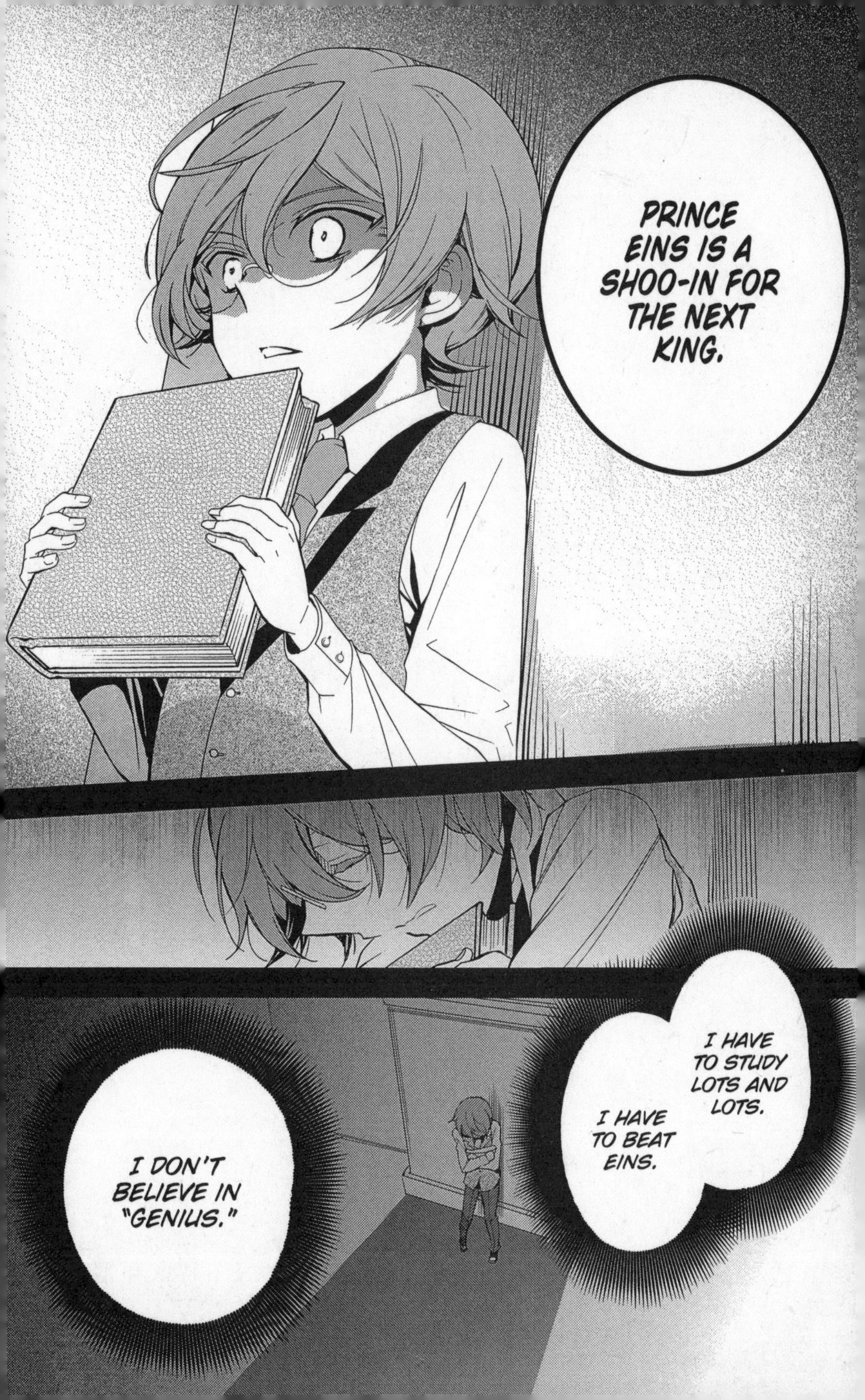
PRINCE EINS IS A SHOO-IN FOR THE NEXT KING.
I HAVE TO STUDY LOTS AND LOTS.
I HAVE TO BEAT EINS.
I DON'T BELIEVE IN "GENIUS."

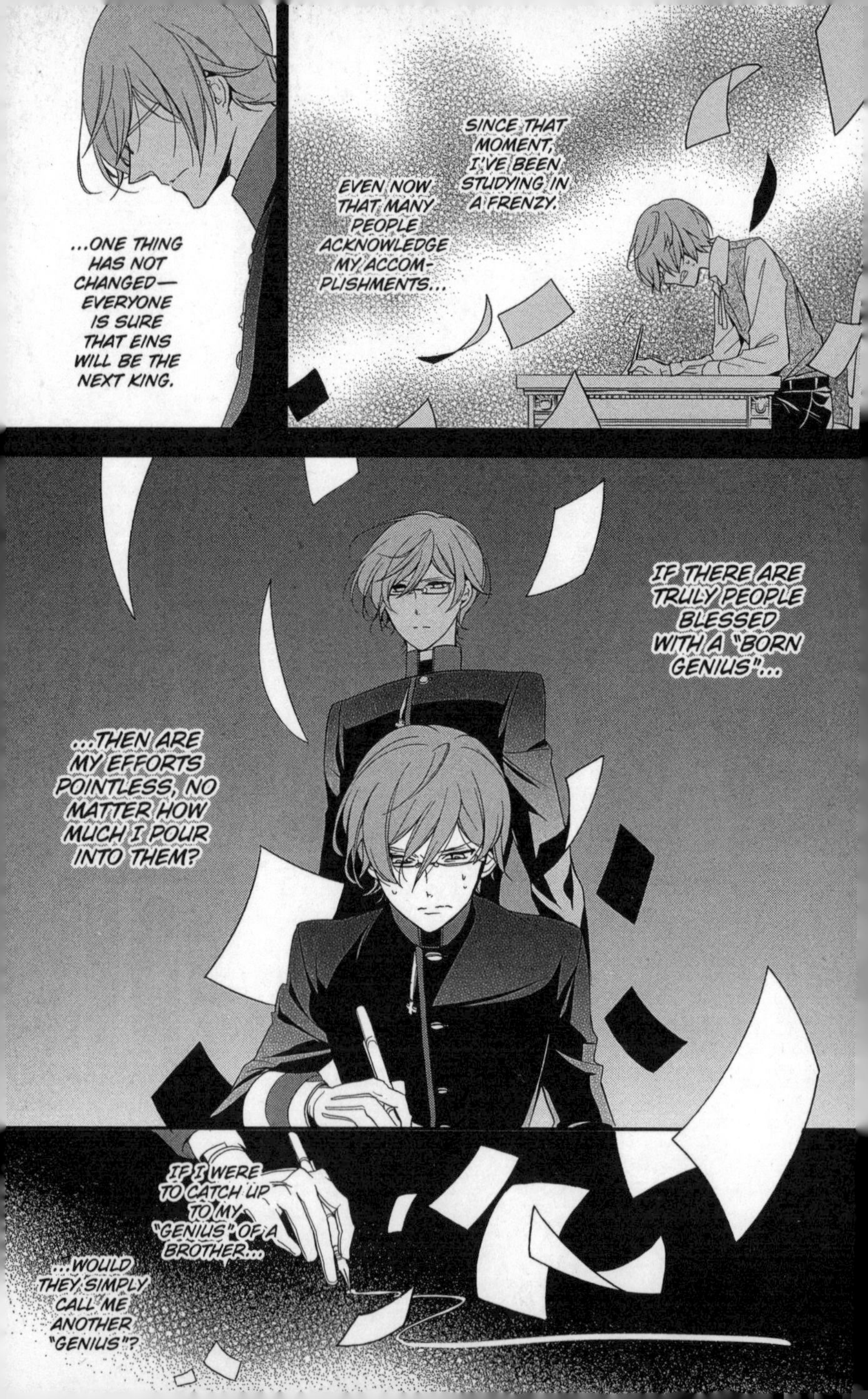
SINCE THAT MOMENT, I'VE BEEN STUDYING IN A FRENZY.
EVEN NOW THAT MANY PEOPLE ACKNOWLEDGE MY ACCOMPLISHMENTS...
...ONE THING HAS NOT CHANGED—EVERYONE IS SURE THAT EINS WILL BE THE NEXT KING.
IF THERE ARE TRULY PEOPLE BLESSED WITH A "BORN GENIUS"...
...THEN ARE MY EFFORTS POINTLESS, NO MATTER HOW MUCH I POUR INTO THEM?
IF I WERE TO CATCH UP TO MY "GENIUS" OF A BROTHER...
...WOULD THEY SIMPLY CALL ME ANOTHER "GENIUS"?

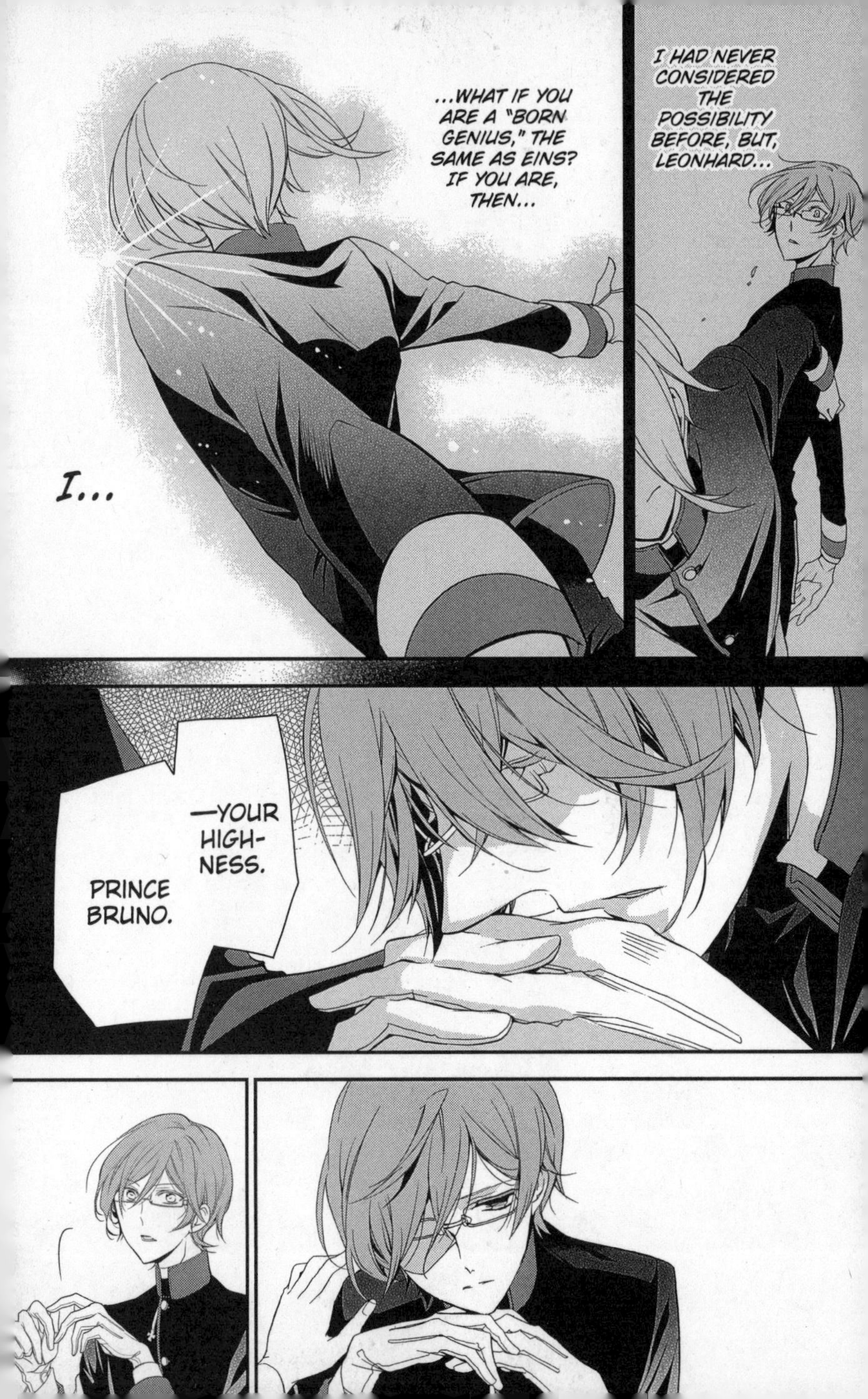
I HAD NEVER CONSIDERED THE POSSIBILITY BEFORE, BUT, LEONHARD...
...WHAT IF YOU ARE A "BORN GENIUS," THE SAME AS EINS? IF YOU ARE, THEN...
I...
—YOUR HIGH-NESS.
PRINCE BRUNO.

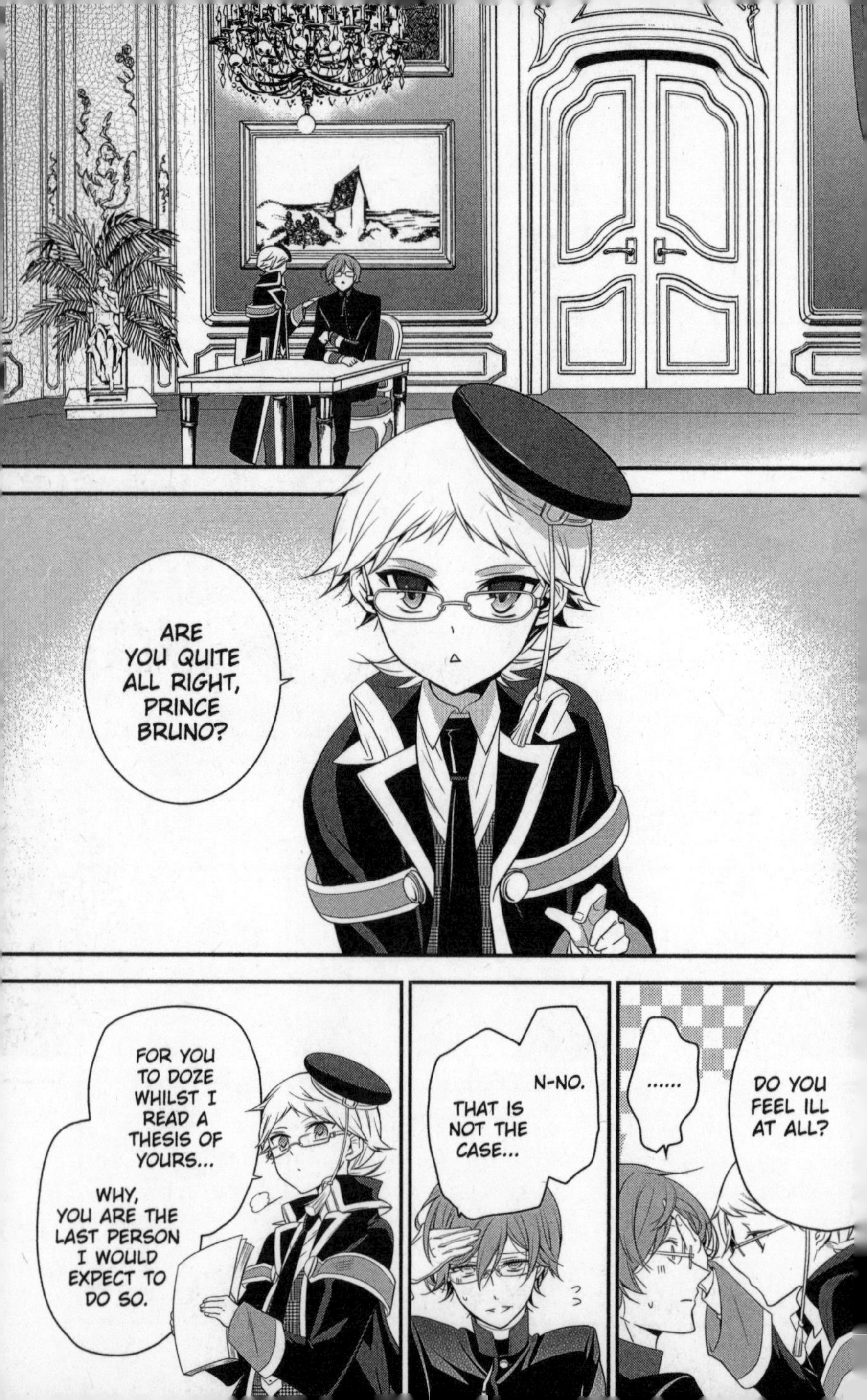
ARE YOU QUITE ALL RIGHT, PRINCE BRUNO?
DO YOU FEEL ILL AT ALL?
......
N-NO.
THAT IS NOT THE CASE...
FOR YOU TO DOZE WHILST I READ A THESIS OF YOURS...
WHY, YOU ARE THE LAST PERSON I WOULD EXPECT TO DO SO.

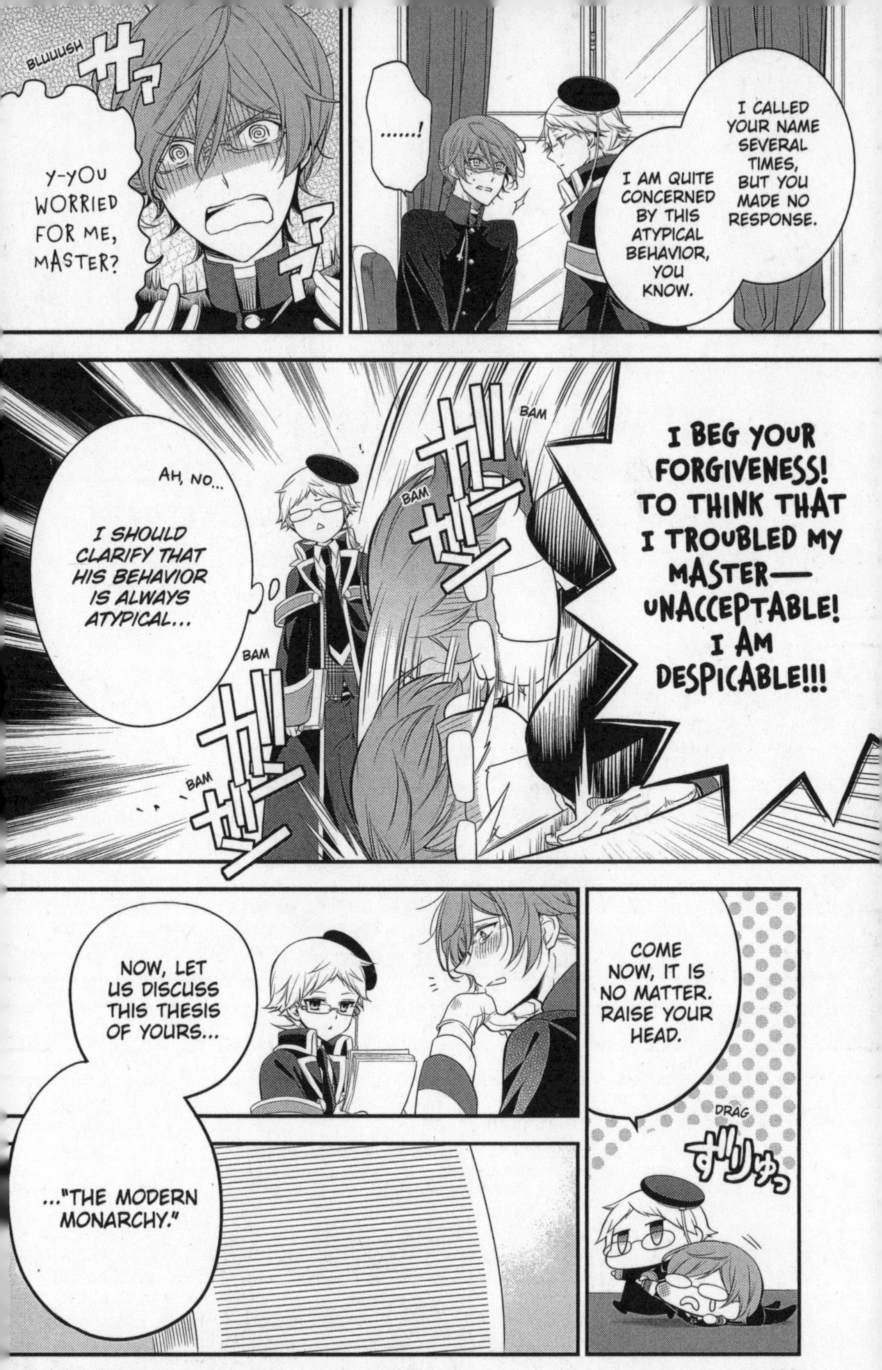
I CALLED YOUR NAME SEVERAL TIMES, BUT YOU MADE NO RESPONSE.
I AM QUITE CONCERNED BY THIS ATYPICAL BEHAVIOR, YOU KNOW.
......!
BLUUUSH
Y-YOU WORRIED FOR ME, MASTER?
I BEG YOUR FORGIVENESS! TO THINK THAT I TROUBLED MY MASTER—UNACCEPTABLE! I AM DESPICABLE!!!
BAM
BAM
AH, NO...
I SHOULD CLARIFY THAT HIS BEHAVIOR IS ALWAYS ATYPICAL...
BAM
BAM
COME NOW, IT IS NO MATTER. RAISE YOUR HEAD.
DRAG
NOW, LET US DISCUSS THIS THESIS OF YOURS...
..."THE MODERN MONARCHY."

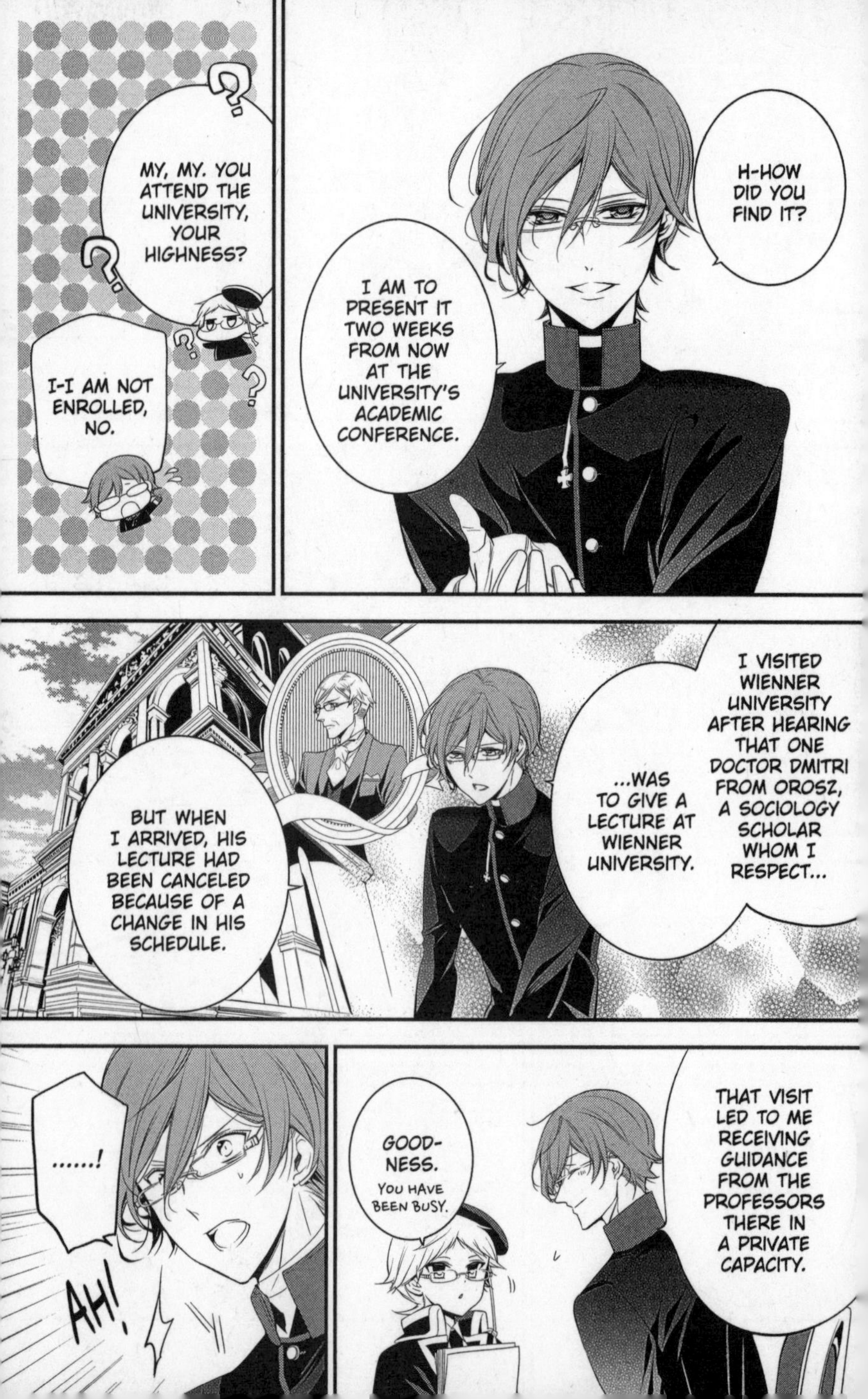
H-HOW DID YOU FIND IT?
I AM TO PRESENT IT TWO WEEKS FROM NOW AT THE UNIVERSITY'S ACADEMIC CONFERENCE.
MY, MY. YOU ATTEND THE UNIVERSITY, YOUR HIGHNESS?
I-I AM NOT ENROLLED, NO.
I VISITED WIENNER UNIVERSITY AFTER HEARING THAT ONE DOCTOR DMITRI FROM OROSZ, A SOCIOLOGY SCHOLAR WHOM I RESPECT...
...WAS TO GIVE A LECTURE AT WIENNER UNIVERSITY.
BUT WHEN I ARRIVED, HIS LECTURE HAD BEEN CANCELED BECAUSE OF A CHANGE IN HIS SCHEDULE.
THAT VISIT LED TO ME RECEIVING GUIDANCE FROM THE PROFESSORS THERE IN A PRIVATE CAPACITY.
GOOD-NESS. YOU HAVE BEEN BUSY.
......!
AH!

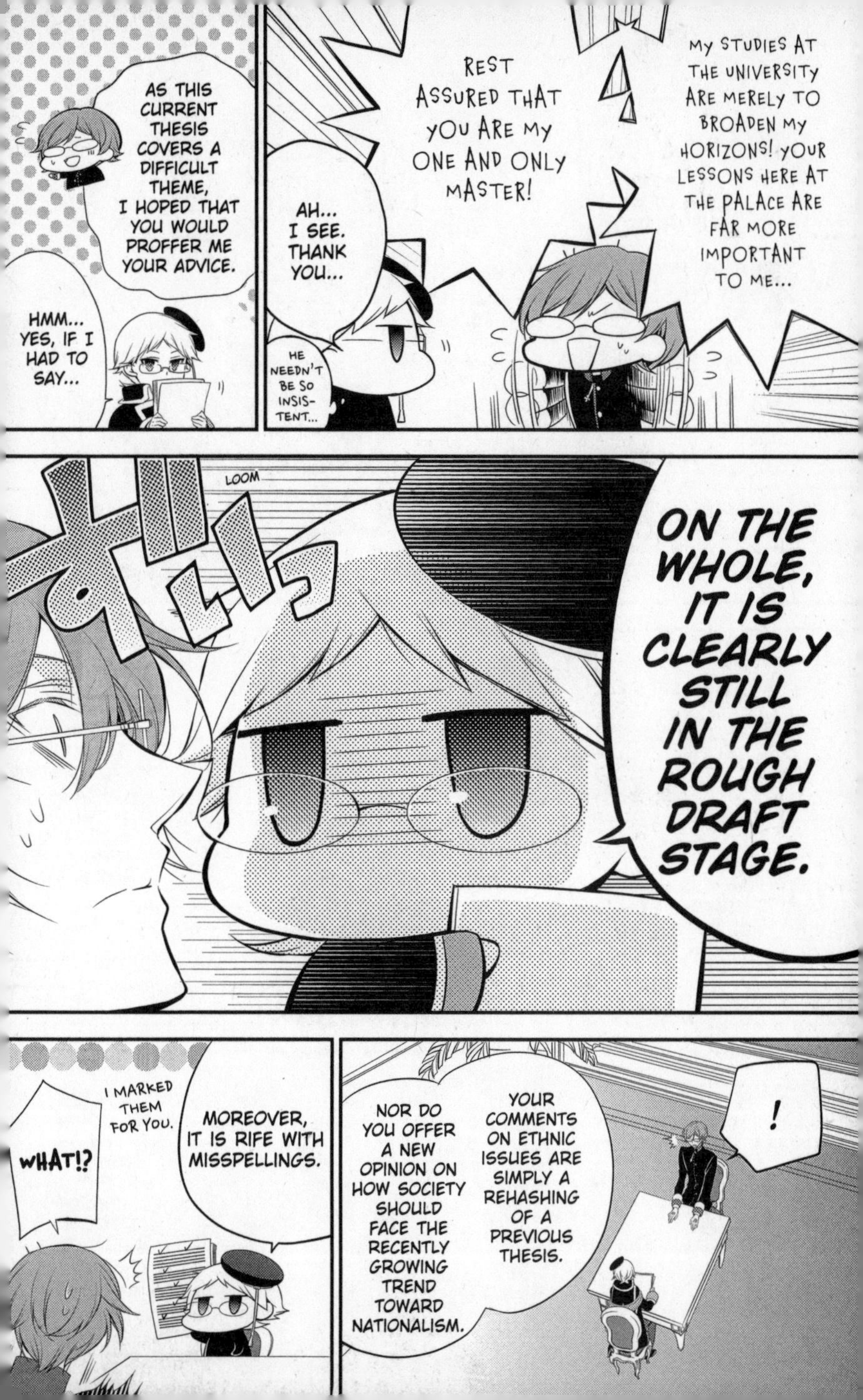
MY STUDIES AT THE UNIVERSITY ARE MERELY TO BROADEN MY HORIZONS! YOUR LESSONS HERE AT THE PALACE ARE FAR MORE IMPORTANT TO ME...
REST ASSURED THAT YOU ARE MY ONE AND ONLY MASTER!
AH... I SEE. THANK YOU...
HE NEEDN'T BE SO INSIS-TENT...
AS THIS CURRENT THESIS COVERS A DIFFICULT THEME, I HOPED THAT YOU WOULD PROFFER ME YOUR ADVICE.
HMM... YES, IF I HAD TO SAY...
ON THE WHOLE, IT IS CLEARLY STILL IN THE ROUGH DRAFT STAGE.
LOOM
!
YOUR COMMENTS ON ETHNIC ISSUES ARE SIMPLY A REHASHING OF A PREVIOUS THESIS.
NOR DO YOU OFFER A NEW OPINION ON HOW SOCIETY SHOULD FACE THE RECENTLY GROWING TREND TOWARD NATIONALISM.
MOREOVER, IT IS RIFE WITH MISSPELLINGS.
I MARKED THEM FOR YOU.
WHAT!?

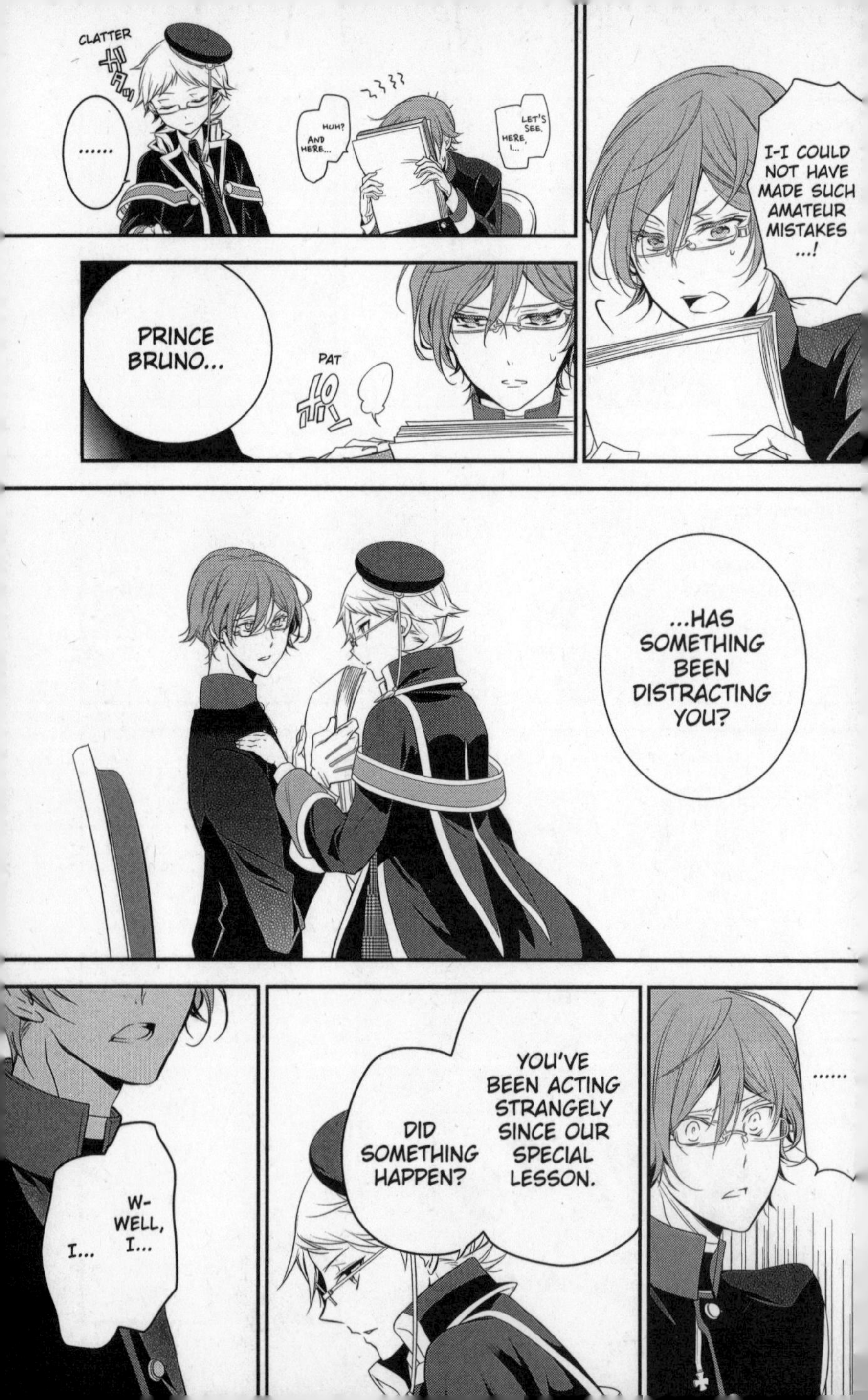
I-I COULD NOT HAVE MADE SUCH AMATEUR MISTAKES ...!
LET'S SEE. HERE, I...
HUH? AND HERE...
CLATTER
......
PAT
PRINCE BRUNO...
...HAS SOMETHING BEEN DISTRACTING YOU?
......
YOU'VE BEEN ACTING STRANGELY SINCE OUR SPECIAL LESSON.
DID SOMETHING HAPPEN?
W-WELL, I...
I...

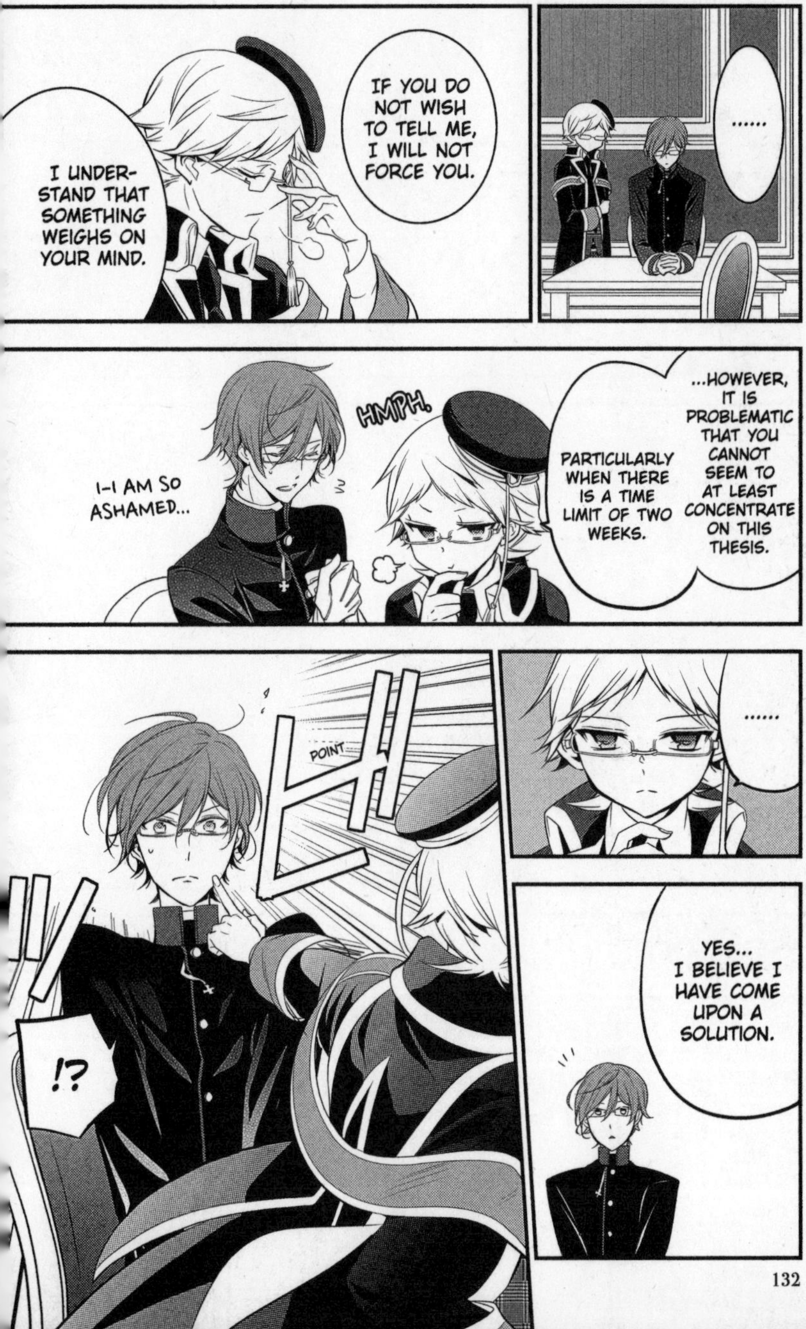

......
IF YOU DO NOT WISH TO TELL ME, I WILL NOT FORCE YOU.
I UNDERSTAND THAT SOMETHING WEIGHS ON YOUR MIND.
...HOWEVER, IT IS PROBLEMATIC THAT YOU CANNOT SEEM TO AT LEAST CONCENTRATE ON THIS THESIS.
PARTICULARLY WHEN THERE IS A TIME LIMIT OF TWO WEEKS.
HMPH.
I-I AM SO ASHAMED...
......
YES... I BELIEVE I HAVE COME UPON A SOLUTION.
POINT
!?

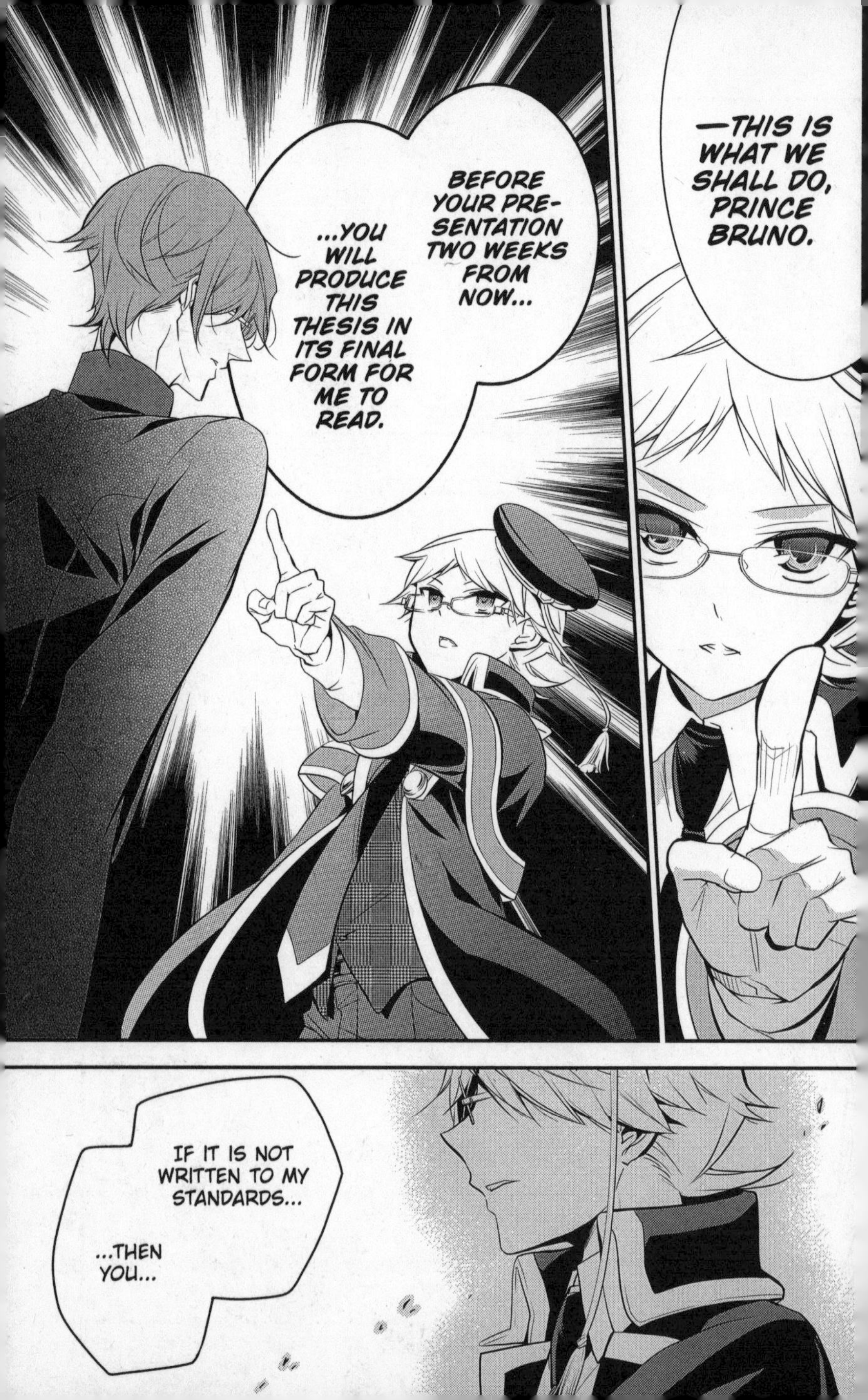
—THIS IS WHAT WE SHALL DO, PRINCE BRUNO.
BEFORE YOUR PRE-SENTATION TWO WEEKS FROM NOW...
...YOU WILL PRODUCE THIS THESIS IN ITS FINAL FORM FOR ME TO READ.
IF IT IS NOT WRITTEN TO MY STANDARDS...
...THEN YOU...

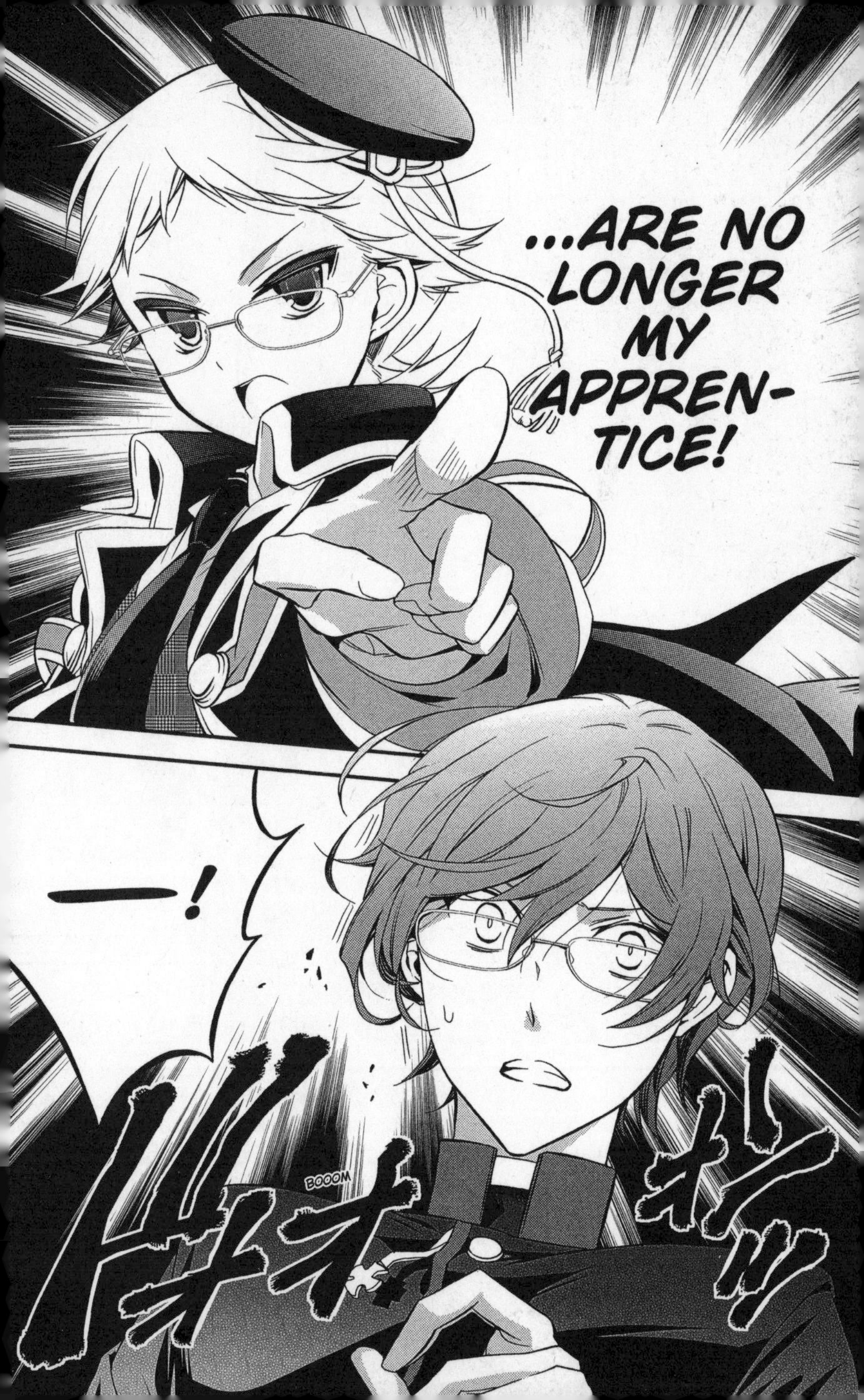
...ARE NO LONGER MY APPREN-TICE!
—!
BOOOM

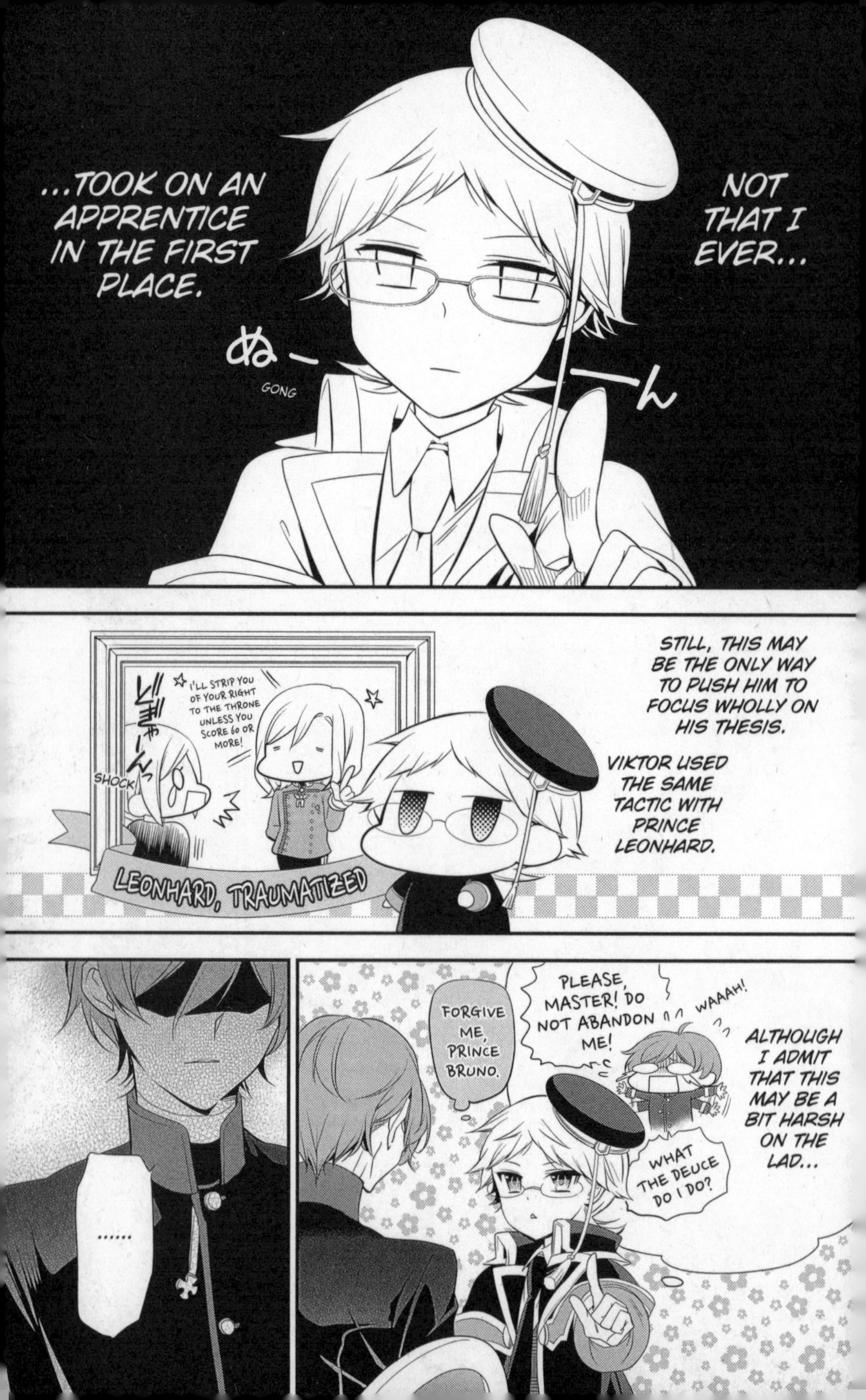
NOT THAT I EVER...
...TOOK ON AN APPRENTICE IN THE FIRST PLACE.
ぬーーん
GONG
STILL, THIS MAY BE THE ONLY WAY TO PUSH HIM TO FOCUS WHOLLY ON HIS THESIS.
VIKTOR USED THE SAME TACTIC WITH PRINCE LEONHARD.
I'LL STRIP YOU OF YOUR RIGHT TO THE THRONE UNLESS YOU SCORE 60 OR MORE!
どぎゃーん
SHOCK
LEONHARD, TRAUMATIZED
ALTHOUGH I ADMIT THAT THIS MAY BE A BIT HARSH ON THE LAD...
PLEASE, MASTER! DO NOT ABANDON ME!
WAAAH!
FORGIVE ME, PRINCE BRUNO.
WHAT THE DEUCE DO I DO?
......

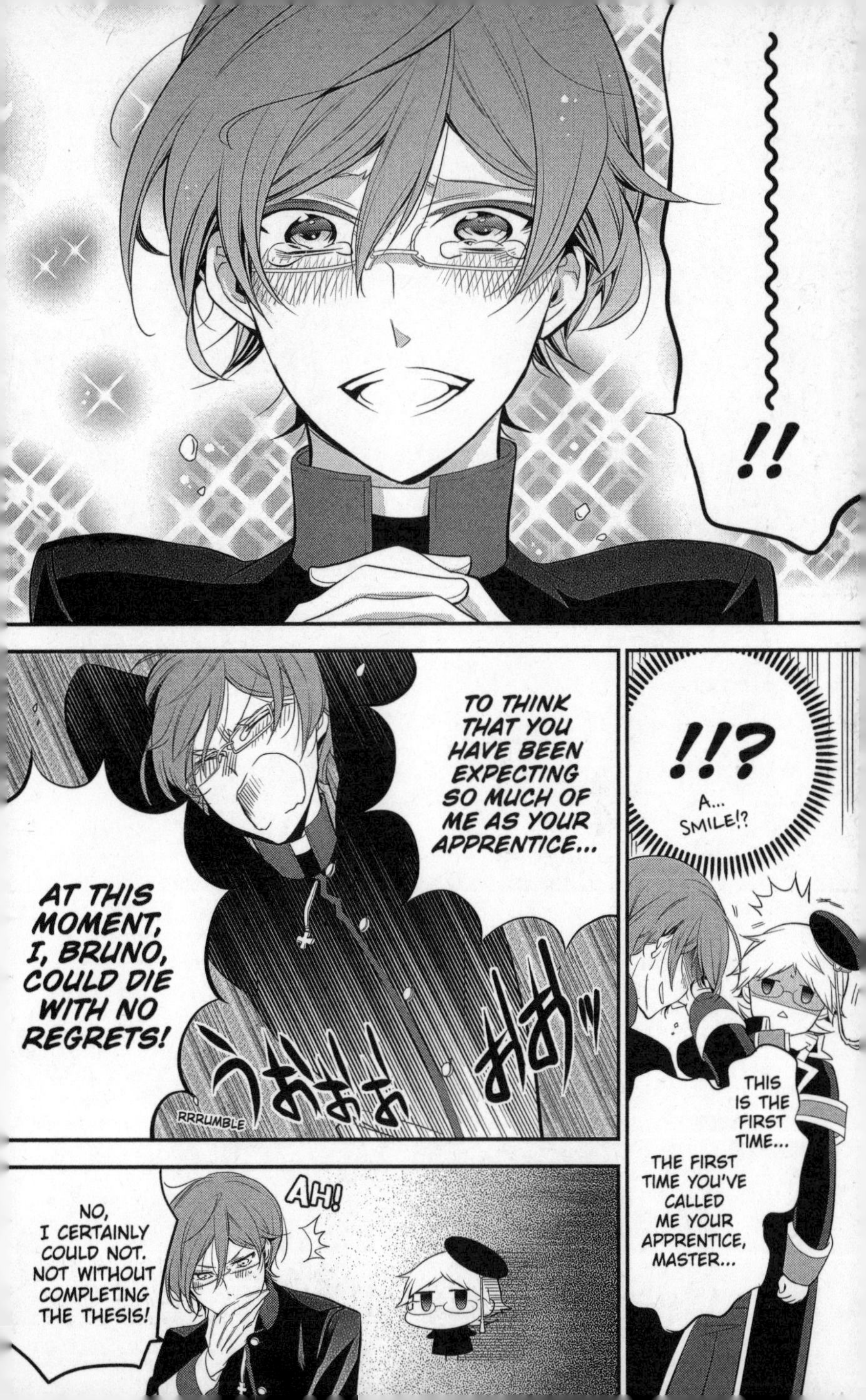
!!
!!?
A... SMILE!?
THIS IS THE FIRST TIME...
THE FIRST TIME YOU'VE CALLED ME YOUR APPRENTICE, MASTER...
TO THINK THAT YOU HAVE BEEN EXPECTING SO MUCH OF ME AS YOUR APPRENTICE...
AT THIS MOMENT, I, BRUNO, COULD DIE WITH NO REGRETS!
RRRUMBLE
AH!
NO, I CERTAINLY COULD NOT. NOT WITHOUT COMPLETING THE THESIS!

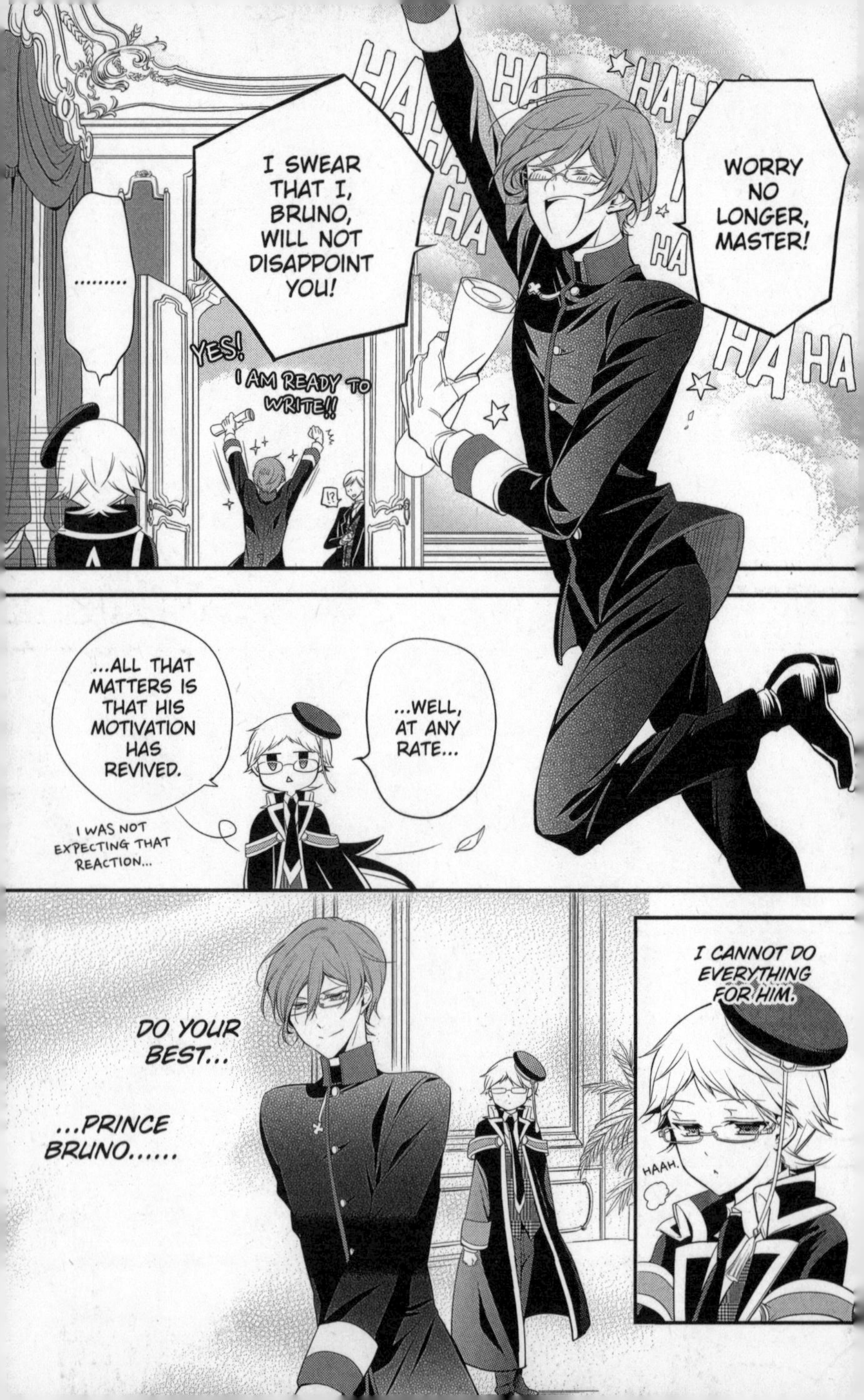
WORRY NO LONGER, MASTER!
HA HA HA HA HA HA HA HA
I SWEAR THAT I, BRUNO, WILL NOT DISAPPOINT YOU!
YES!
I AM READY TO WRITE!!
!?
....
...WELL, AT ANY RATE...
...ALL THAT MATTERS IS THAT HIS MOTIVATION HAS REVIVED.
I WAS NOT EXPECTING THAT REACTION...
I CANNOT DO EVERYTHING FOR HIM.
HAAH.
DO YOUR BEST...
...PRINCE BRUNO......

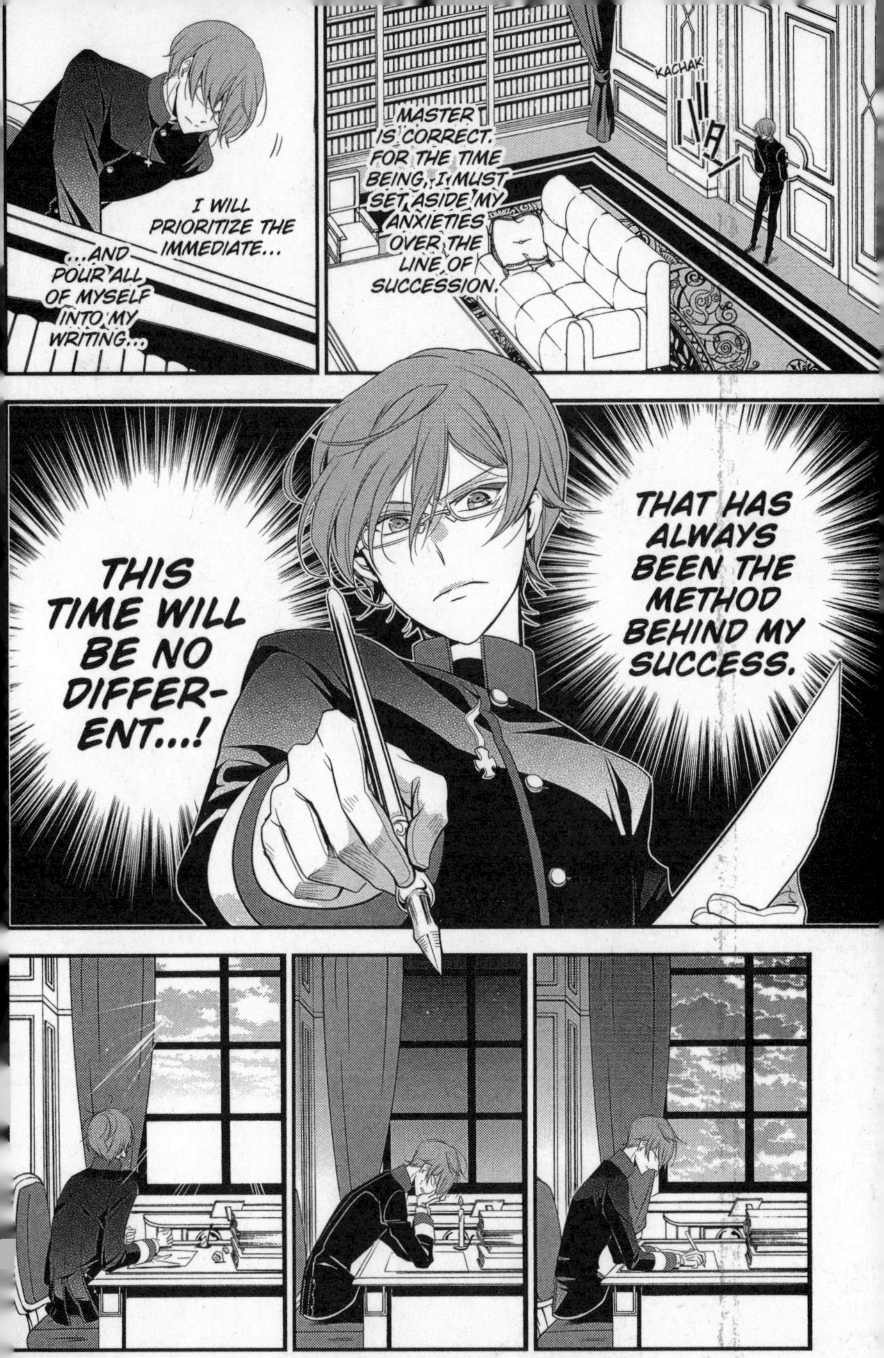
KACHAK
MASTER IS CORRECT. FOR THE TIME BEING, I MUST SET ASIDE MY ANXIETIES OVER THE LINE OF SUCCESSION.
I WILL PRIORITIZE THE IMMEDIATE...
...AND POUR ALL OF MYSELF INTO MY WRITING...
THAT HAS ALWAYS BEEN THE METHOD BEHIND MY SUCCESS.
THIS TIME WILL BE NO DIFFER-ENT...!

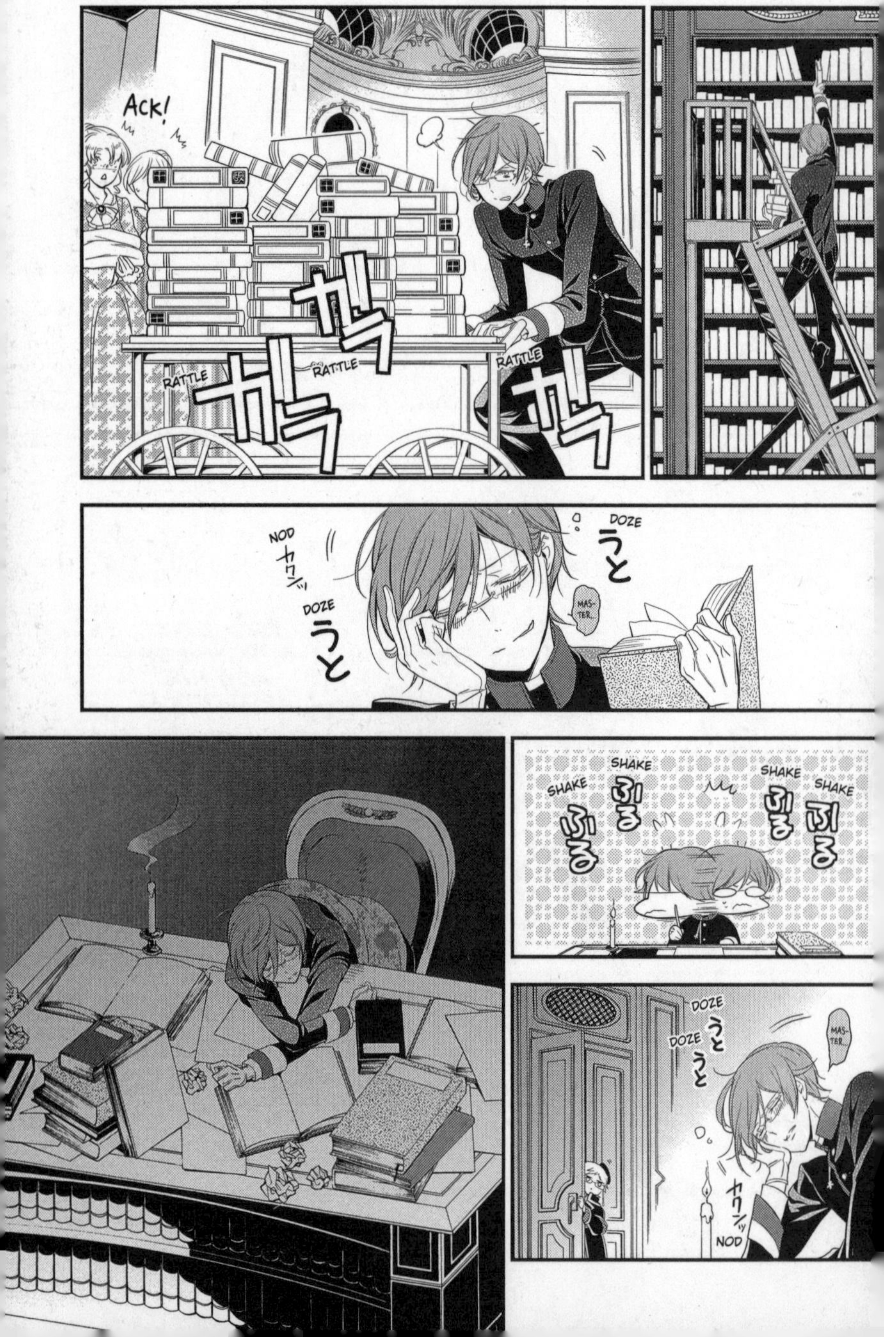
RATTLE
ガラ
RATTLE
ガラ
RATTLE
ガラ
ACK!
DOZE
うと
MAS-TER...
NOD
カクンッ
DOZE
うと
SHAKE
ふる
SHAKE
ふる
SHAKE
ふる
SHAKE
ふる
MAS-TER...
DOZE
うと
DOZE
うと
カクンッ
NOD

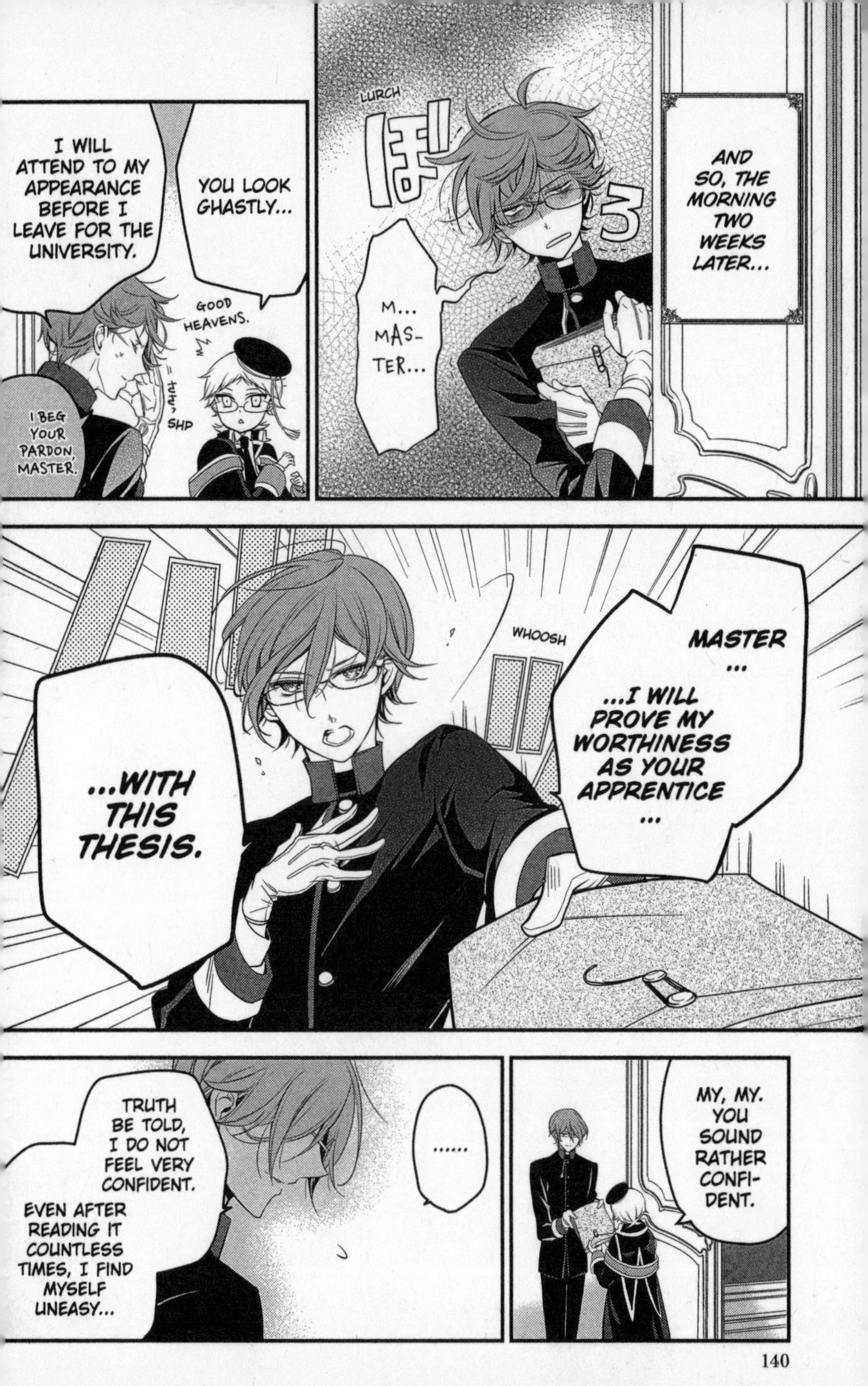
AND SO, THE MORNING TWO WEEKS LATER...
LURCH
ぼ
M... MAS-TER...
YOU LOOK GHASTLY...
GOOD HEAVENS.
SHP
I WILL ATTEND TO MY APPEARANCE BEFORE I LEAVE FOR THE UNIVERSITY.
I BEG YOUR PARDON, MASTER.
WHOOSH
MASTER ...
...I WILL PROVE MY WORTHINESS AS YOUR APPRENTICE ...
...WITH THIS THESIS.
MY, MY. YOU SOUND RATHER CONFI-DENT.
......
TRUTH BE TOLD, I DO NOT FEEL VERY CONFIDENT.
EVEN AFTER READING IT COUNTLESS TIMES, I FIND MYSELF UNEASY...

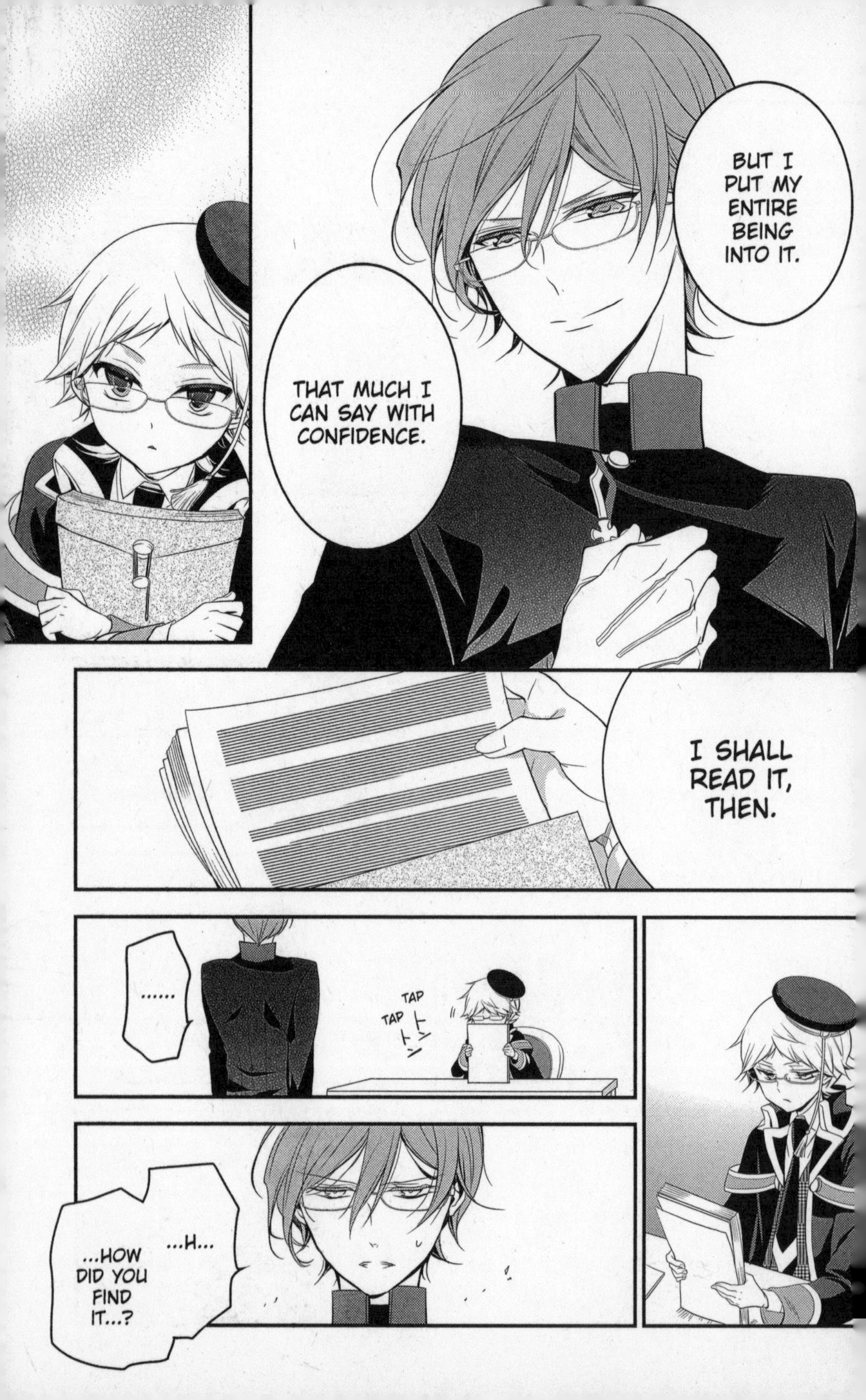
BUT I PUT MY ENTIRE BEING INTO IT.
THAT MUCH I CAN SAY WITH CONFIDENCE.
I SHALL READ IT, THEN.
......
TAP
TAP
...H...
...HOW DID YOU FIND IT...?

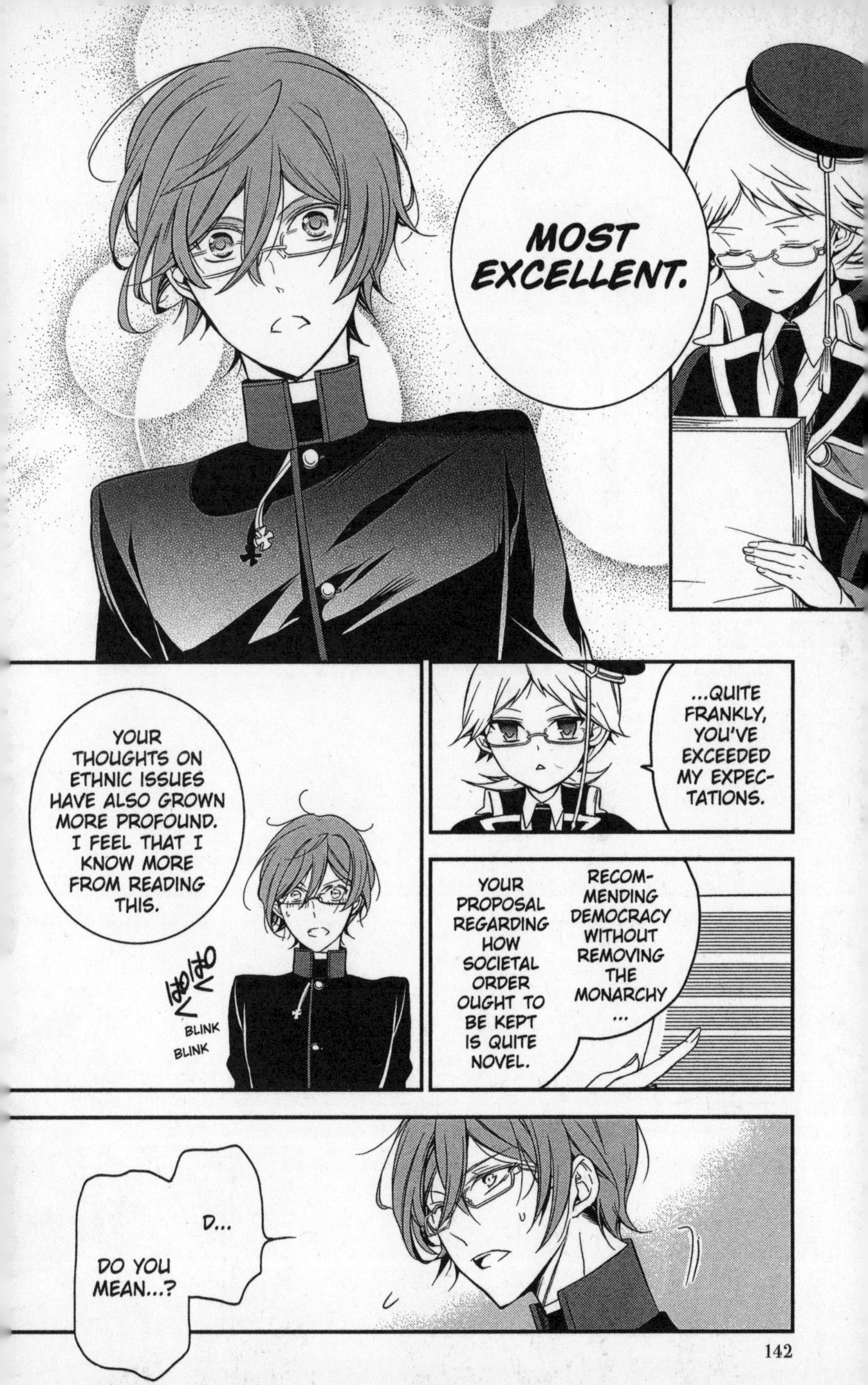
MOST EXCELLENT.
...QUITE FRANKLY, YOU'VE EXCEEDED MY EXPEC-TATIONS.
RECOM-MENDING DEMOCRACY WITHOUT REMOVING THE MONARCHY ...
YOUR PROPOSAL REGARDING HOW SOCIETAL ORDER OUGHT TO BE KEPT IS QUITE NOVEL.
YOUR THOUGHTS ON ETHNIC ISSUES HAVE ALSO GROWN MORE PROFOUND. I FEEL THAT I KNOW MORE FROM READING THIS.
BLINK BLINK
D... DO YOU MEAN...?

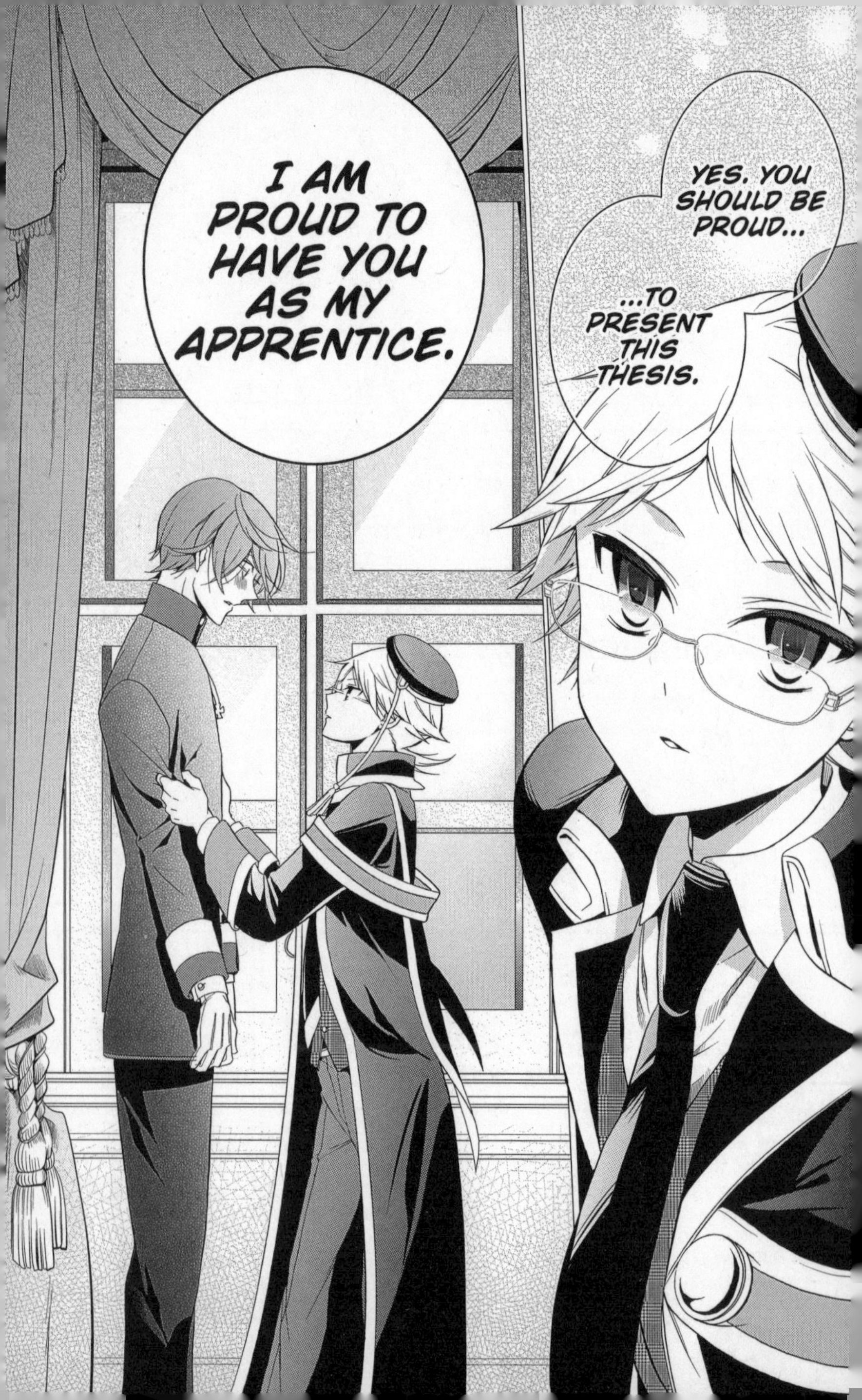
YES. YOU SHOULD BE PROUD...
...TO PRESENT THIS THESIS.
I AM PROUD TO HAVE YOU AS MY APPRENTICE.

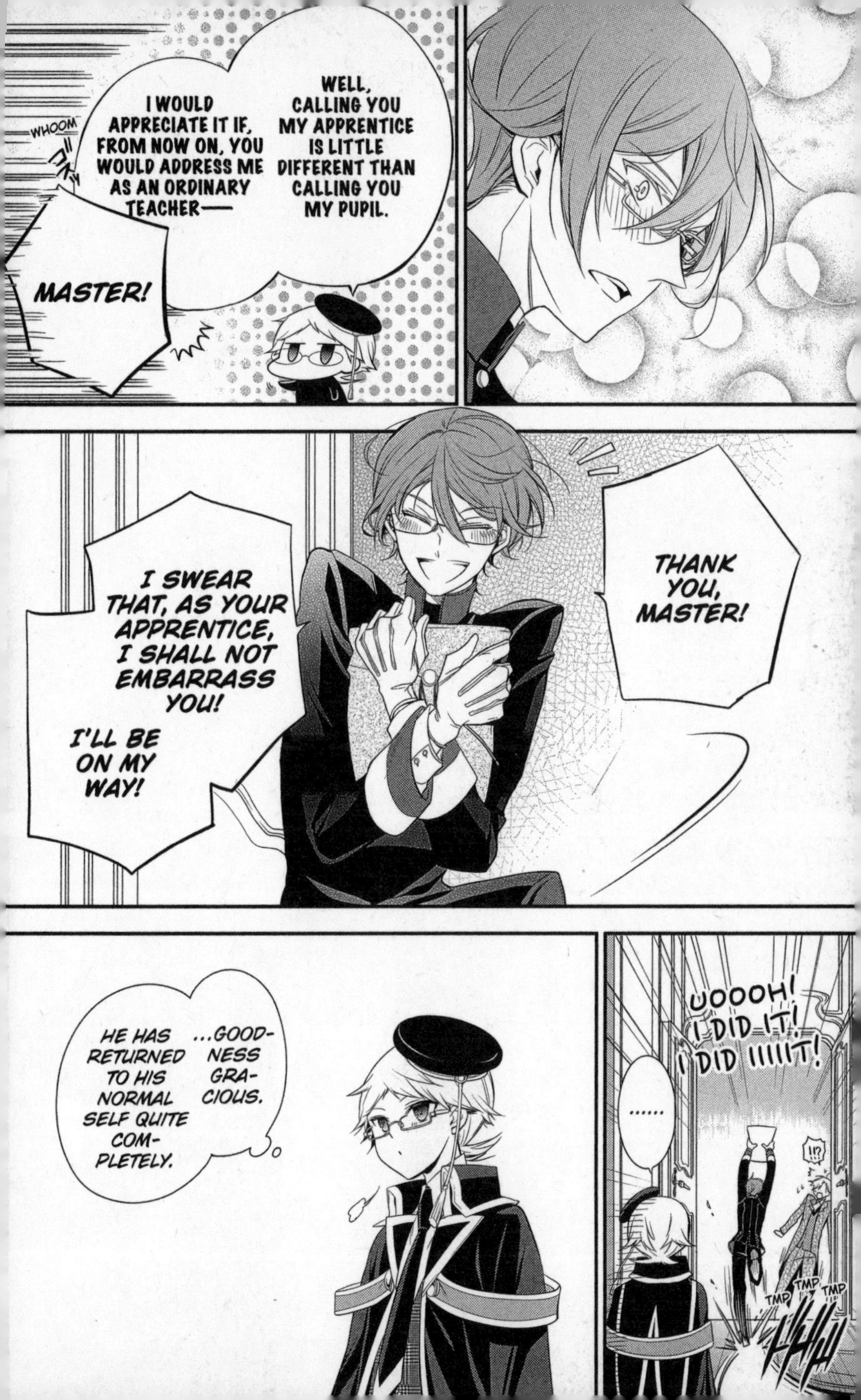
WELL, CALLING YOU MY APPRENTICE IS LITTLE DIFFERENT THAN CALLING YOU MY PUPIL.
I WOULD APPRECIATE IT IF, FROM NOW ON, YOU WOULD ADDRESS ME AS AN ORDINARY TEACHER—
WHOOM
MASTER!
THANK YOU, MASTER!
I SWEAR THAT, AS YOUR APPRENTICE, I SHALL NOT EMBARRASS YOU!
I'LL BE ON MY WAY!
UOOOH! I DID IT! I DID IIIIIT!
......
!!?
TMP TMP TMP
...GOODNESS GRACIOUS.
HE HAS RETURNED TO HIS NORMAL SELF QUITE COMPLETELY.

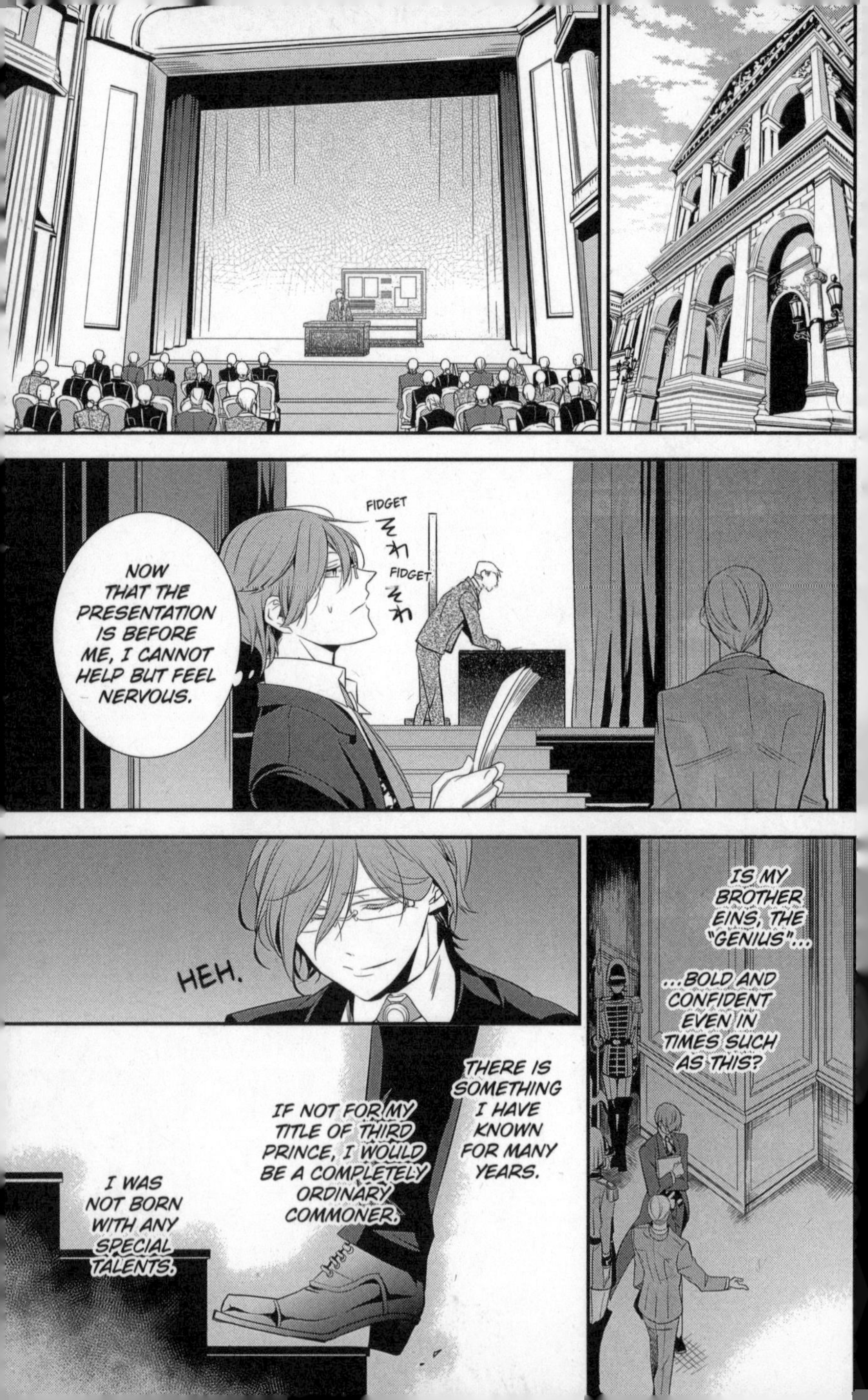
FIDGET
FIDGET
NOW THAT THE PRESENTATION IS BEFORE ME, I CANNOT HELP BUT FEEL NERVOUS.
IS MY BROTHER EINS, THE "GENIUS"...
...BOLD AND CONFIDENT EVEN IN TIMES SUCH AS THIS?
HEH.
THERE IS SOMETHING I HAVE KNOWN FOR MANY YEARS.
IF NOT FOR MY TITLE OF THIRD PRINCE, I WOULD BE A COMPLETELY ORDINARY COMMONER.
I WAS NOT BORN WITH ANY SPECIAL TALENTS.

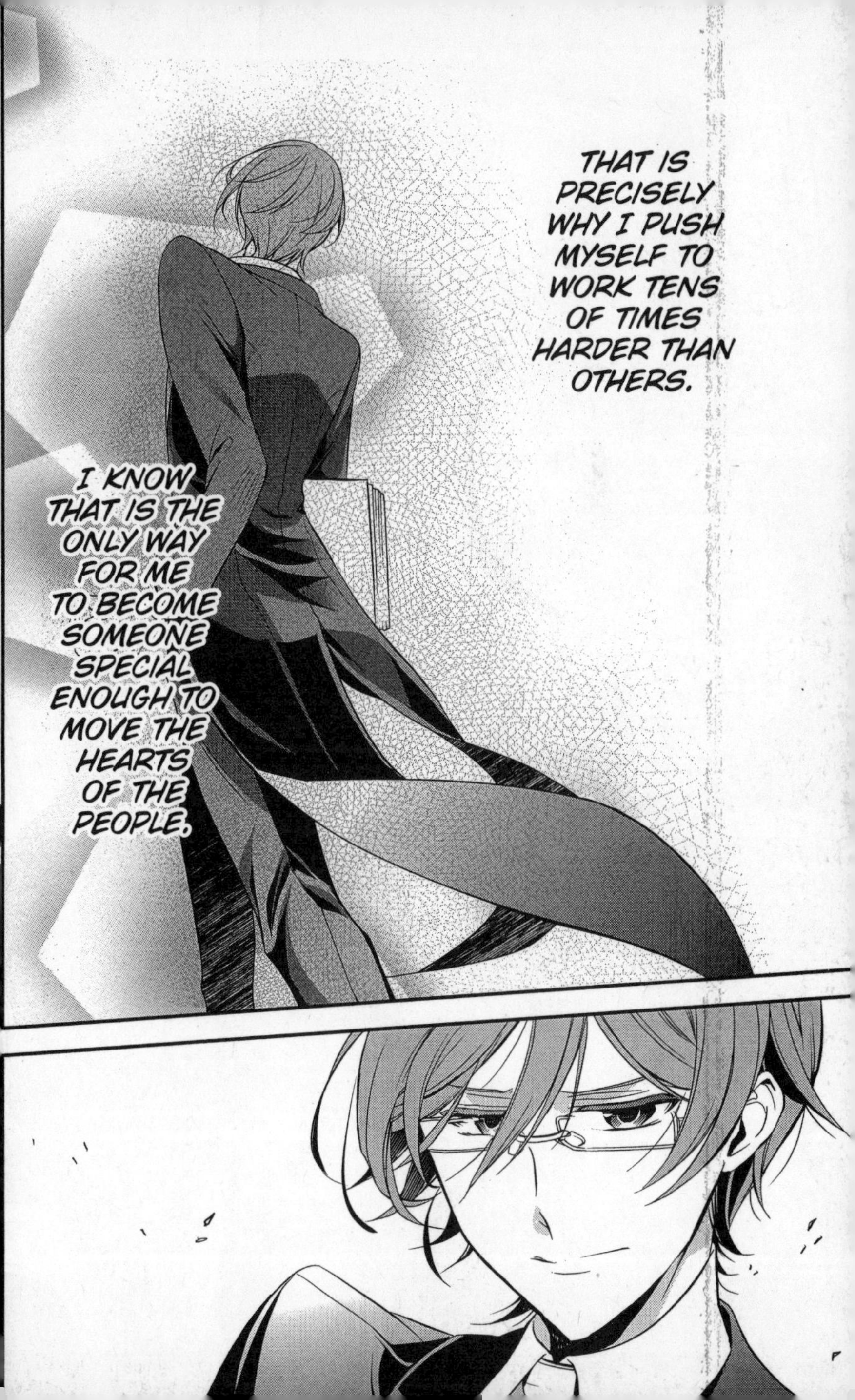
THAT IS PRECISELY WHY I PUSH MYSELF TO WORK TENS OF TIMES HARDER THAN OTHERS.
I KNOW THAT IS THE ONLY WAY FOR ME TO BECOME SOMEONE SPECIAL ENOUGH TO MOVE THE HEARTS OF THE PEOPLE.

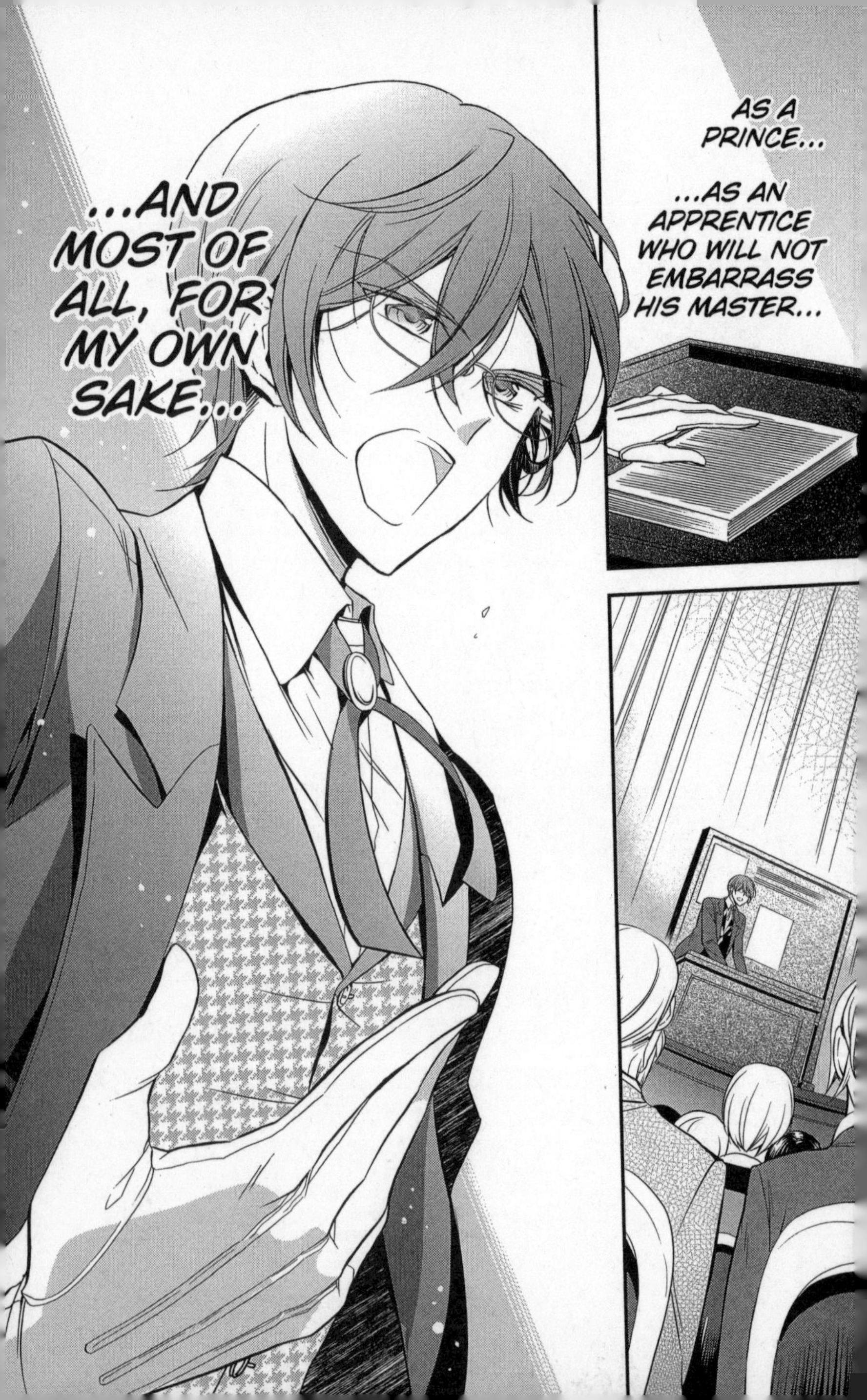
AS A PRINCE...
...AS AN APPRENTICE WHO WILL NOT EMBARRASS HIS MASTER...
...AND MOST OF ALL, FOR MY OWN SAKE...

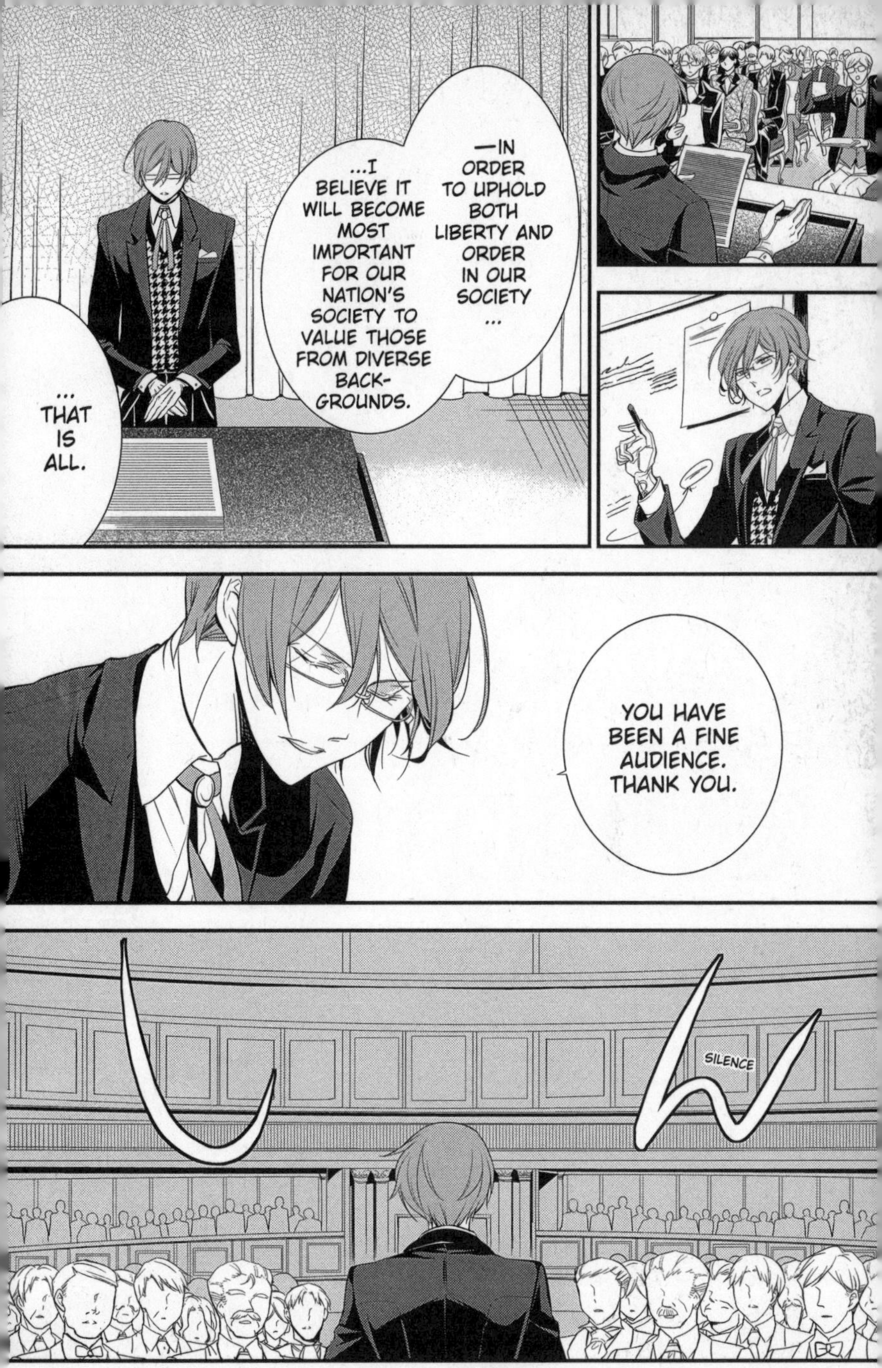
—IN ORDER TO UPHOLD BOTH LIBERTY AND ORDER IN OUR SOCIETY ...
...I BELIEVE IT WILL BECOME MOST IMPORTANT FOR OUR NATION'S SOCIETY TO VALUE THOSE FROM DIVERSE BACK-GROUNDS.
... THAT IS ALL.
YOU HAVE BEEN A FINE AUDIENCE. THANK YOU.
SILENCE

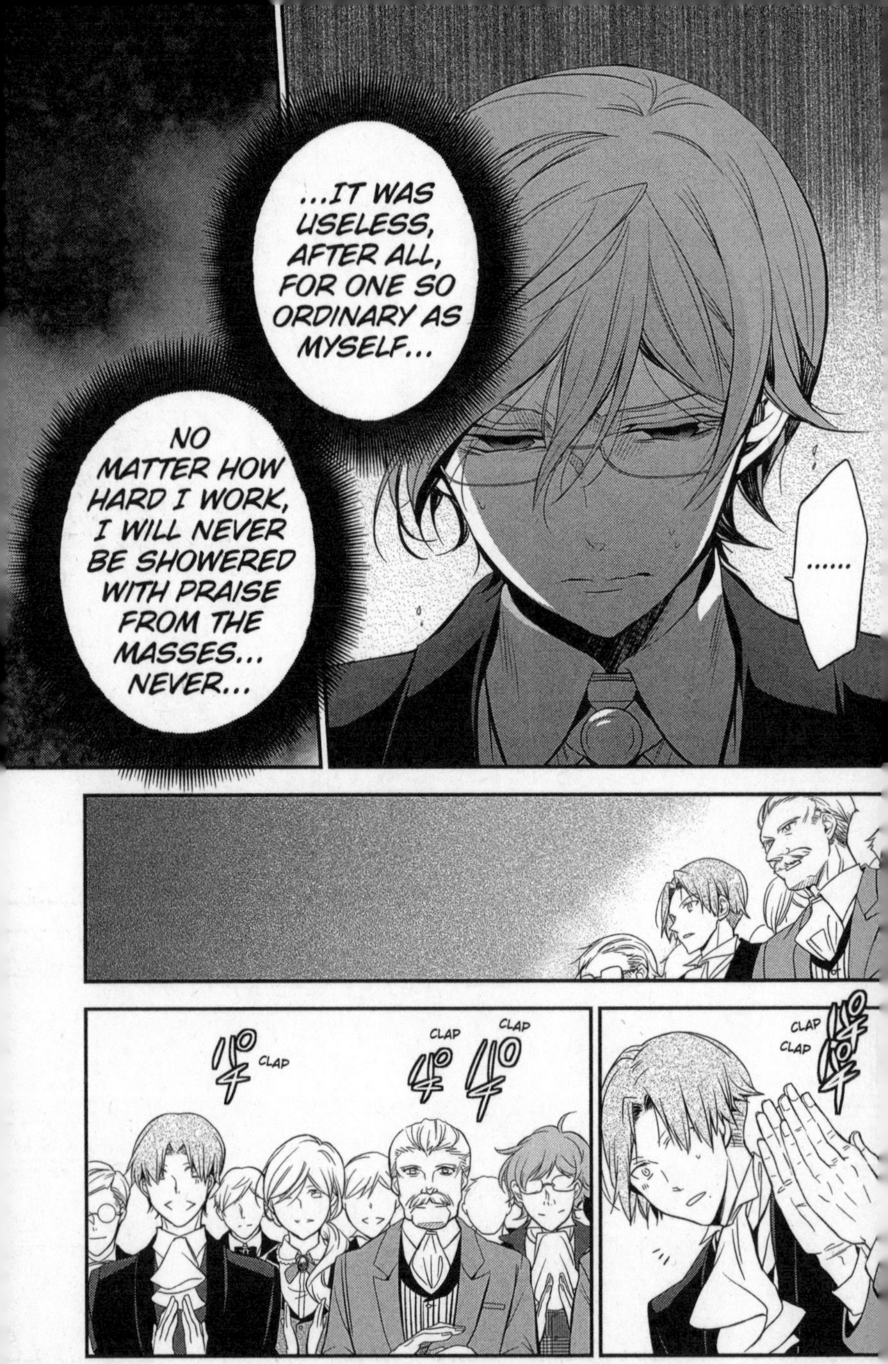
...IT WAS USELESS, AFTER ALL, FOR ONE SO ORDINARY AS MYSELF...
NO MATTER HOW HARD I WORK, I WILL NEVER BE SHOWERED WITH PRAISE FROM THE MASSES... NEVER...
......
CLAP
CLAP
CLAP
CLAP
CLAP

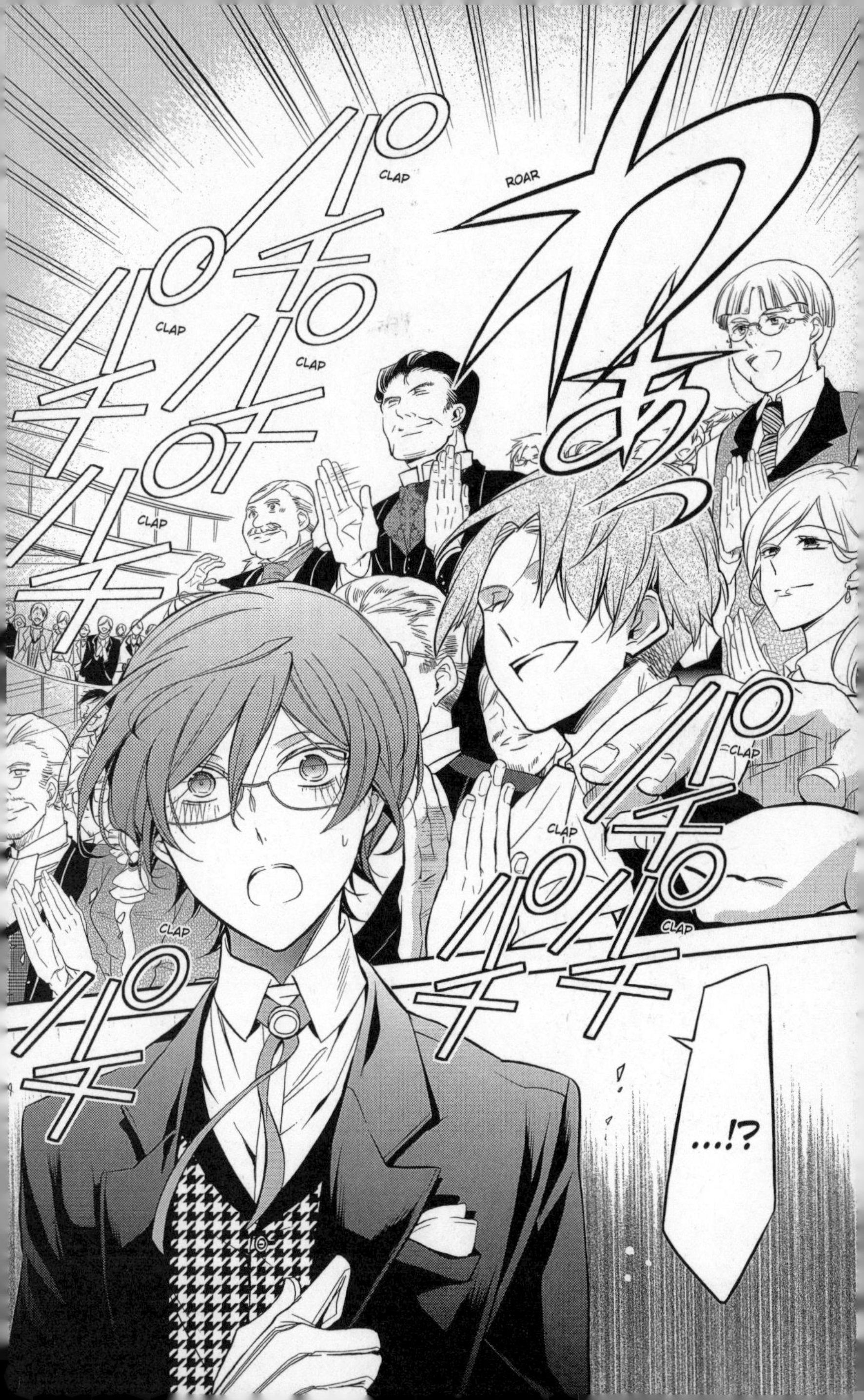

ROAR
CLAP
CLAP
CLAP
CLAP
CLAP
CLAP
CLAP
...!?
CLAP

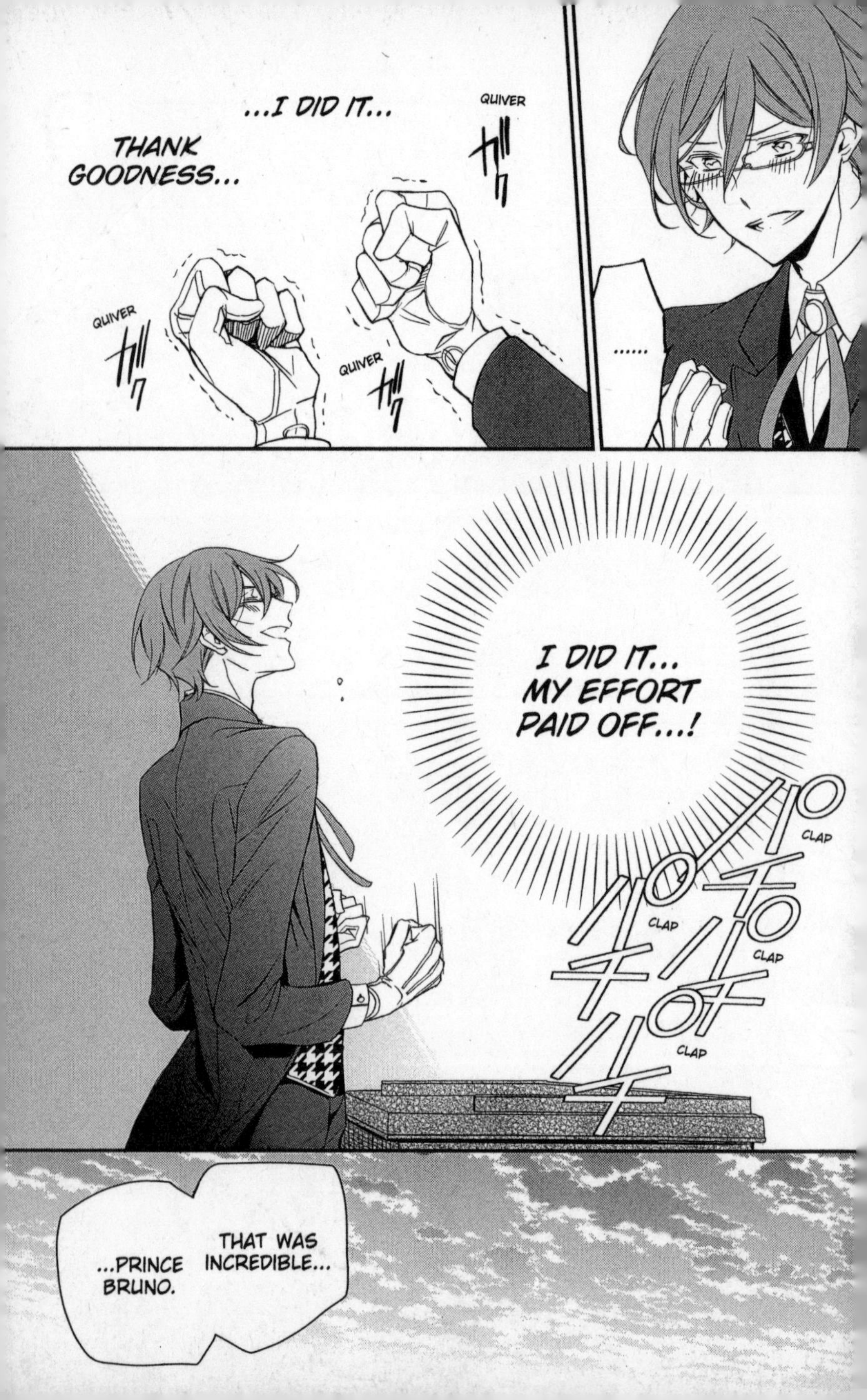
......
...I DID IT...
THANK GOODNESS...
QUIVER
ガク
QUIVER
ガク
QUIVER
ガク
I DID IT... MY EFFORT PAID OFF...!
CLAP
CLAP
CLAP
CLAP
パチパチ
パチパチ
THAT WAS INCREDIBLE...
...PRINCE BRUNO.

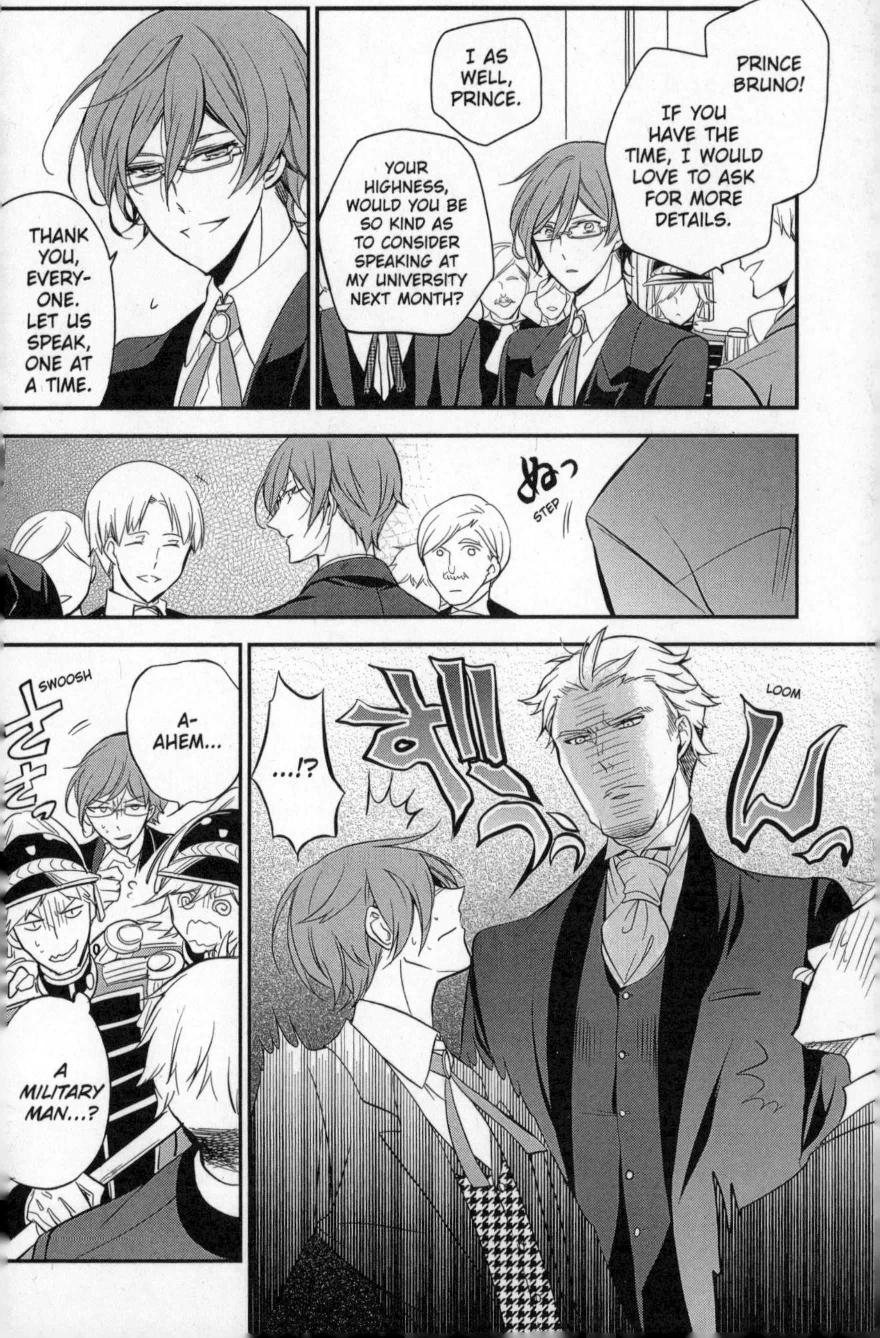
PRINCE BRUNO!
IF YOU HAVE THE TIME, I WOULD LOVE TO ASK FOR MORE DETAILS.
I AS WELL, PRINCE.
YOUR HIGHNESS, WOULD YOU BE SO KIND AS TO CONSIDER SPEAKING AT MY UNIVERSITY NEXT MONTH?
THANK YOU, EVERY-ONE. LET US SPEAK, ONE AT A TIME.
ぬっ
STEP
LOOM
...!?
SWOOSH
A-AHEM...
A MILITARY MAN...?

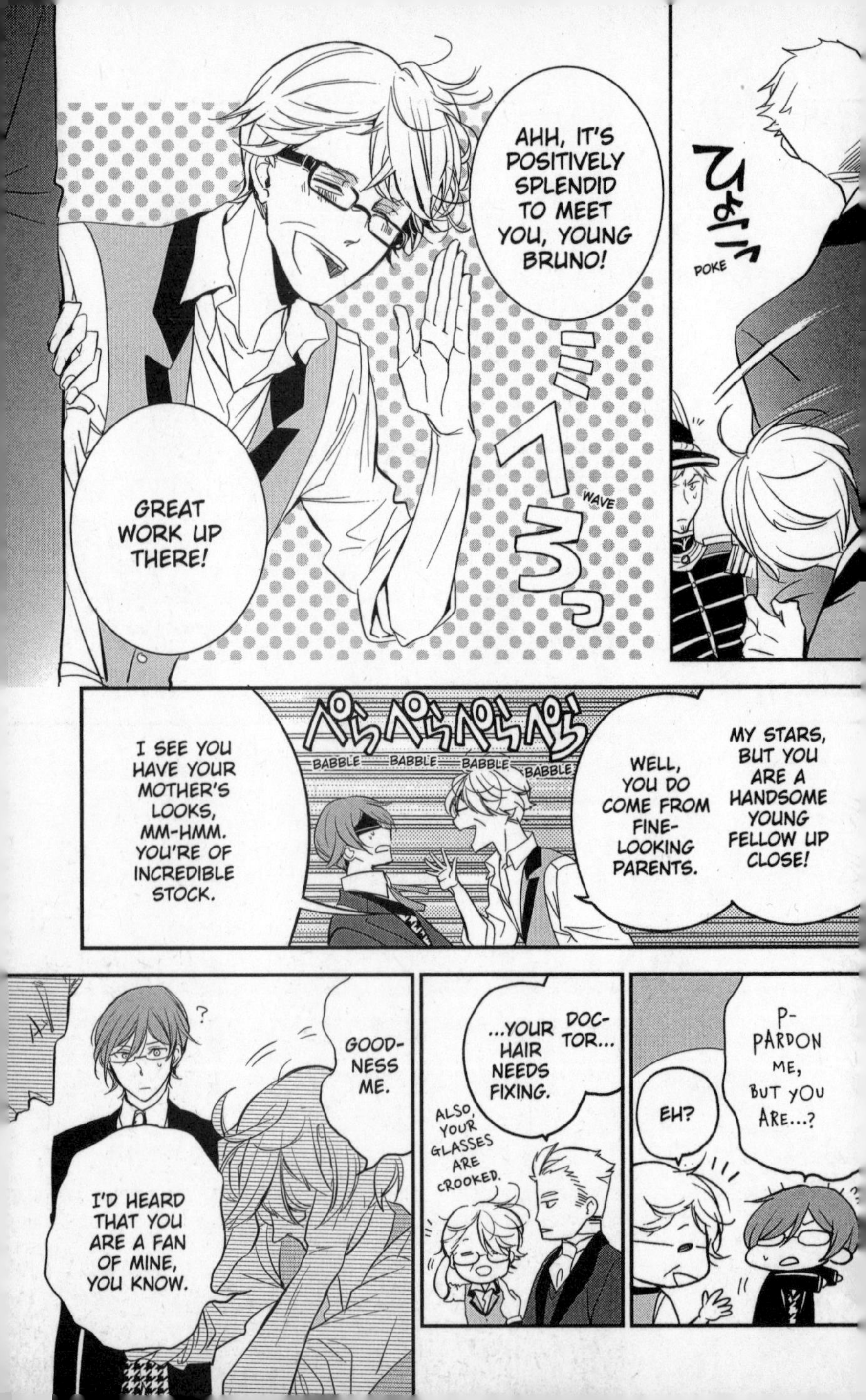
POKE
AHH, IT'S POSITIVELY SPLENDID TO MEET YOU, YOUNG BRUNO!
WAVE
GREAT WORK UP THERE!
MY STARS, BUT YOU ARE A HANDSOME YOUNG FELLOW UP CLOSE!
WELL, YOU DO COME FROM FINE-LOOKING PARENTS.
ぺらぺらぺらぺら
BABBLE BABBLE BABBLE BABBLE
I SEE YOU HAVE YOUR MOTHER'S LOOKS, MM-HMM. YOU'RE OF INCREDIBLE STOCK.
P-PARDON ME, BUT YOU ARE...?
EH?
DOCTOR...
...YOUR HAIR NEEDS FIXING.
ALSO, YOUR GLASSES ARE CROOKED.
GOODNESS ME.
I'D HEARD THAT YOU ARE A FAN OF MINE, YOU KNOW.

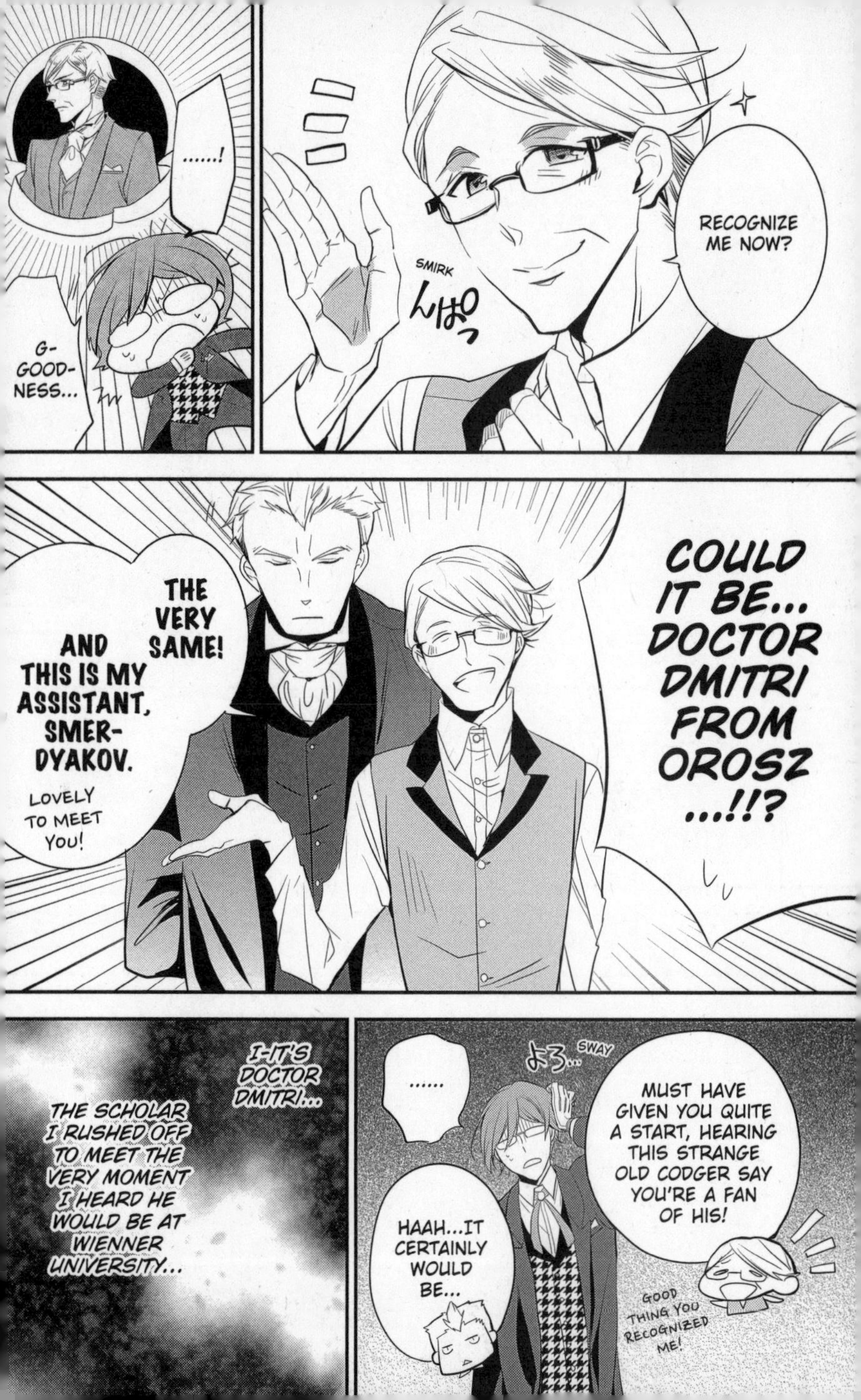
RECOGNIZE ME NOW?
SMIRK
んぱっ
......!
G-GOODNESS...
COULD IT BE... DOCTOR DMITRI FROM OROSZ ...!!?
THE VERY SAME!
AND THIS IS MY ASSISTANT, SMER-DYAKOV.
LOVELY TO MEET YOU!
MUST HAVE GIVEN YOU QUITE A START, HEARING THIS STRANGE OLD CODGER SAY YOU'RE A FAN OF HIS!
よろ... SWAY
......
HAAH...IT CERTAINLY WOULD BE...
GOOD THING YOU RECOGNIZED ME!
I-IT'S DOCTOR DMITRI...
THE SCHOLAR I RUSHED OFF TO MEET THE VERY MOMENT I HEARD HE WOULD BE AT WIENNER UNIVERSITY...

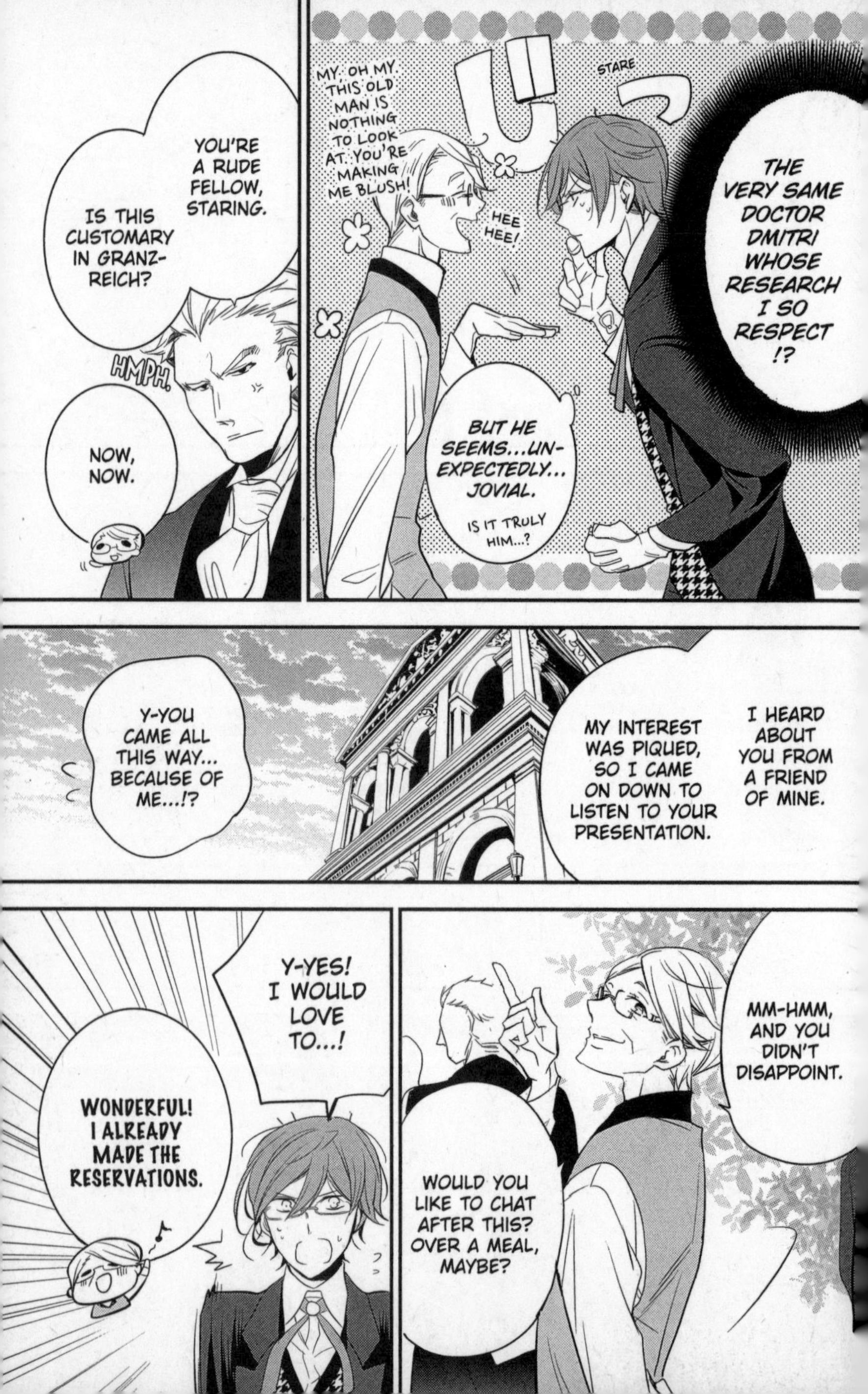
STARE
THE VERY SAME DOCTOR DMITRI WHOSE RESEARCH I SO RESPECT !?
MY, OH MY. THIS OLD MAN IS NOTHING TO LOOK AT. YOU'RE MAKING ME BLUSH!
HEE HEE!
BUT HE SEEMS...UN-EXPECTEDLY... JOVIAL.
IS IT TRULY HIM...?
YOU'RE A RUDE FELLOW, STARING.
IS THIS CUSTOMARY IN GRANZ-REICH?
HMPH.
NOW, NOW.
I HEARD ABOUT YOU FROM A FRIEND OF MINE.
MY INTEREST WAS PIQUED, SO I CAME ON DOWN TO LISTEN TO YOUR PRESENTATION.
Y-YOU CAME ALL THIS WAY... BECAUSE OF ME...!?
MM-HMM, AND YOU DIDN'T DISAPPOINT.
WOULD YOU LIKE TO CHAT AFTER THIS? OVER A MEAL, MAYBE?
Y-YES! I WOULD LOVE TO...!
WONDERFUL! I ALREADY MADE THE RESERVATIONS.

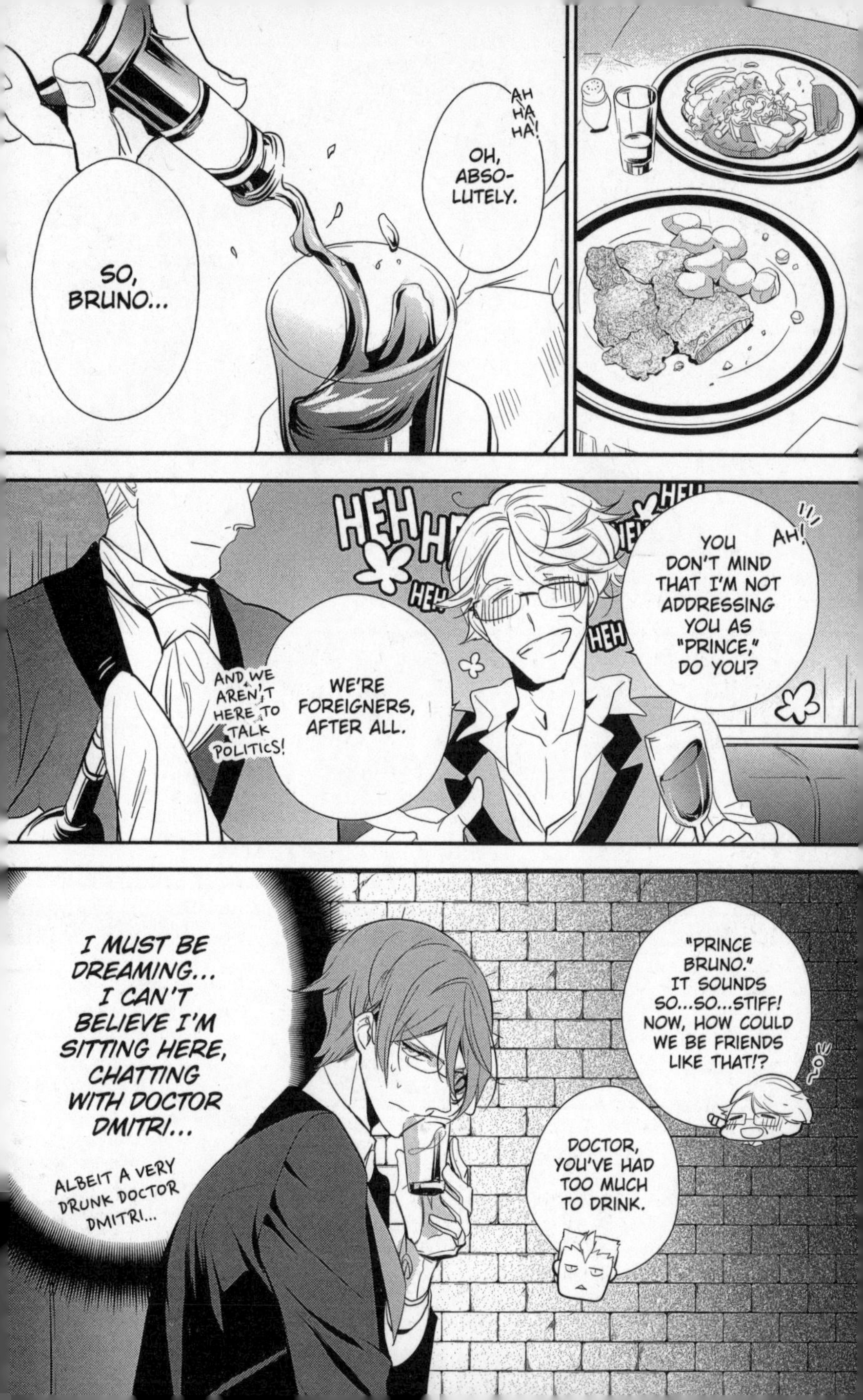
AH HA HA!
OH, ABSO-LUTELY.
SO, BRUNO...
HEH HEH HEH HEH HEH
AH!
YOU DON'T MIND THAT I'M NOT ADDRESSING YOU AS "PRINCE," DO YOU?
WE'RE FOREIGNERS, AFTER ALL.
AND WE AREN'T HERE TO TALK POLITICS!
"PRINCE BRUNO." IT SOUNDS SO...SO...STIFF! NOW, HOW COULD WE BE FRIENDS LIKE THAT!?
I MUST BE DREAMING... I CAN'T BELIEVE I'M SITTING HERE, CHATTING WITH DOCTOR DMITRI...
DOCTOR, YOU'VE HAD TOO MUCH TO DRINK.
ALBEIT A VERY DRUNK DOCTOR DMITRI...

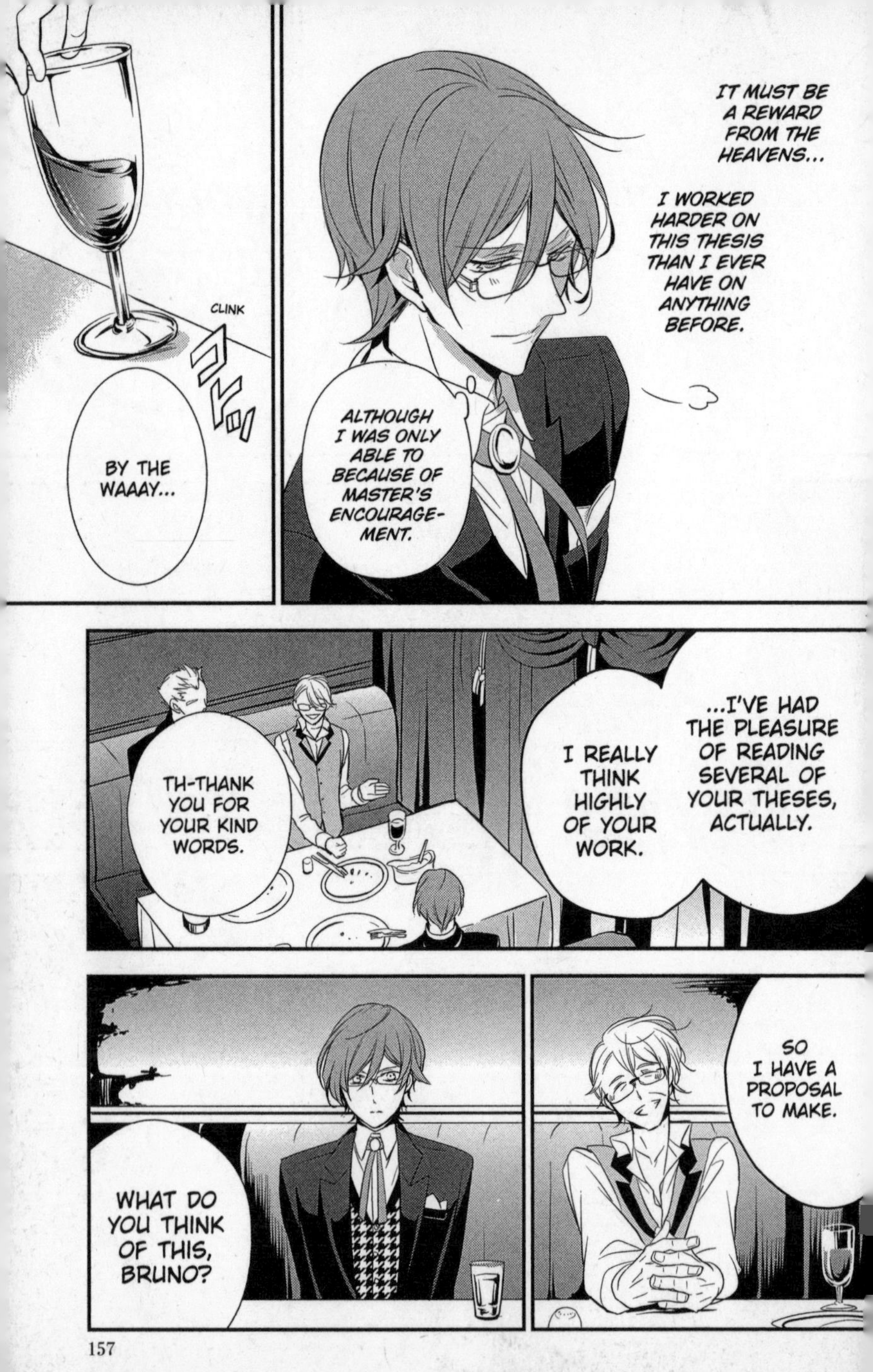
IT MUST BE A REWARD FROM THE HEAVENS...
I WORKED HARDER ON THIS THESIS THAN I EVER HAVE ON ANYTHING BEFORE.
ALTHOUGH I WAS ONLY ABLE TO BECAUSE OF MASTER'S ENCOURAGE-MENT.
CLINK
BY THE WAAAY...
...I'VE HAD THE PLEASURE OF READING SEVERAL OF YOUR THESES, ACTUALLY.
I REALLY THINK HIGHLY OF YOUR WORK.
TH-THANK YOU FOR YOUR KIND WORDS.
SO I HAVE A PROPOSAL TO MAKE.
WHAT DO YOU THINK OF THIS, BRUNO?

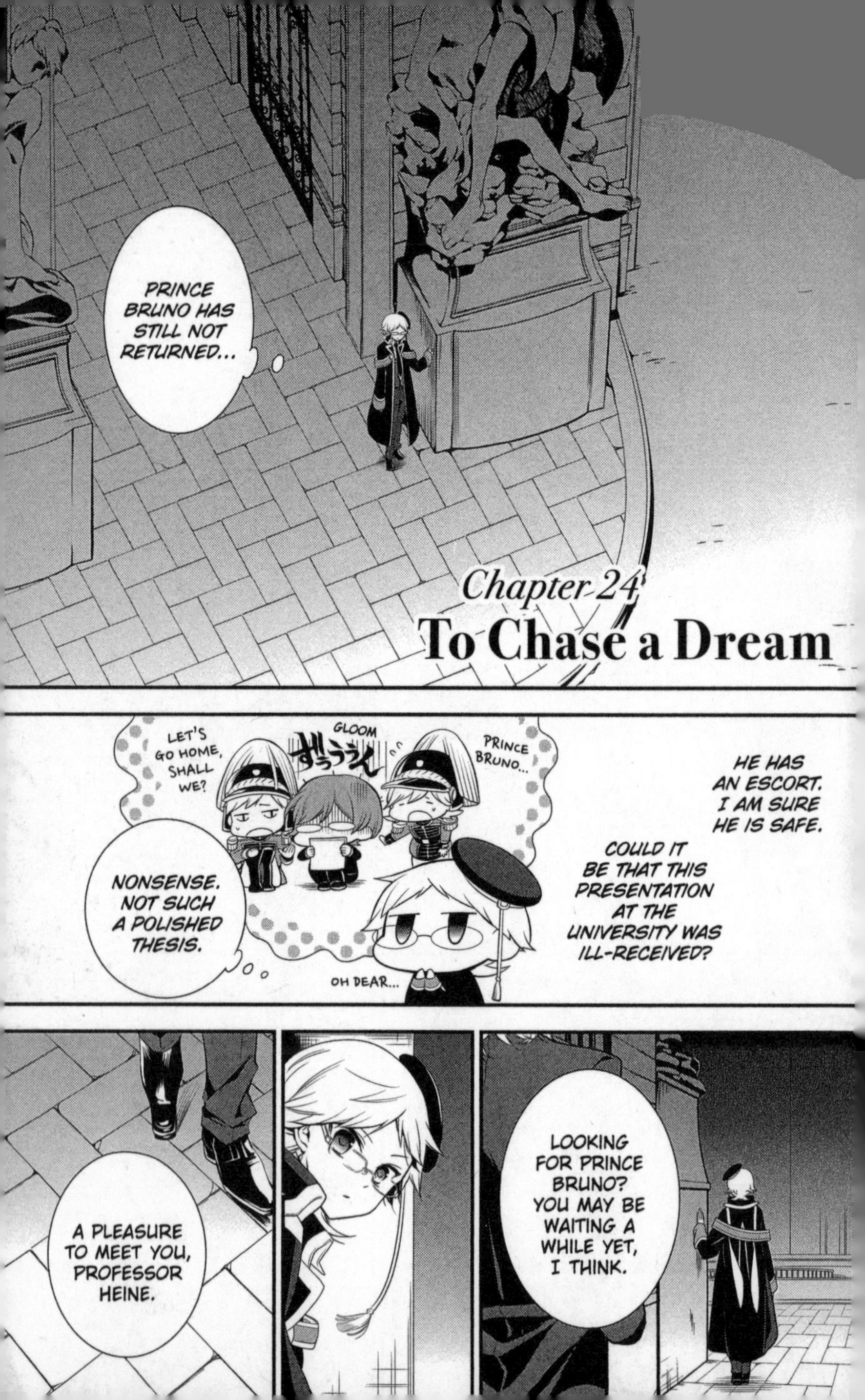
PRINCE BRUNO HAS STILL NOT RETURNED...
Chapter 24
To Chase a Dream
HE HAS AN ESCORT. I AM SURE HE IS SAFE.
COULD IT BE THAT THIS PRESENTATION AT THE UNIVERSITY WAS ILL-RECEIVED?
PRINCE BRUNO...
GLOOM
LET'S GO HOME, SHALL WE?
NONSENSE. NOT SUCH A POLISHED THESIS.
OH DEAR...
LOOKING FOR PRINCE BRUNO? YOU MAY BE WAITING A WHILE YET, I THINK.
A PLEASURE TO MEET YOU, PROFESSOR HEINE.

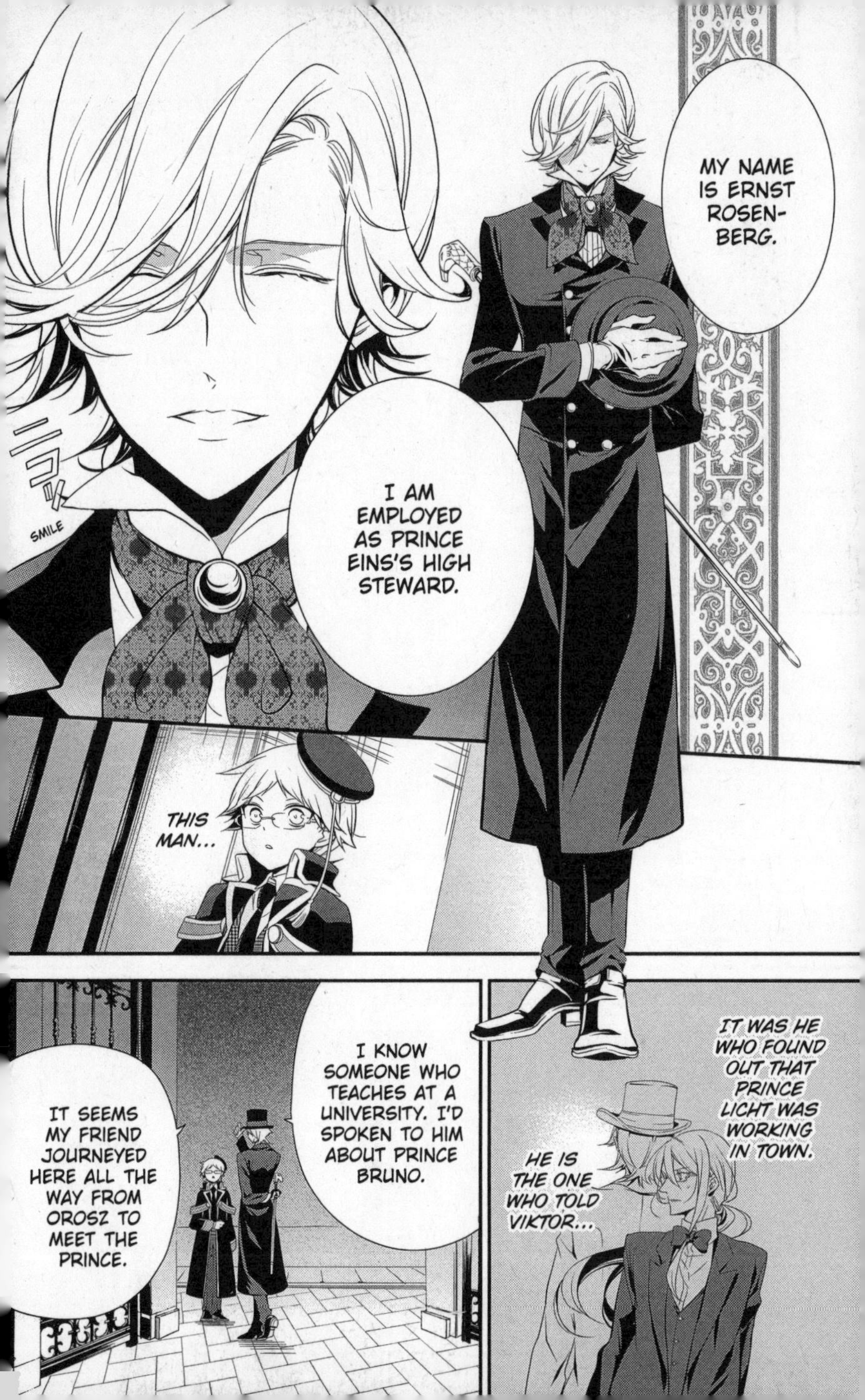
MY NAME IS ERNST ROSEN-BERG.
I AM EMPLOYED AS PRINCE EINS'S HIGH STEWARD.
SMILE
THIS MAN...
IT WAS HE WHO FOUND OUT THAT PRINCE LICHT WAS WORKING IN TOWN.
HE IS THE ONE WHO TOLD VIKTOR...
I KNOW SOMEONE WHO TEACHES AT A UNIVERSITY. I'D SPOKEN TO HIM ABOUT PRINCE BRUNO.
IT SEEMS MY FRIEND JOURNEYED HERE ALL THE WAY FROM OROSZ TO MEET THE PRINCE.

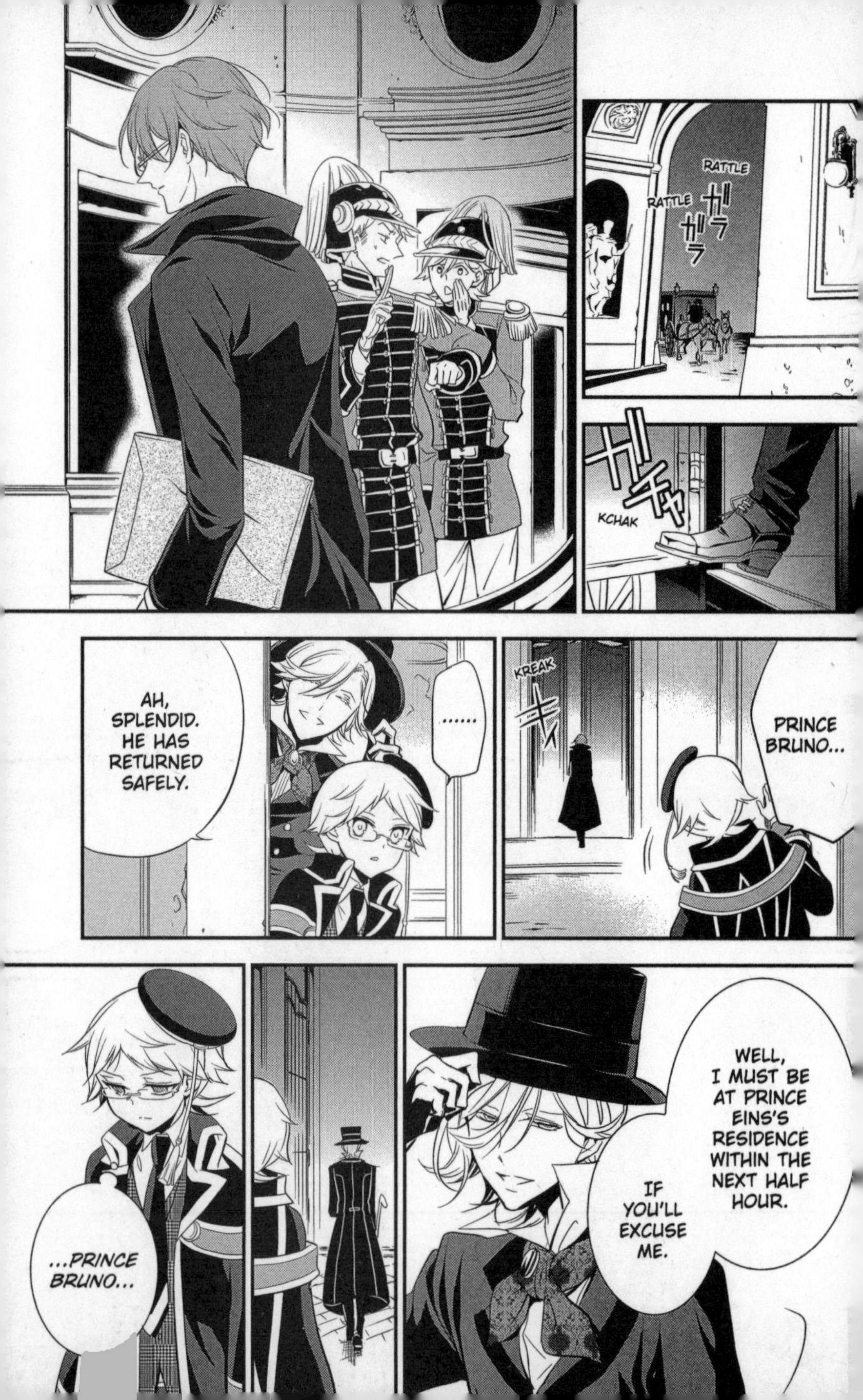
RATTLE
RATTLE
ガラ
ガラ
ガチャ
KCHAK
KREAK
PRINCE BRUNO...
......
AH, SPLENDID. HE HAS RETURNED SAFELY.
WELL, I MUST BE AT PRINCE EINS'S RESIDENCE WITHIN THE NEXT HALF HOUR.
IF YOU'LL EXCUSE ME.
...PRINCE BRUNO...

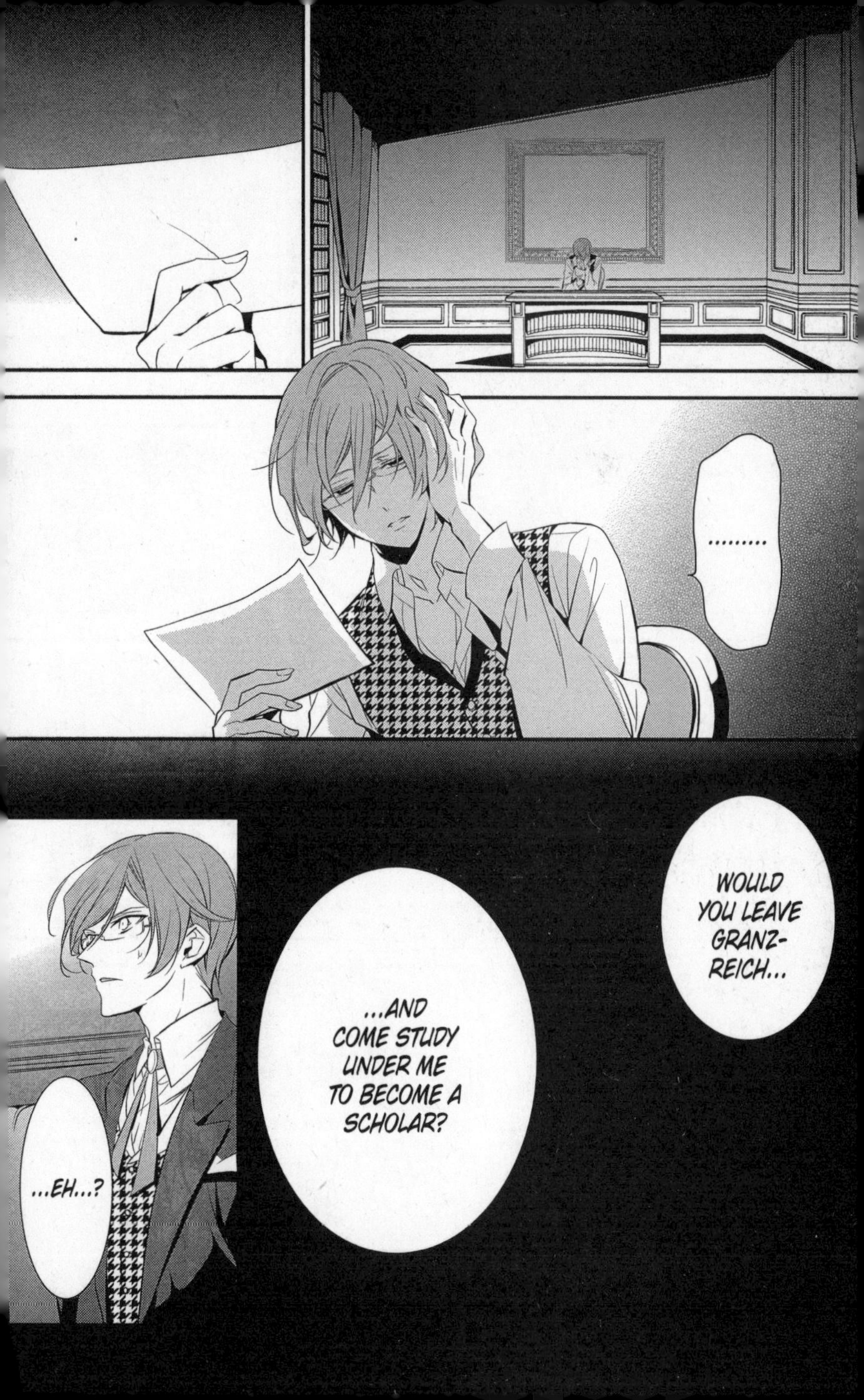
....
WOULD YOU LEAVE GRANZ-REICH...
...AND COME STUDY UNDER ME TO BECOME A SCHOLAR?
...EH...?

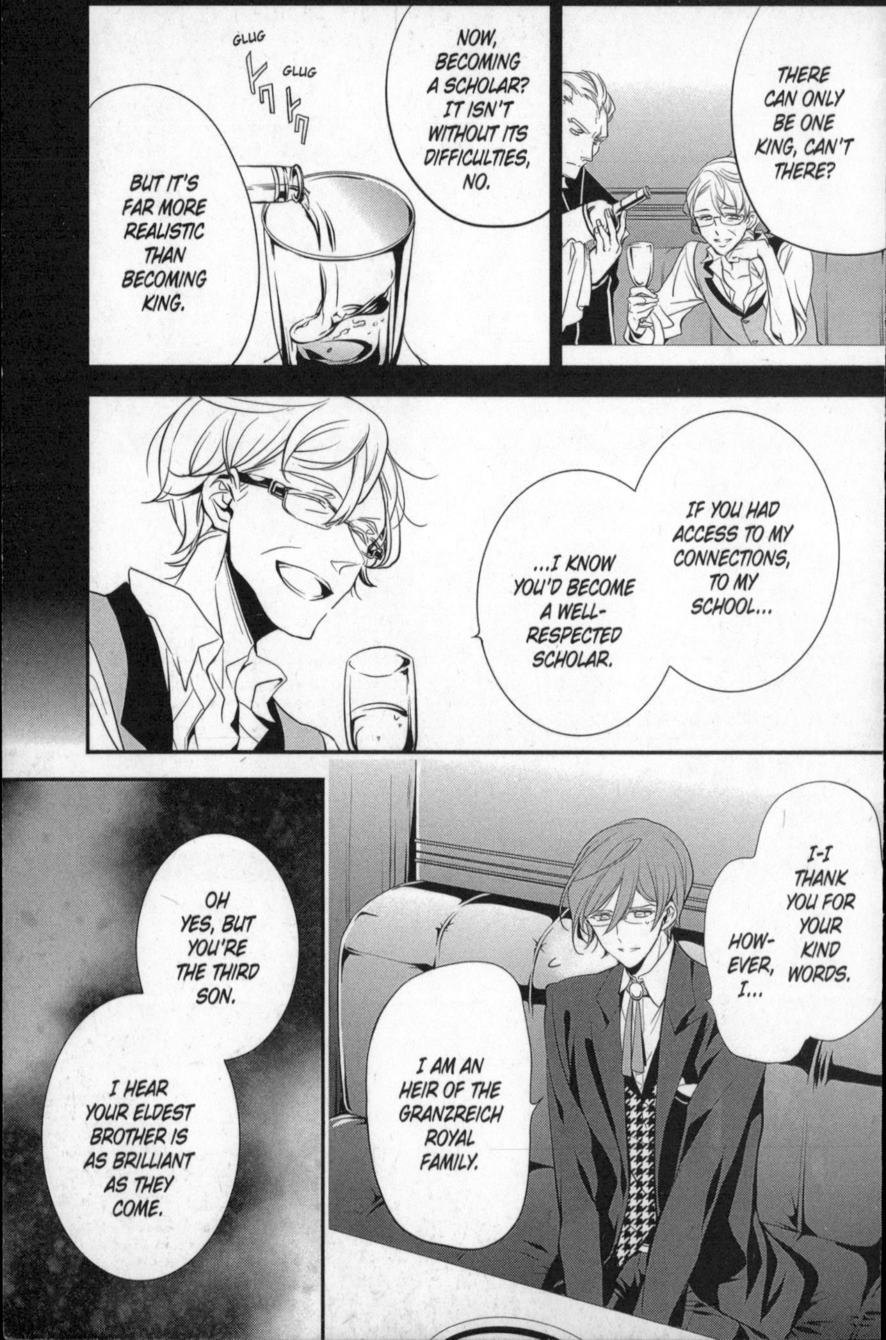
THERE CAN ONLY BE ONE KING, CAN'T THERE?
NOW, BECOMING A SCHOLAR? IT ISN'T WITHOUT ITS DIFFICULTIES, NO.
GLUG
GLUG
BUT IT'S FAR MORE REALISTIC THAN BECOMING KING.
IF YOU HAD ACCESS TO MY CONNECTIONS, TO MY SCHOOL...
...I KNOW YOU'D BECOME A WELL-RESPECTED SCHOLAR.
I-I THANK YOU FOR YOUR KIND WORDS.
HOW-EVER, I...
I AM AN HEIR OF THE GRANZREICH ROYAL FAMILY.
OH YES, BUT YOU'RE THE THIRD SON.
I HEAR YOUR ELDEST BROTHER IS AS BRILLIANT AS THEY COME.

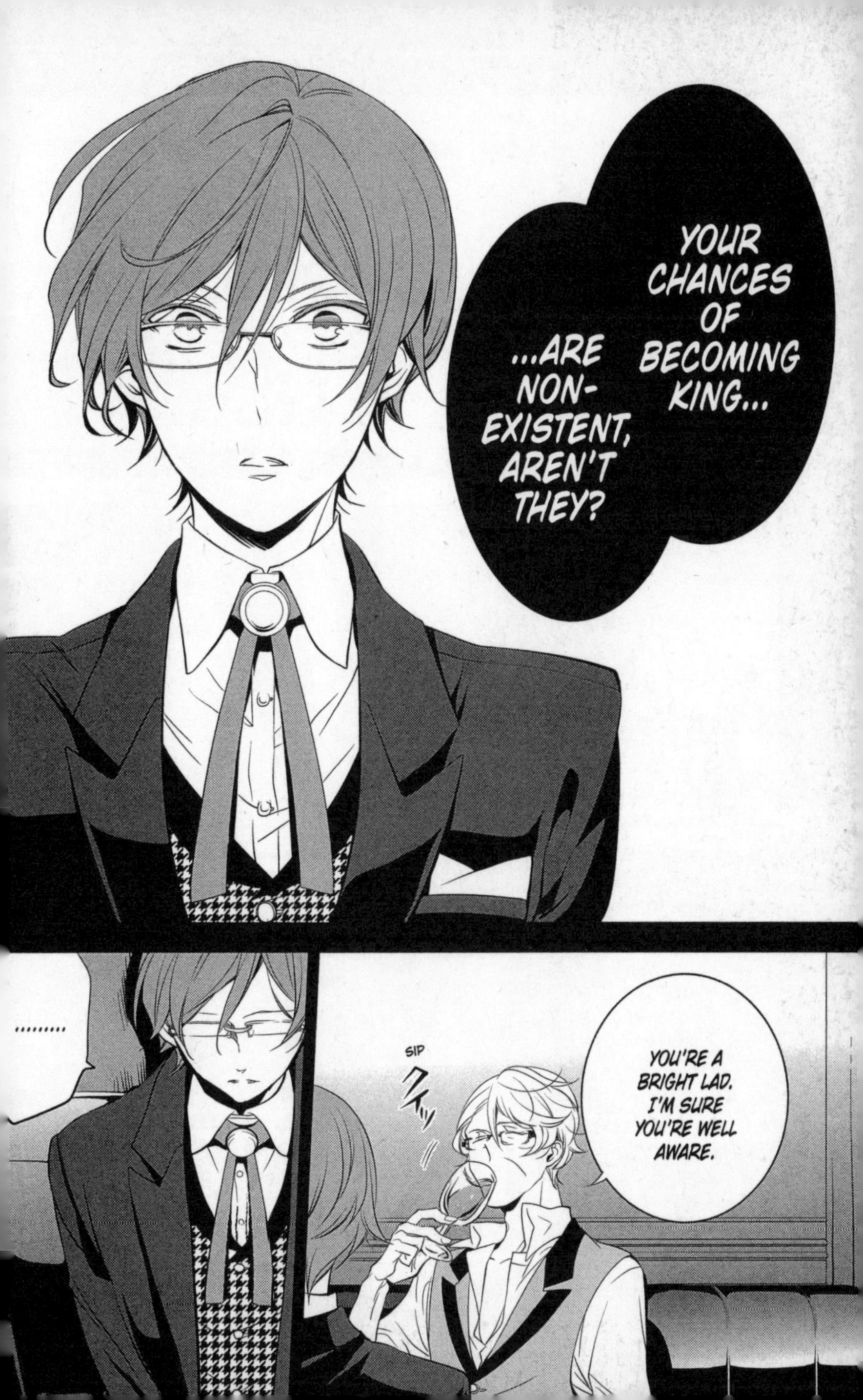
YOUR CHANCES OF BECOMING KING...
...ARE NON-EXISTENT, AREN'T THEY?
YOU'RE A BRIGHT LAD. I'M SURE YOU'RE WELL AWARE.
SIP
....

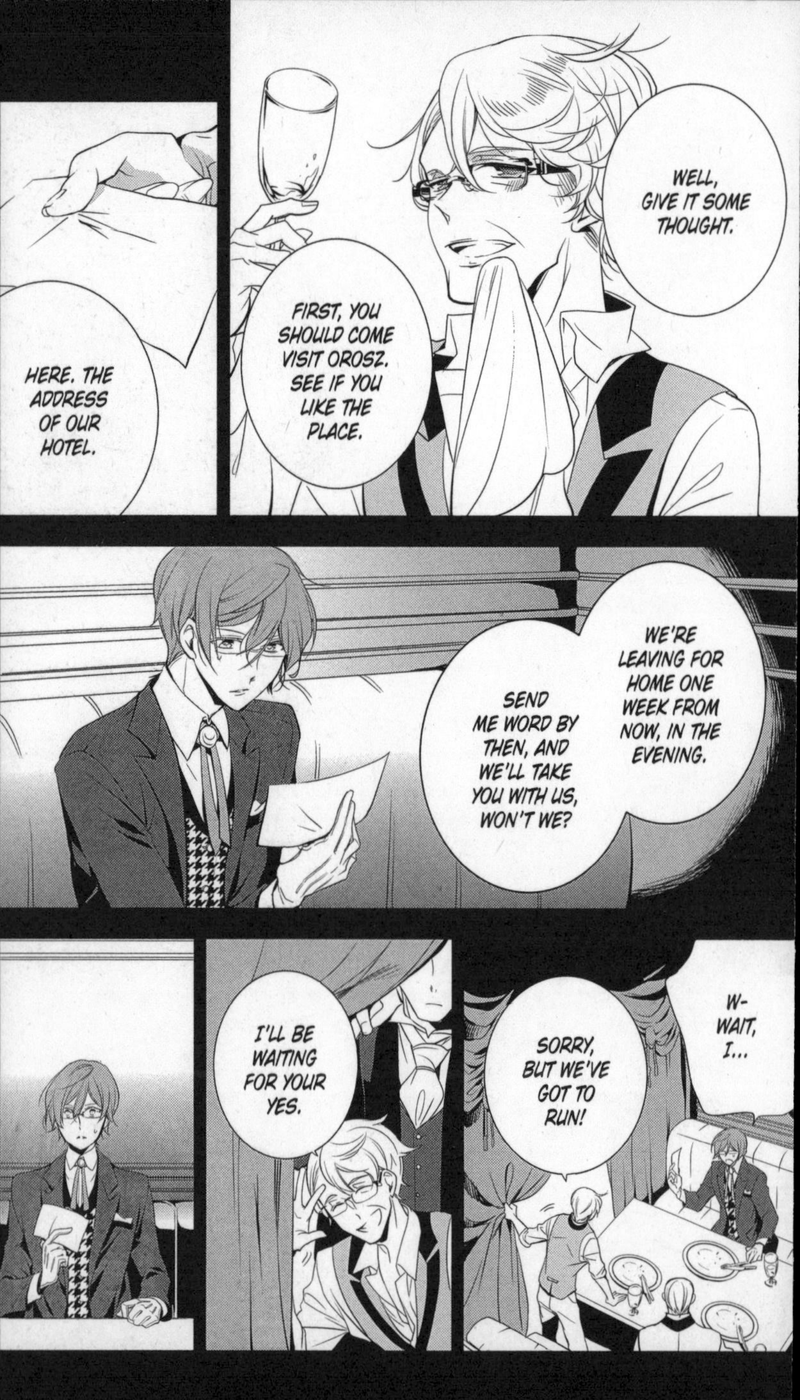
WELL, GIVE IT SOME THOUGHT.
FIRST, YOU SHOULD COME VISIT OROSZ. SEE IF YOU LIKE THE PLACE.
HERE. THE ADDRESS OF OUR HOTEL.
WE'RE LEAVING FOR HOME ONE WEEK FROM NOW, IN THE EVENING.
SEND ME WORD BY THEN, AND WE'LL TAKE YOU WITH US, WON'T WE?
W-WAIT, I...
SORRY, BUT WE'VE GOT TO RUN!
I'LL BE WAITING FOR YOUR YES.

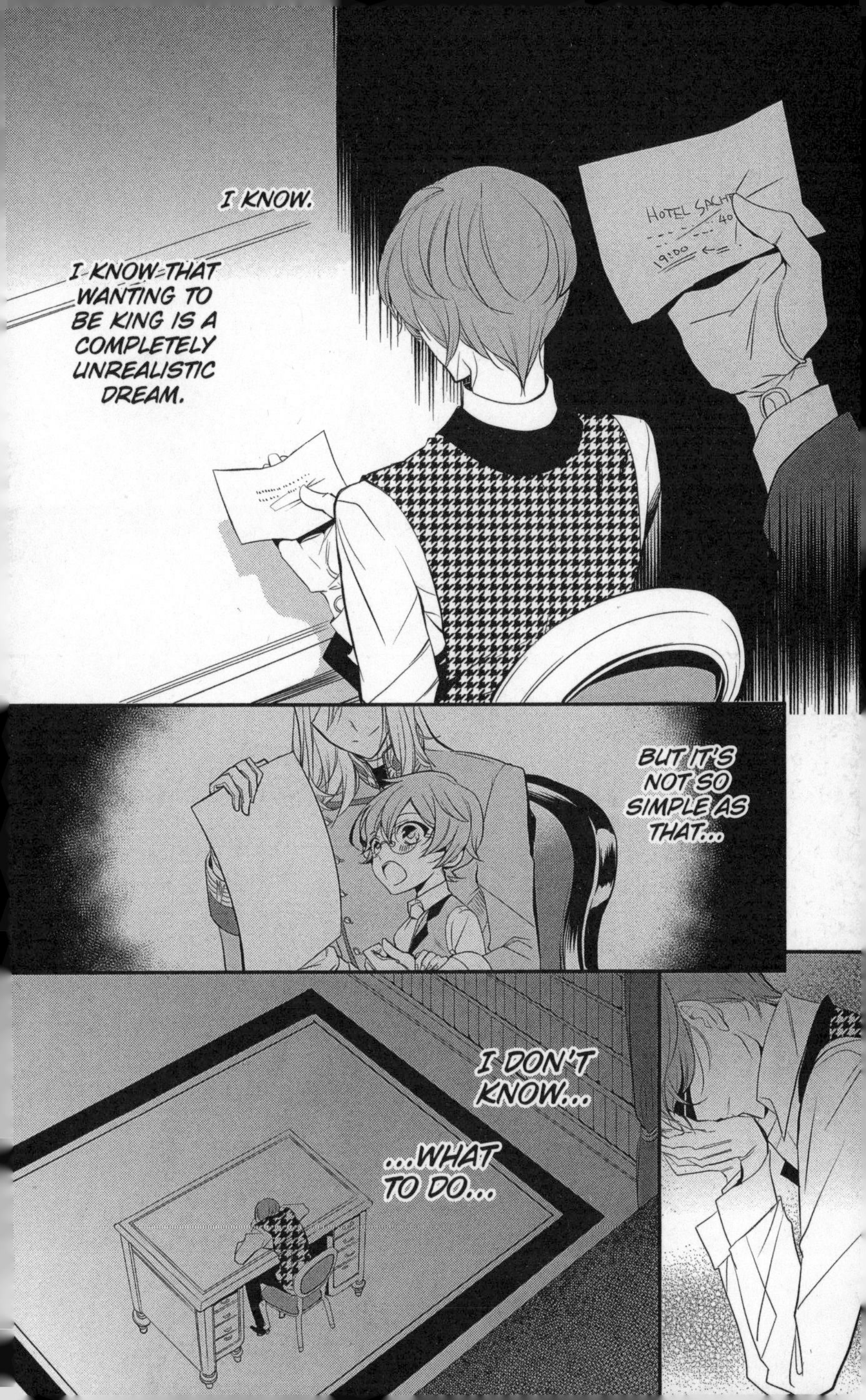
I KNOW.
I KNOW THAT WANTING TO BE KING IS A COMPLETELY UNREALISTIC DREAM.
BUT IT'S NOT SO SIMPLE AS THAT...
I DON'T KNOW...
...WHAT TO DO...

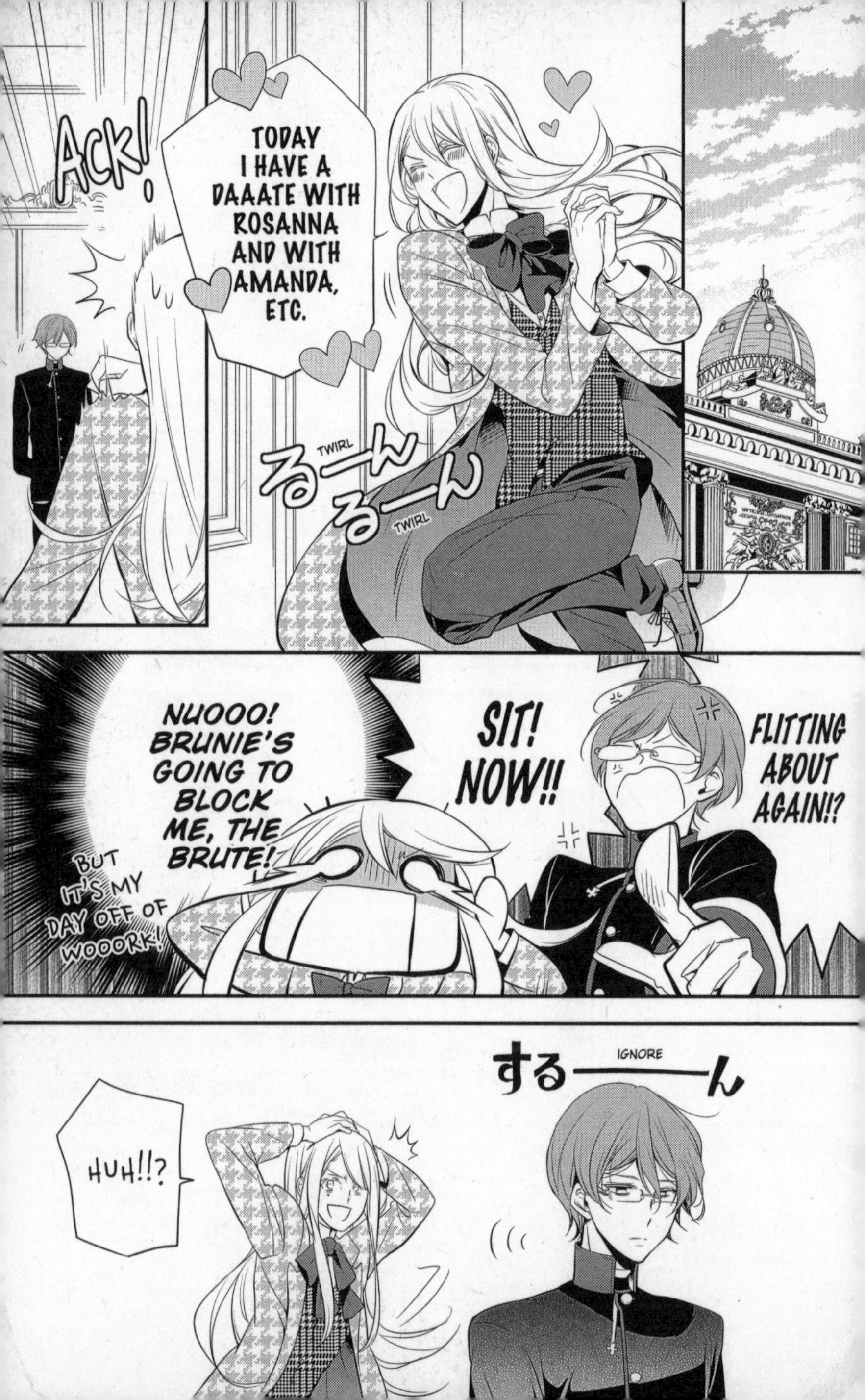
TODAY I HAVE A DAAATE WITH ROSANNA AND WITH AMANDA, ETC.
るーん TWIRL
るーん TWIRL
ACK!
FLITTING ABOUT AGAIN!?
SIT! NOW!!
NUOOO! BRUNIE'S GOING TO BLOCK ME, THE BRUTE!
BUT IT'S MY DAY OFF OF WOOORK!
するーーん IGNORE
HUH!!?

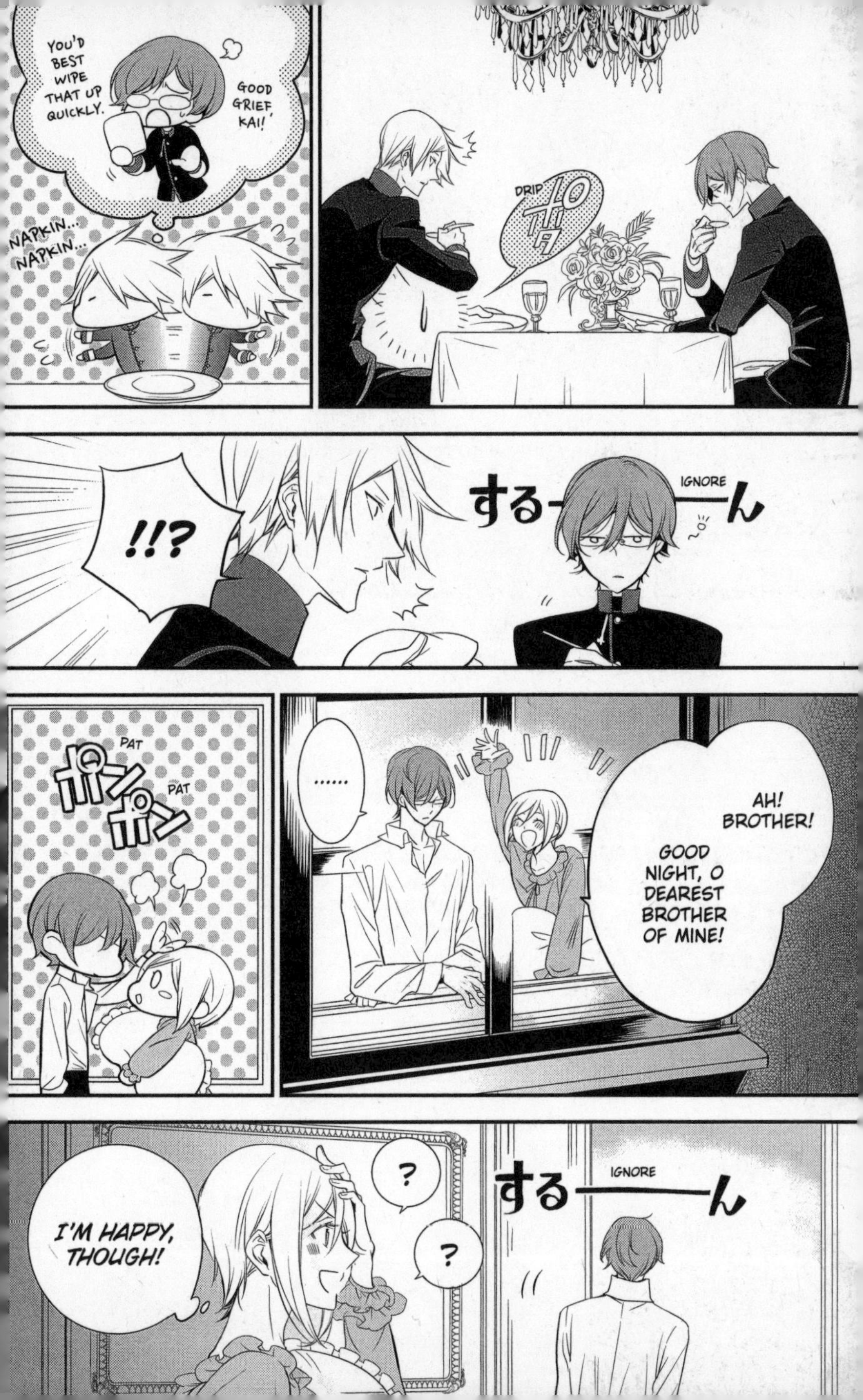
DRIP
GOOD GRIEF KAI!
YOU'D BEST WIPE THAT UP QUICKLY.
NAPKIN... NAPKIN...
するーーん
IGNORE
!!?
AH! BROTHER!
GOOD NIGHT, O DEAREST BROTHER OF MINE!
......
ポンポン
PAT PAT
するーーん
IGNORE
?
?
I'M HAPPY, THOUGH!

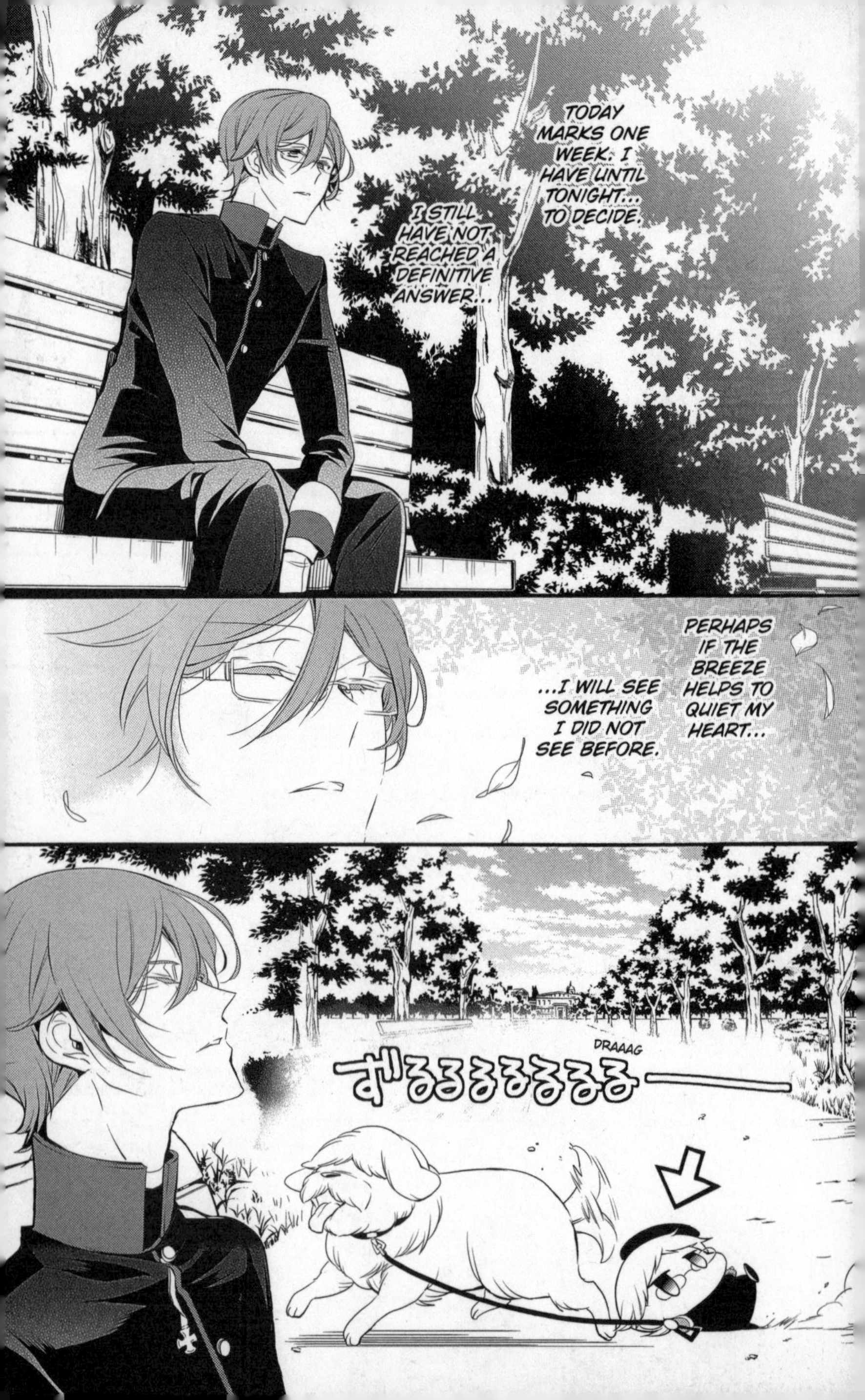
TODAY MARKS ONE WEEK. I HAVE UNTIL TONIGHT... TO DECIDE.
I STILL HAVE NOT REACHED A DEFINITIVE ANSWER...
PERHAPS IF THE BREEZE HELPS TO QUIET MY HEART...
...I WILL SEE SOMETHING I DID NOT SEE BEFORE.
ずるるるるるるるるー
DRAAAG

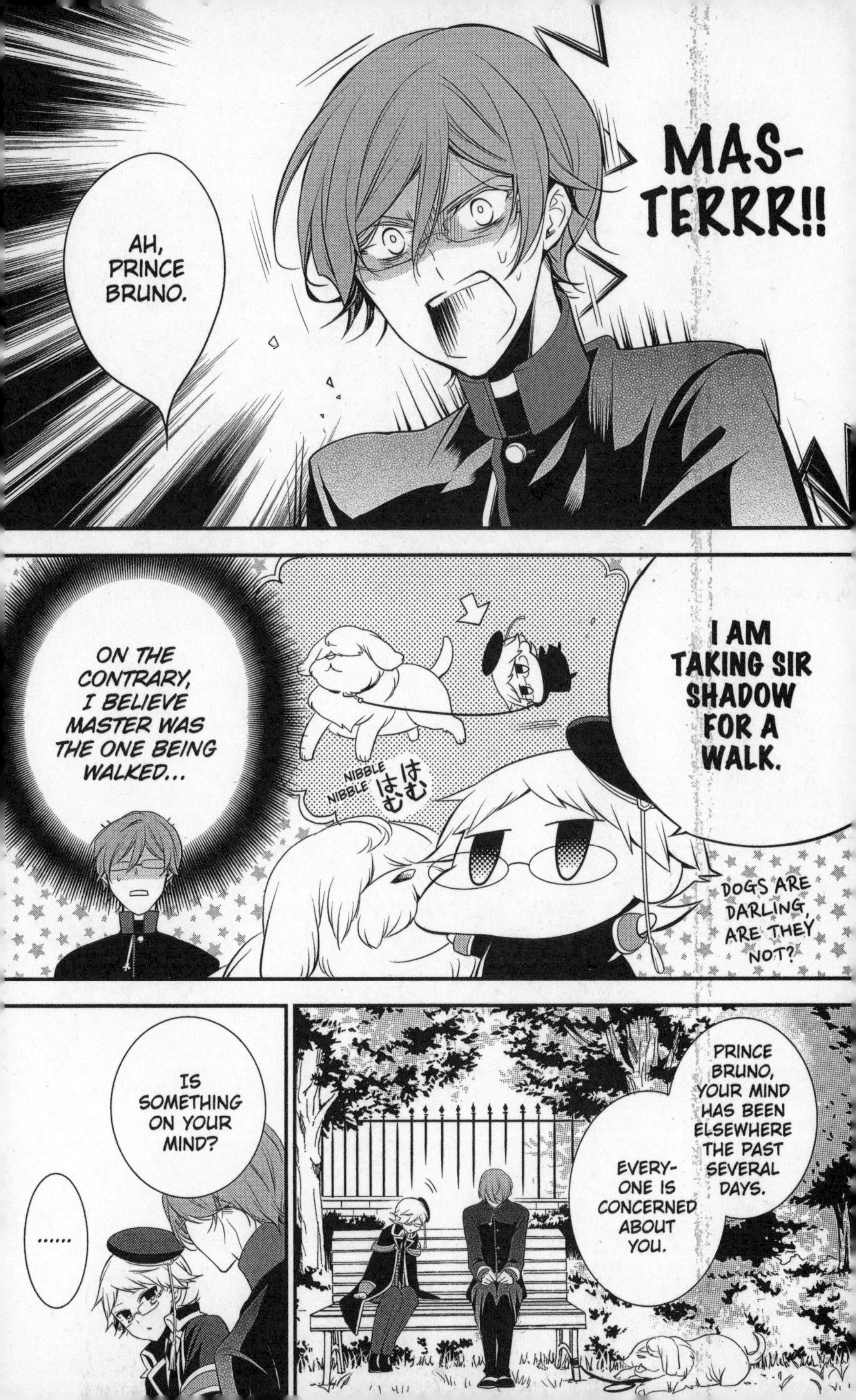
MAS-TERRR!!
AH, PRINCE BRUNO.
I AM TAKING SIR SHADOW FOR A WALK.
NIBBLE NIBBLE はむはむ
DOGS ARE DARLING, ARE THEY NOT?
ON THE CONTRARY, I BELIEVE MASTER WAS THE ONE BEING WALKED...
PRINCE BRUNO, YOUR MIND HAS BEEN ELSEWHERE THE PAST SEVERAL DAYS.
EVERY-ONE IS CONCERNED ABOUT YOU.
IS SOMETHING ON YOUR MIND?
......

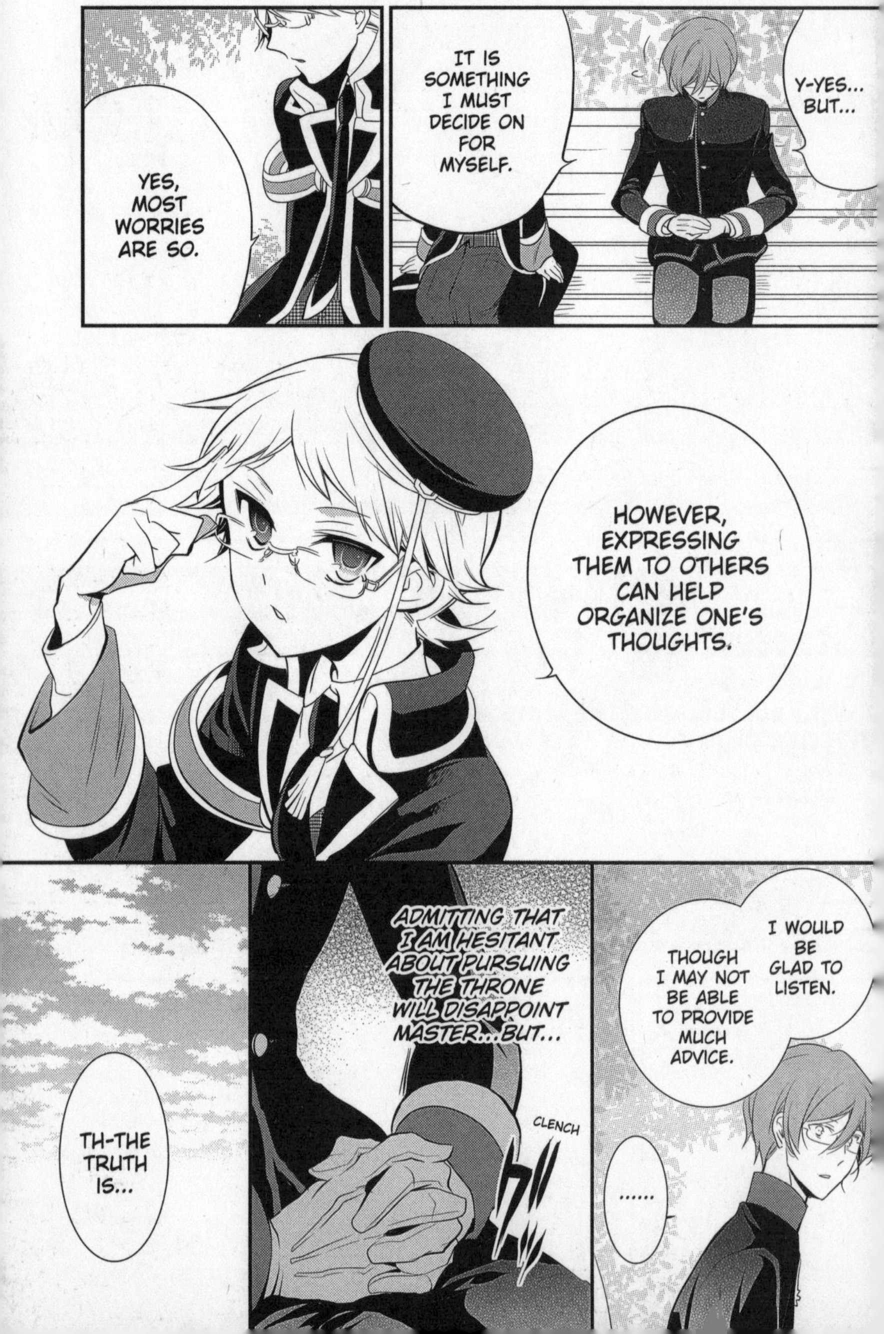
Y-YES... BUT...
IT IS SOMETHING I MUST DECIDE ON FOR MYSELF.
YES, MOST WORRIES ARE SO.
HOWEVER, EXPRESSING THEM TO OTHERS CAN HELP ORGANIZE ONE'S THOUGHTS.
I WOULD BE GLAD TO LISTEN.
THOUGH I MAY NOT BE ABLE TO PROVIDE MUCH ADVICE.
......
ADMITTING THAT I AM HESITANT ABOUT PURSUING THE THRONE WILL DISAPPOINT MASTER... BUT...
CLENCH
TH-THE TRUTH IS...

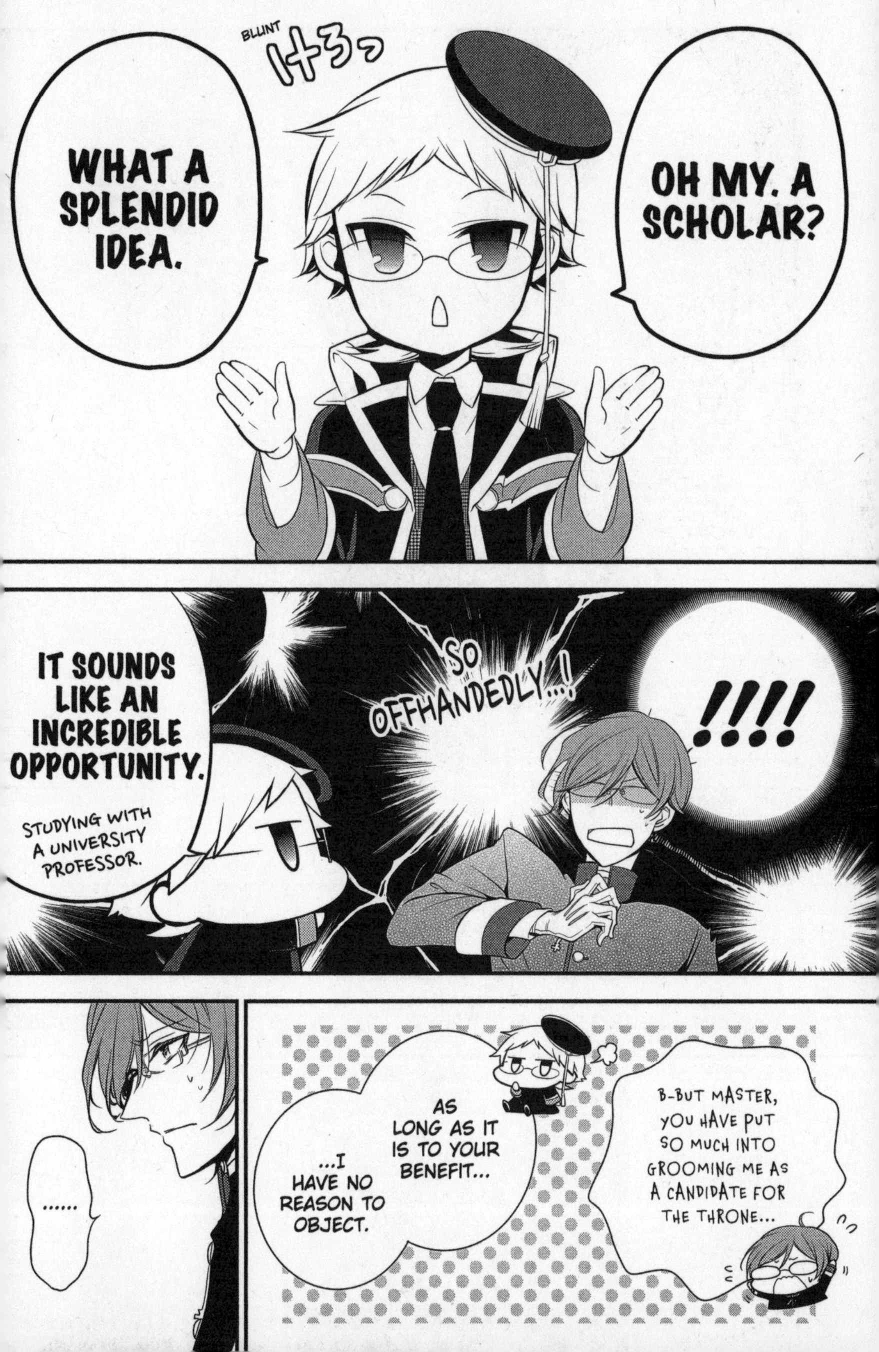

OH MY. A SCHOLAR?
BLUNT
WHAT A SPLENDID IDEA.
!!!!
SO OFFHANDEDLY...!
IT SOUNDS LIKE AN INCREDIBLE OPPORTUNITY.
STUDYING WITH A UNIVERSITY PROFESSOR.
B-BUT MASTER, YOU HAVE PUT SO MUCH INTO GROOMING ME AS A CANDIDATE FOR THE THRONE...
AS LONG AS IT IS TO YOUR BENEFIT...
...I HAVE NO REASON TO OBJECT.
......

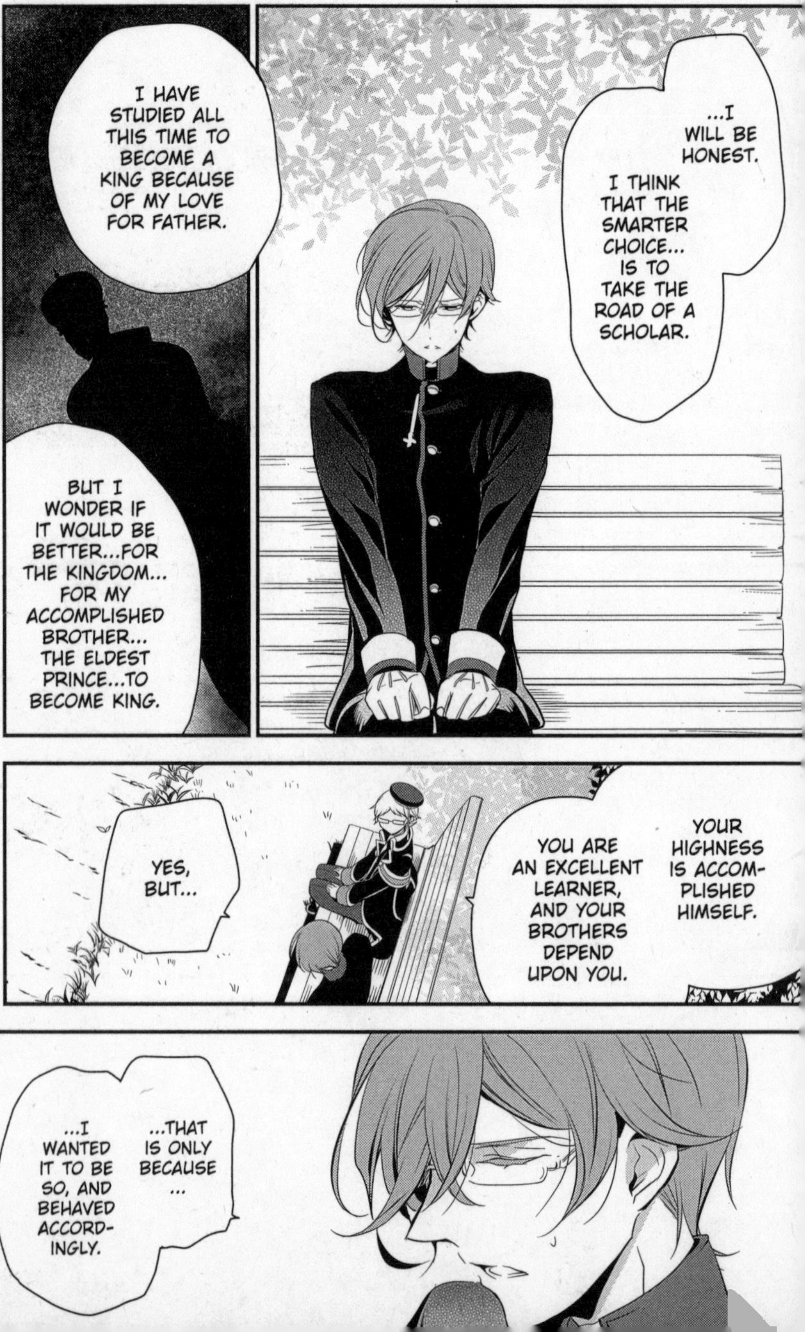
...I WILL BE HONEST.
I THINK THAT THE SMARTER CHOICE... IS TO TAKE THE ROAD OF A SCHOLAR.
I HAVE STUDIED ALL THIS TIME TO BECOME A KING BECAUSE OF MY LOVE FOR FATHER.
BUT I WONDER IF IT WOULD BE BETTER...FOR THE KINGDOM... FOR MY ACCOMPLISHED BROTHER... THE ELDEST PRINCE...TO BECOME KING.
YOUR HIGHNESS IS ACCOM-PLISHED HIMSELF.
YOU ARE AN EXCELLENT LEARNER, AND YOUR BROTHERS DEPEND UPON YOU.
YES, BUT...
...THAT IS ONLY BECAUSE...
...I WANTED IT TO BE SO, AND BEHAVED ACCORD-INGLY.

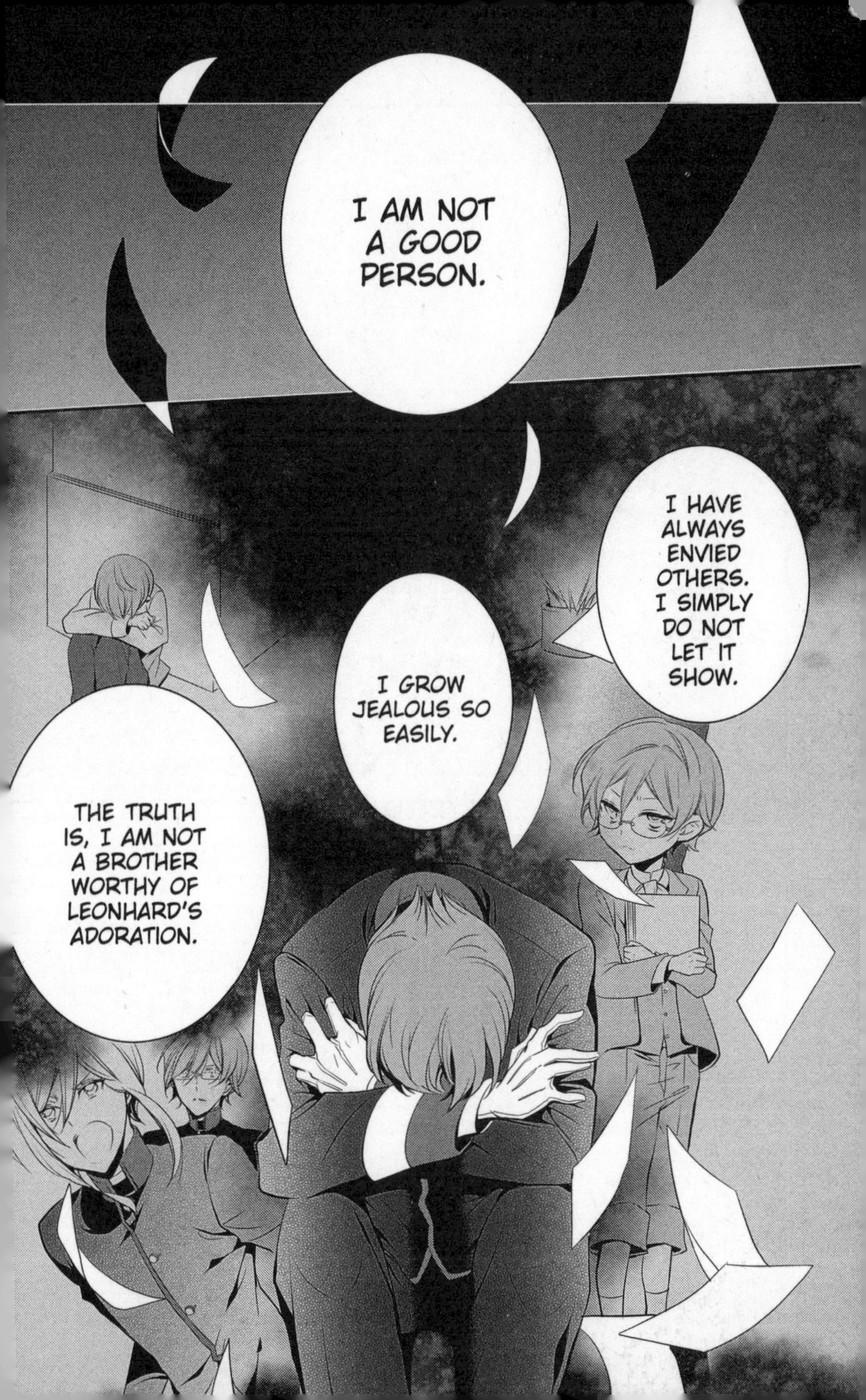
I AM NOT A GOOD PERSON.
I HAVE ALWAYS ENVIED OTHERS. I SIMPLY DO NOT LET IT SHOW.
I GROW JEALOUS SO EASILY.
THE TRUTH IS, I AM NOT A BROTHER WORTHY OF LEONHARD'S ADORATION.

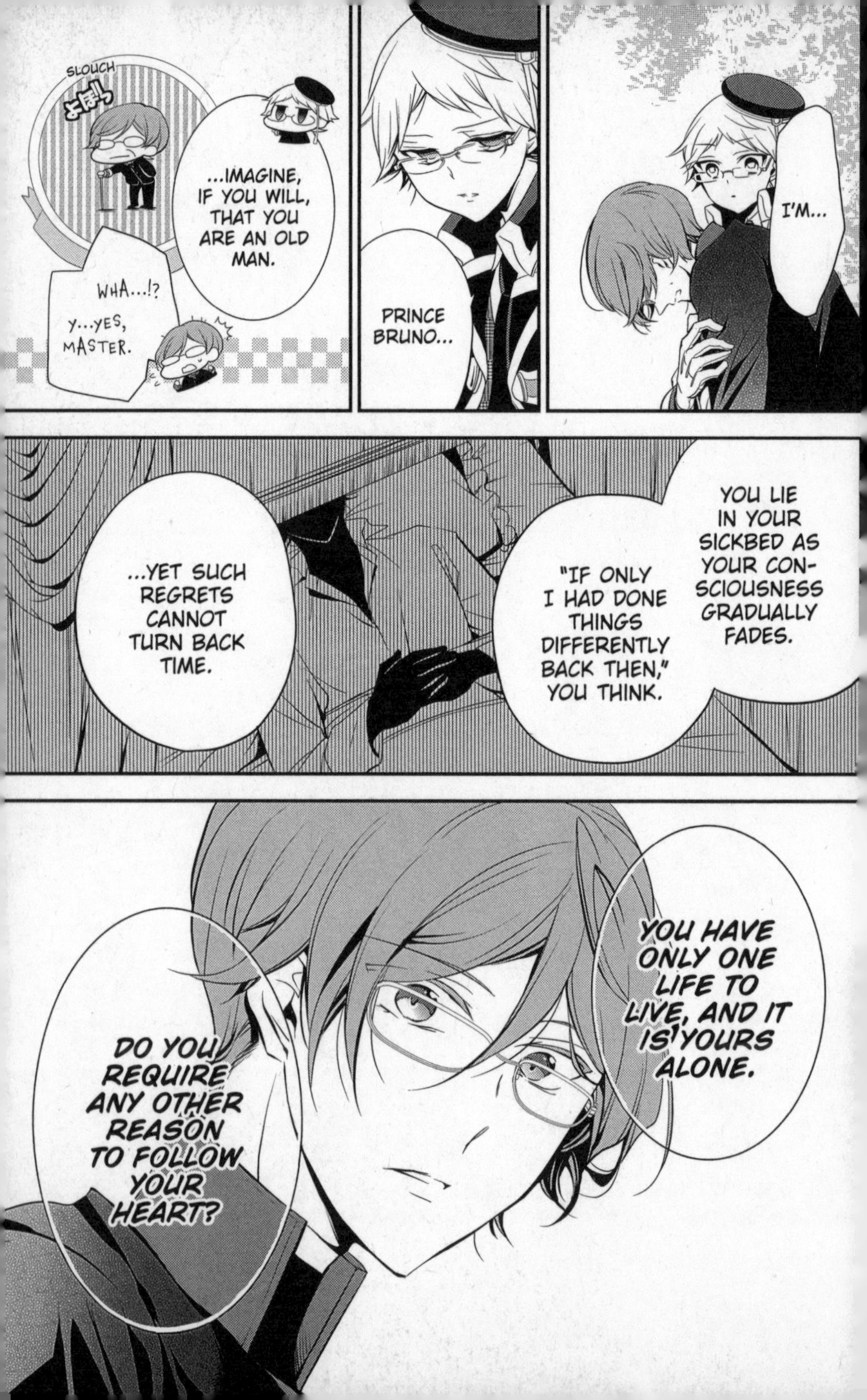
I'M...
PRINCE BRUNO...
...IMAGINE, IF YOU WILL, THAT YOU ARE AN OLD MAN.
SLOUCH
WHA...!? Y...YES, MASTER.
YOU LIE IN YOUR SICKBED AS YOUR CON-SCIOUSNESS GRADUALLY FADES.
"IF ONLY I HAD DONE THINGS DIFFERENTLY BACK THEN," YOU THINK.
...YET SUCH REGRETS CANNOT TURN BACK TIME.
YOU HAVE ONLY ONE LIFE TO LIVE, AND IT IS YOURS ALONE.
DO YOU REQUIRE ANY OTHER REASON TO FOLLOW YOUR HEART?

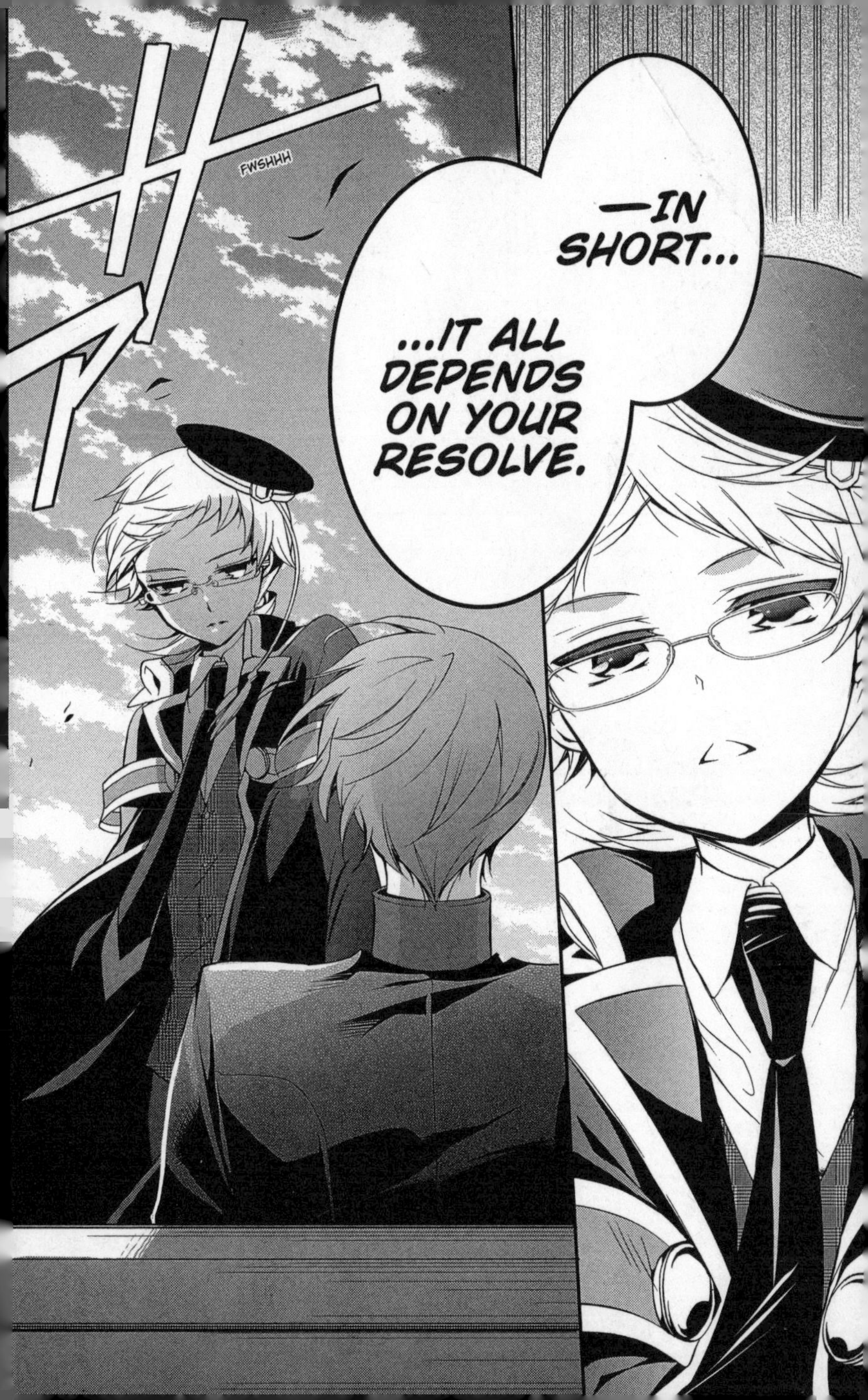
—IN SHORT...
...IT ALL DEPENDS ON YOUR RESOLVE.
FWSHHH

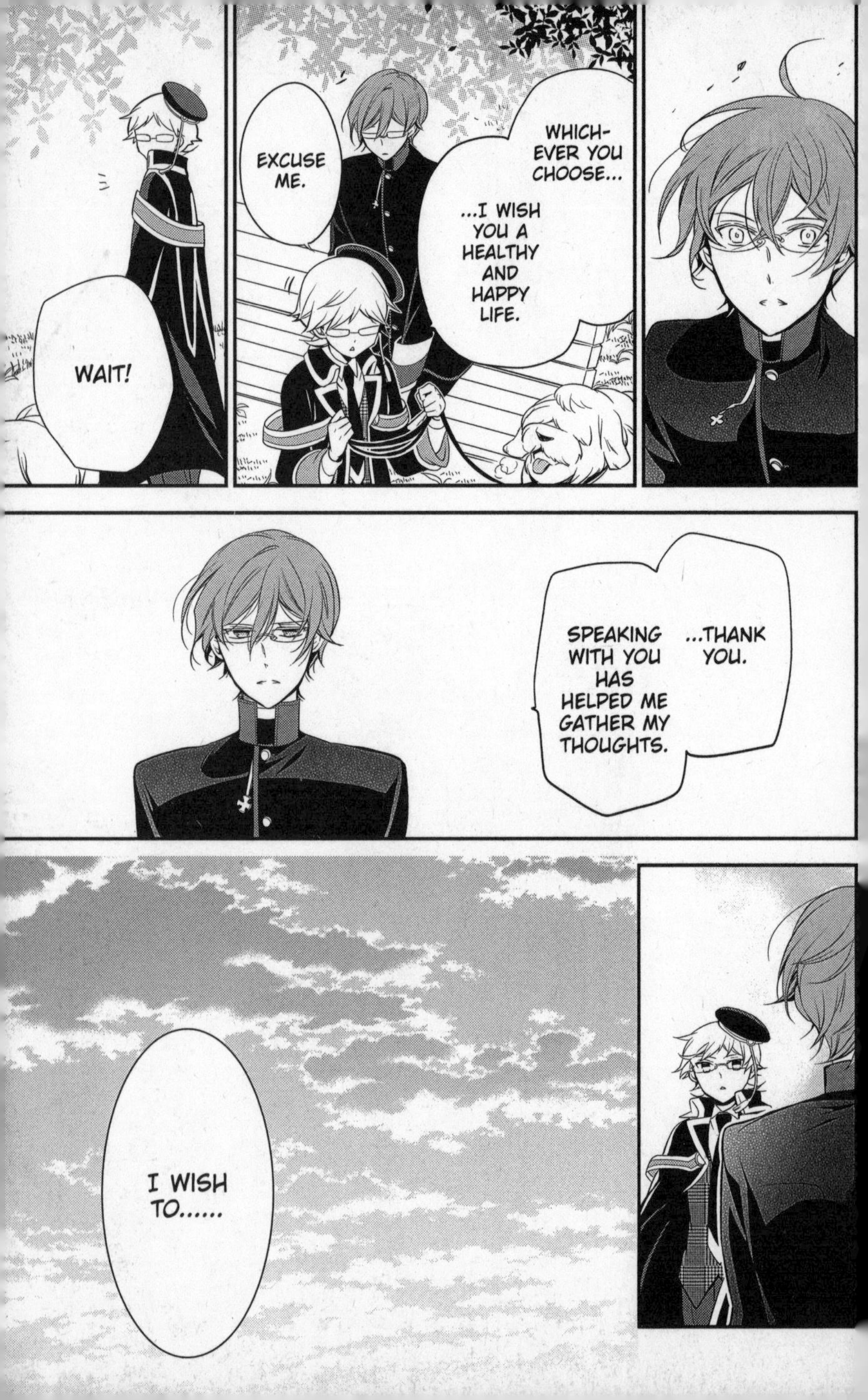
WHICH-EVER YOU CHOOSE...
...I WISH YOU A HEALTHY AND HAPPY LIFE.
EXCUSE ME.
WAIT!
...THANK YOU.
SPEAKING WITH YOU HAS HELPED ME GATHER MY THOUGHTS.
I WISH TO......

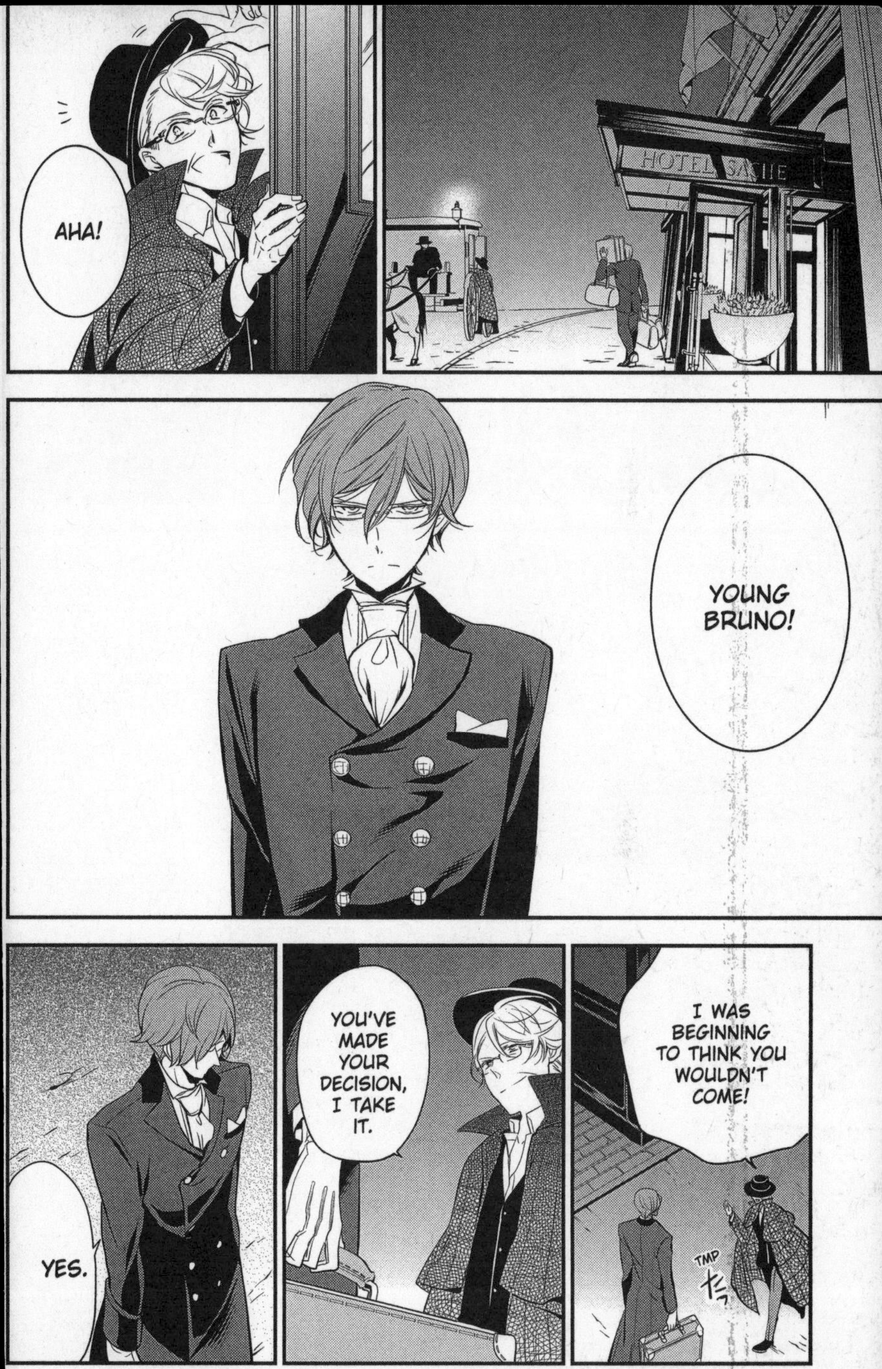
AHA!
YOUNG BRUNO!
I WAS BEGINNING TO THINK YOU WOULDN'T COME!
TMP
YOU'VE MADE YOUR DECISION, I TAKE IT.
YES.

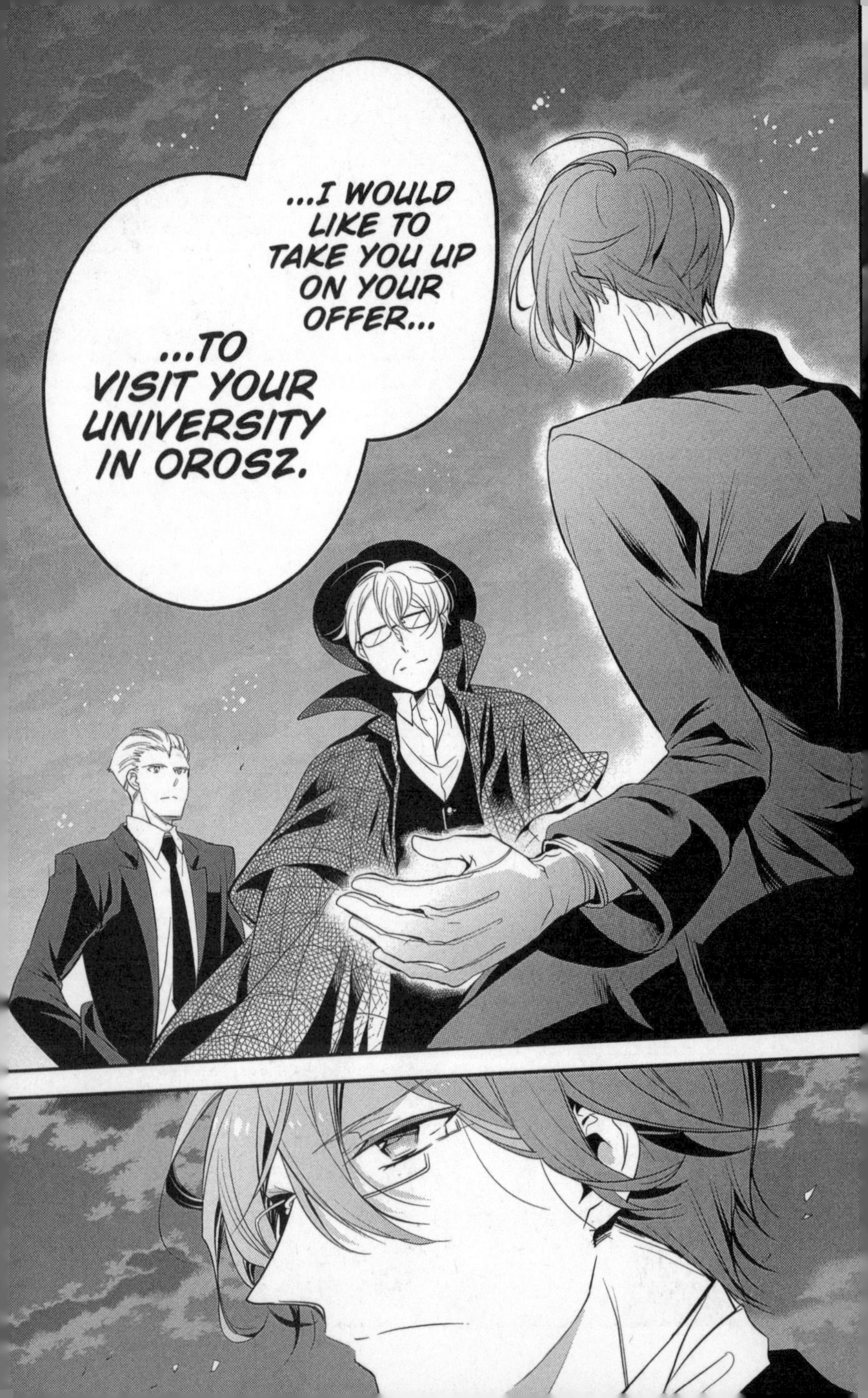
...I WOULD LIKE TO TAKE YOU UP ON YOUR OFFER...
...TO VISIT YOUR UNIVERSITY IN OROSZ.

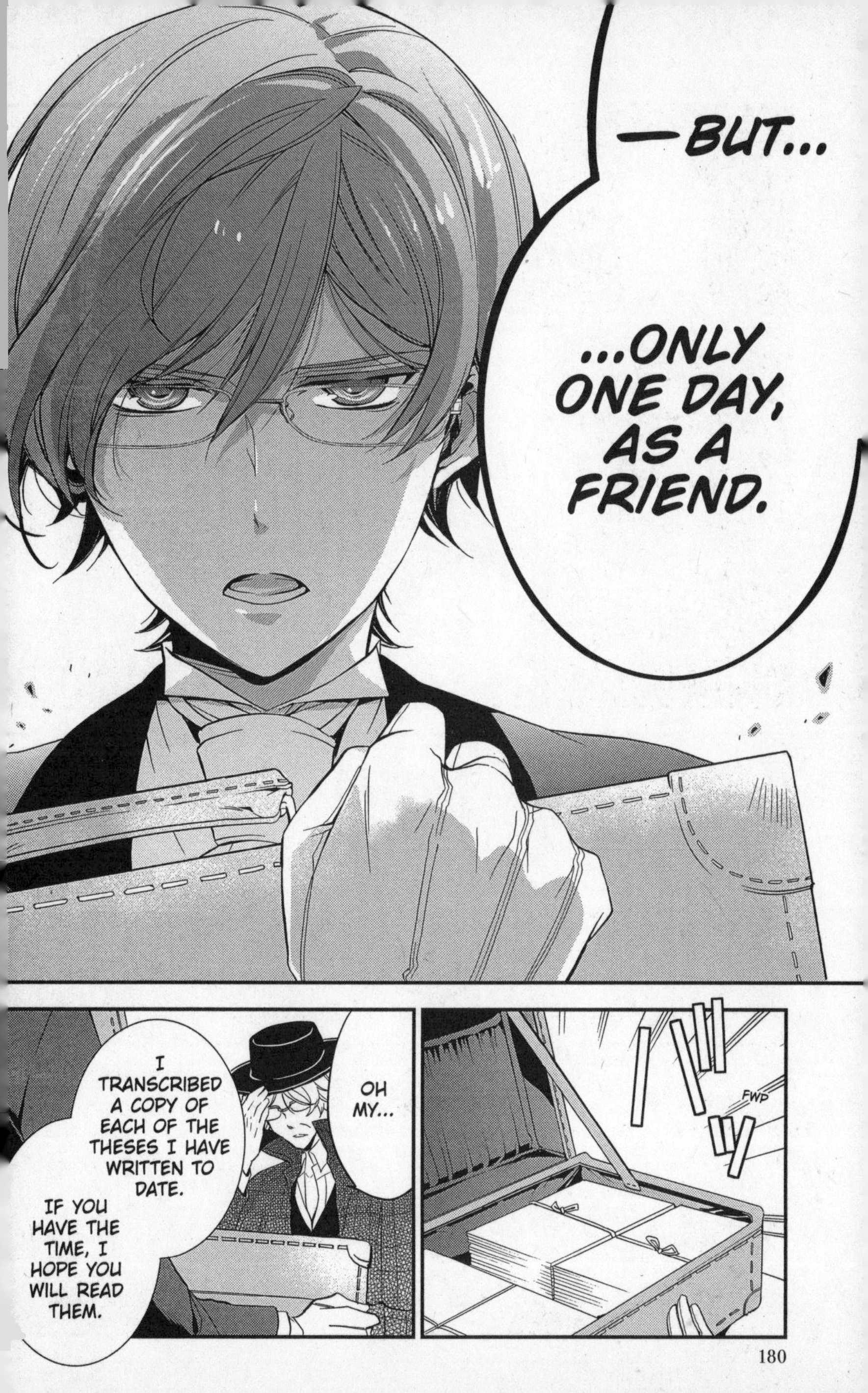
—BUT...
...ONLY ONE DAY, AS A FRIEND.
FWP
OH MY...
I TRANSCRIBED A COPY OF EACH OF THE THESES I HAVE WRITTEN TO DATE.
IF YOU HAVE THE TIME, I HOPE YOU WILL READ THEM.

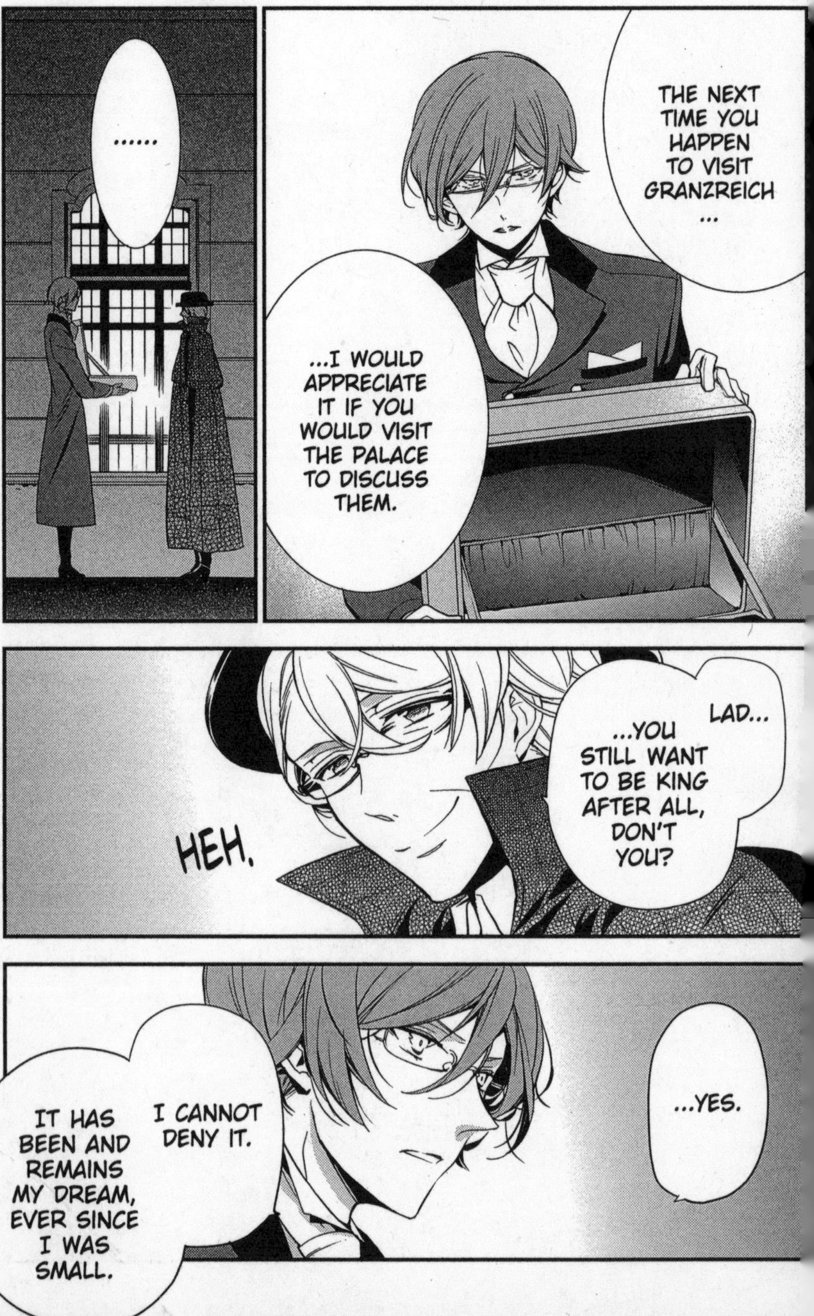
THE NEXT TIME YOU HAPPEN TO VISIT GRANZREICH ...
...I WOULD APPRECIATE IT IF YOU WOULD VISIT THE PALACE TO DISCUSS THEM.
......
LAD...
...YOU STILL WANT TO BE KING AFTER ALL, DON'T YOU?
HEH.
...YES.
I CANNOT DENY IT.
IT HAS BEEN AND REMAINS MY DREAM, EVER SINCE I WAS SMALL.

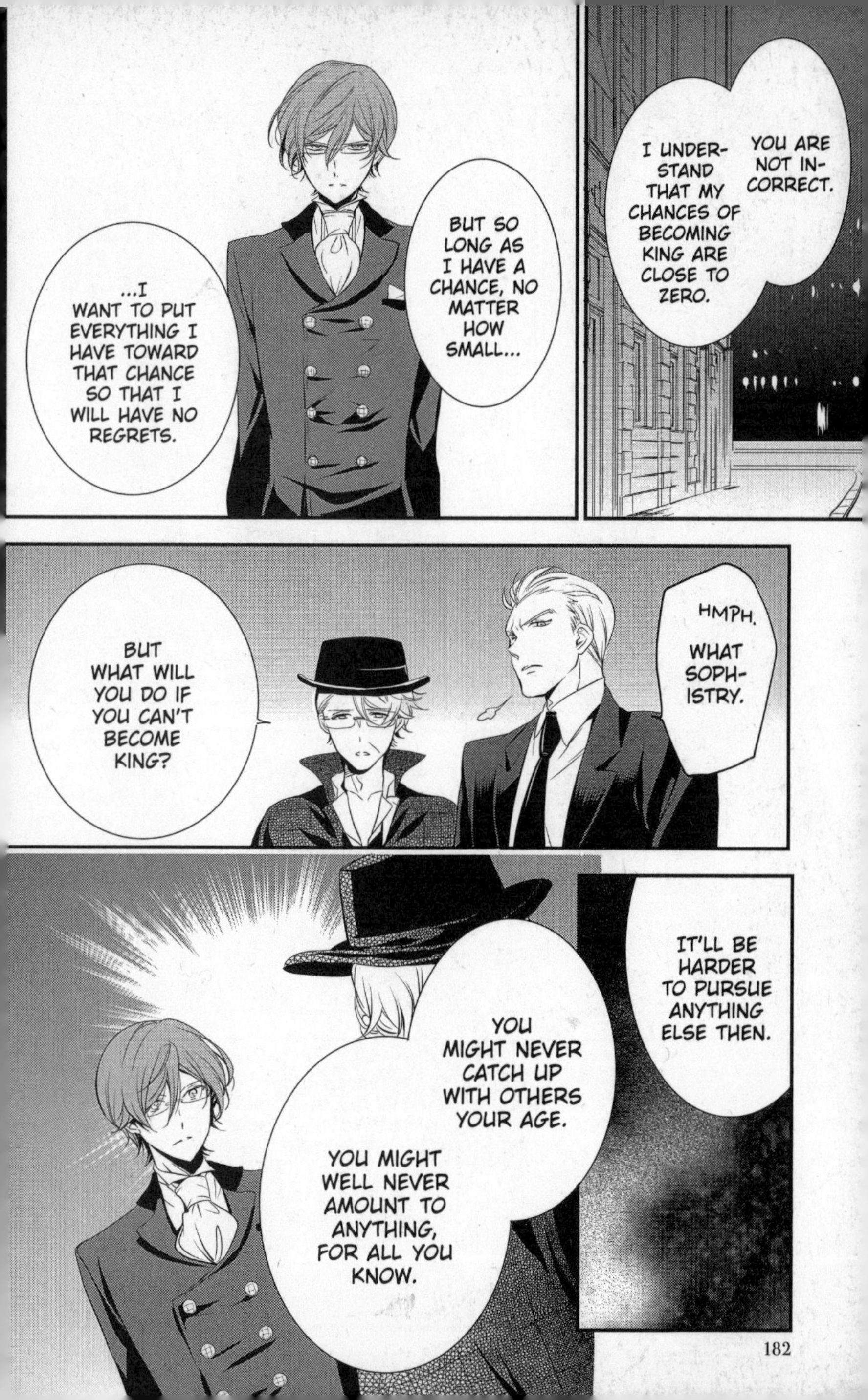
YOU ARE NOT IN-CORRECT.
I UNDER-STAND THAT MY CHANCES OF BECOMING KING ARE CLOSE TO ZERO.
BUT SO LONG AS I HAVE A CHANCE, NO MATTER HOW SMALL...
...I WANT TO PUT EVERYTHING I HAVE TOWARD THAT CHANCE SO THAT I WILL HAVE NO REGRETS.
HMPH.
WHAT SOPH-ISTRY.
BUT WHAT WILL YOU DO IF YOU CAN'T BECOME KING?
IT'LL BE HARDER TO PURSUE ANYTHING ELSE THEN.
YOU MIGHT NEVER CATCH UP WITH OTHERS YOUR AGE.
YOU MIGHT WELL NEVER AMOUNT TO ANYTHING, FOR ALL YOU KNOW.

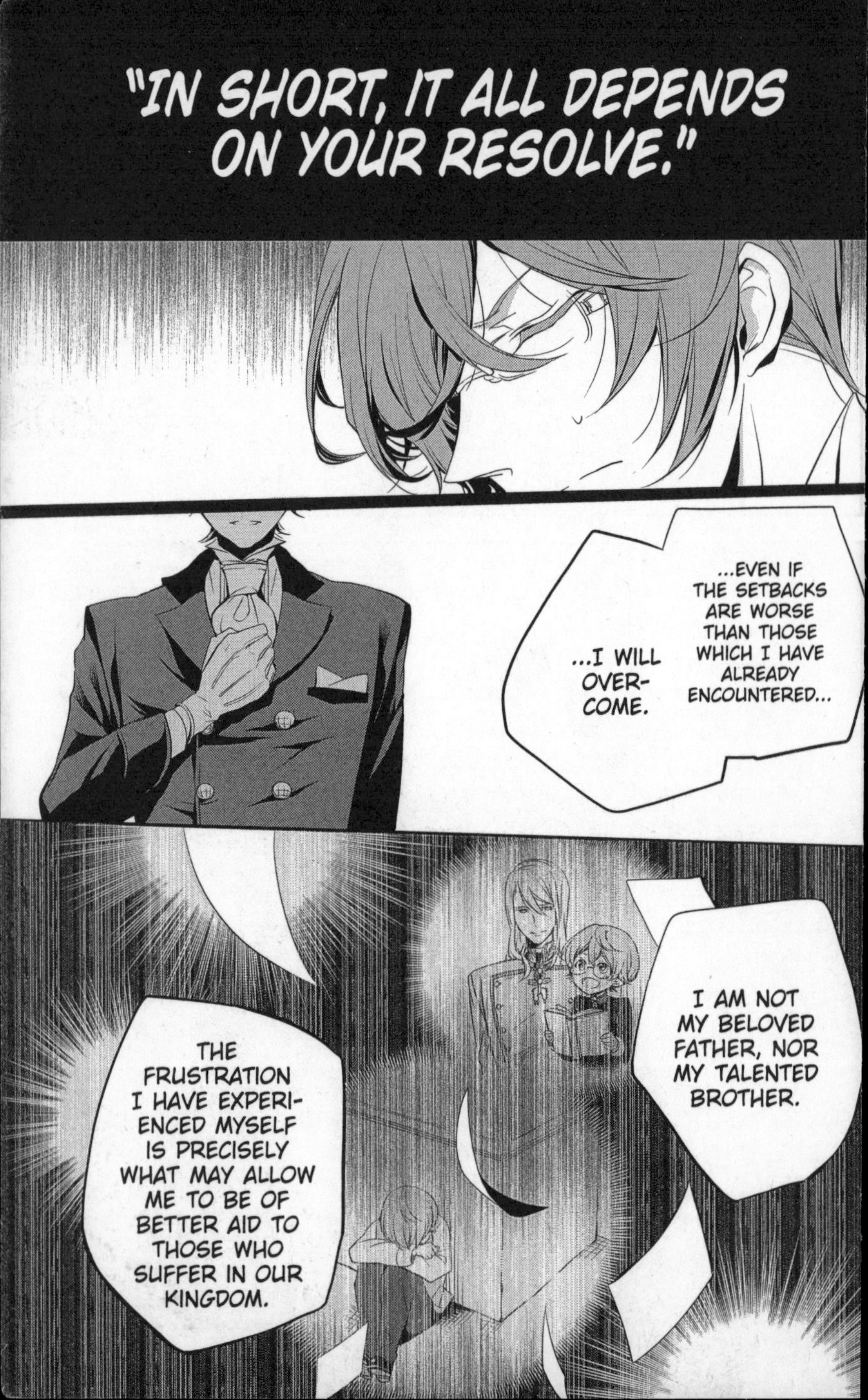
"IN SHORT, IT ALL DEPENDS ON YOUR RESOLVE."
...EVEN IF THE SETBACKS ARE WORSE THAN THOSE WHICH I HAVE ALREADY ENCOUNTERED...
...I WILL OVERCOME.
I AM NOT MY BELOVED FATHER, NOR MY TALENTED BROTHER.
THE FRUSTRATION I HAVE EXPERIENCED MYSELF IS PRECISELY WHAT MAY ALLOW ME TO BE OF BETTER AID TO THOSE WHO SUFFER IN OUR KINGDOM.

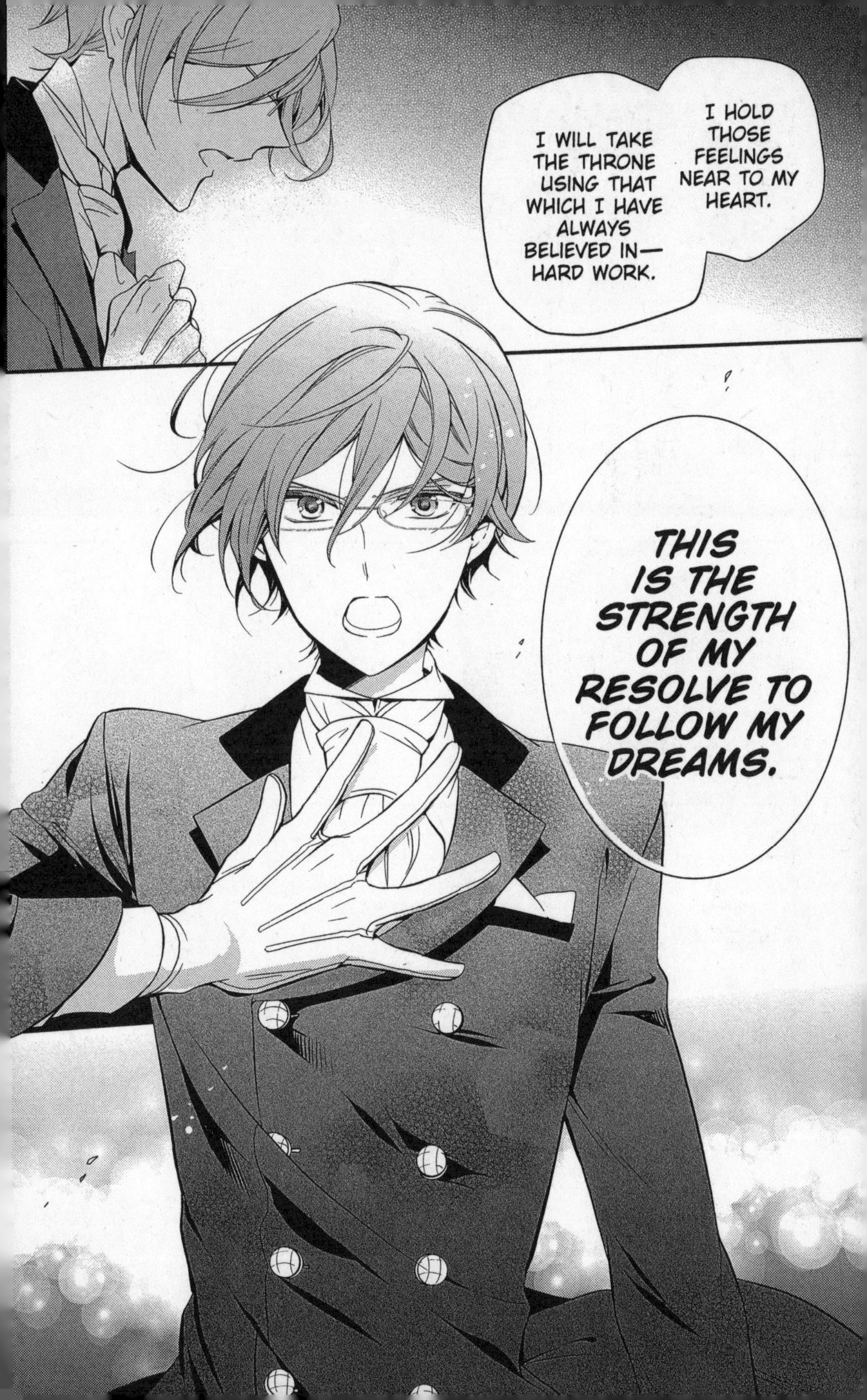
I HOLD THOSE FEELINGS NEAR TO MY HEART.
I WILL TAKE THE THRONE USING THAT WHICH I HAVE ALWAYS BELIEVED IN— HARD WORK.
THIS IS THE STRENGTH OF MY RESOLVE TO FOLLOW MY DREAMS.

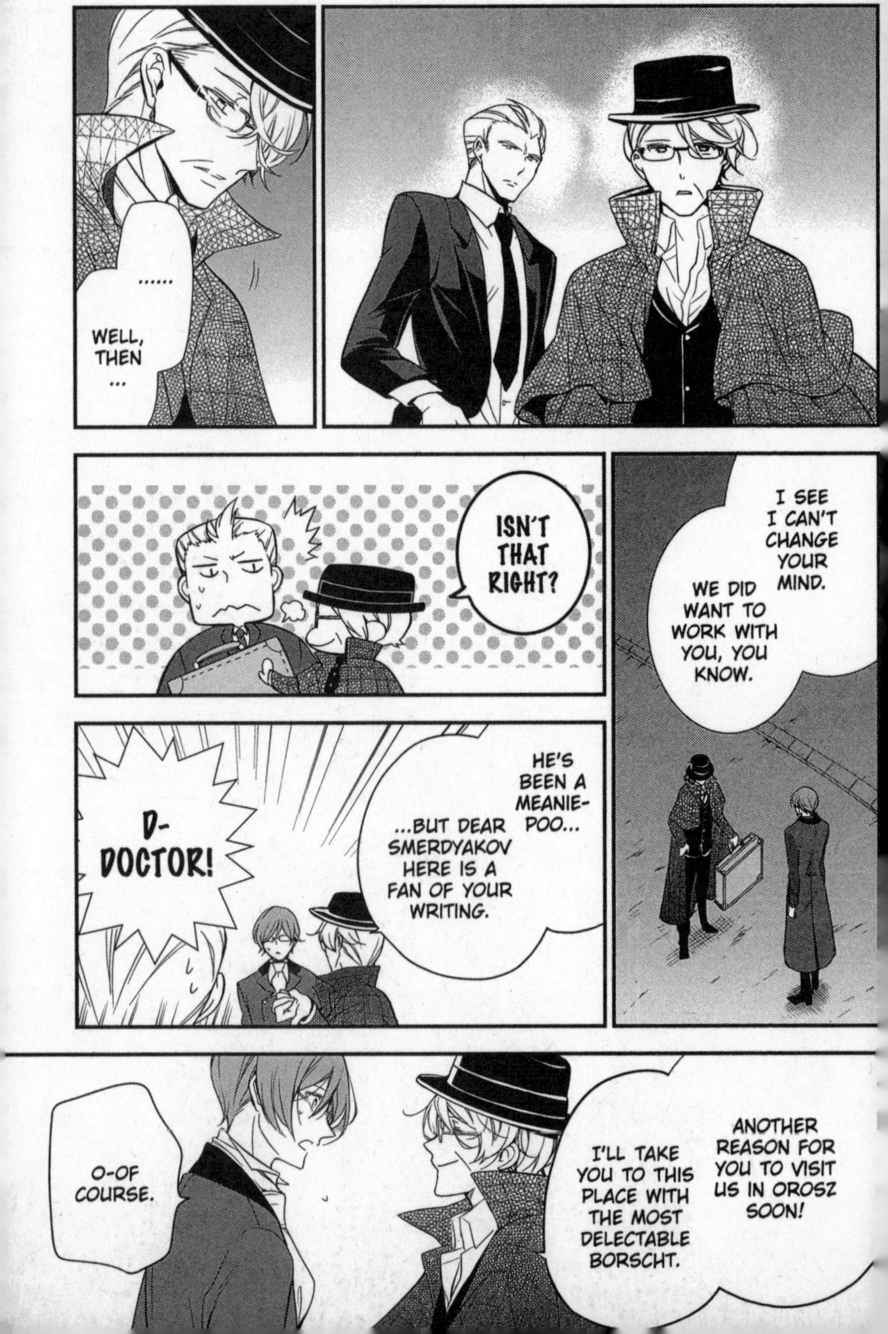
......
WELL, THEN ...
I SEE I CAN'T CHANGE YOUR MIND.
WE DID WANT TO WORK WITH YOU, YOU KNOW.
ISN'T THAT RIGHT?
HE'S BEEN A MEANIE-POO...
...BUT DEAR SMERDYAKOV HERE IS A FAN OF YOUR WRITING.
D-DOCTOR!
ANOTHER REASON FOR YOU TO VISIT US IN OROSZ SOON!
I'LL TAKE YOU TO THIS PLACE WITH THE MOST DELECTABLE BORSCHT.
O-OF COURSE.

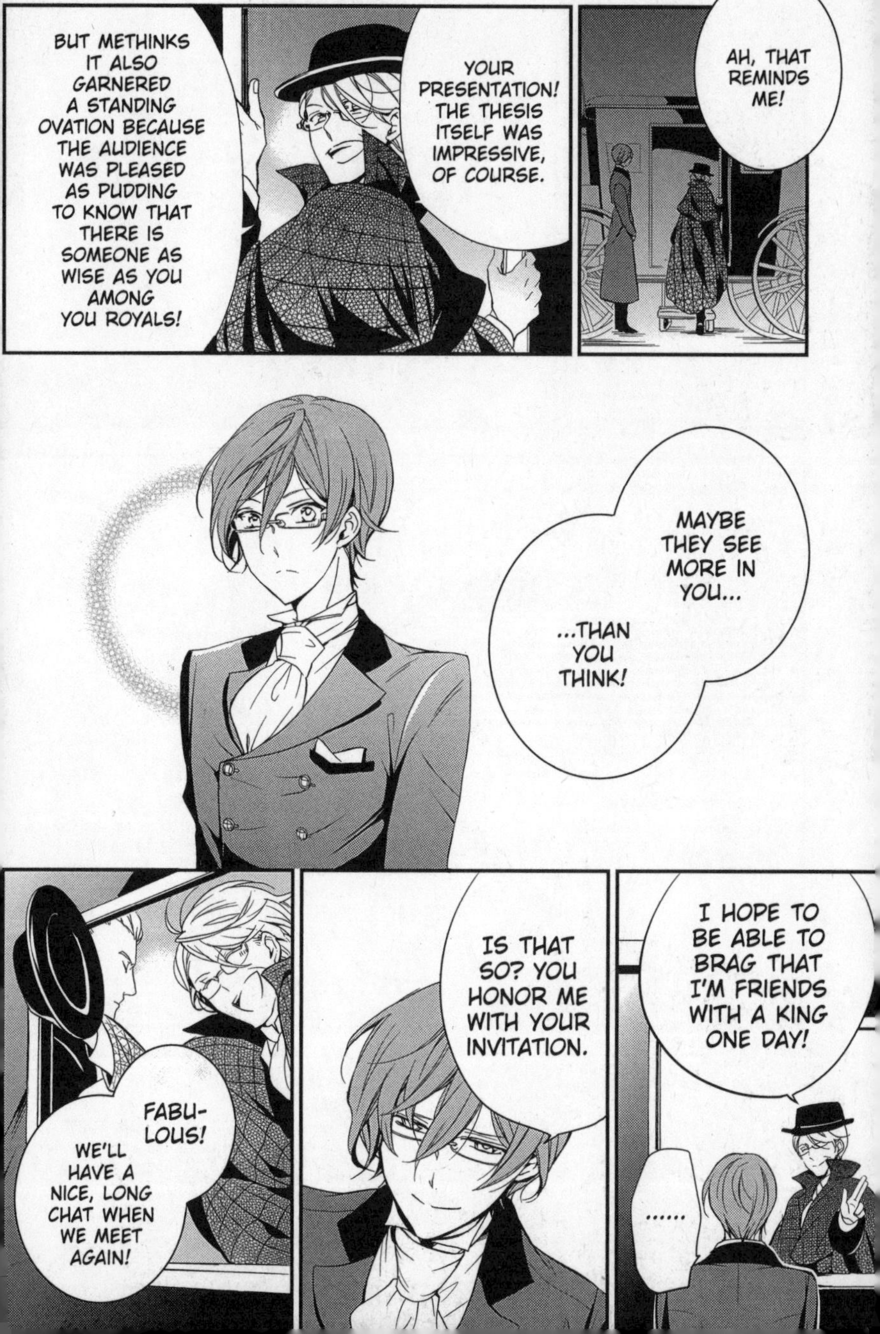

AH, THAT REMINDS ME!
YOUR PRESENTATION! THE THESIS ITSELF WAS IMPRESSIVE, OF COURSE.
BUT METHINKS IT ALSO GARNERED A STANDING OVATION BECAUSE THE AUDIENCE WAS PLEASED AS PUDDING TO KNOW THAT THERE IS SOMEONE AS WISE AS YOU AMONG YOU ROYALS!
MAYBE THEY SEE MORE IN YOU...
...THAN YOU THINK!
I HOPE TO BE ABLE TO BRAG THAT I'M FRIENDS WITH A KING ONE DAY!
......
IS THAT SO? YOU HONOR ME WITH YOUR INVITATION.
FABU-LOUS!
WE'LL HAVE A NICE, LONG CHAT WHEN WE MEET AGAIN!

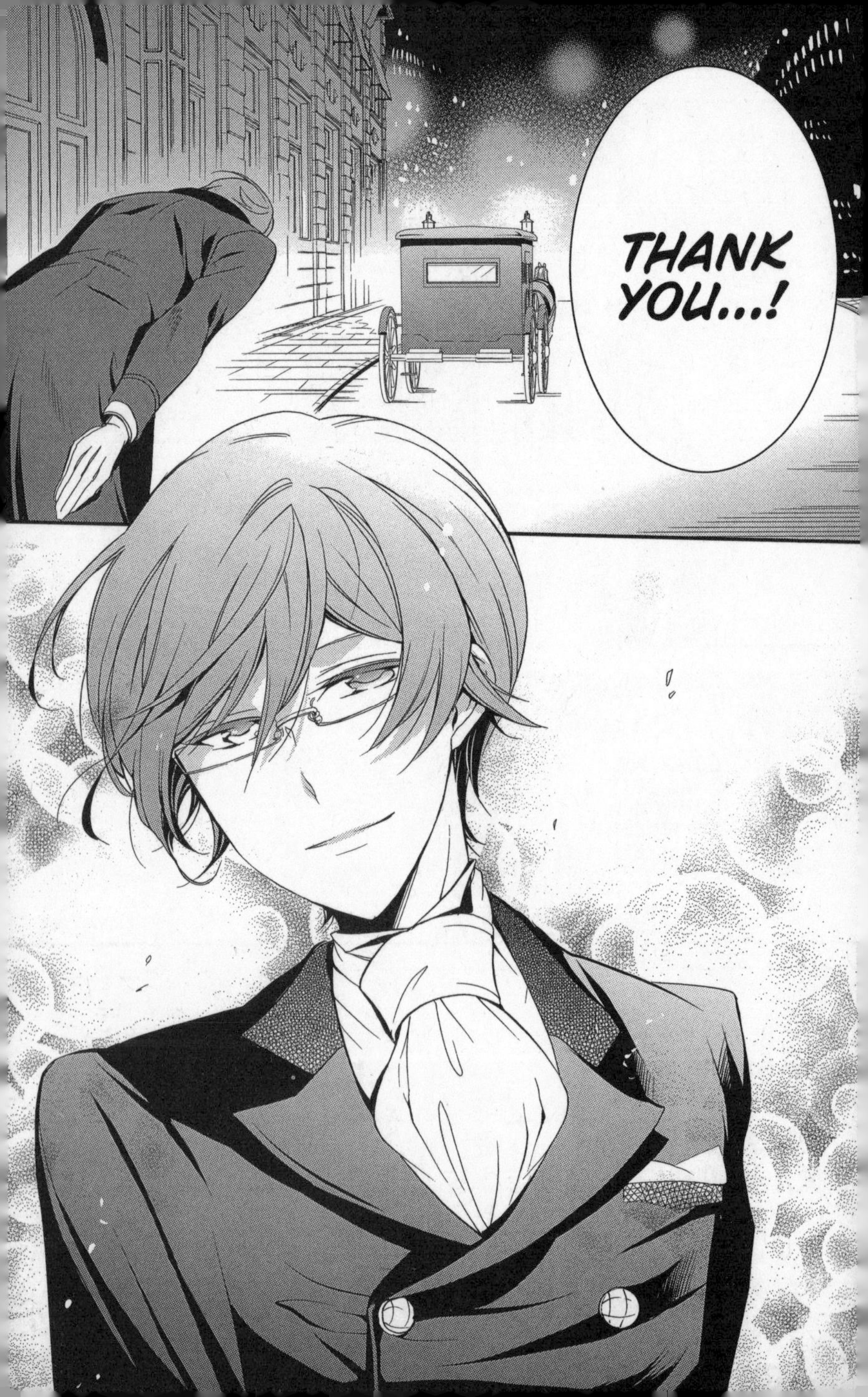
THANK YOU...!

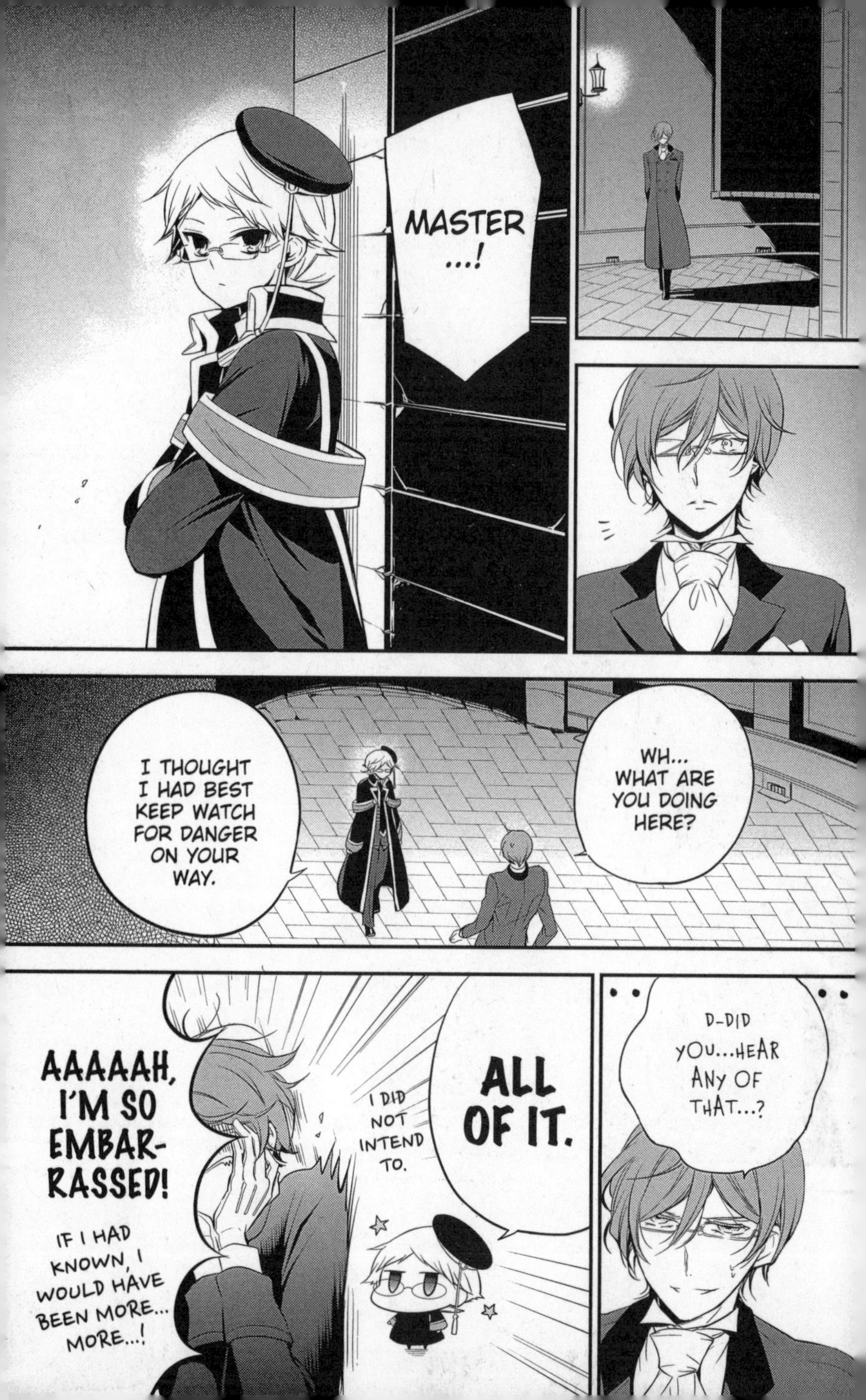
MASTER ...!
WH... WHAT ARE YOU DOING HERE?
I THOUGHT I HAD BEST KEEP WATCH FOR DANGER ON YOUR WAY.
D-DID YOU...HEAR ANY OF THAT...?
ALL OF IT.
I DID NOT INTEND TO.
AAAAAH, I'M SO EMBARRASSED!
IF I HAD KNOWN, I WOULD HAVE BEEN MORE... MORE...!

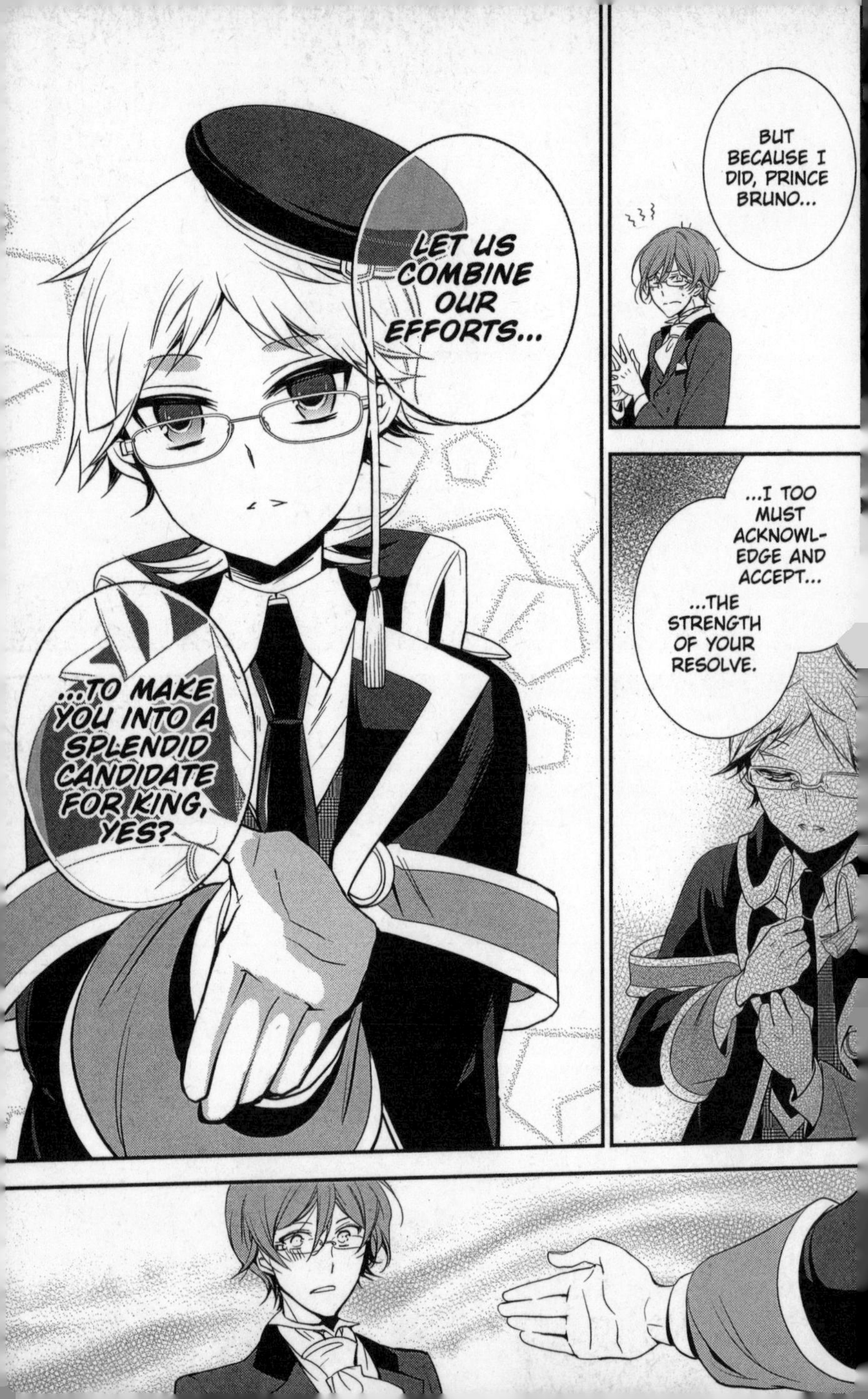
BUT BECAUSE I DID, PRINCE BRUNO...
...I TOO MUST ACKNOWL-EDGE AND ACCEPT...
...THE STRENGTH OF YOUR RESOLVE.
LET US COMBINE OUR EFFORTS...
...TO MAKE YOU INTO A SPLENDID CANDIDATE FOR KING, YES?

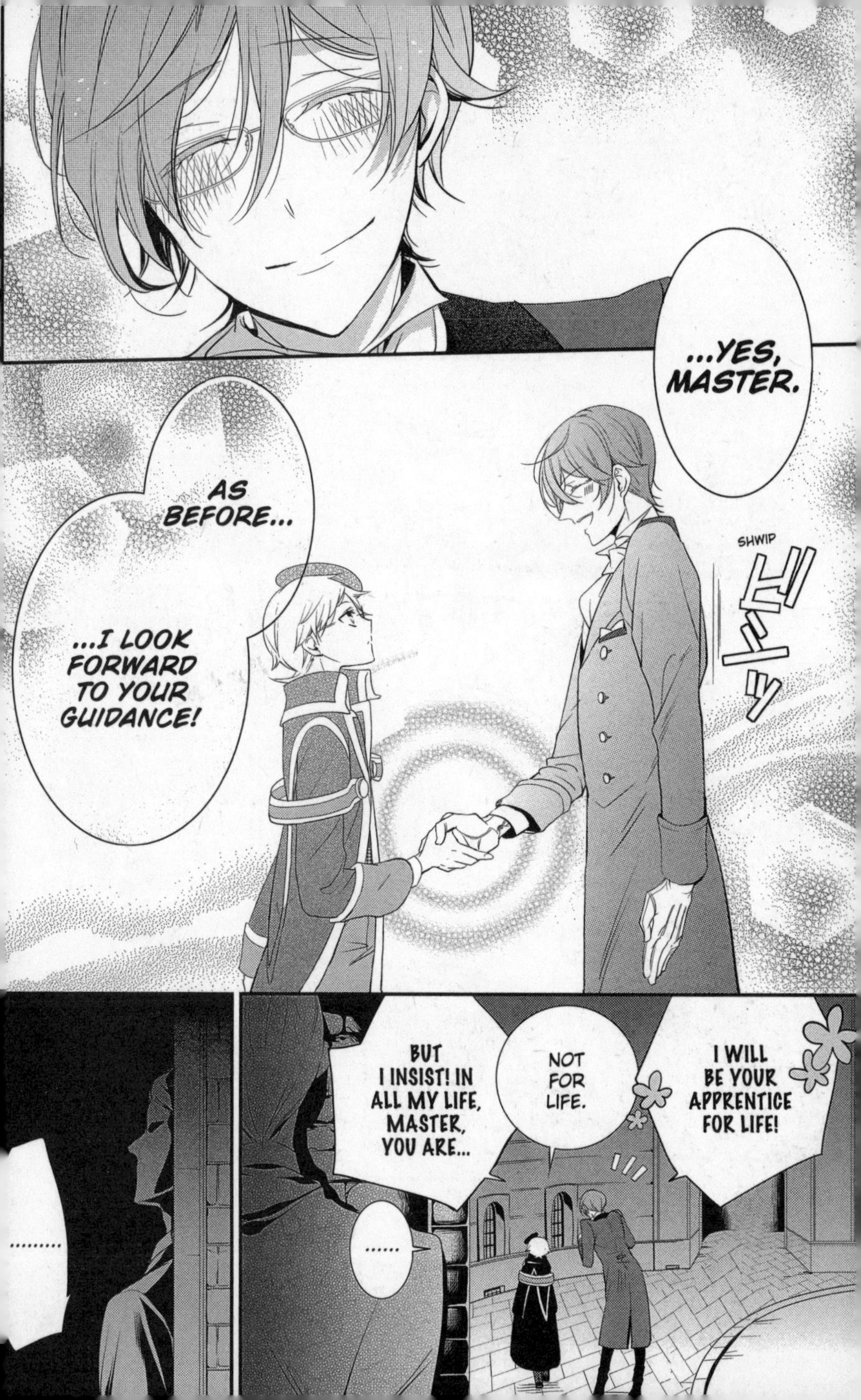
...YES, MASTER.
SHWIP
AS BEFORE...
...I LOOK FORWARD TO YOUR GUIDANCE!
I WILL BE YOUR APPRENTICE FOR LIFE!
NOT FOR LIFE.
BUT I INSIST! IN ALL MY LIFE, MASTER, YOU ARE...
......
....

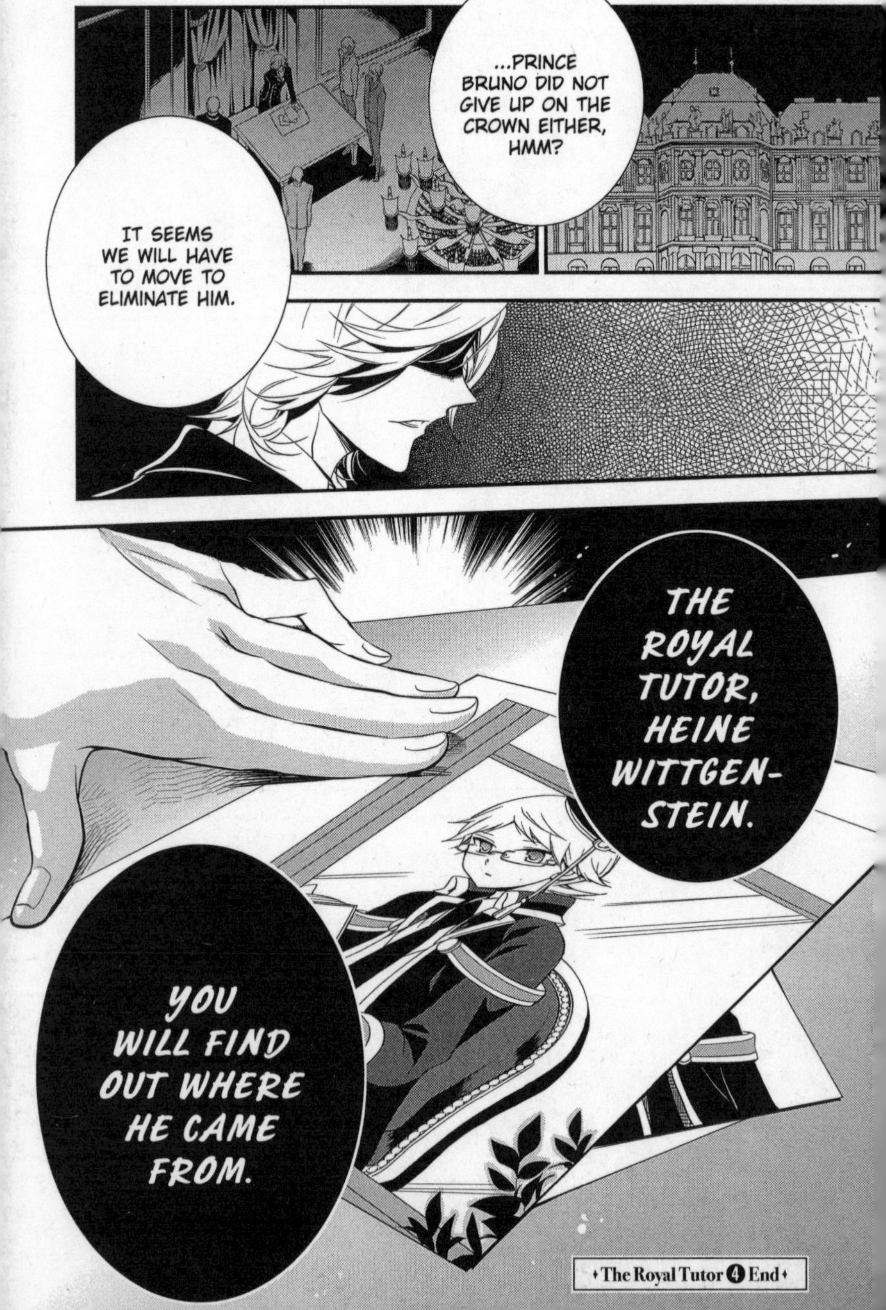
...PRINCE BRUNO DID NOT GIVE UP ON THE CROWN EITHER, HMM?
IT SEEMS WE WILL HAVE TO MOVE TO ELIMINATE HIM.
THE ROYAL TUTOR, HEINE WITTGEN-STEIN.
YOU WILL FIND OUT WHERE HE CAME FROM.
The Royal Tutor 4 End

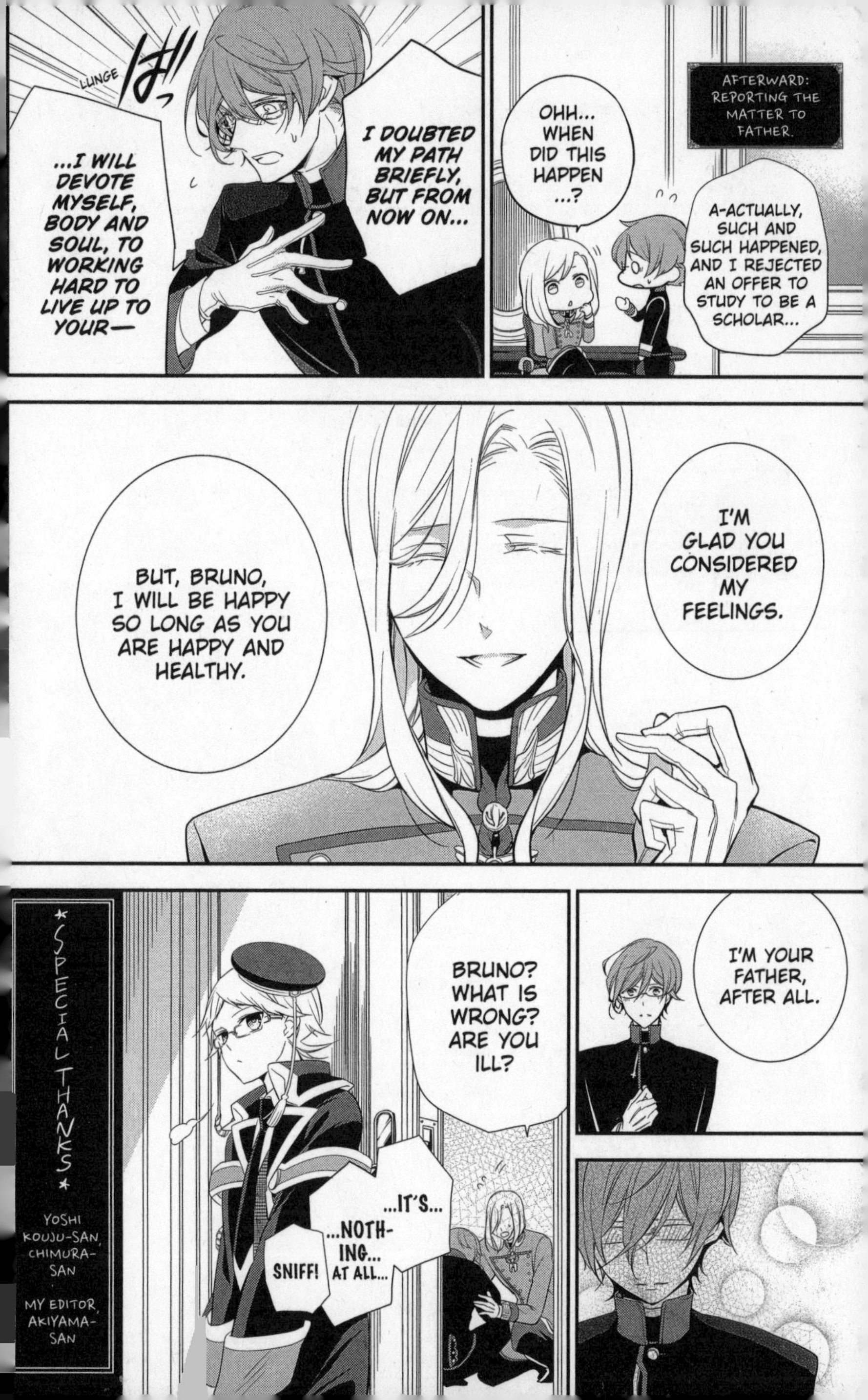
AFTERWARD: REPORTING THE MATTER TO FATHER.
OHH... WHEN DID THIS HAPPEN ...?
A-ACTUALLY, SUCH AND SUCH HAPPENED, AND I REJECTED AN OFFER TO STUDY TO BE A SCHOLAR...
LUNGE
I DOUBTED MY PATH BRIEFLY, BUT FROM NOW ON...
...I WILL DEVOTE MYSELF, BODY AND SOUL, TO WORKING HARD TO LIVE UP TO YOUR—
I'M GLAD YOU CONSIDERED MY FEELINGS.
BUT, BRUNO, I WILL BE HAPPY SO LONG AS YOU ARE HAPPY AND HEALTHY.
I'M YOUR FATHER, AFTER ALL.
BRUNO? WHAT IS WRONG? ARE YOU ILL?
...IT'S...
...NOTHING... AT ALL...
SNIFF!
SPECIAL THANKS
YOSHI KOUJU-SAN, CHIMURA-SAN
MY EDITOR, AKIYAMA-SAN

Translation Notes

Page 77
Arsène Lupin: Heine's fictional account of his sordid past draws from the name Arsène Lupin, a gentleman thief featured in the novels and short stories of Maurice Leblanc beginning in the early 1900s.

Page 95
Prunksaal: In our world, the Prunksaal is the name of the building in the Hofburg Palace in which the Austrian National Library resides.

Page 160
High steward: As high steward, Count Ernst would oversee Prince Eins's household—basically, he is the head of Prince Eins's servants.

Page 185
Borscht: A Ukranian soup common in Eastern Europe, traditionally made from meat/bone stock, vegetables, and beetroot juice.

Inside Back Cover
Daifuku: A kind of *mochi* (sticky rice cake) with a sweet filling, usually red bean paste.

The Royal Tuto

Translation: Amanda Haley • Lette...

THE ROYAL TUTOR Vol. 4 ©2015 Higasa Akai/SQUARE ENIX CO., LTD. First published in Japan in 2015 by SQUARE ENIX CO., LTD. English translation rights arranged with SQUARE ENIX CO., LTD. and Yen Press, LLC through Tuttle-Mori Agency, Inc., Tokyo.

English translation ©2015 by SQUARE ENIX CO., LTD.

Yen Press
1290 Avenue of the Americas
New York, NY 10104

Visit us at yenpress.com
facebook.com/yenpress
twitter.com/yenpress
yenpress.tumblr.com
instagram.com/yenpress

First Yen Press Print Edition: November 2017
Originally published as an eBook in October 2015 by Yen Press.

Yen Press is an imprint of Yen Press, LLC.
The Yen Press name and logo are trademarks of Yen Press, LLC.

The publisher is not responsible for websites (or their content) that are not owned by the publisher.

Library of Congress Control Number: 2017938422

ISBN: 978-0-316-41287-2 (paperback)

10 9 8 7 6 5 4 3 2 1

BVG

Printed in the United States of America